TIGER & BUNNY 2

ART BY **MIZUKI SAKAKIBARA**

PLANNING / STORY **SUNRISE** | ORIGINAL SCRIPT **Masafumi Nishida**

ORIGINAL CHARACTER AND HERO DESIGN **Masakazu Katsura**

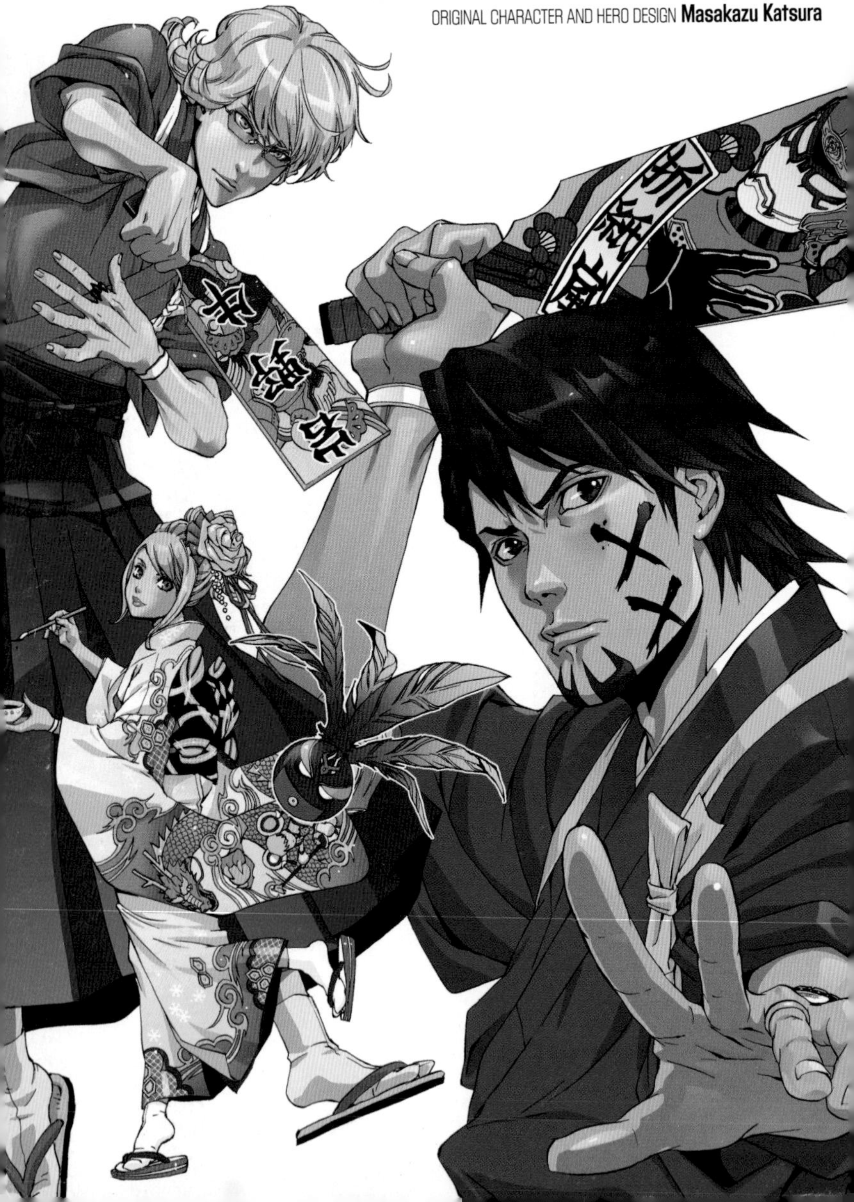

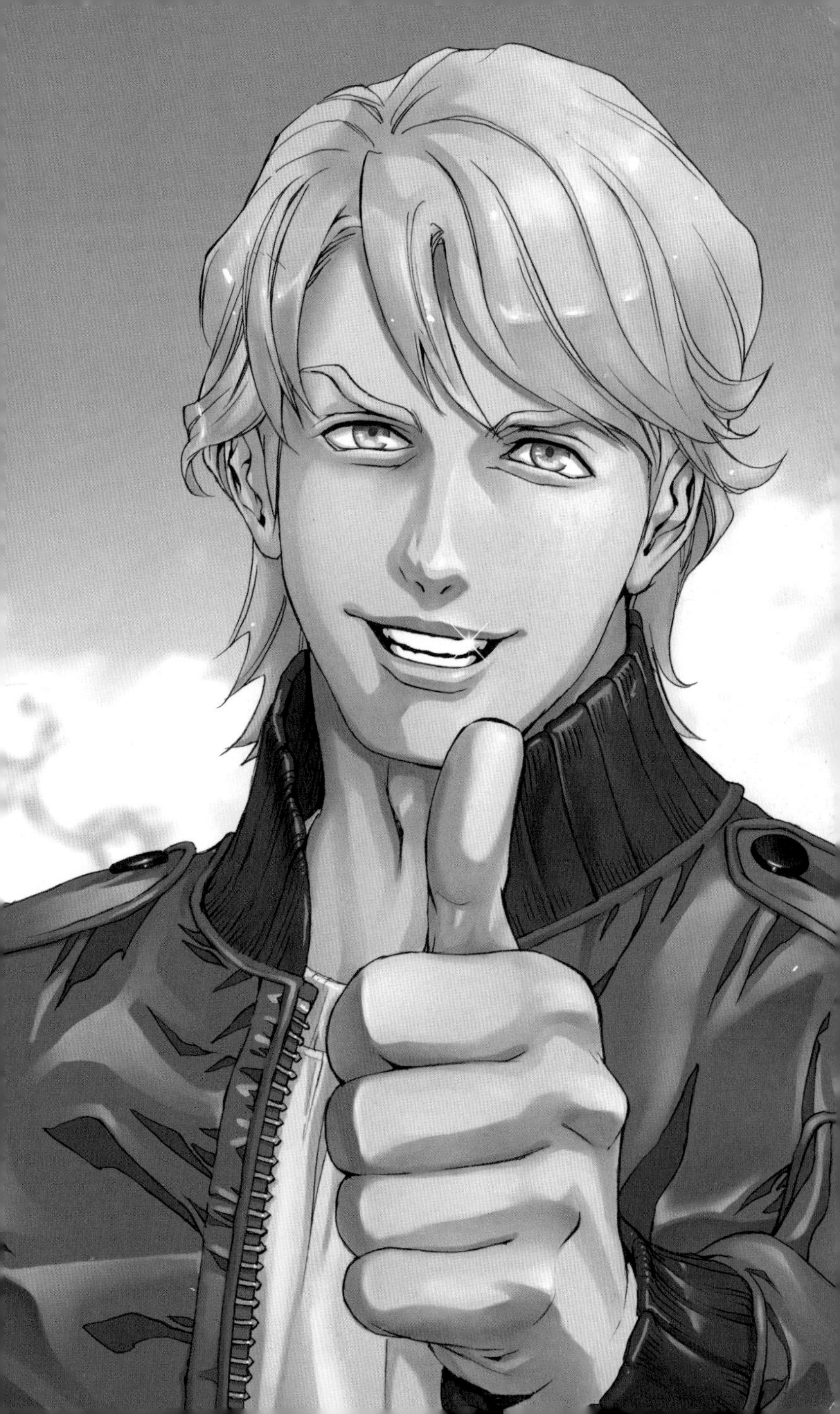

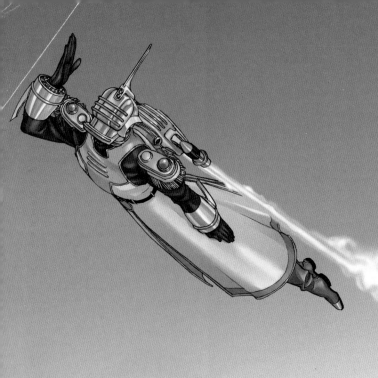

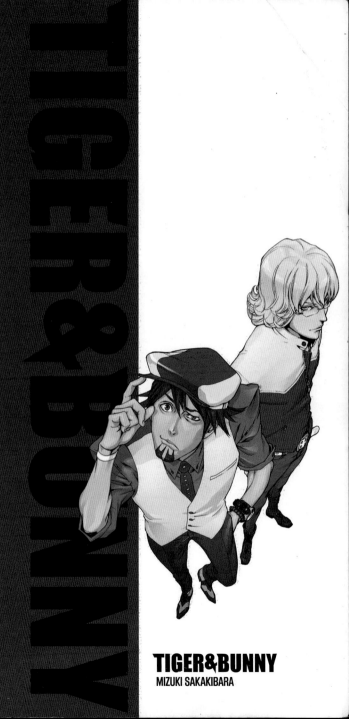

TIGER&BUNNY

MIZUKI SAKAKIBARA

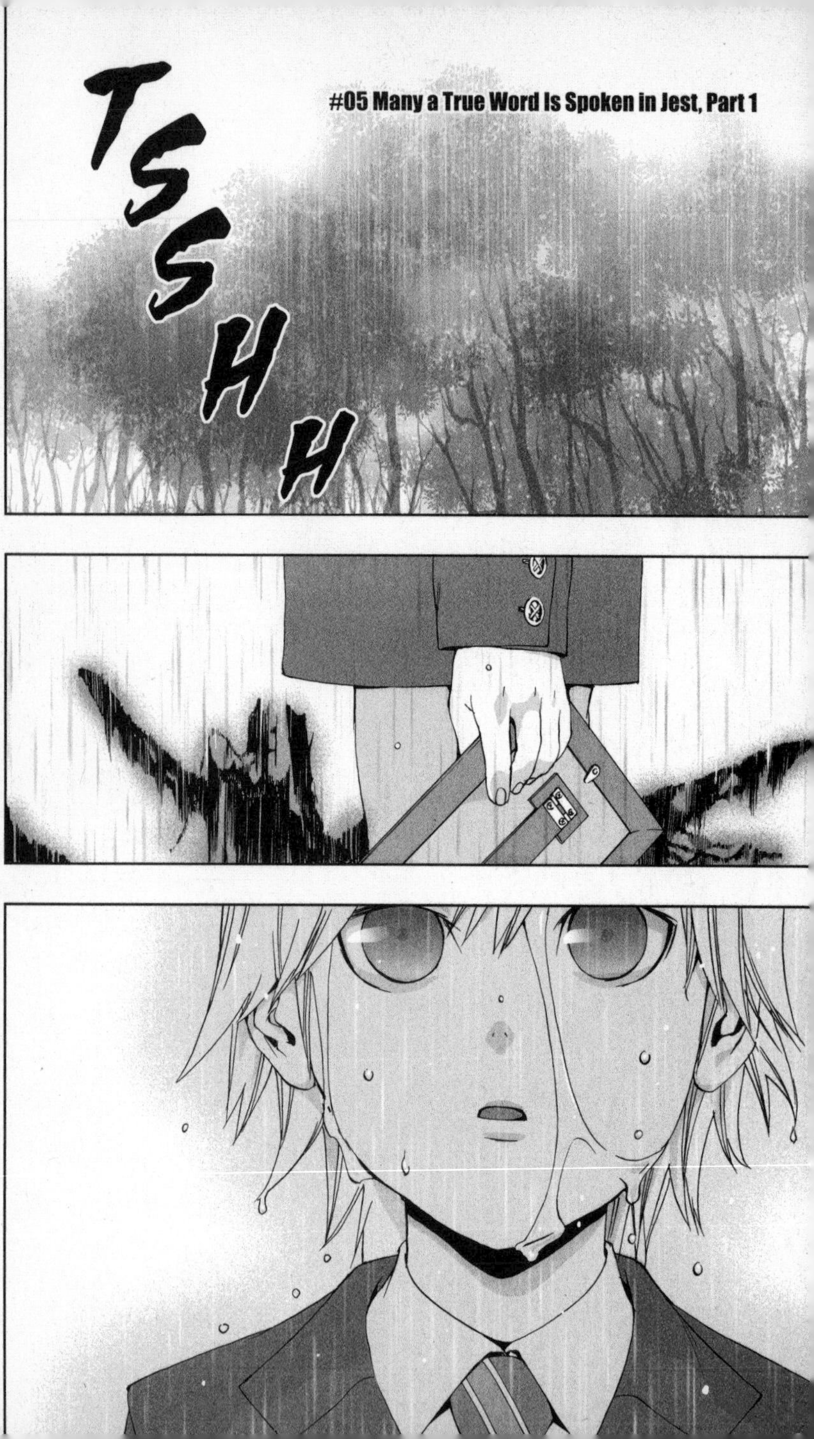
#05 Many a True Word Is Spoken in Jest, Part 1
TSSHH

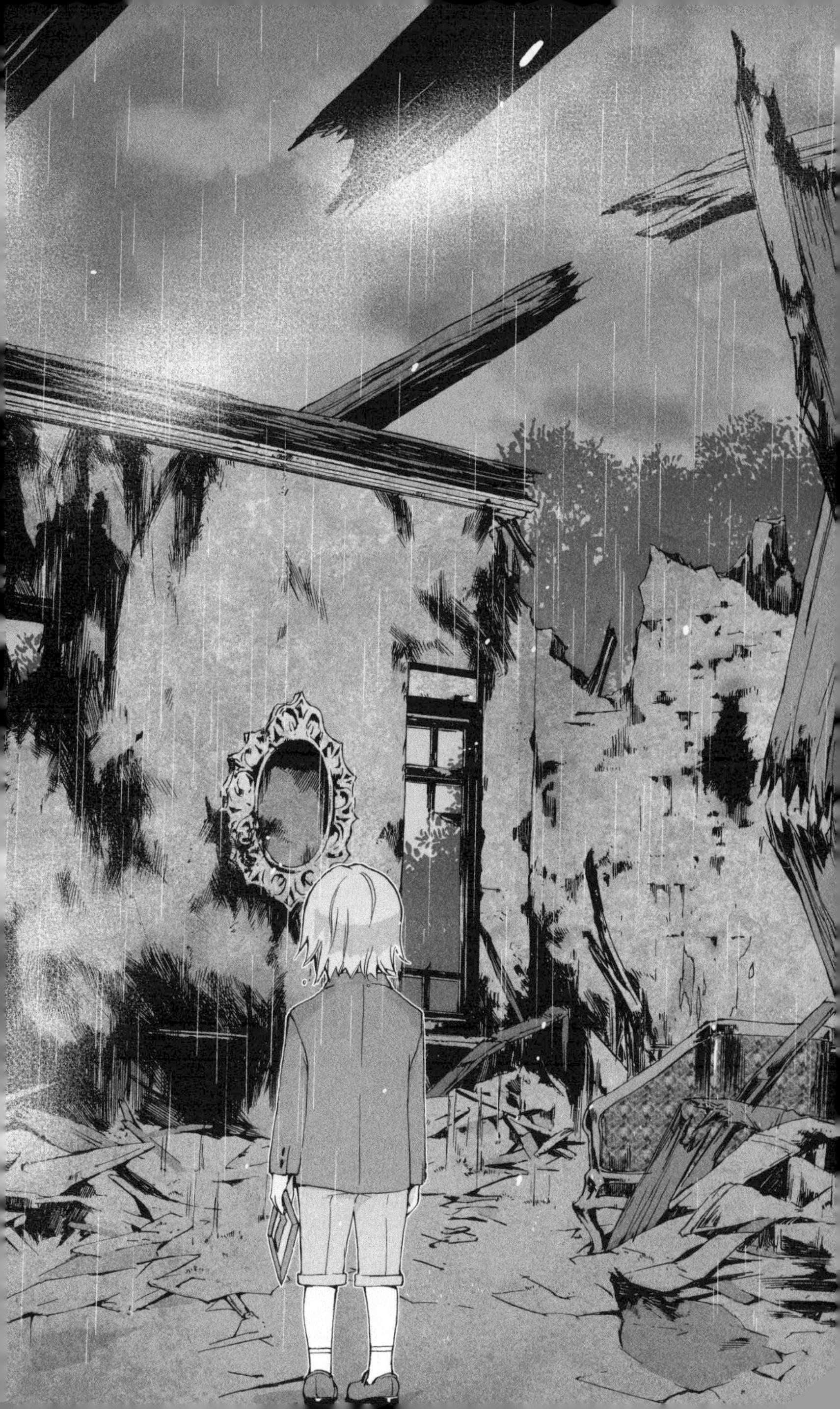

#05 Many a True Word Is Spoken in Jest, Part 1

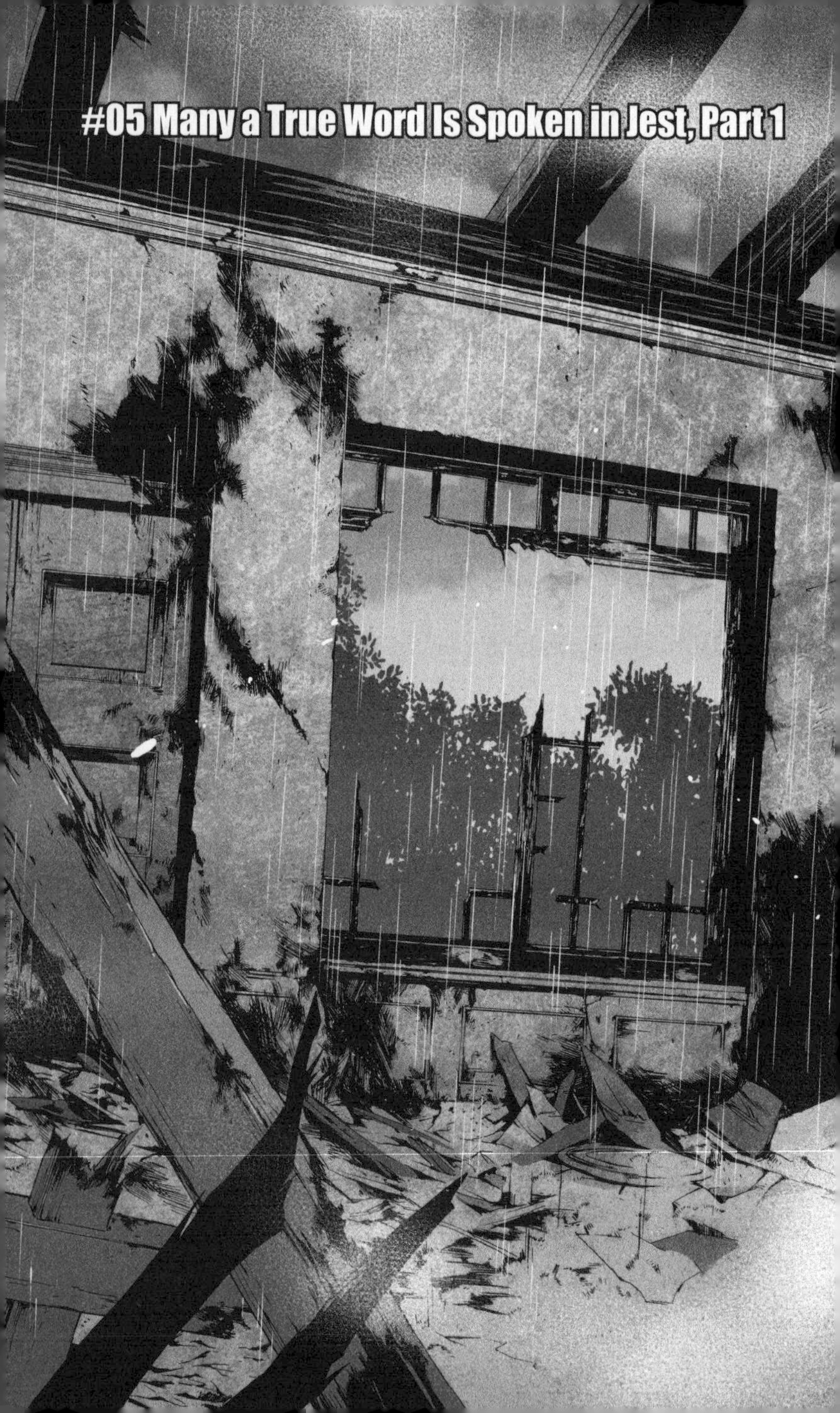

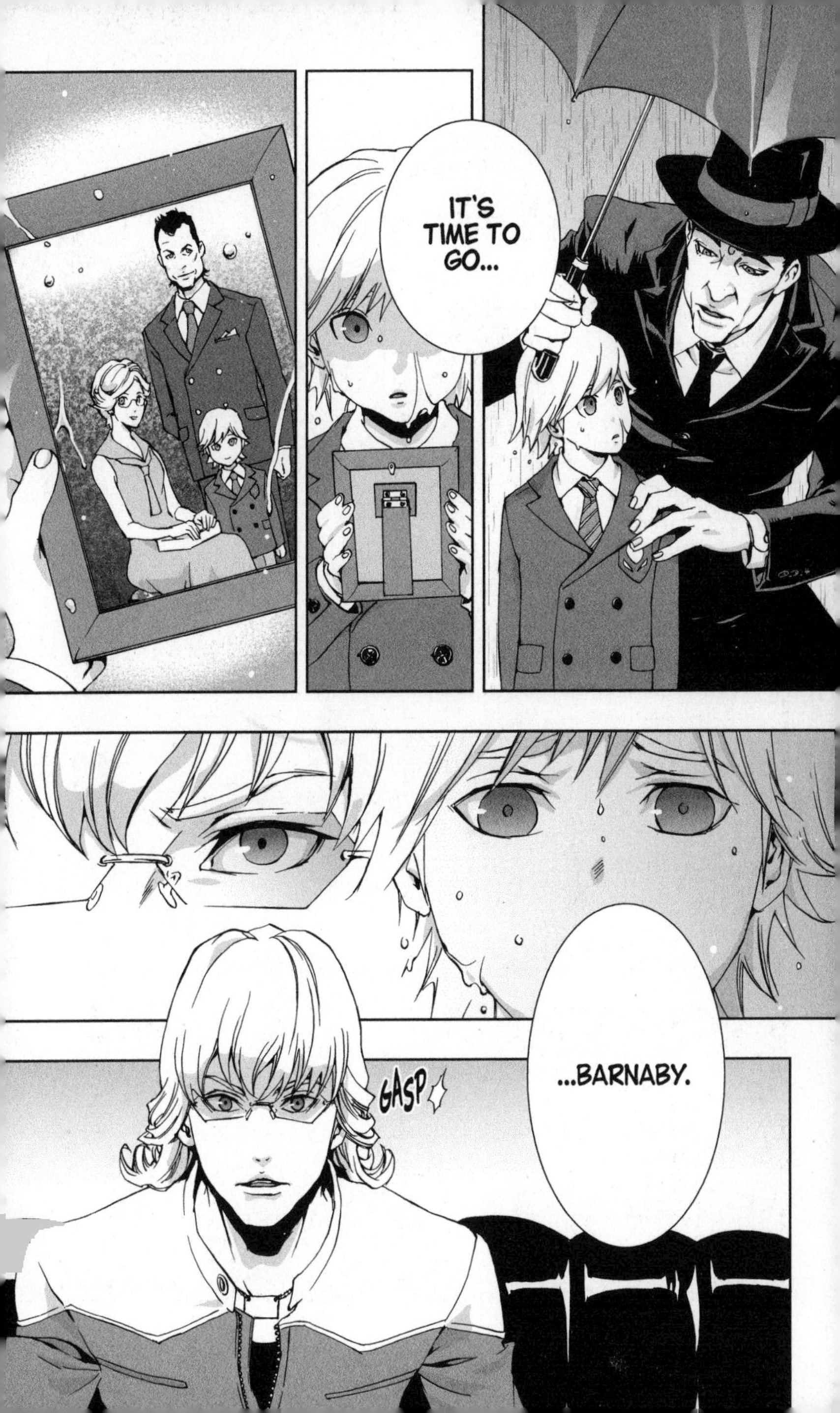
IT'S TIME TO GO...
...BARNABY.
GASP

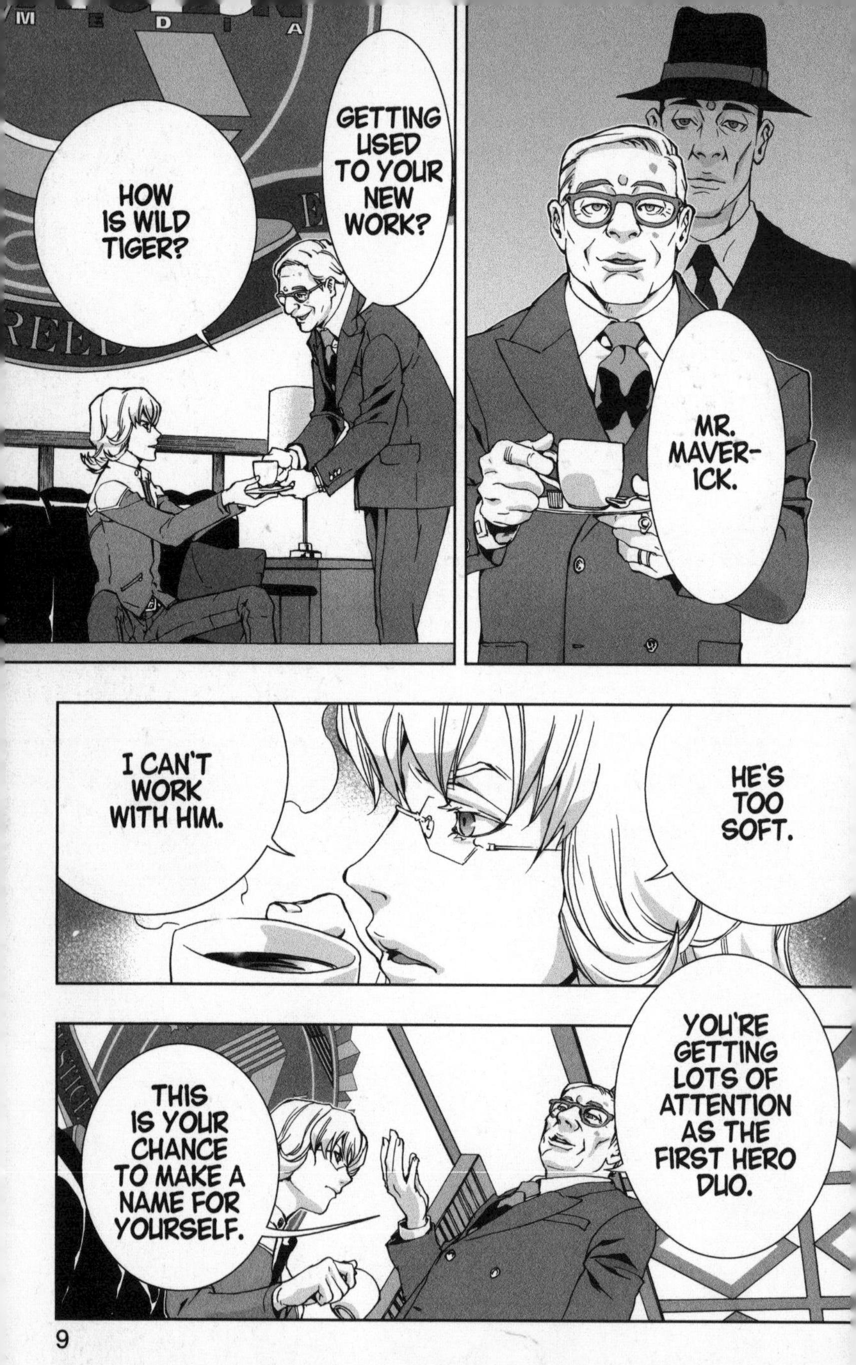
MR. MAVERICK.
GETTING USED TO YOUR NEW WORK?
HOW IS WILD TIGER?
HE'S TOO SOFT.
I CAN'T WORK WITH HIM.
YOU'RE GETTING LOTS OF ATTENTION AS THE FIRST HERO DUO.
THIS IS YOUR CHANCE TO MAKE A NAME FOR YOURSELF.

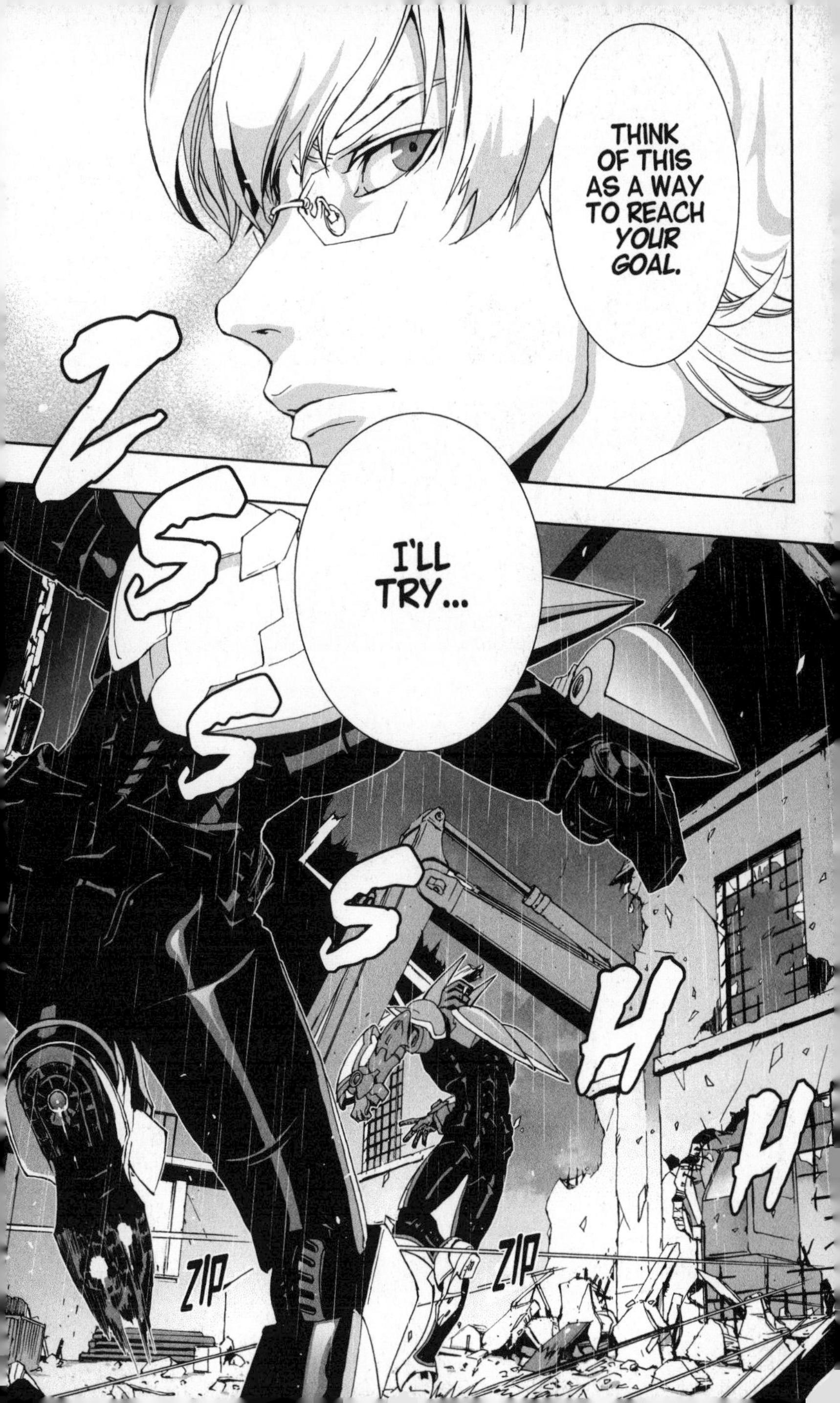
THINK OF THIS AS A WAY TO REACH YOUR GOAL.
I'LL TRY...
ZSSSHH
ZIP
ZIP

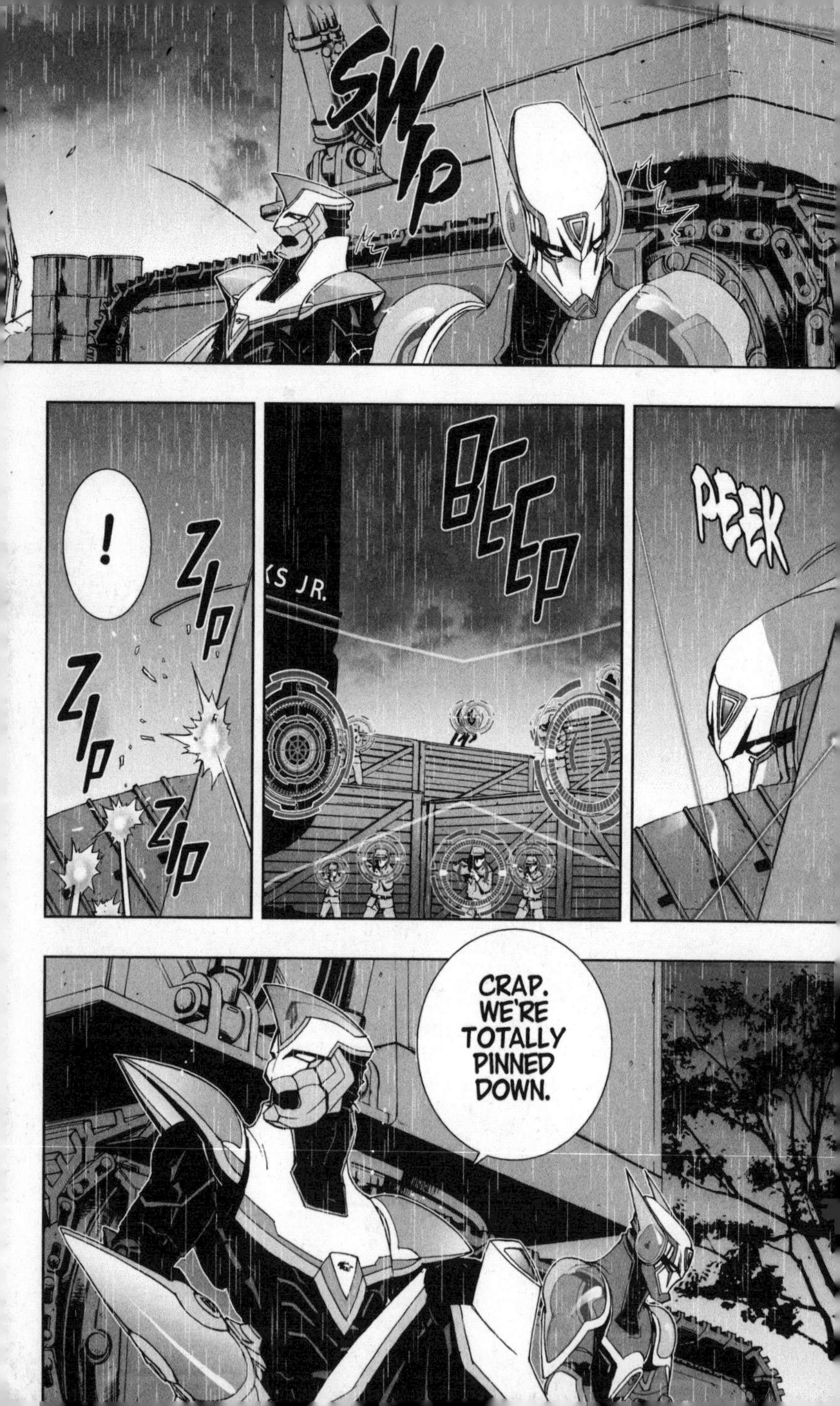
SWIP
PEEK
BEEP
KS JR.
!
ZIP
ZIP
ZIP
CRAP. WE'RE TOTALLY PINNED DOWN.

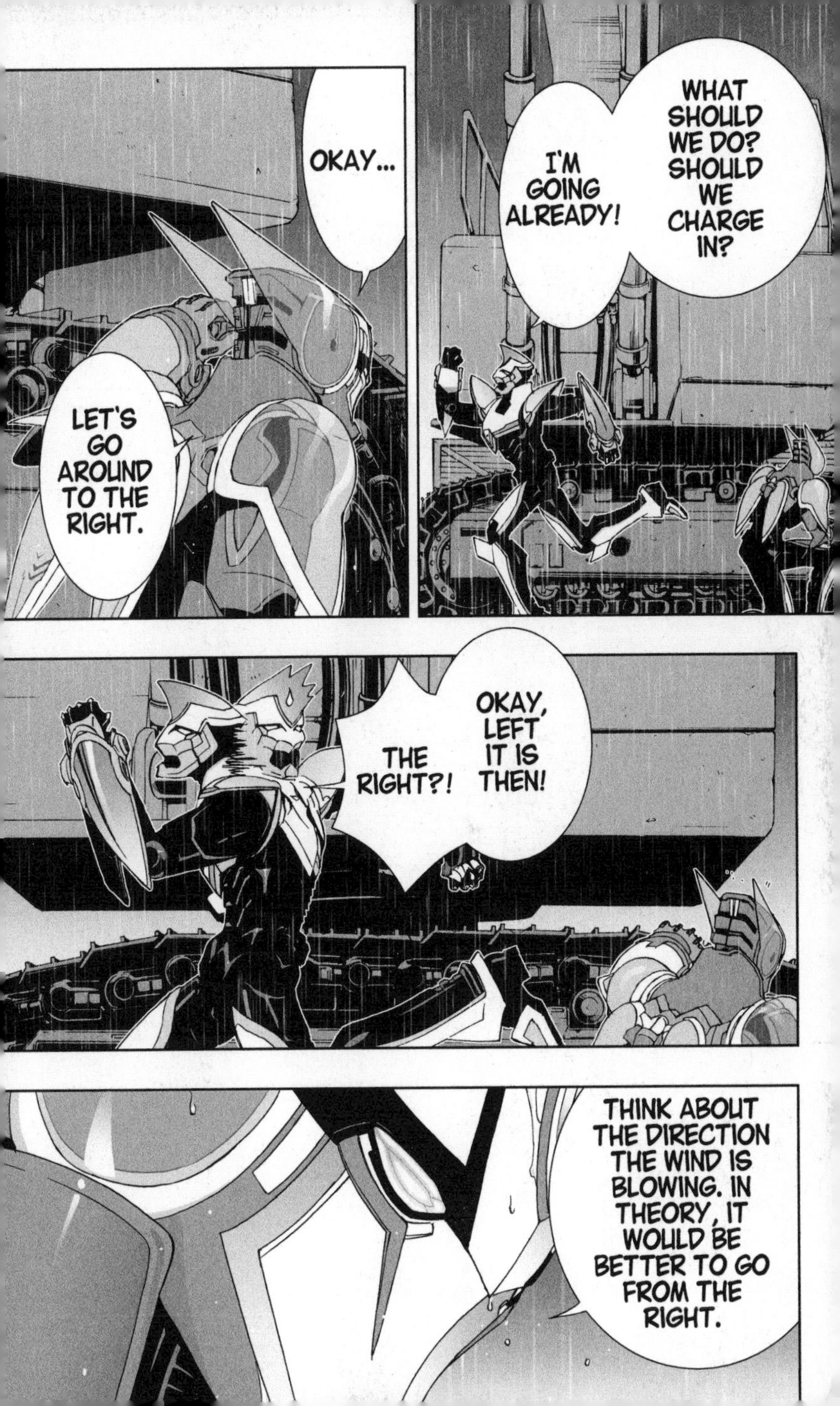
WHAT SHOULD WE DO? SHOULD WE CHARGE IN?
I'M GOING ALREADY!
OKAY...
LET'S GO AROUND TO THE RIGHT.
OKAY, LEFT IT IS THEN!
THE RIGHT?!
THINK ABOUT THE DIRECTION THE WIND IS BLOWING. IN THEORY, IT WOULD BE BETTER TO GO FROM THE RIGHT.

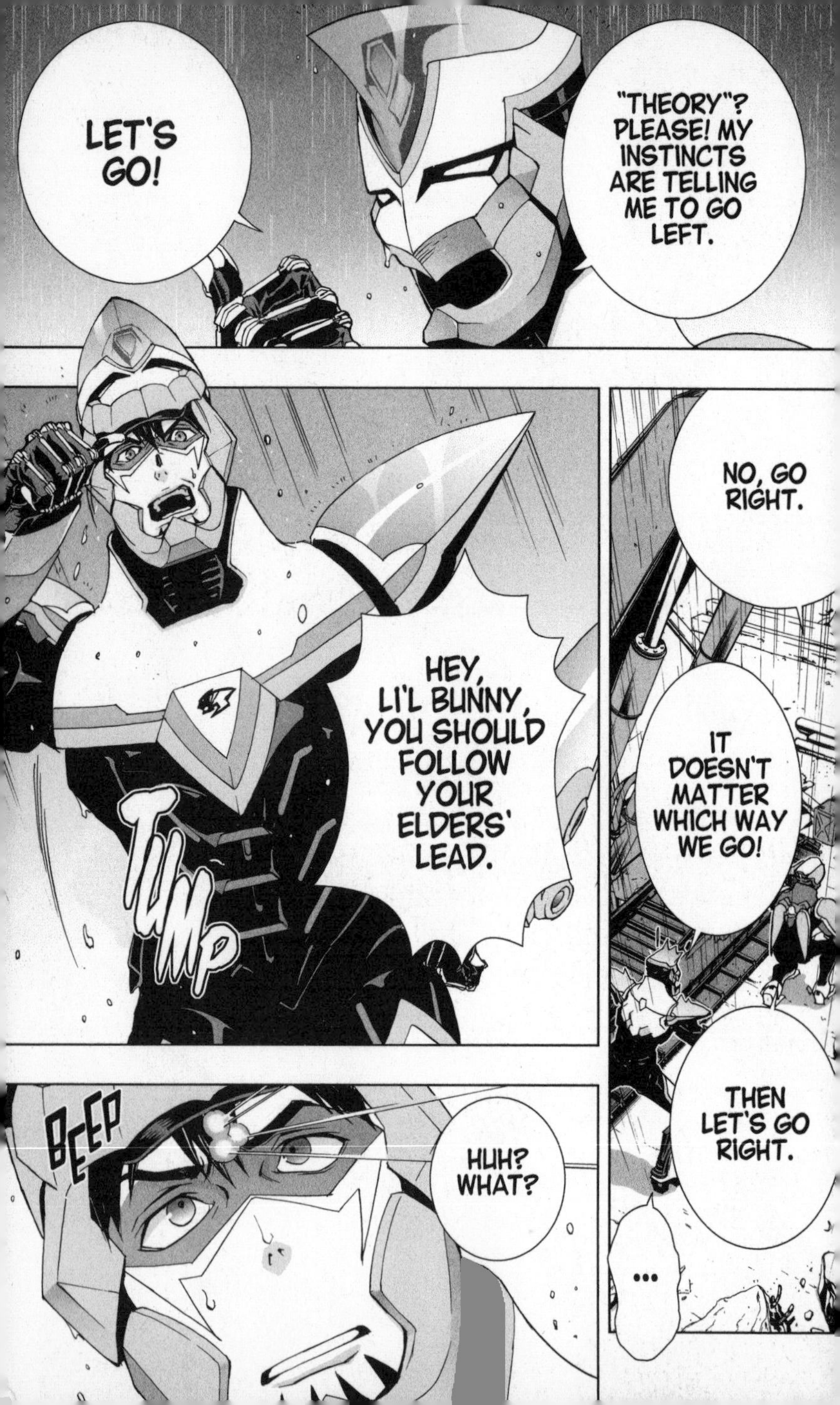
"THEORY"? PLEASE! MY INSTINCTS ARE TELLING ME TO GO LEFT.
LET'S GO!
NO, GO RIGHT.
IT DOESN'T MATTER WHICH WAY WE GO!
THEN LET'S GO RIGHT.
...
HEY, LI'L BUNNY, YOU SHOULD FOLLOW YOUR ELDERS' LEAD.
TUMP
BEEP
HUH? WHAT?

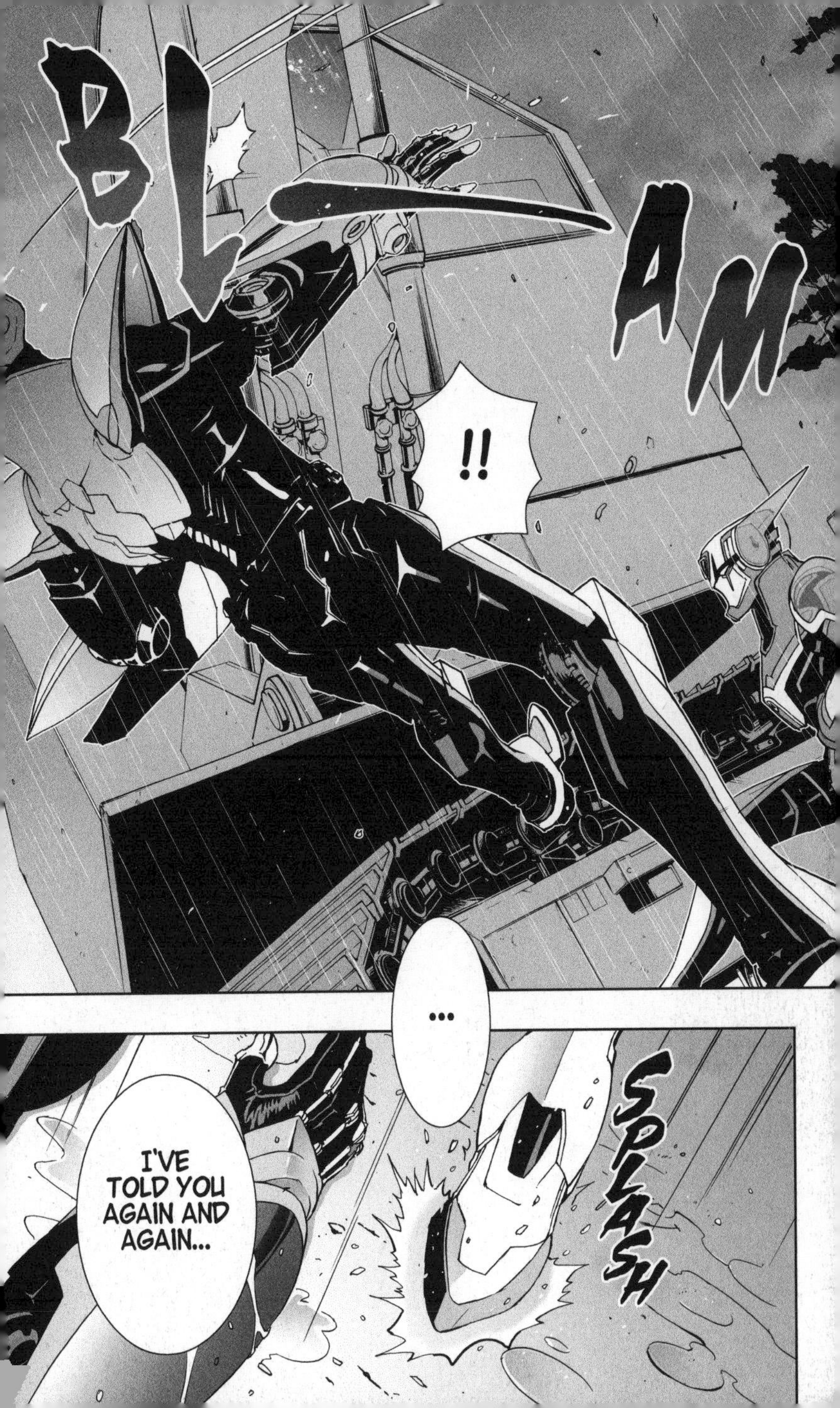
BLAM
!!
...
SPLASH
I'VE TOLD YOU AGAIN AND AGAIN...

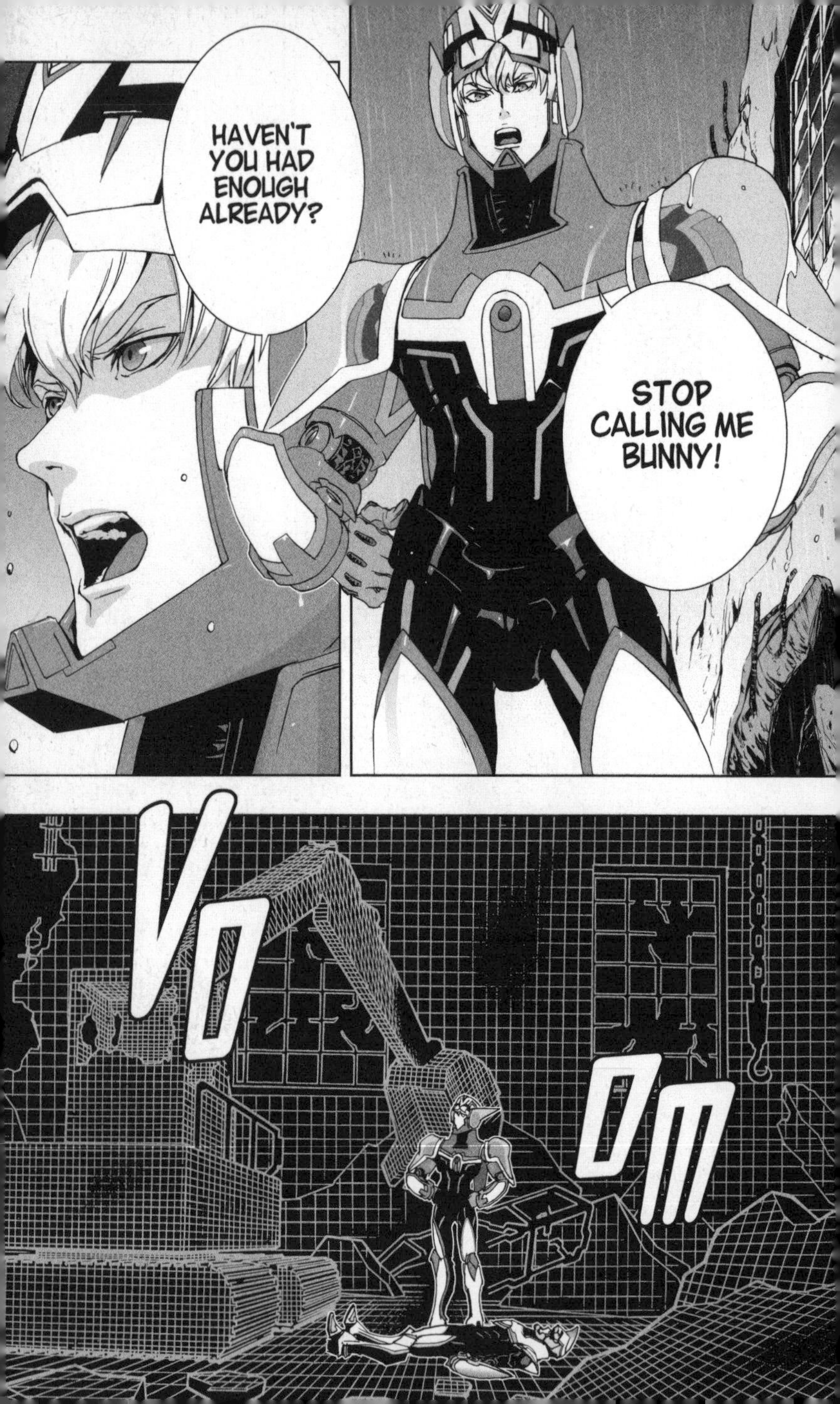
STOP CALLING ME BUNNY!
HAVEN'T YOU HAD ENOUGH ALREADY?
VOOM

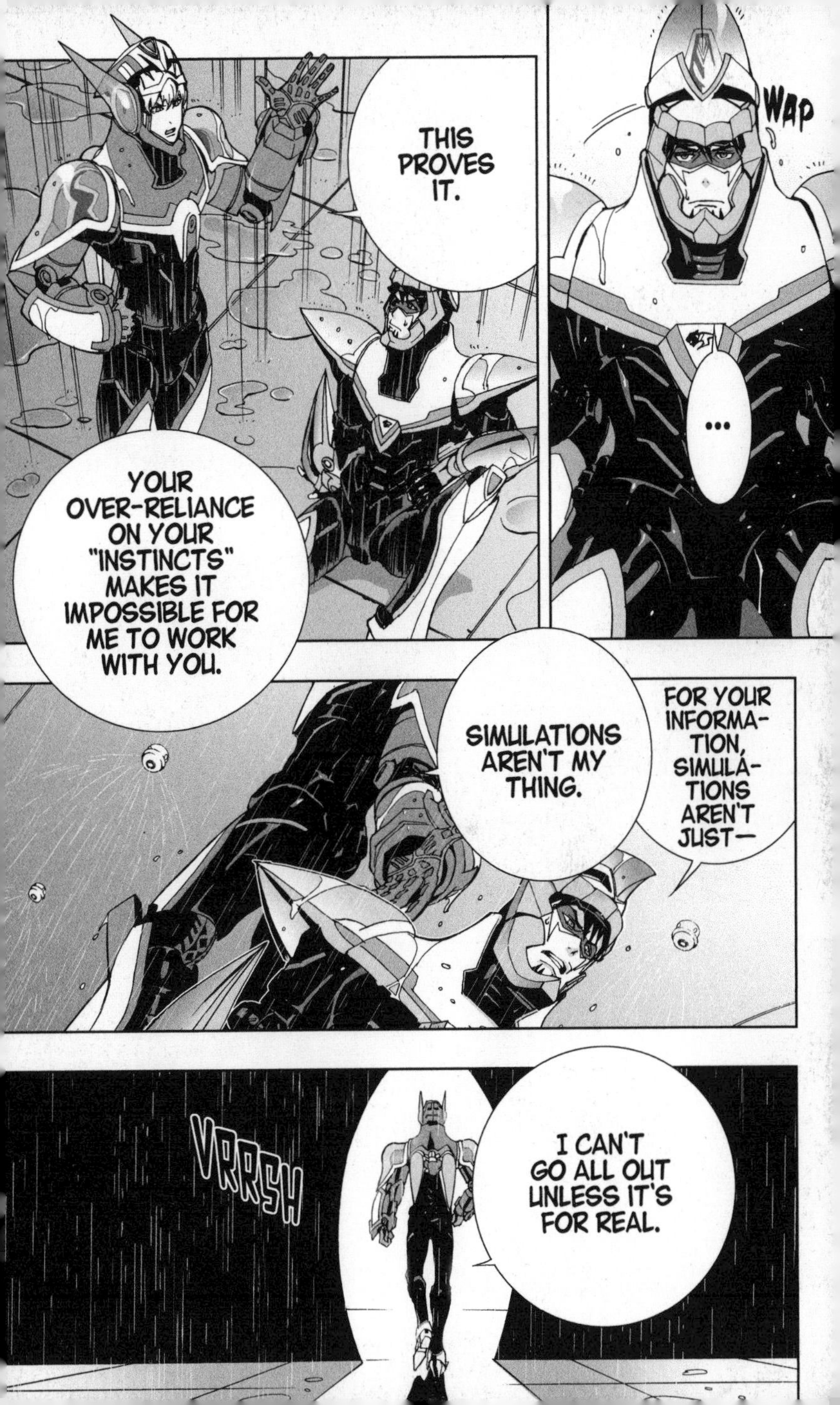
WAP
...
THIS PROVES IT.
YOUR OVER-RELIANCE ON YOUR "INSTINCTS" MAKES IT IMPOSSIBLE FOR ME TO WORK WITH YOU.
FOR YOUR INFORMATION, SIMULATIONS AREN'T JUST—
SIMULATIONS AREN'T MY THING.
I CAN'T GO ALL OUT UNLESS IT'S FOR REAL.
VRRSH

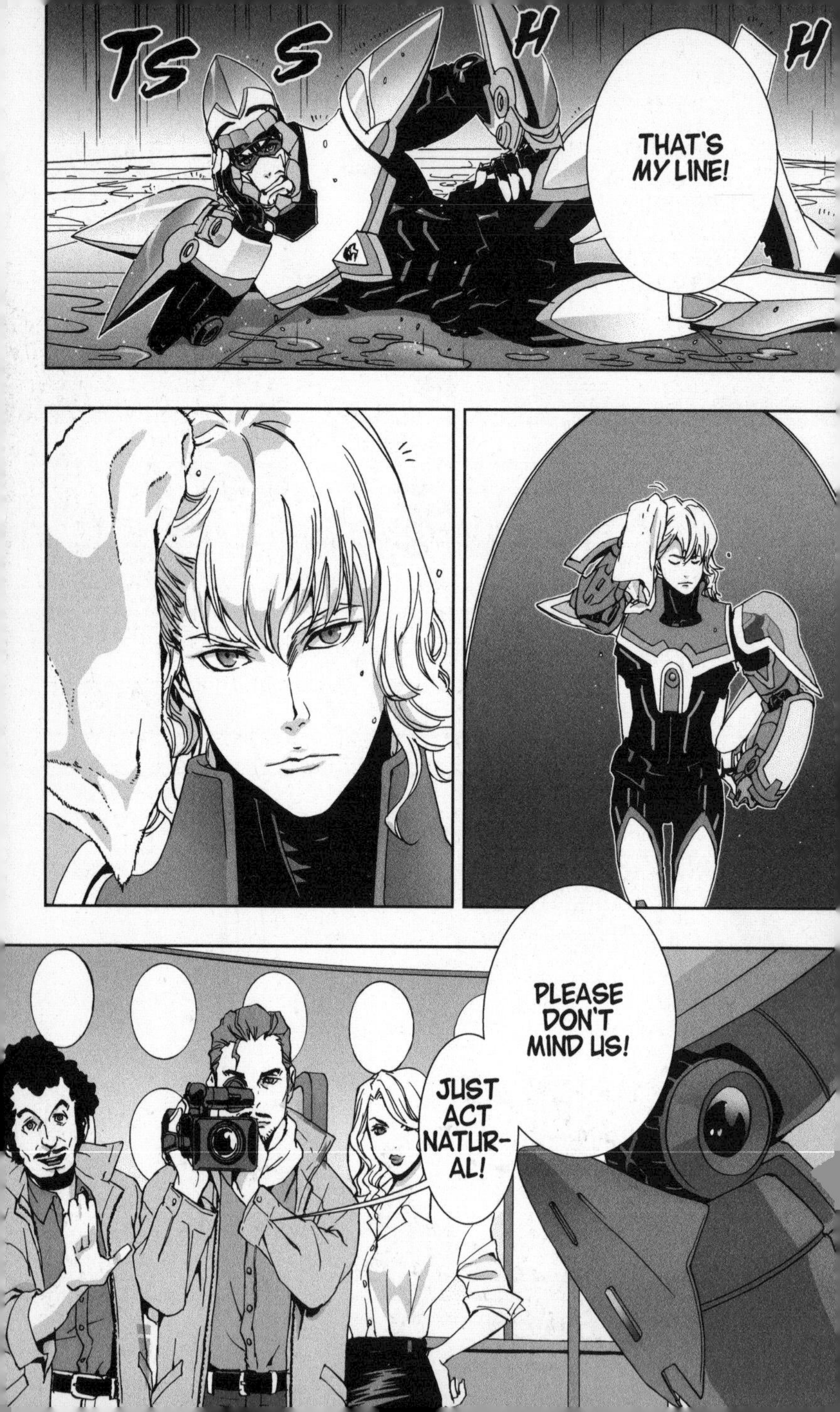
TSSHH
THAT'S MY LINE!
PLEASE DON'T MIND US!
JUST ACT NATUR-AL!

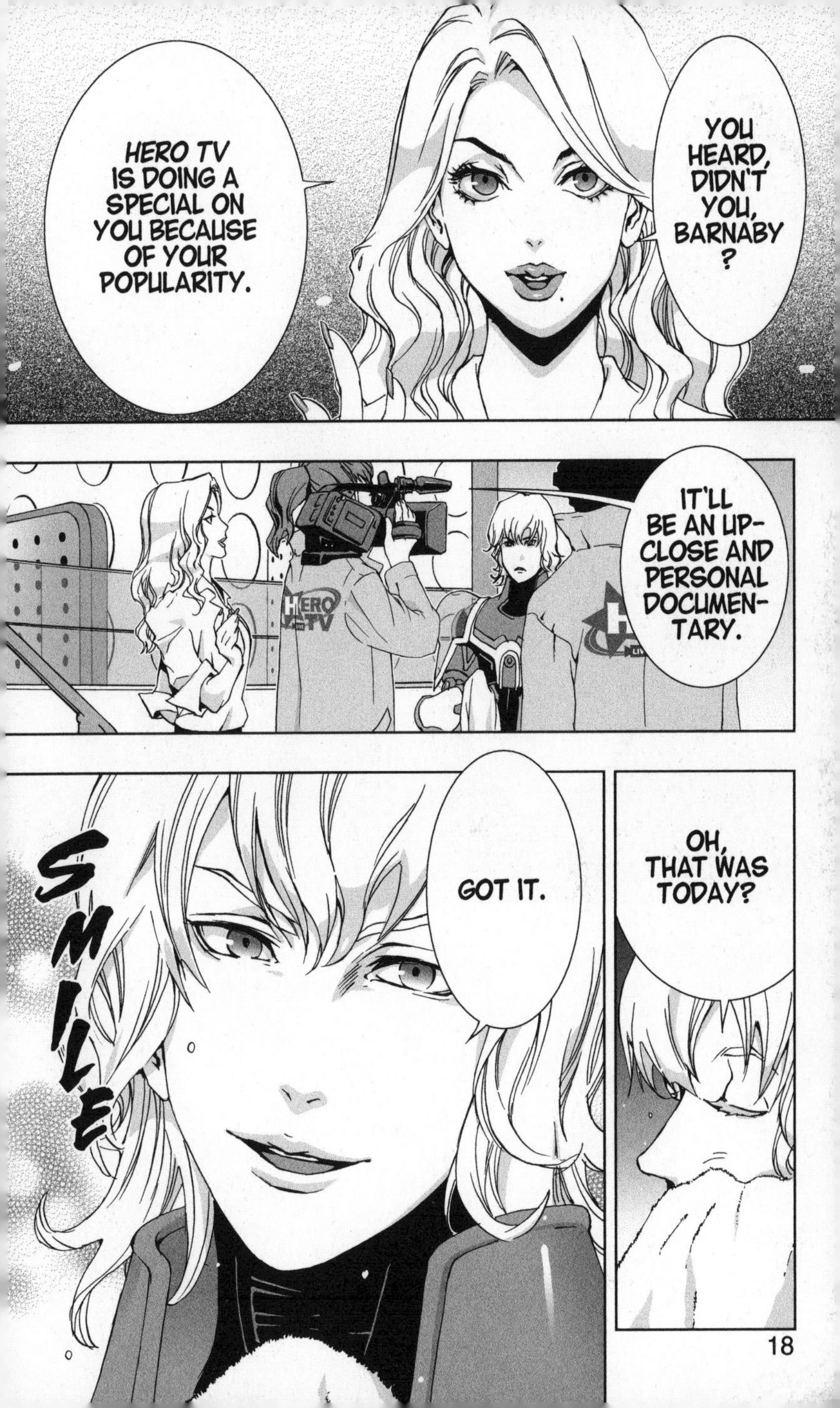
YOU HEARD, DIDN'T YOU, BARNABY?
HERO TV IS DOING A SPECIAL ON YOU BECAUSE OF YOUR POPULARITY.
IT'LL BE AN UP-CLOSE AND PERSONAL DOCUMENTARY.
OH, THAT WAS TODAY?
GOT IT.
SMILE

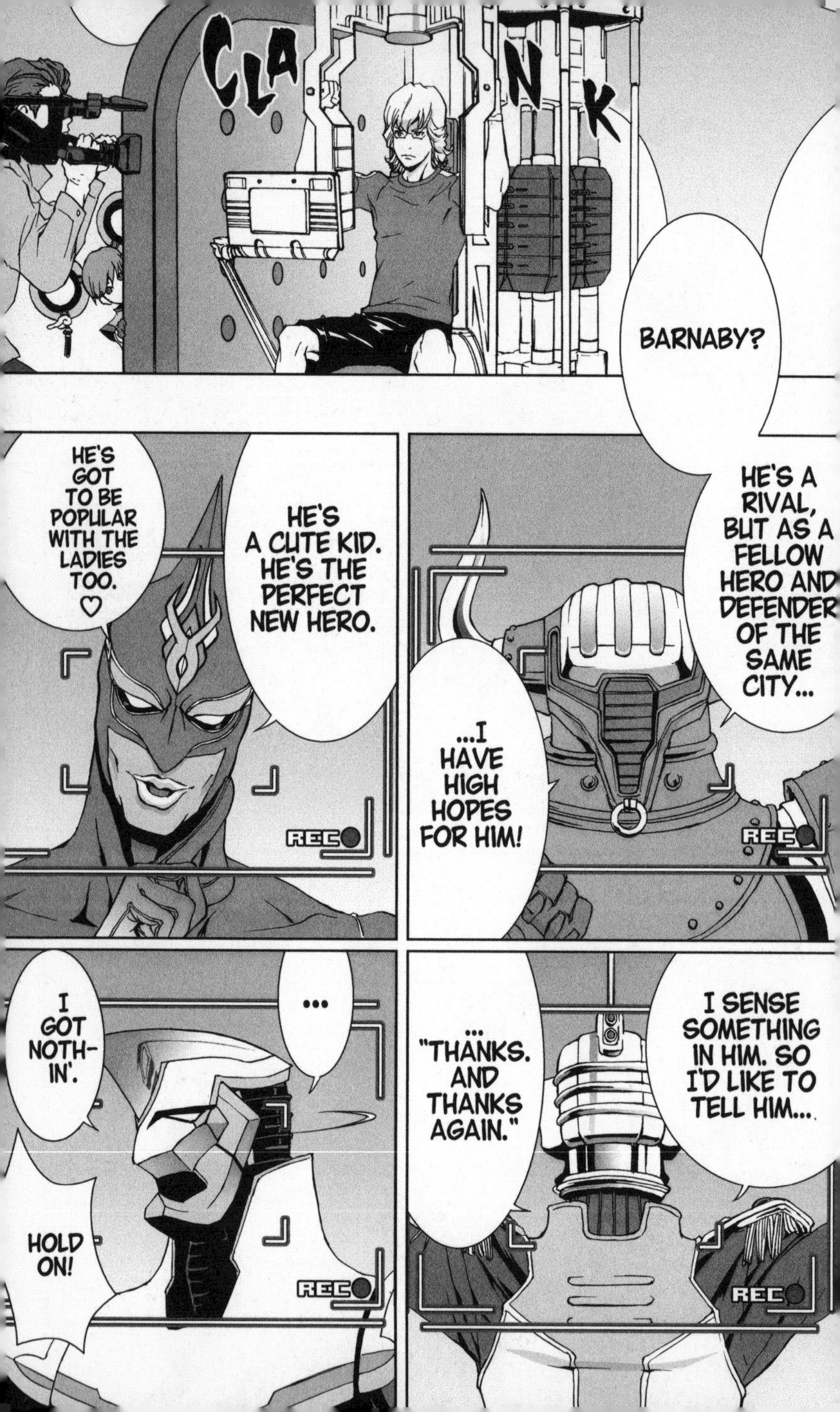
CLANK
BARNABY?
HE'S A RIVAL, BUT AS A FELLOW HERO AND DEFENDER OF THE SAME CITY...
...I HAVE HIGH HOPES FOR HIM!
HE'S A CUTE KID. HE'S THE PERFECT NEW HERO.
HE'S GOT TO BE POPULAR WITH THE LADIES TOO. ♡
I SENSE SOMETHING IN HIM. SO I'D LIKE TO TELL HIM...
..."THANKS. AND THANKS AGAIN."
...
I GOT NOTH-IN'.
HOLD ON!

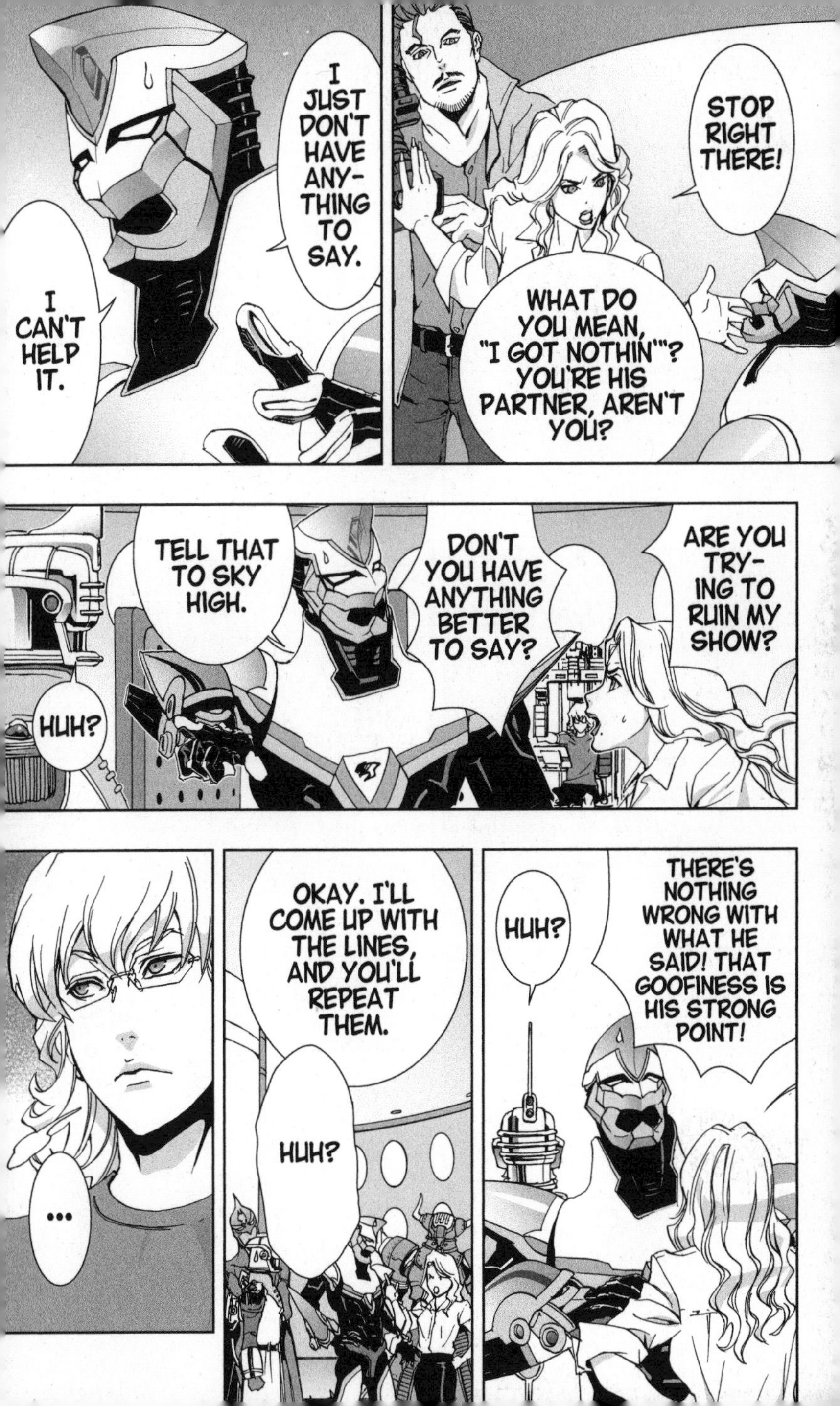
STOP RIGHT THERE!
WHAT DO YOU MEAN, "I GOT NOTHIN'"? YOU'RE HIS PARTNER, AREN'T YOU?
I JUST DON'T HAVE ANY-THING TO SAY.
I CAN'T HELP IT.
ARE YOU TRY-ING TO RUIN MY SHOW?
DON'T YOU HAVE ANYTHING BETTER TO SAY?
TELL THAT TO SKY HIGH.
HUH?
THERE'S NOTHING WRONG WITH WHAT HE SAID! THAT GOOFINESS IS HIS STRONG POINT!
HUH?
OKAY. I'LL COME UP WITH THE LINES, AND YOU'LL REPEAT THEM.
HUH?
...

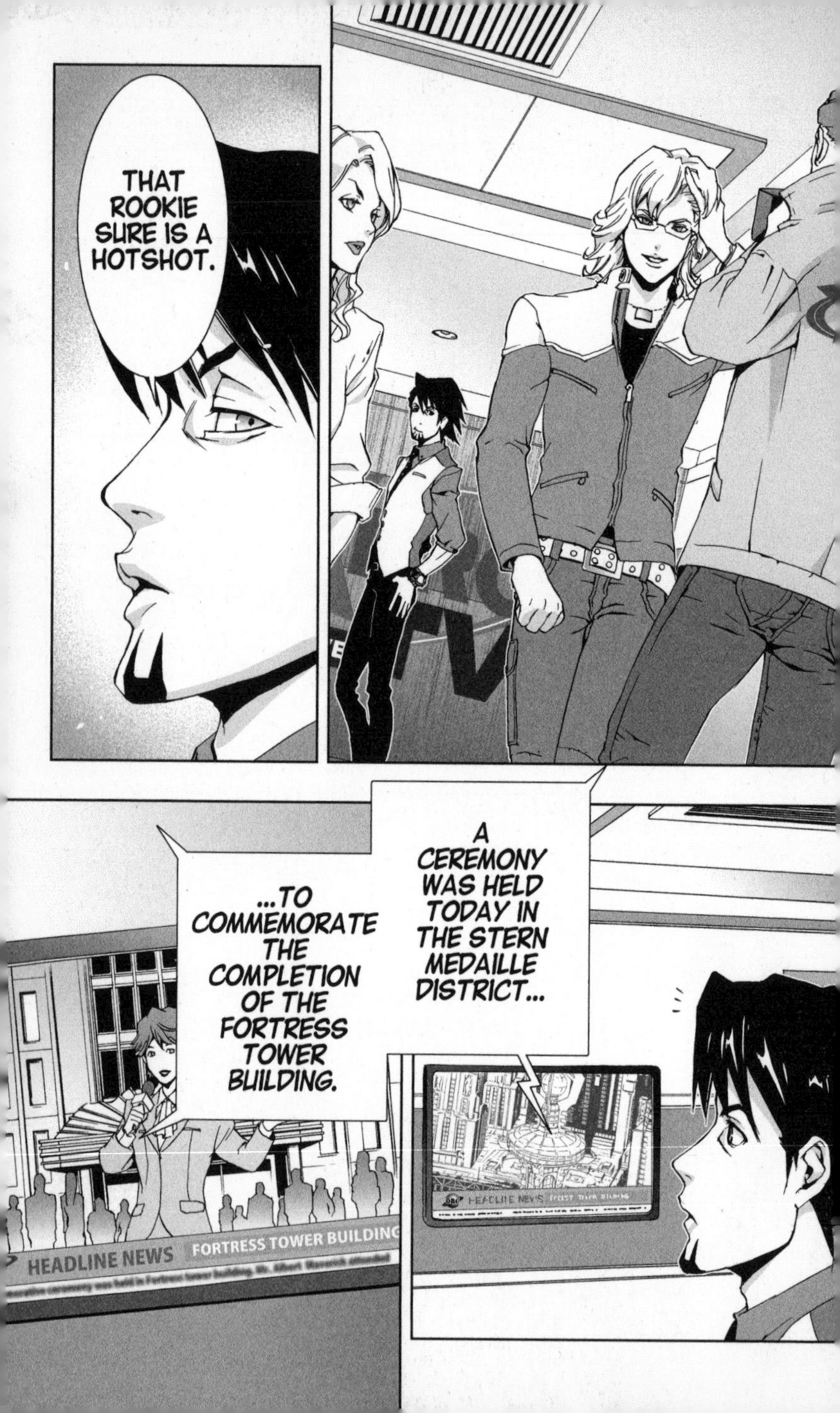
THAT ROOKIE SURE IS A HOTSHOT.
A CEREMONY WAS HELD TODAY IN THE STERN MEDAILLE DISTRICT...
...TO COMMEMORATE THE COMPLETION OF THE FORTRESS TOWER BUILDING.
HEADLINE NEWS
FORTRESS TOWER BUILDING

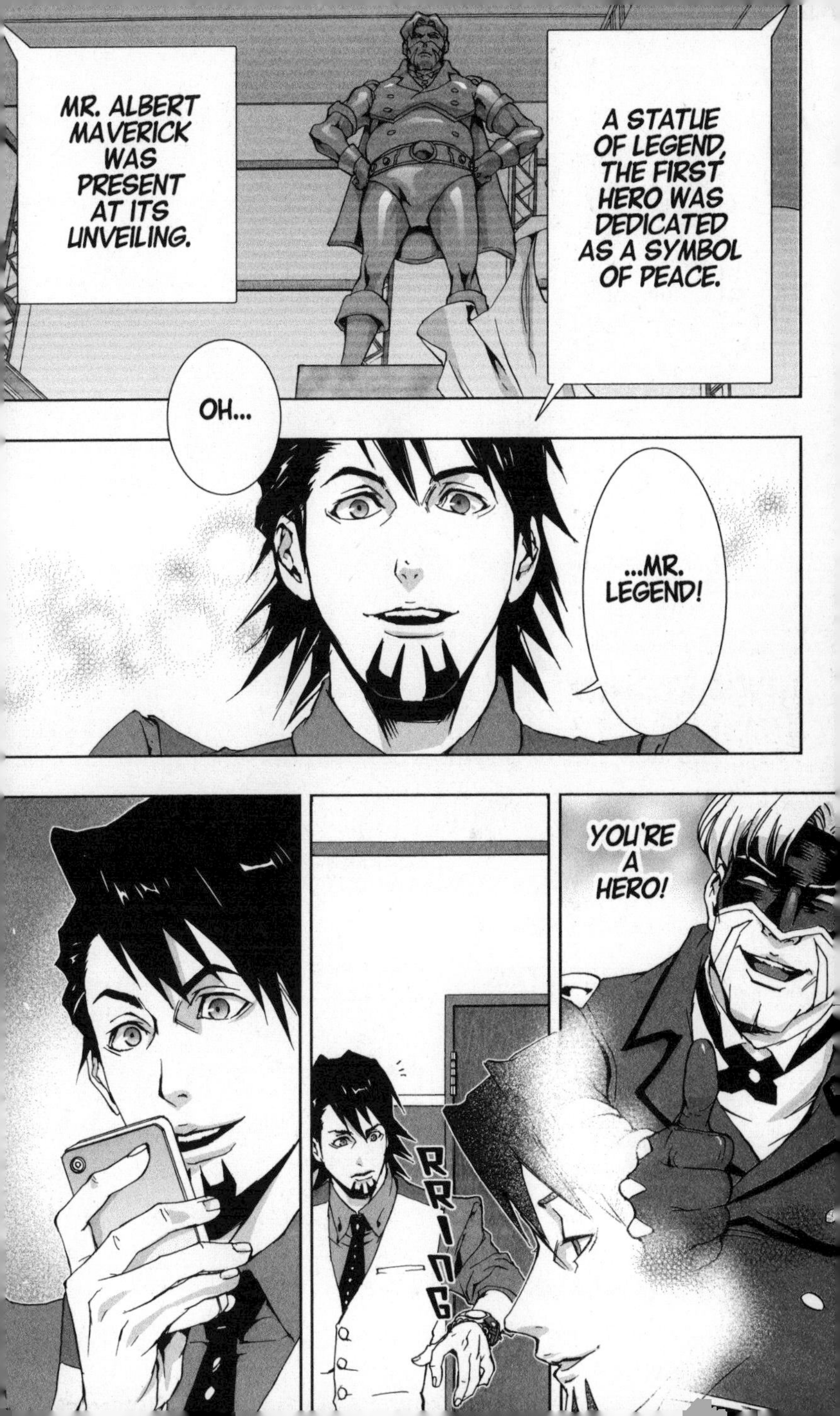
A STATUE OF LEGEND, THE FIRST HERO WAS DEDICATED AS A SYMBOL OF PEACE.
MR. ALBERT MAVERICK WAS PRESENT AT ITS UNVEILING.
OH...
...MR. LEGEND!
YOU'RE A HERO!
RRING

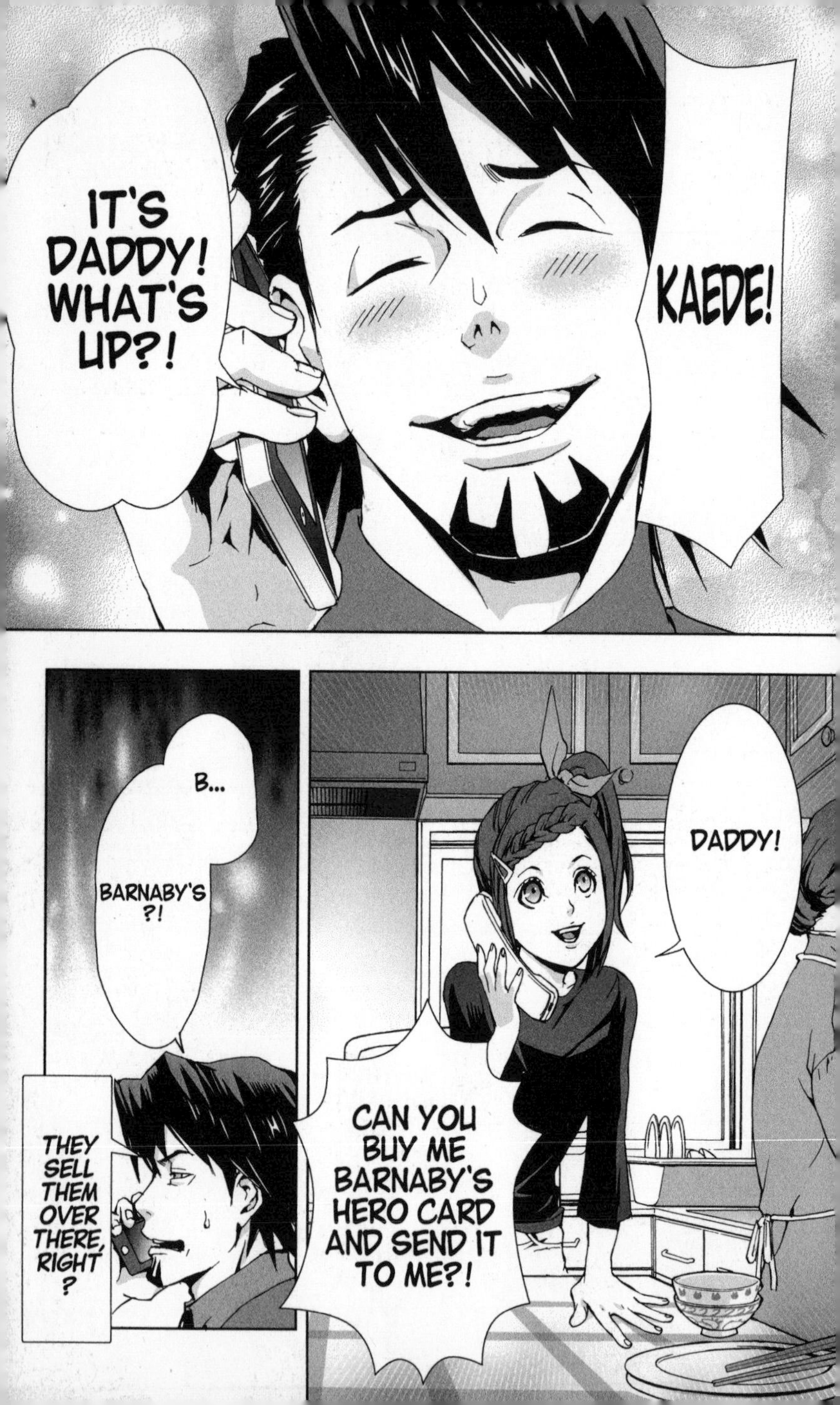
KAEDE!
IT'S DADDY! WHAT'S UP?!
DADDY!
CAN YOU BUY ME BARNABY'S HERO CARD AND SEND IT TO ME?!
B...
BARNABY'S ?!
THEY SELL THEM OVER THERE, RIGHT?

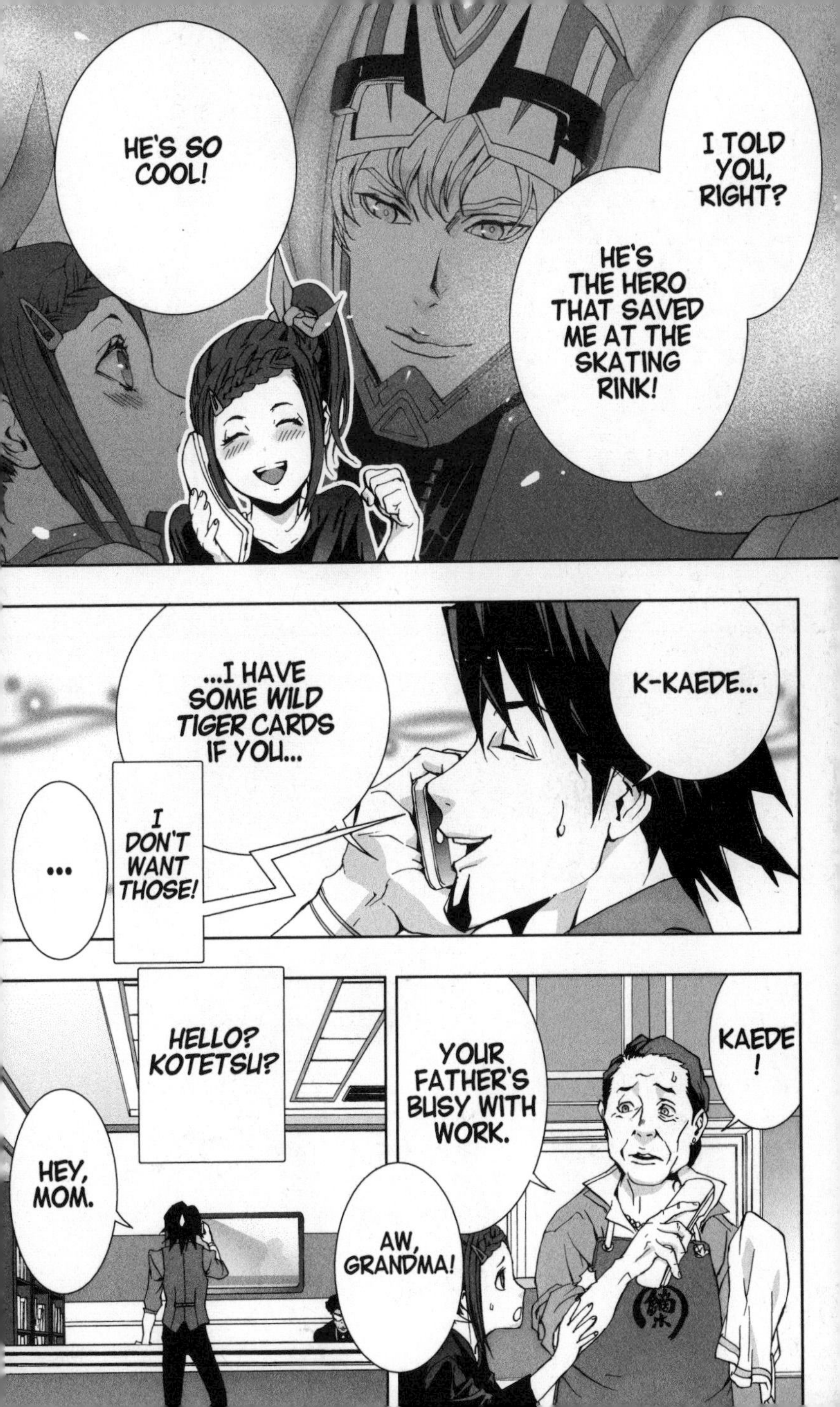
I TOLD YOU, RIGHT?
HE'S THE HERO THAT SAVED ME AT THE SKATING RINK!
HE'S SO COOL!
K-KAEDE...
...I HAVE SOME WILD TIGER CARDS IF YOU...
I DON'T WANT THOSE!
...
KAEDE!
YOUR FATHER'S BUSY WITH WORK.
AW, GRANDMA!
HELLO? KOTETSU?
HEY, MOM.

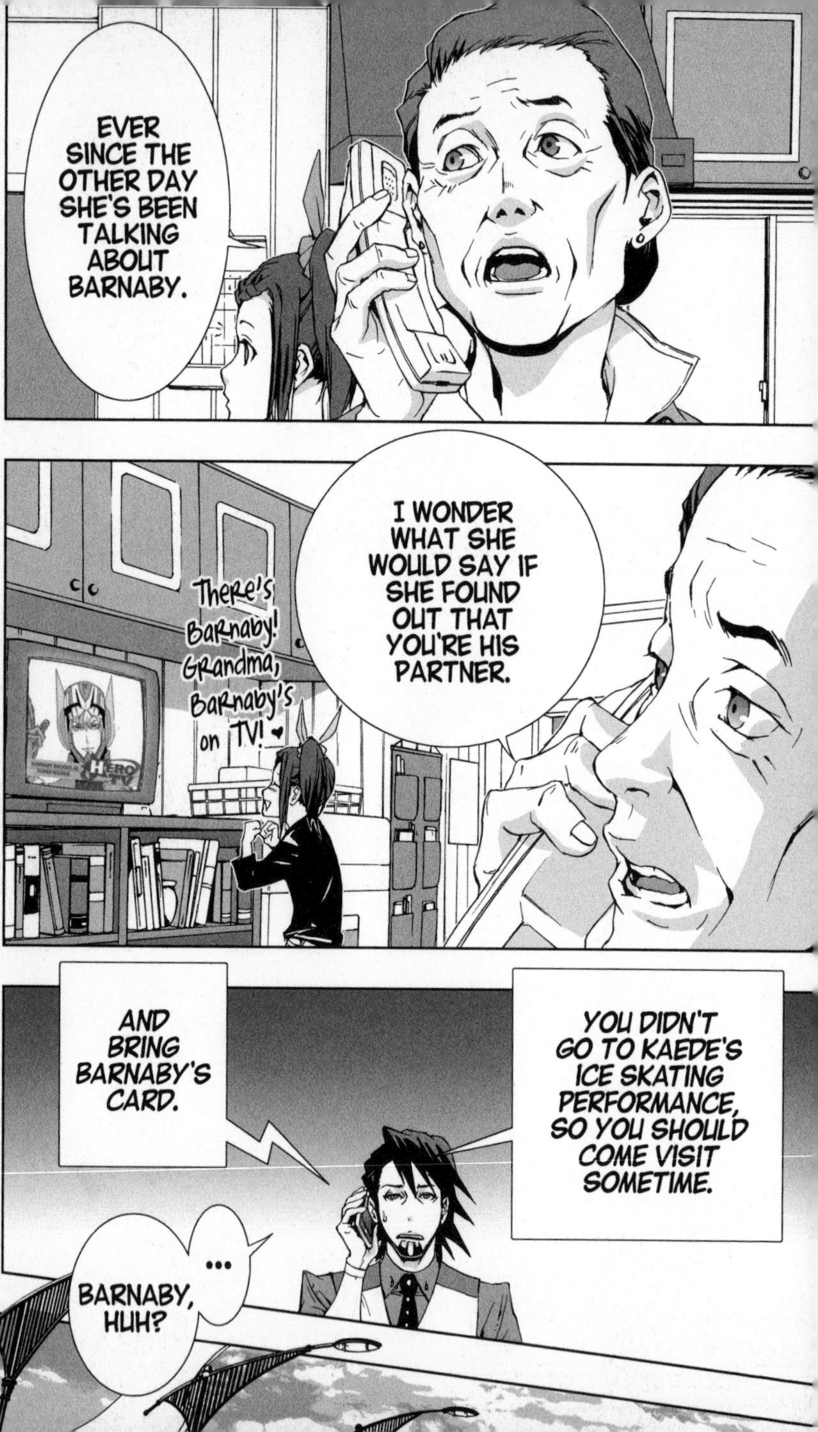
EVER SINCE THE OTHER DAY SHE'S BEEN TALKING ABOUT BARNABY.
I WONDER WHAT SHE WOULD SAY IF SHE FOUND OUT THAT YOU'RE HIS PARTNER.
There's Barnaby! Grandma, Barnaby's on TV! ♥
HERO TV
YOU DIDN'T GO TO KAEDE'S ICE SKATING PERFORMANCE, SO YOU SHOULD COME VISIT SOMETIME.
AND BRING BARNABY'S CARD.
... BARNABY, HUH?

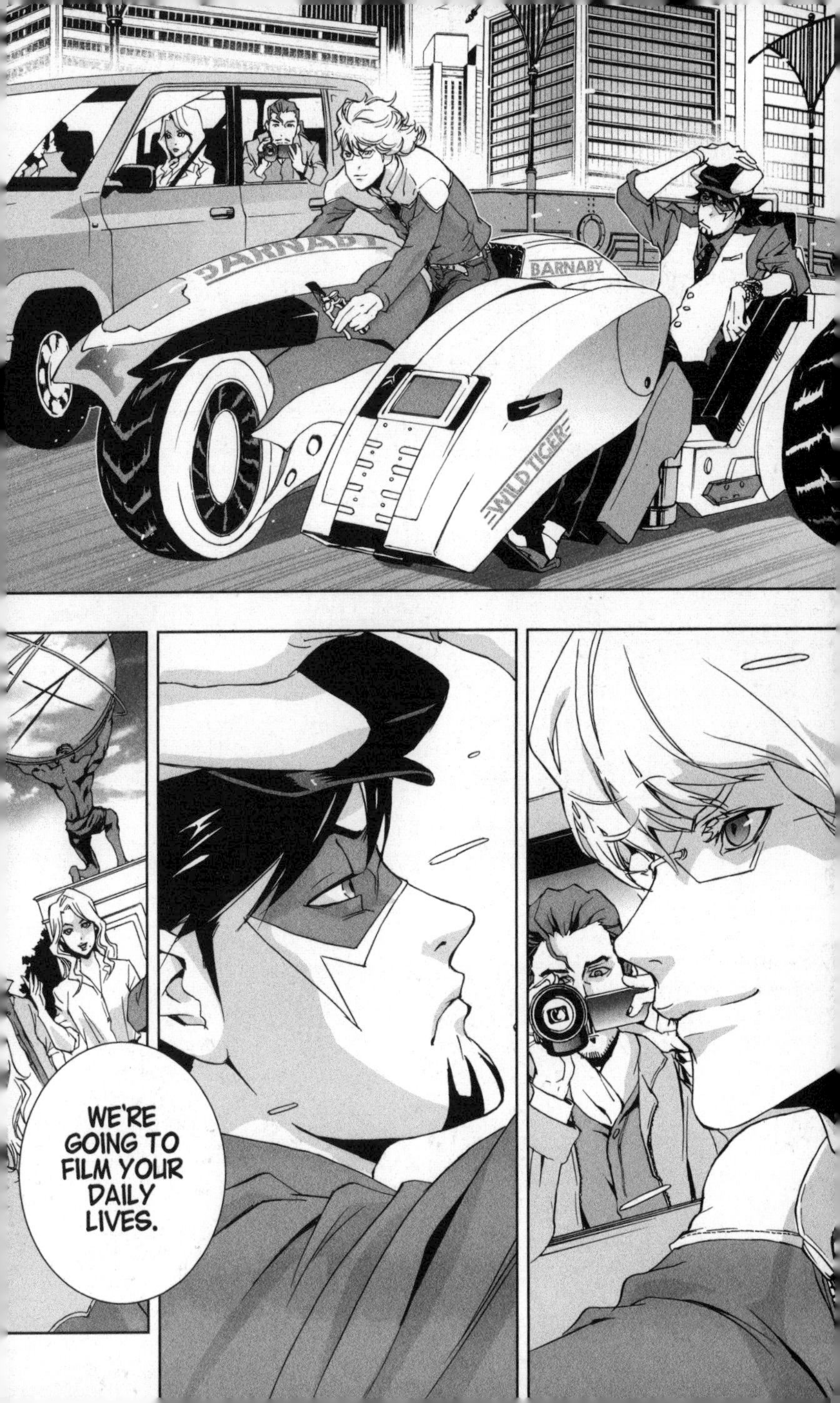
BARNABY
BARNABY
WILD TIGER
WE'RE GOING TO FILM YOUR DAILY LIVES.

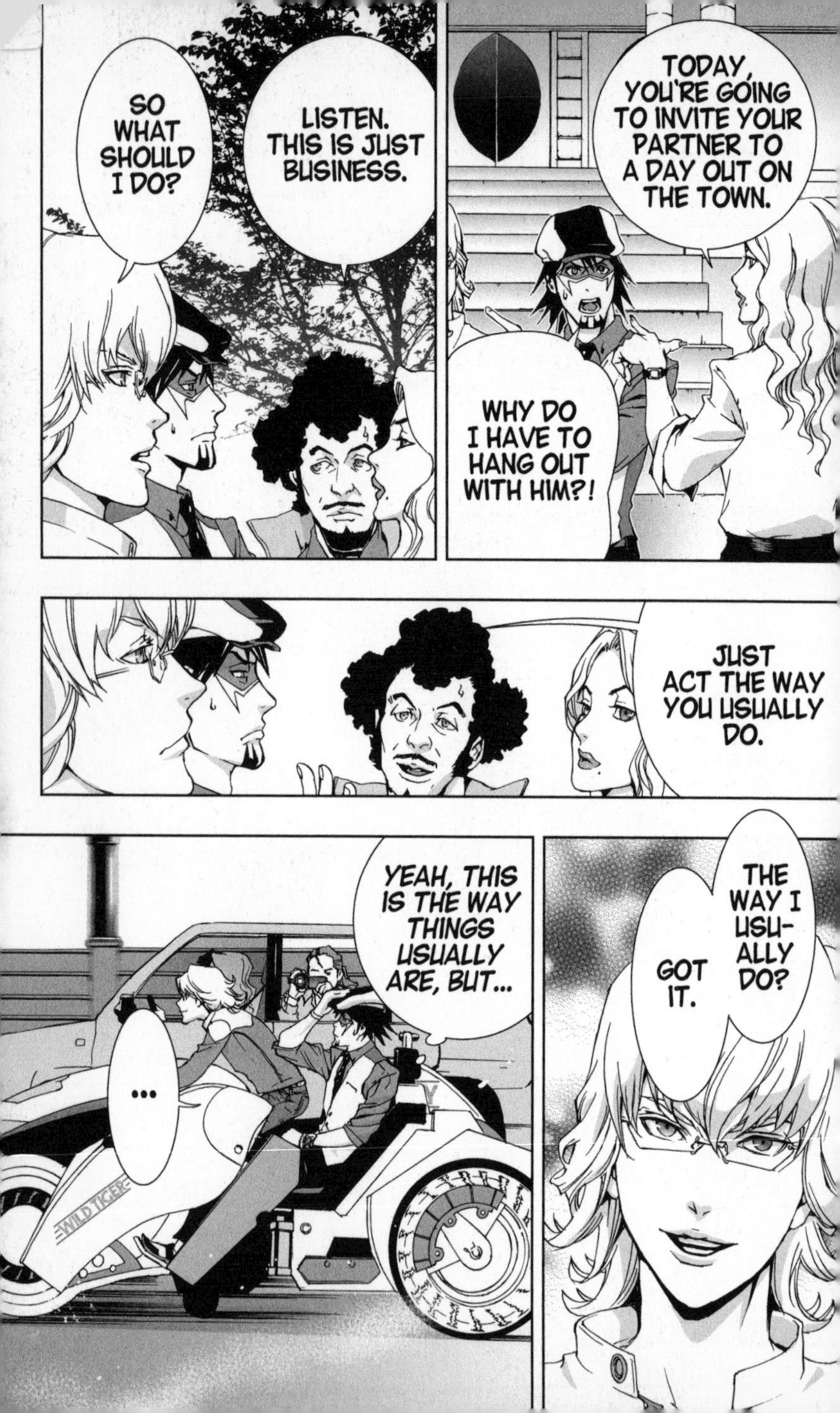
TODAY, YOU'RE GOING TO INVITE YOUR PARTNER TO A DAY OUT ON THE TOWN.
WHY DO I HAVE TO HANG OUT WITH HIM?!
LISTEN. THIS IS JUST BUSINESS.
SO WHAT SHOULD I DO?
JUST ACT THE WAY YOU USUALLY DO.
THE WAY I USU-ALLY DO?
GOT IT.
YEAH, THIS IS THE WAY THINGS USUALLY ARE, BUT...
...
WILD TIGER

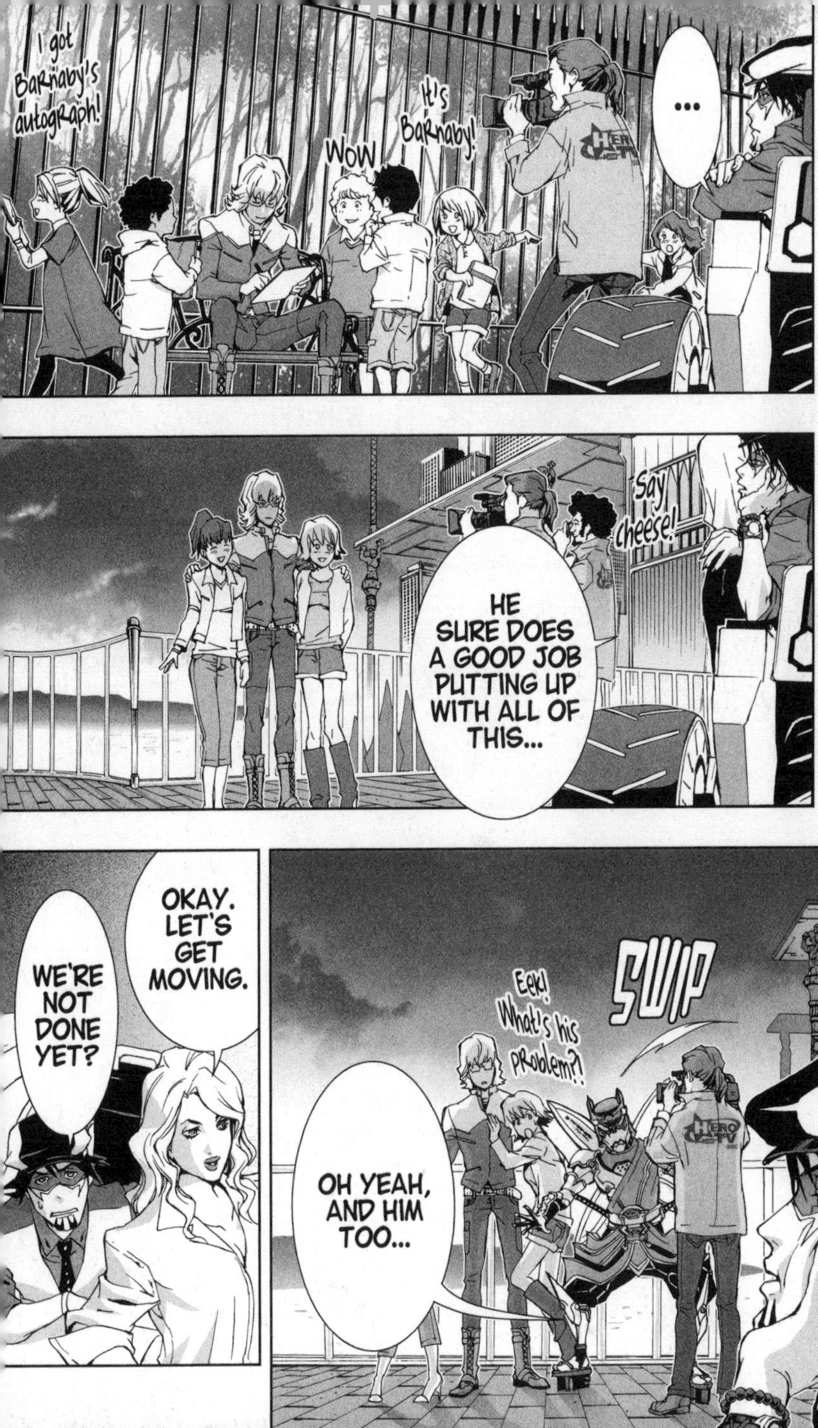
...
It's Barnaby!
WOW
I got Barnaby's autograph!
Say cheese!
HE SURE DOES A GOOD JOB PUTTING UP WITH ALL OF THIS...
SWIP
Eek! What's his problem?!
OH YEAH, AND HIM TOO...
OKAY. LET'S GET MOVING.
WE'RE NOT DONE YET?

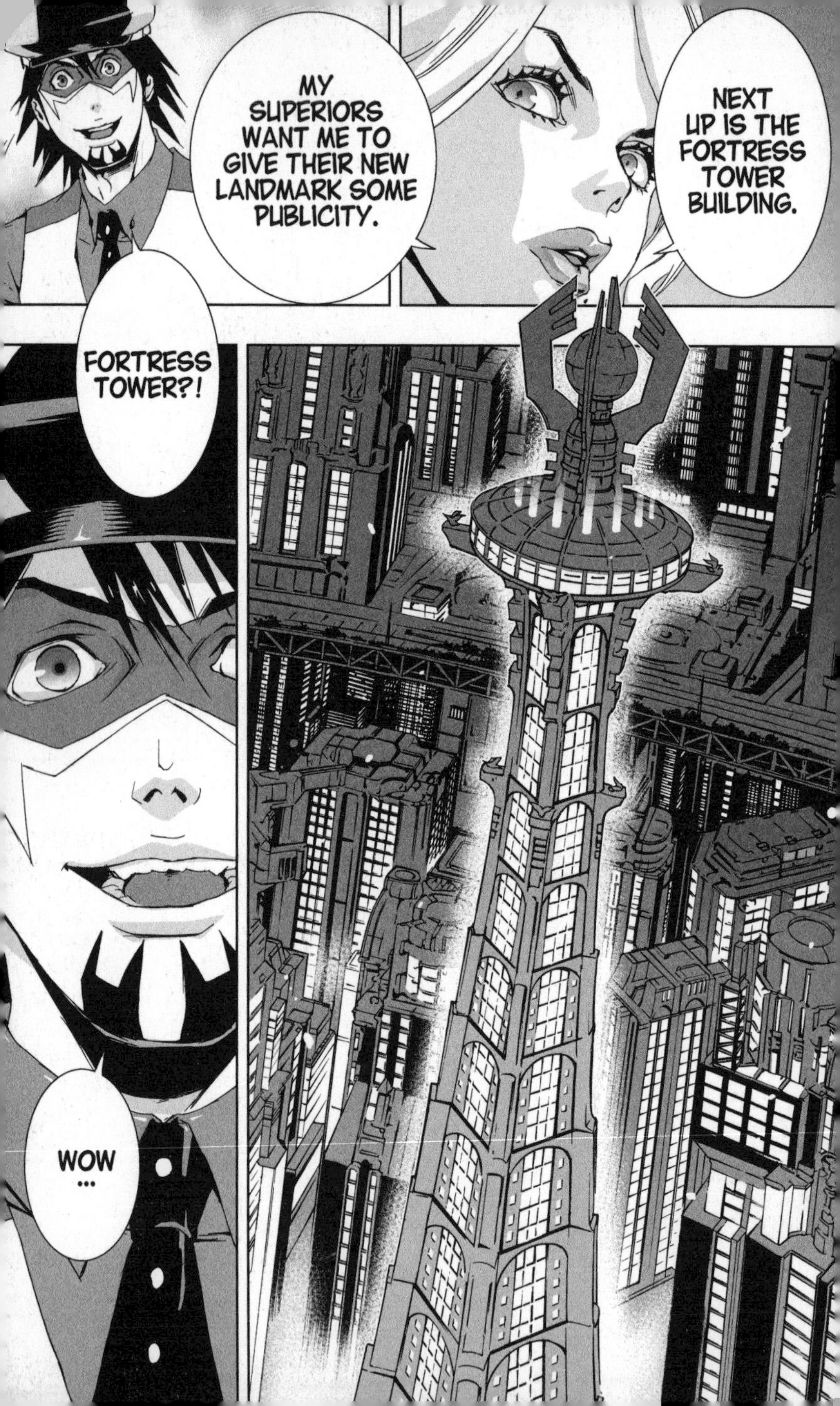
NEXT UP IS THE FORTRESS TOWER BUILDING.
MY SUPERIORS WANT ME TO GIVE THEIR NEW LANDMARK SOME PUBLICITY.
FORTRESS TOWER?!
WOW ...

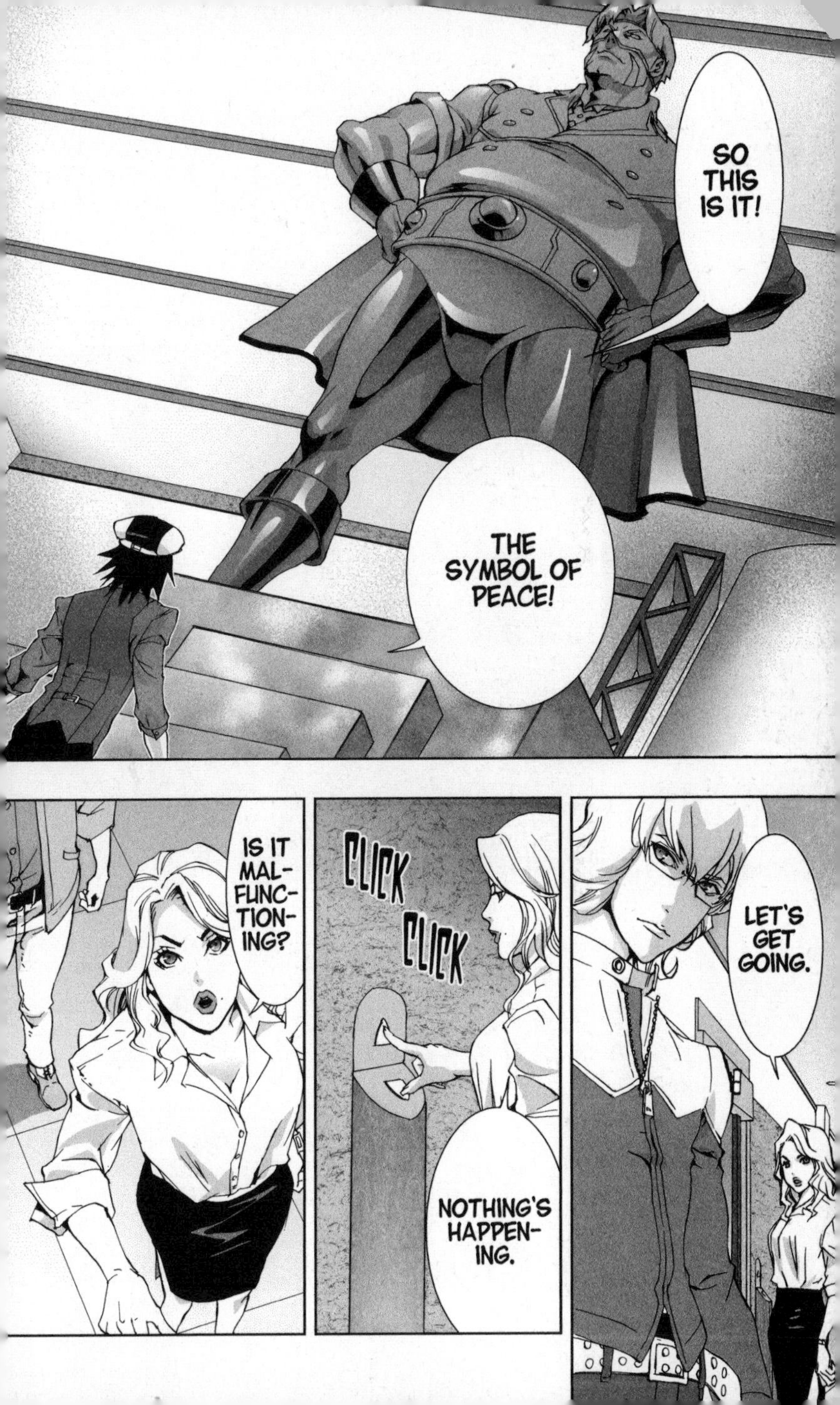
SO THIS IS IT!
THE SYMBOL OF PEACE!
LET'S GET GOING.
CLICK
CLICK
NOTHING'S HAPPEN-ING.
IS IT MAL-FUNC-TION-ING?

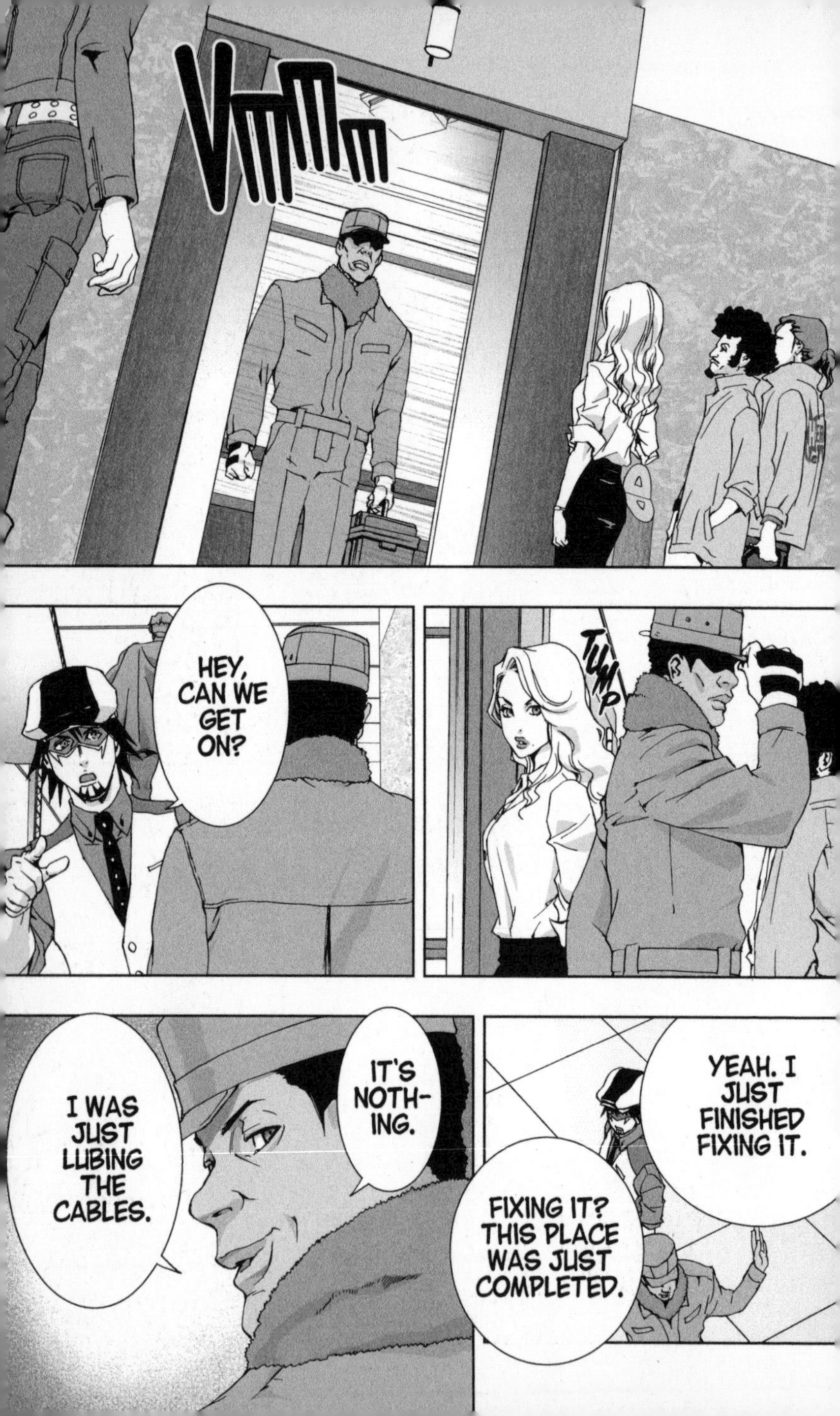
VMMM
TUMP
HEY, CAN WE GET ON?
YEAH. I JUST FINISHED FIXING IT.
FIXING IT? THIS PLACE WAS JUST COMPLETED.
IT'S NOTH-ING.
I WAS JUST LUBING THE CABLES.

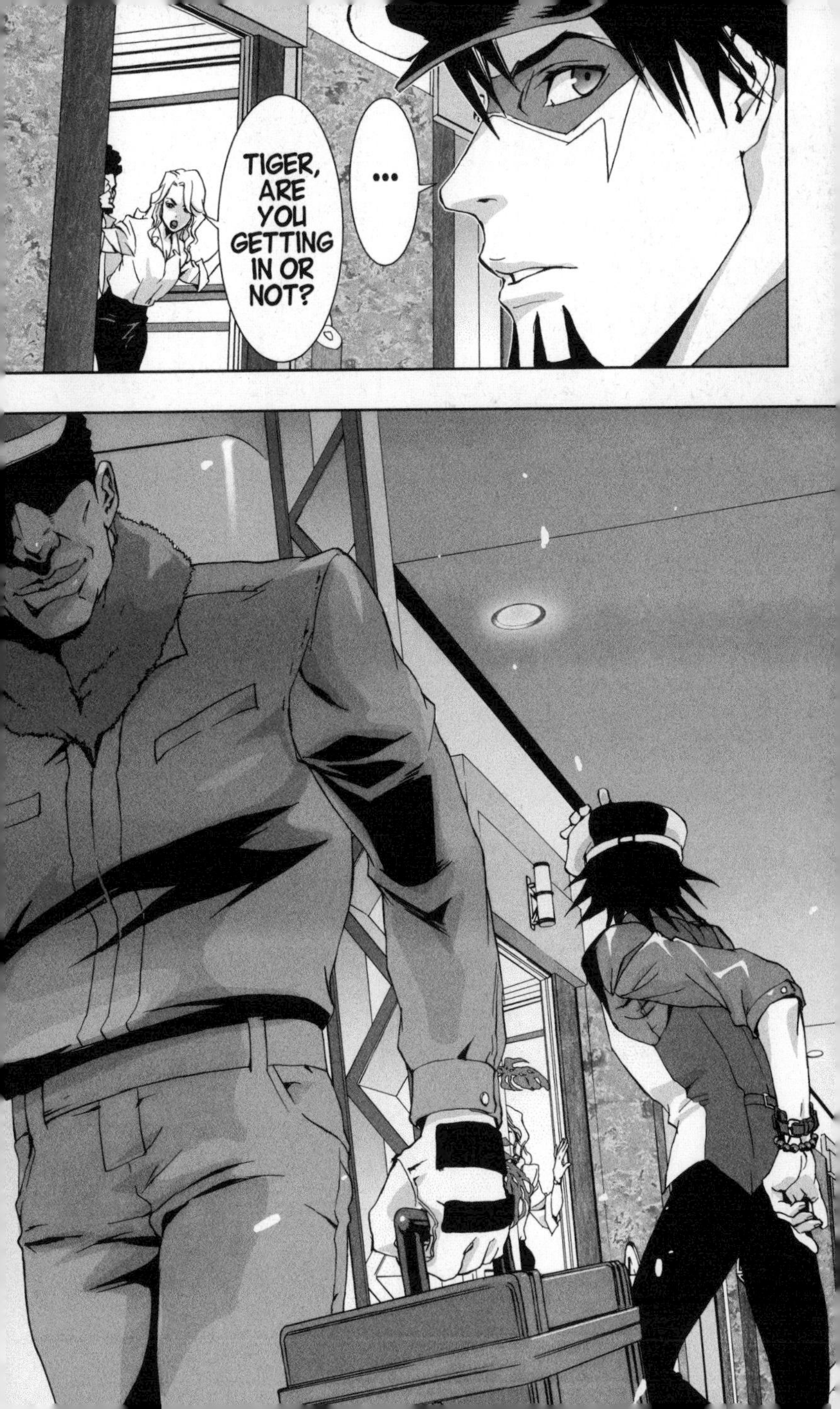
...
TIGER, ARE YOU GETTING IN OR NOT?

#06 Many a True Word Is Spoken in Jest, Part 2

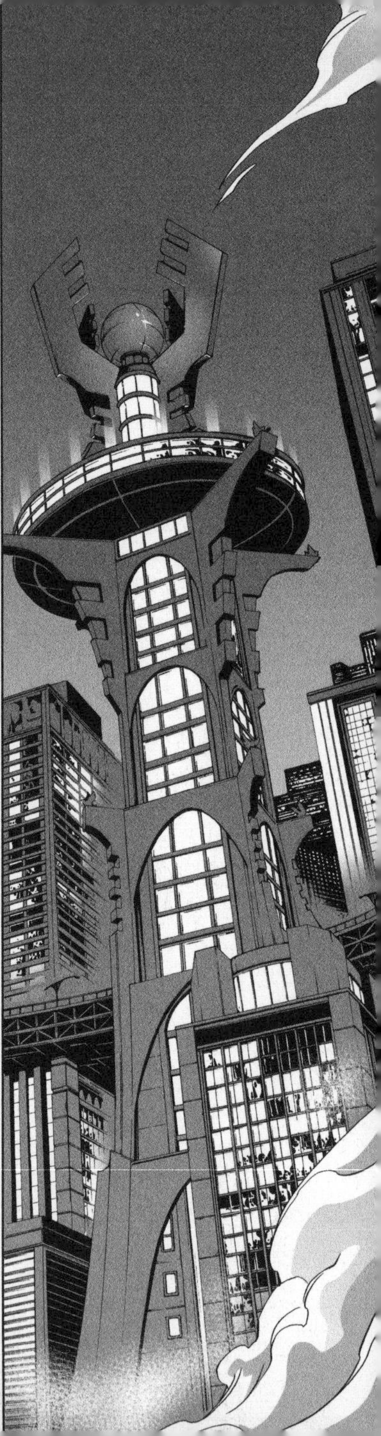

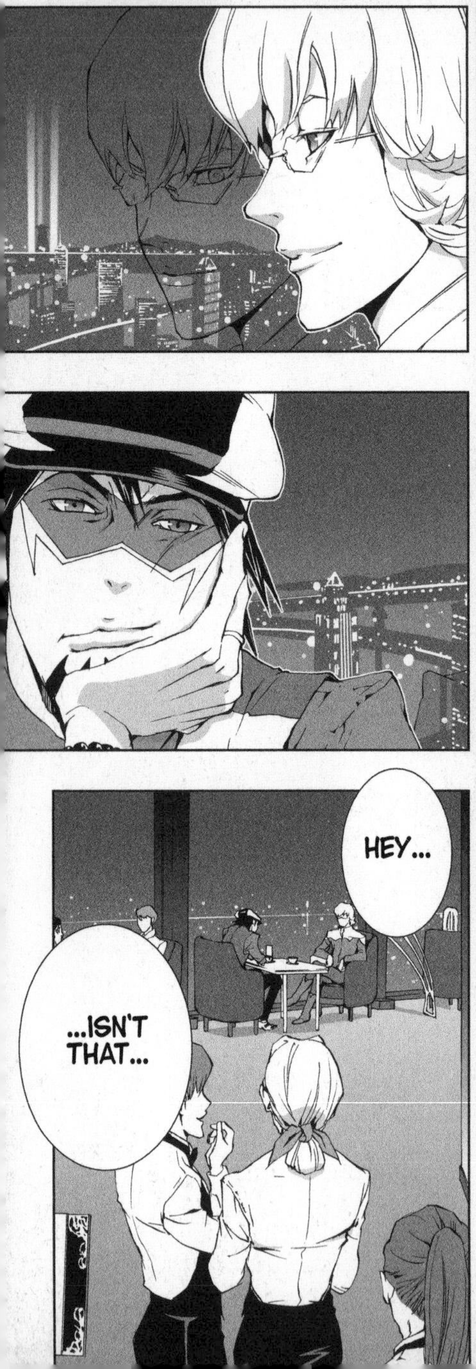
HEY...
...ISN'T THAT...

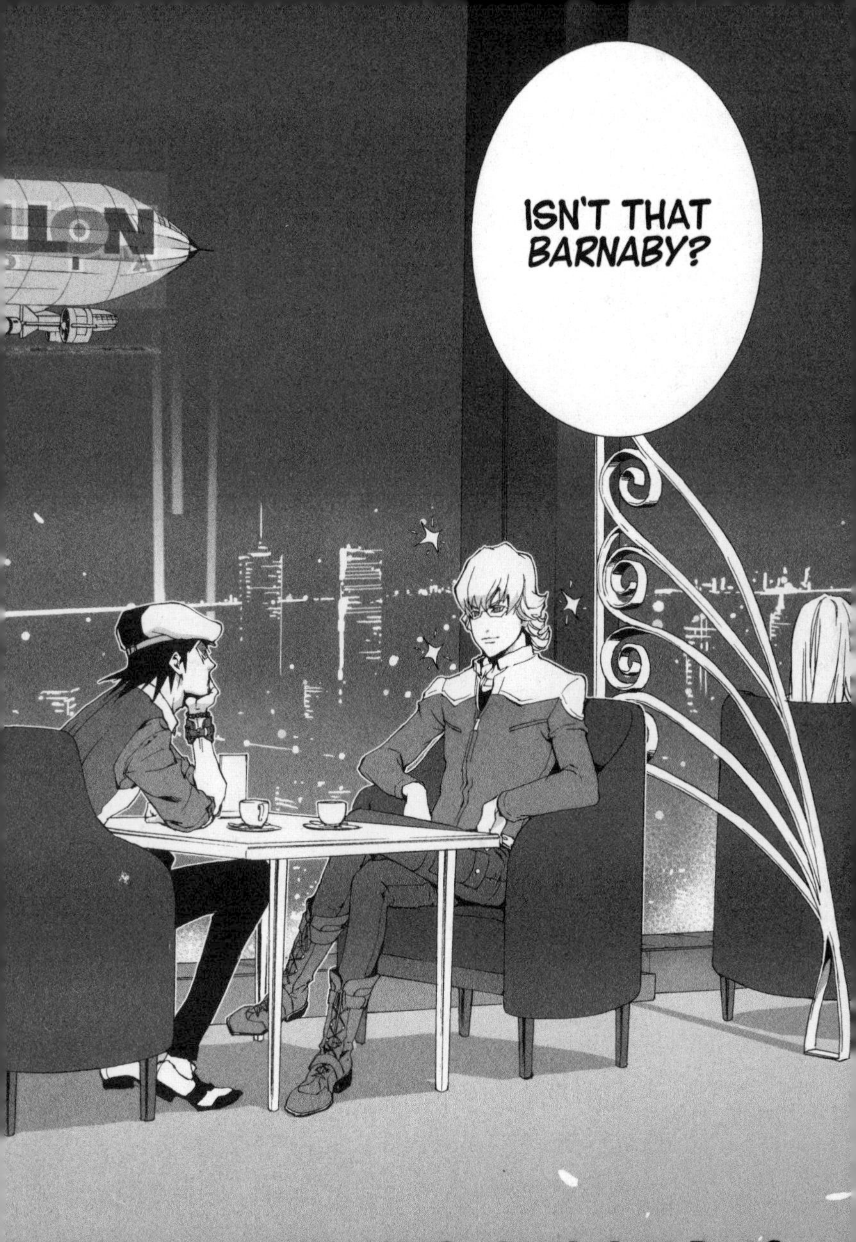
ISN'T THAT BARNABY?

#06 Many a True Word Is Spoken in Jest, Part 2

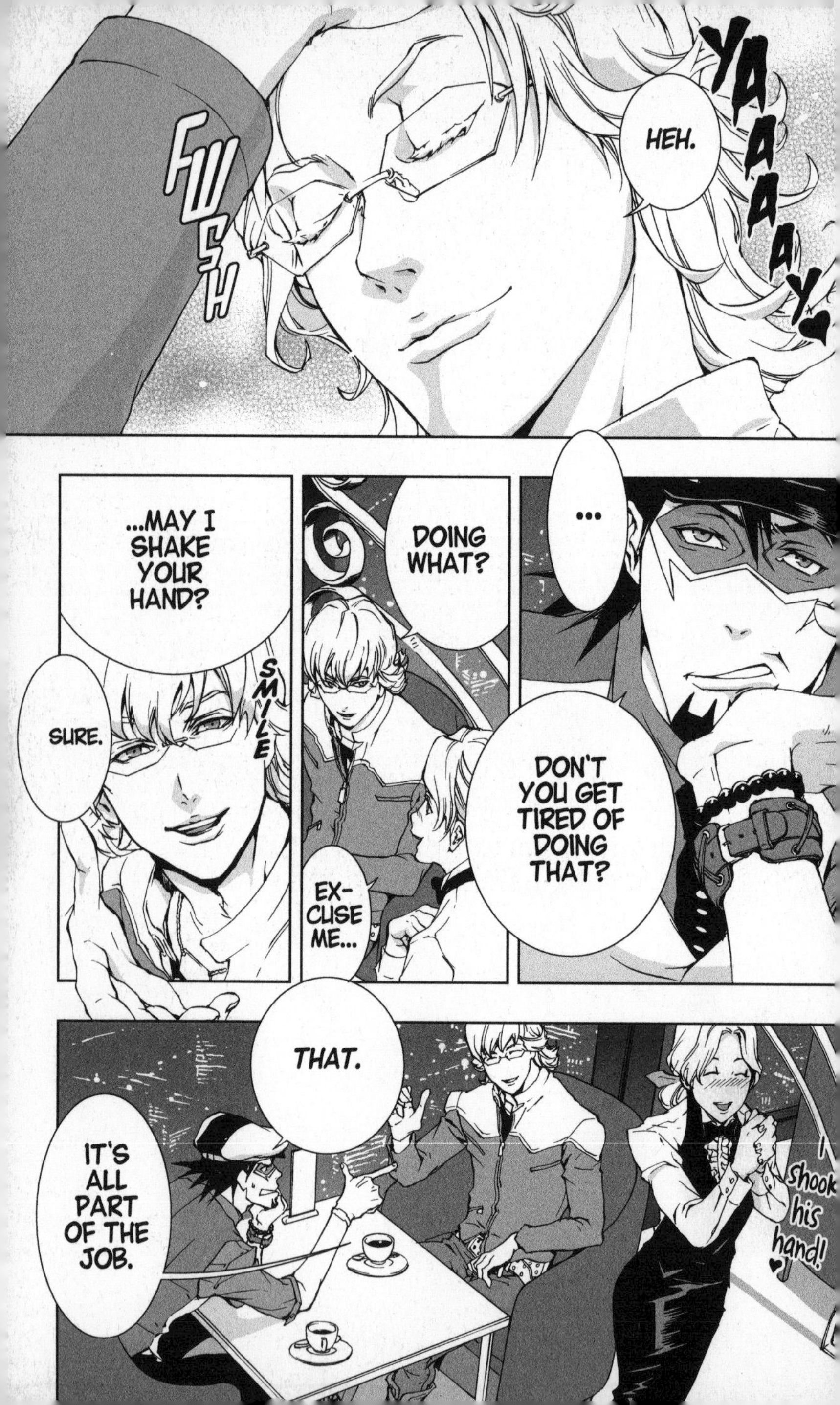
YAAAAY♥
HEH.
FWSH
...
DON'T YOU GET TIRED OF DOING THAT?
DOING WHAT?
EX-CUSE ME...
...MAY I SHAKE YOUR HAND?
SMILE
SURE.
I shook his hand! ♥
THAT.
IT'S ALL PART OF THE JOB.

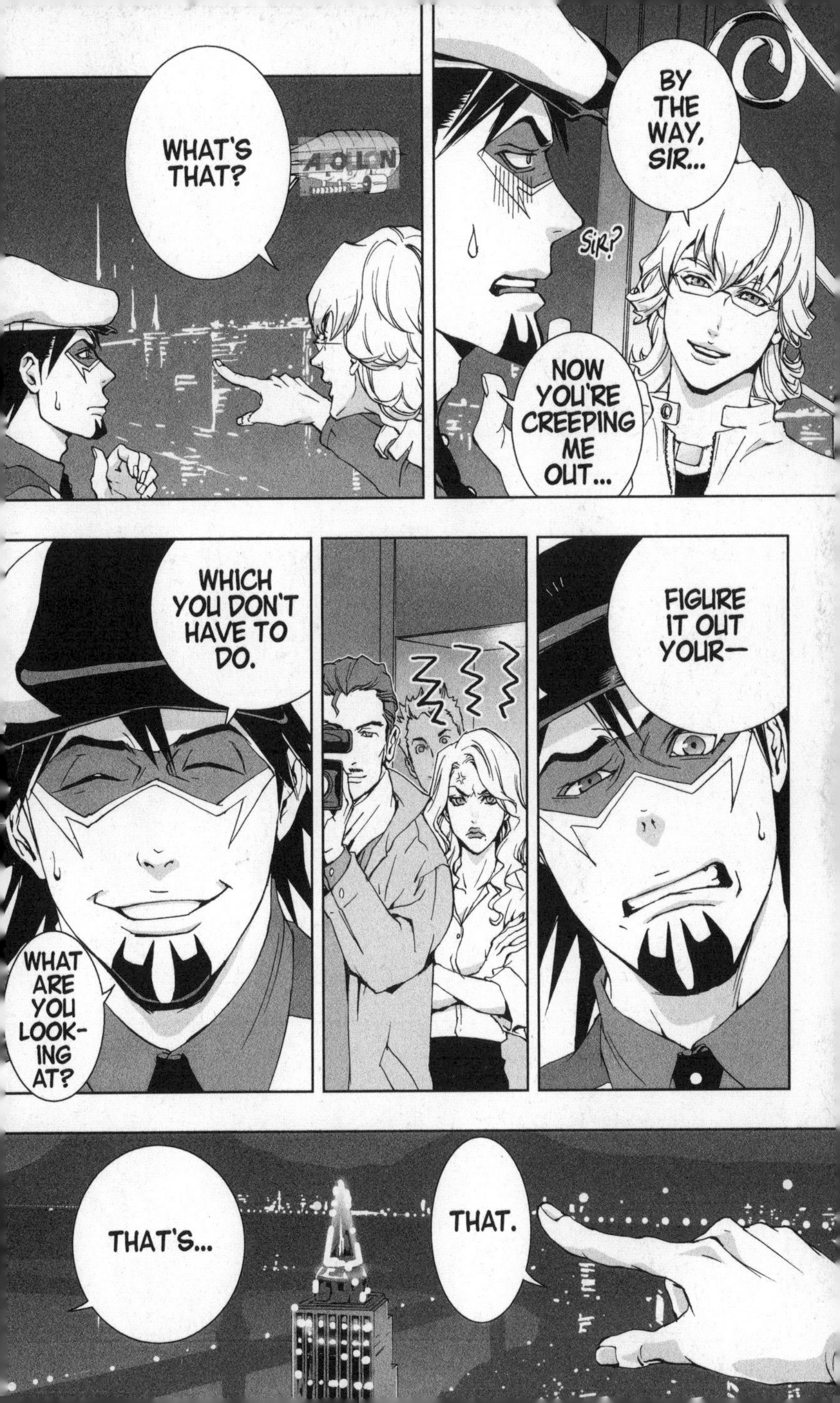
BY THE WAY, SIR...
SIR?
NOW YOU'RE CREEPING ME OUT...
WHAT'S THAT?
FIGURE IT OUT YOUR—
WHICH YOU DON'T HAVE TO DO.
WHAT ARE YOU LOOK-ING AT?
THAT.
THAT'S...

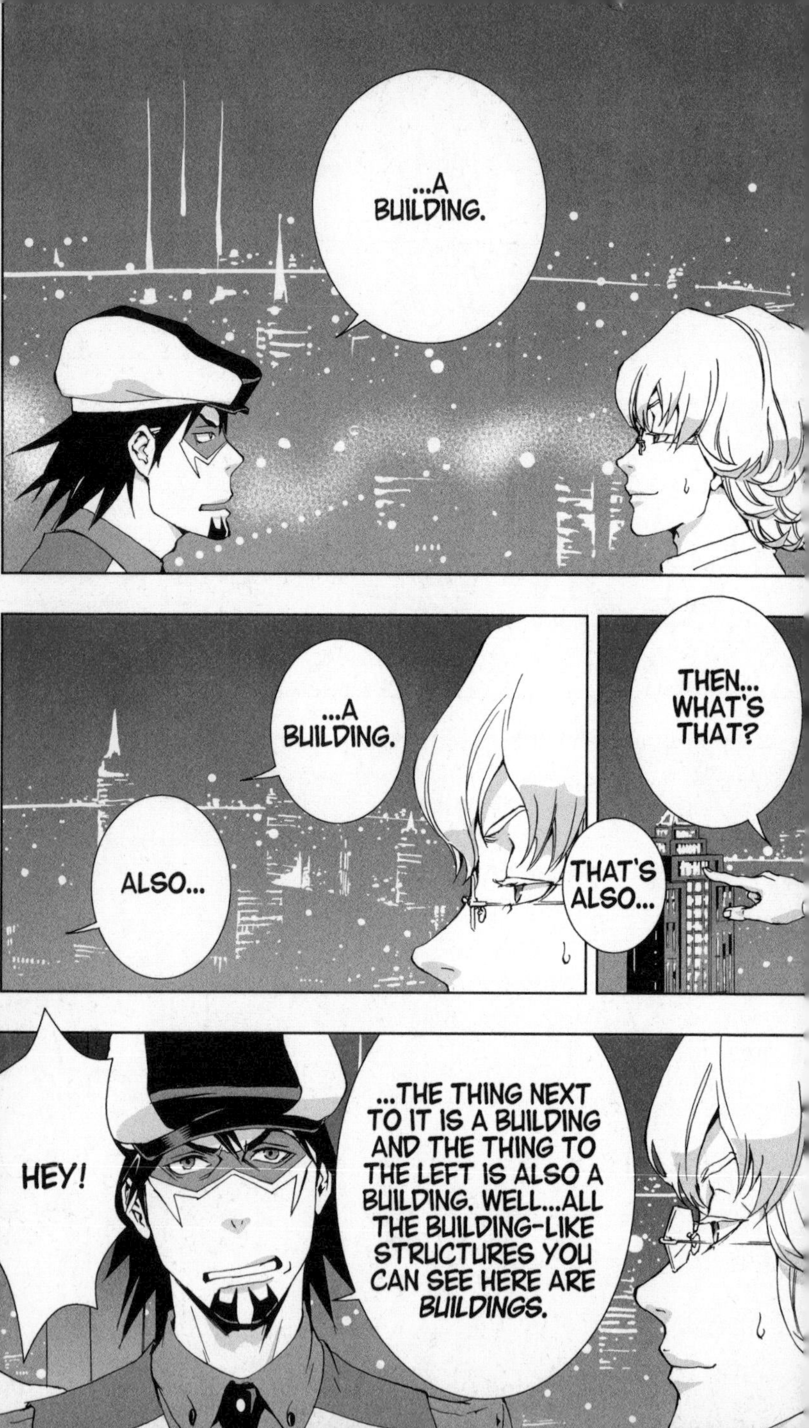
...A BUILDING.
THEN... WHAT'S THAT?
THAT'S ALSO...
...A BUILDING.
ALSO...
...THE THING NEXT TO IT IS A BUILDING AND THE THING TO THE LEFT IS ALSO A BUILDING. WELL...ALL THE BUILDING-LIKE STRUCTURES YOU CAN SEE HERE ARE BUILDINGS.
HEY!

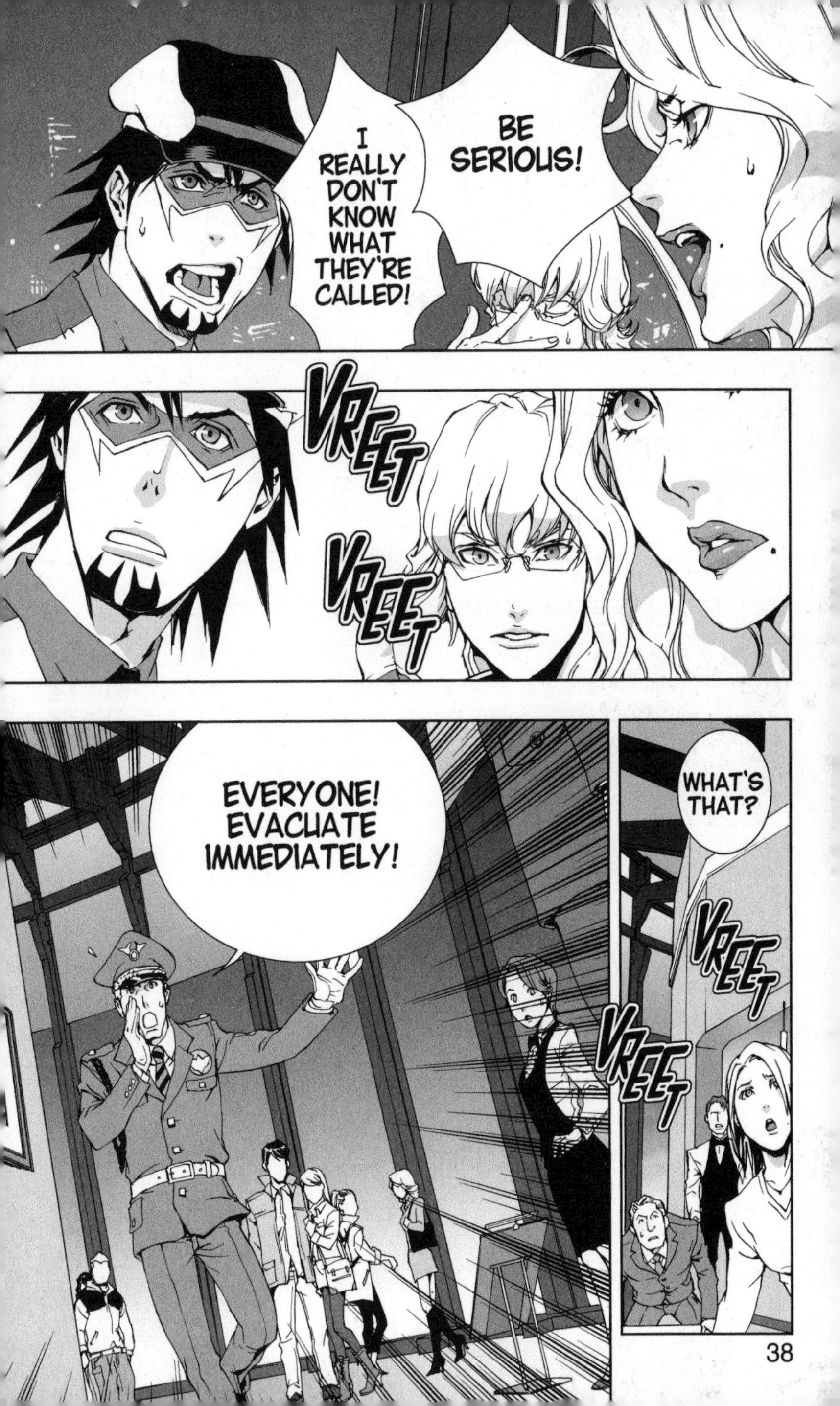
BE SERIOUS!
I REALLY DON'T KNOW WHAT THEY'RE CALLED!
VREET
VREET
WHAT'S THAT?
VREET
VREET
EVERYONE! EVACUATE IMMEDIATELY!

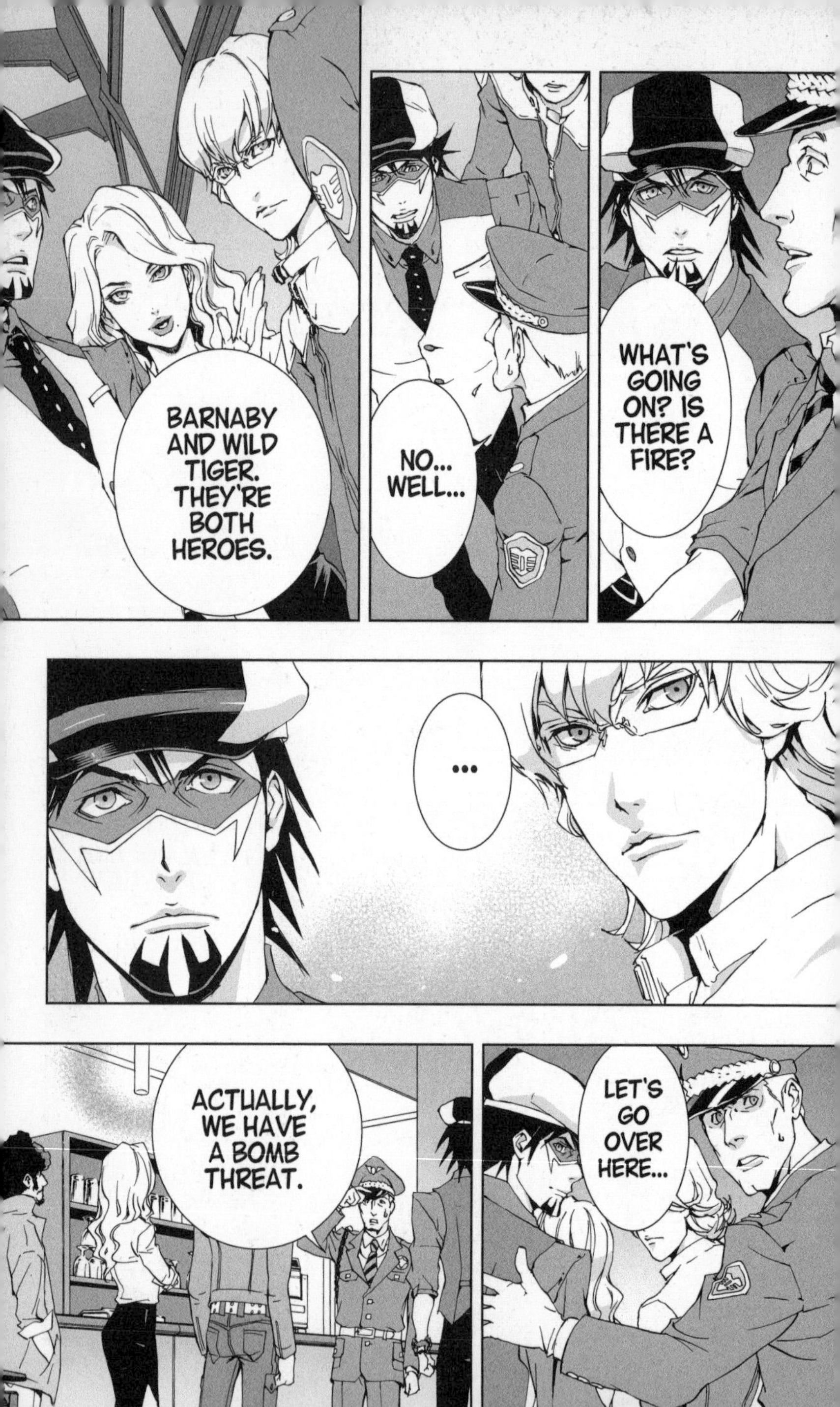
WHAT'S GOING ON? IS THERE A FIRE?
NO... WELL...
BARNABY AND WILD TIGER. THEY'RE BOTH HEROES.
...
LET'S GO OVER HERE...
ACTUALLY, WE HAVE A BOMB THREAT.

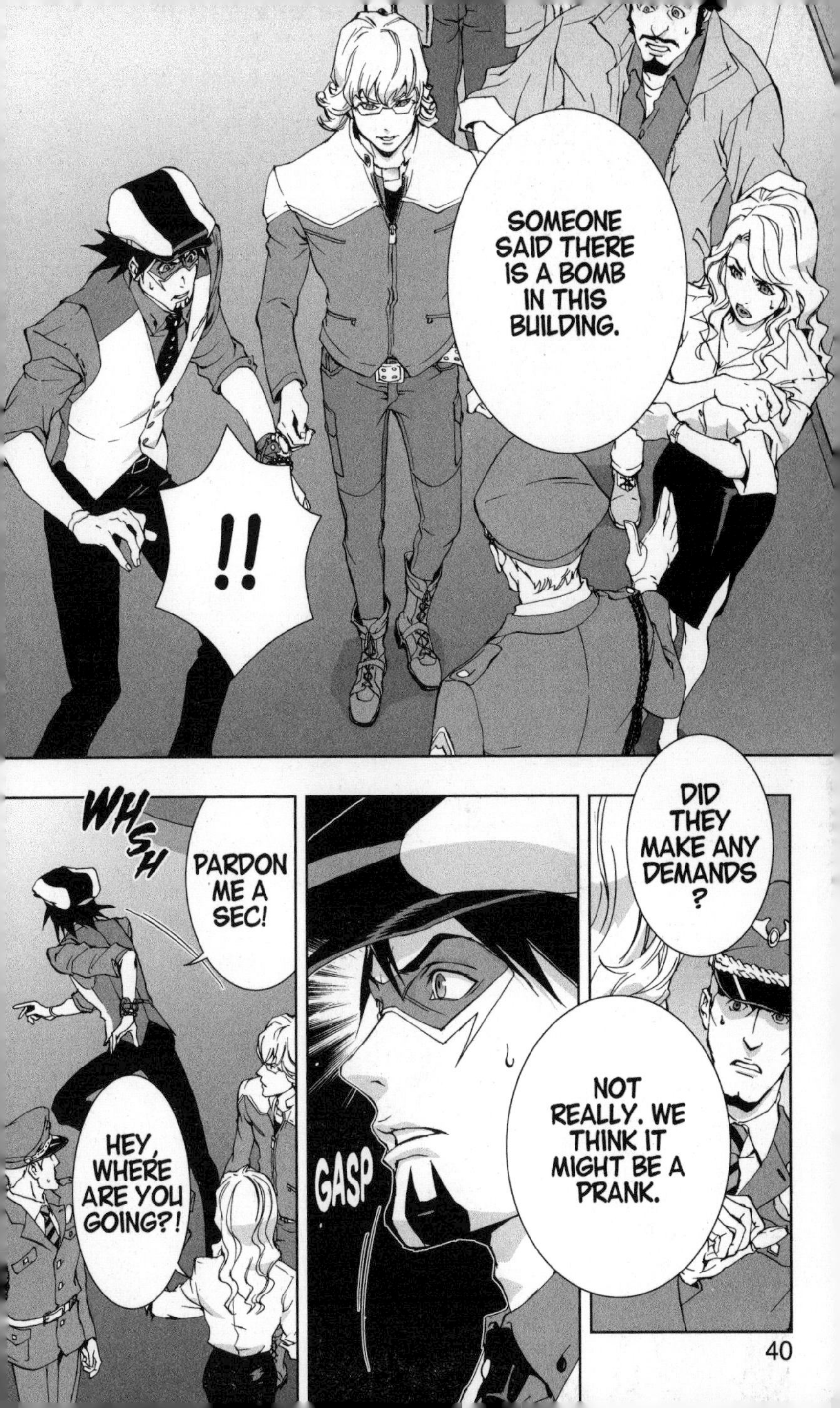
SOMEONE SAID THERE IS A BOMB IN THIS BUILDING.
!!
DID THEY MAKE ANY DEMANDS?
NOT REALLY. WE THINK IT MIGHT BE A PRANK.
GASP
WHSH
PARDON ME A SEC!
HEY, WHERE ARE YOU GOING?!

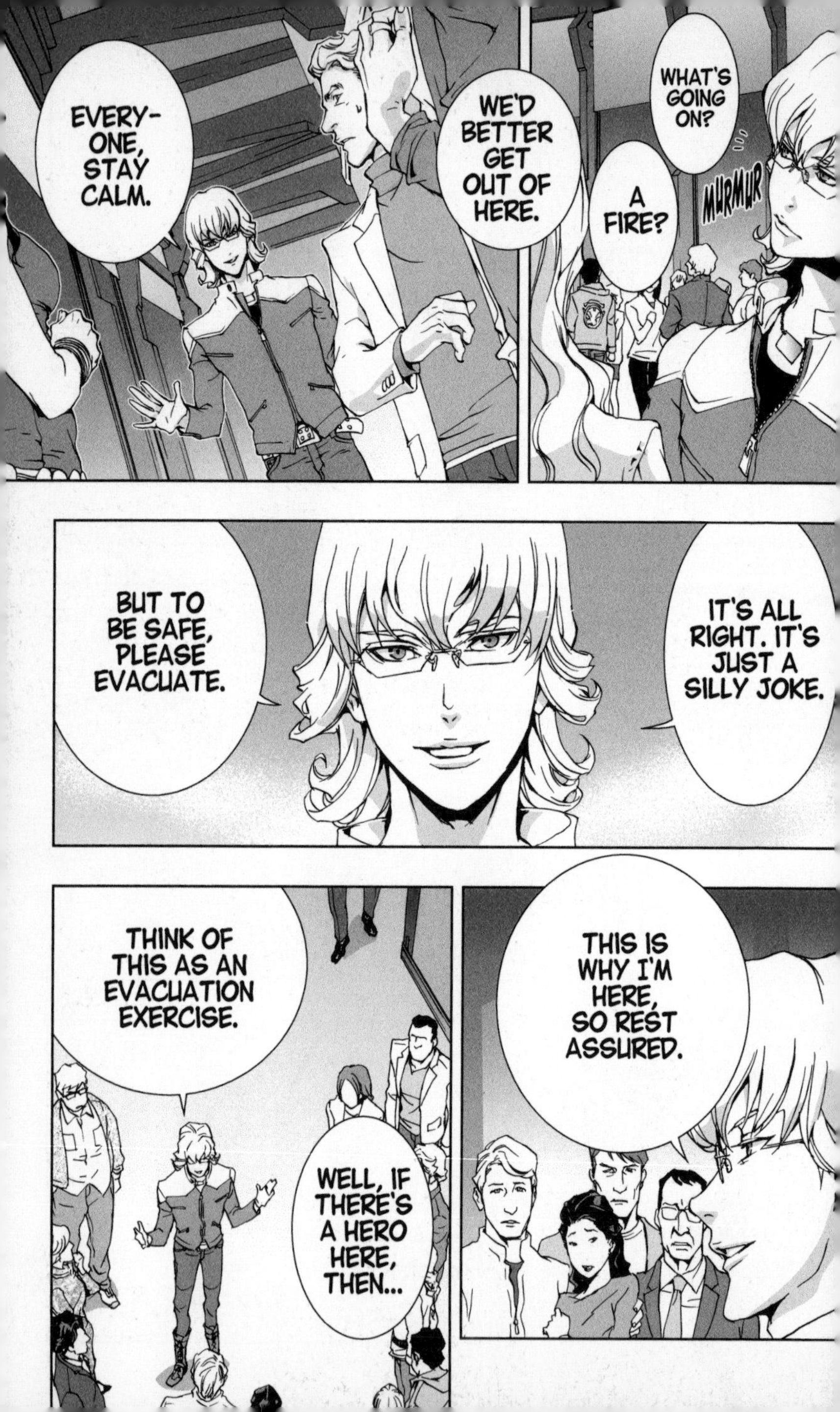
WHAT'S GOING ON?
MURMUR
A FIRE?
WE'D BETTER GET OUT OF HERE.
EVERY-ONE, STAY CALM.
IT'S ALL RIGHT. IT'S JUST A SILLY JOKE.
BUT TO BE SAFE, PLEASE EVACUATE.
THIS IS WHY I'M HERE, SO REST ASSURED.
THINK OF THIS AS AN EVACUATION EXERCISE.
WELL, IF THERE'S A HERO HERE, THEN...

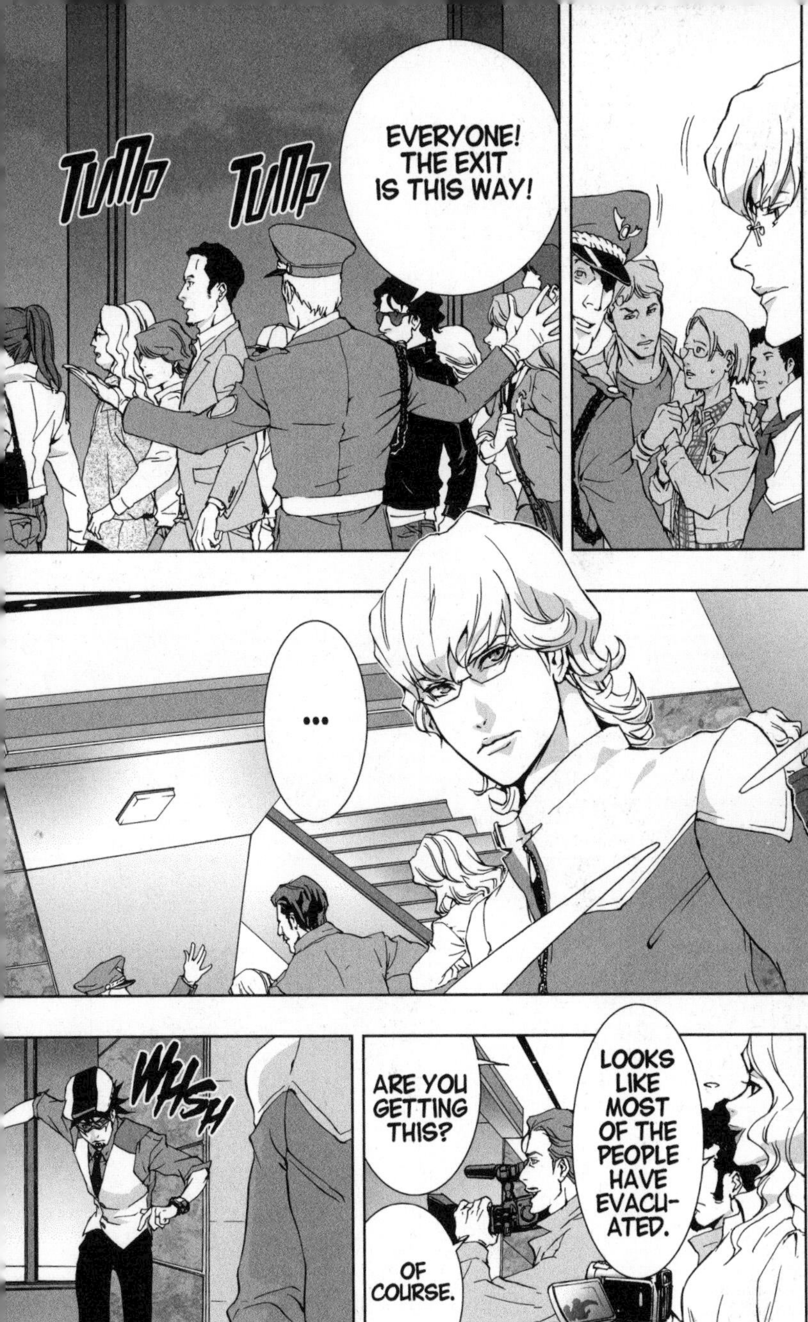
EVERYONE! THE EXIT IS THIS WAY!
TUMP
TUMP
...
LOOKS LIKE MOST OF THE PEOPLE HAVE EVACU-ATED.
ARE YOU GETTING THIS?
OF COURSE.
WHSH

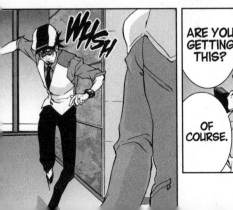

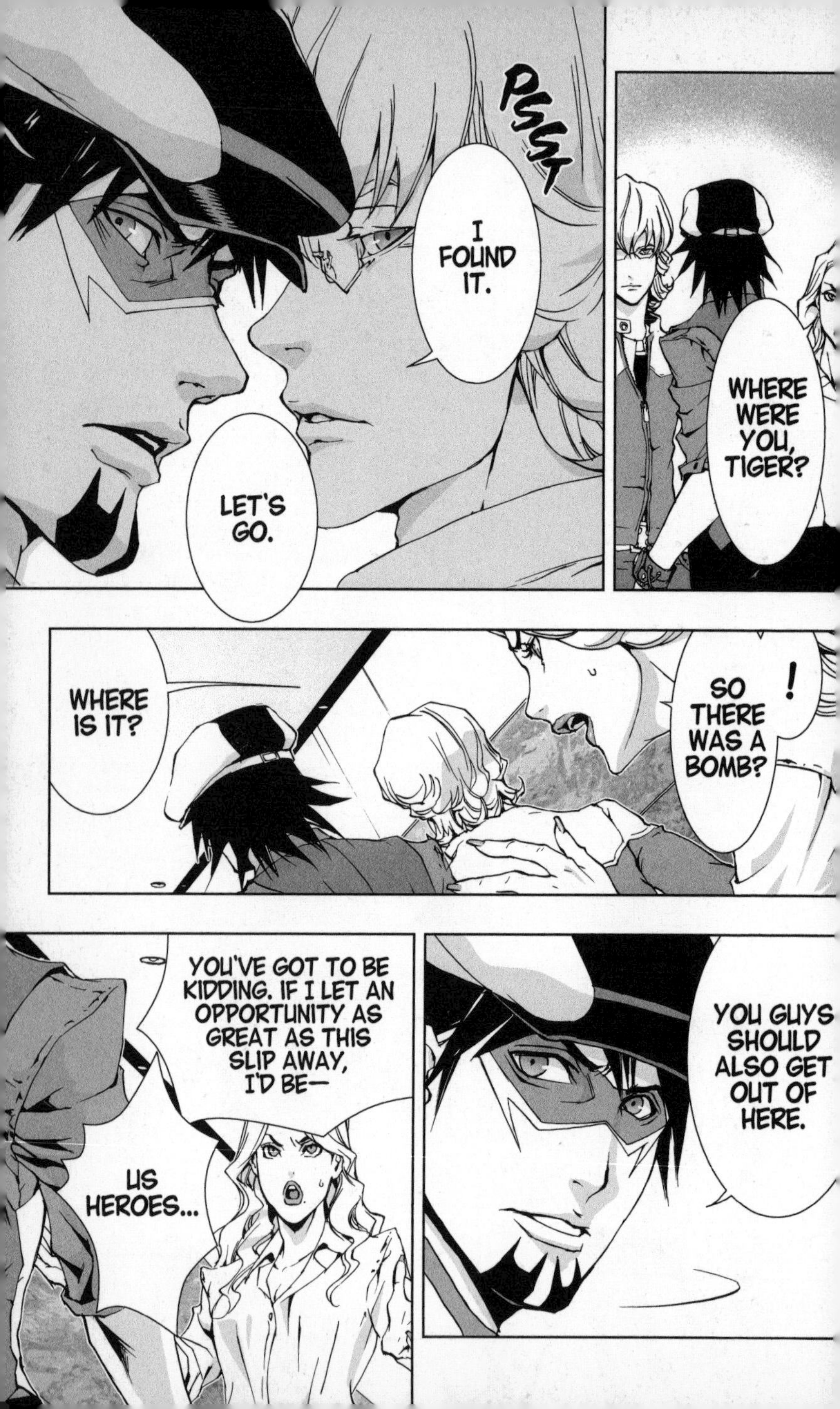
WHERE WERE YOU, TIGER?
PSSST
I FOUND IT.
LET'S GO.
!
SO THERE WAS A BOMB?
WHERE IS IT?
YOU GUYS SHOULD ALSO GET OUT OF HERE.
YOU'VE GOT TO BE KIDDING. IF I LET AN OPPORTUNITY AS GREAT AS THIS SLIP AWAY, I'D BE—
US HEROES...

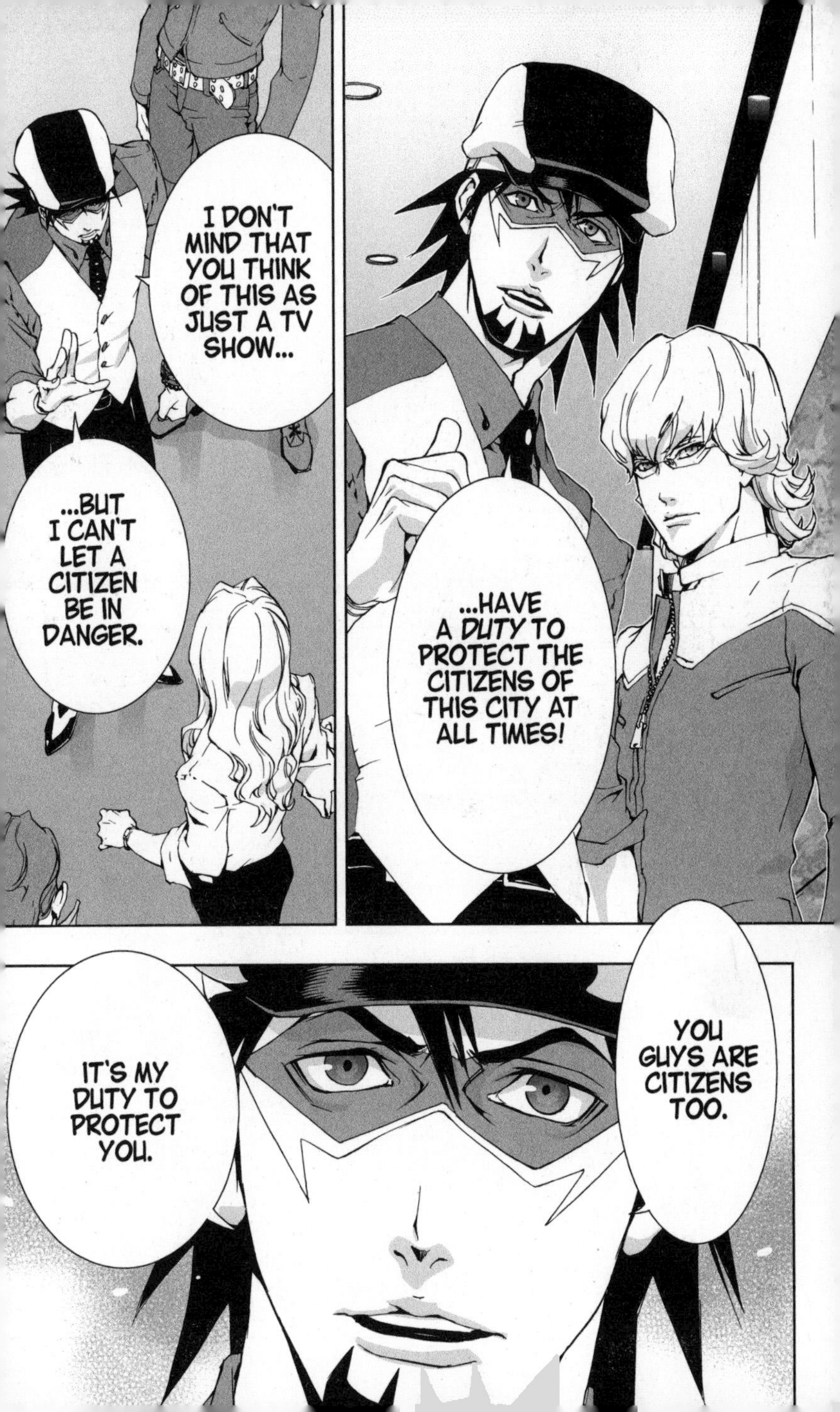
...HAVE A DUTY TO PROTECT THE CITIZENS OF THIS CITY AT ALL TIMES!
I DON'T MIND THAT YOU THINK OF THIS AS JUST A TV SHOW...
...BUT I CAN'T LET A CITIZEN BE IN DANGER.
YOU GUYS ARE CITIZENS TOO.
IT'S MY DUTY TO PROTECT YOU.

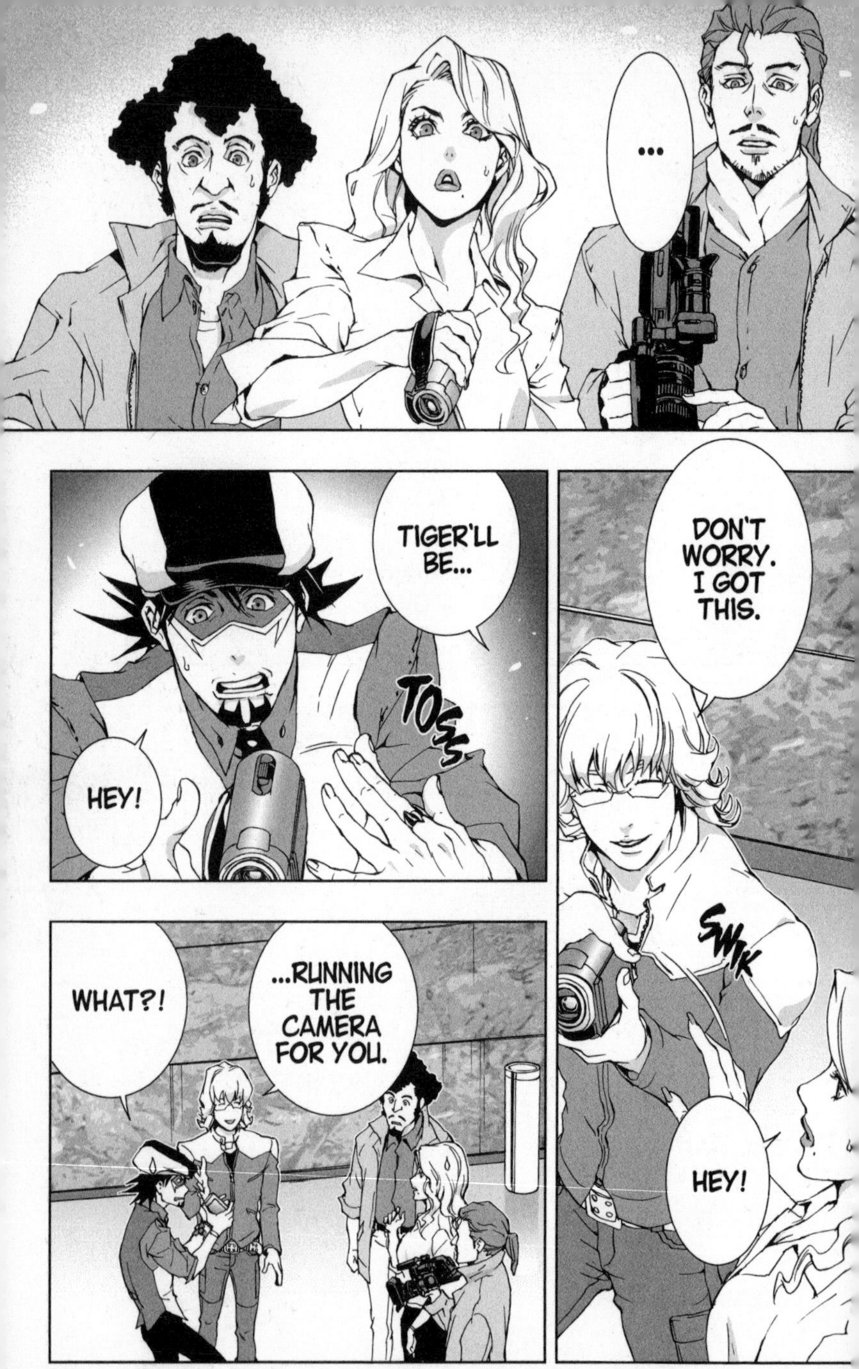
...
DON'T WORRY. I GOT THIS.
SNIK
HEY!
TIGER'LL BE...
TOSS
HEY!
...RUNNING THE CAMERA FOR YOU.
WHAT?!

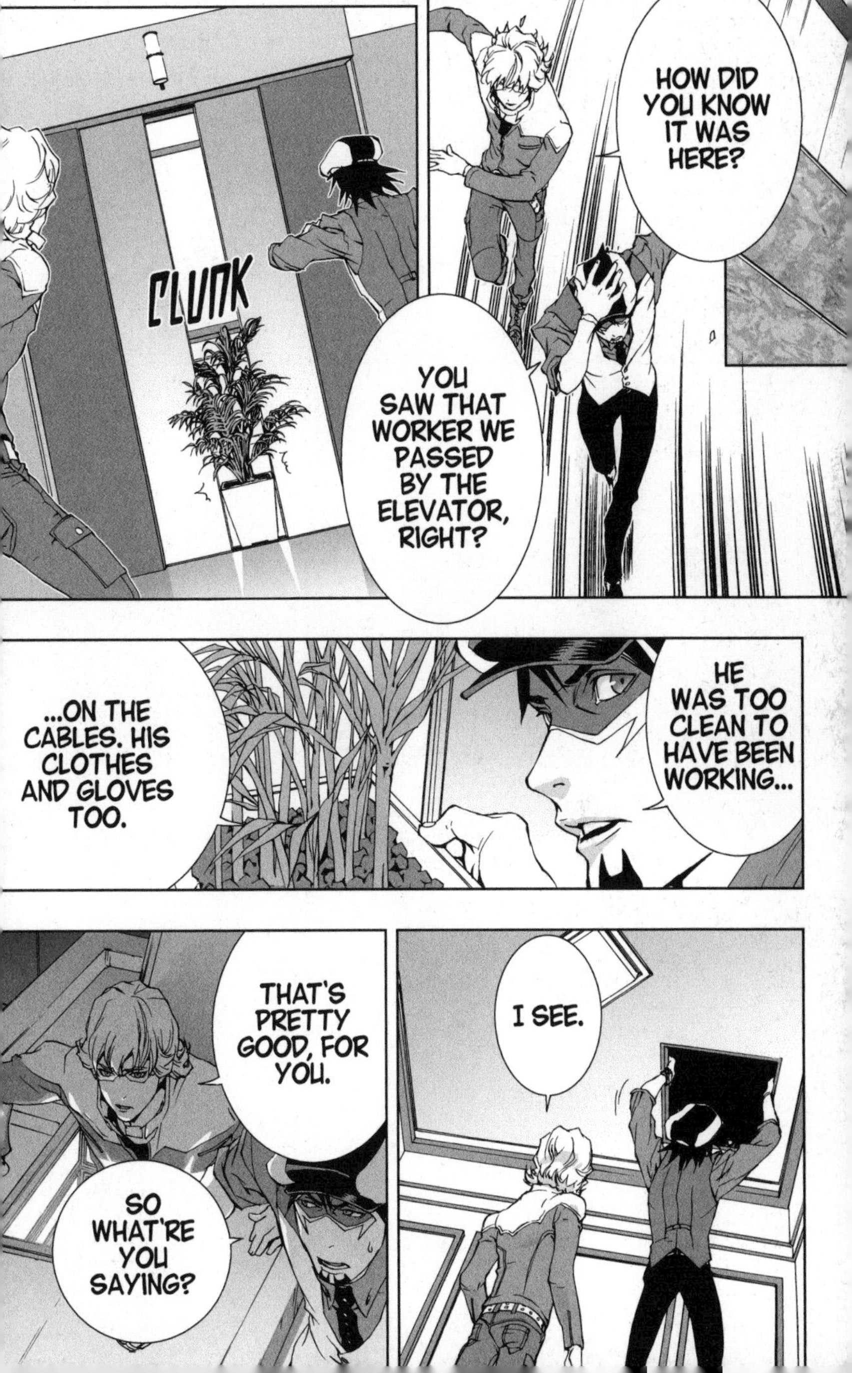
HOW DID YOU KNOW IT WAS HERE?
YOU SAW THAT WORKER WE PASSED BY THE ELEVATOR, RIGHT?
CLUNK
HE WAS TOO CLEAN TO HAVE BEEN WORKING...
...ON THE CABLES. HIS CLOTHES AND GLOVES TOO.
I SEE.
THAT'S PRETTY GOOD, FOR YOU.
SO WHAT'RE YOU SAYING?

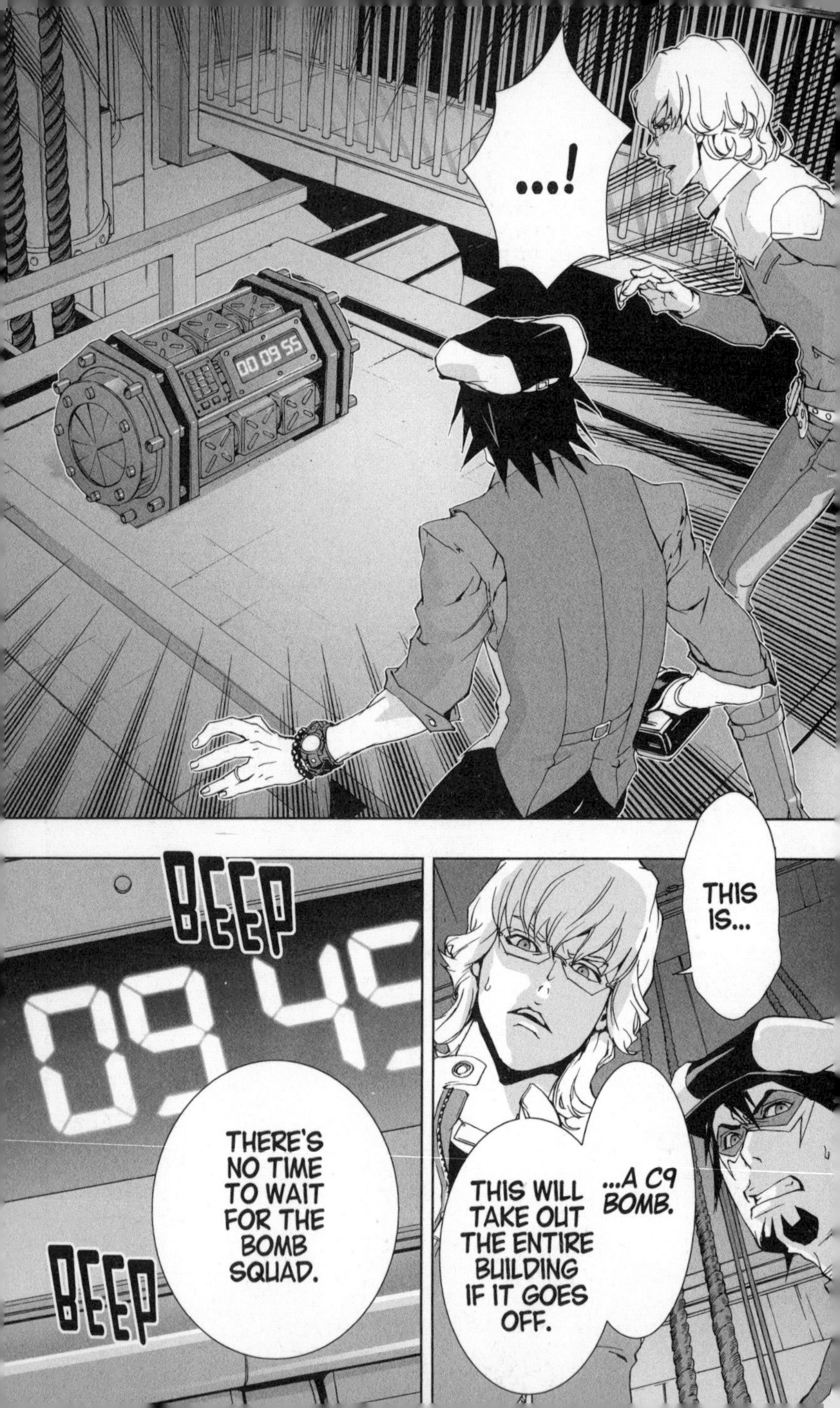
...!
00 09 55
THIS IS...
...A C9 BOMB.
THIS WILL TAKE OUT THE ENTIRE BUILDING IF IT GOES OFF.
BEEP
THERE'S NO TIME TO WAIT FOR THE BOMB SQUAD.
BEEP

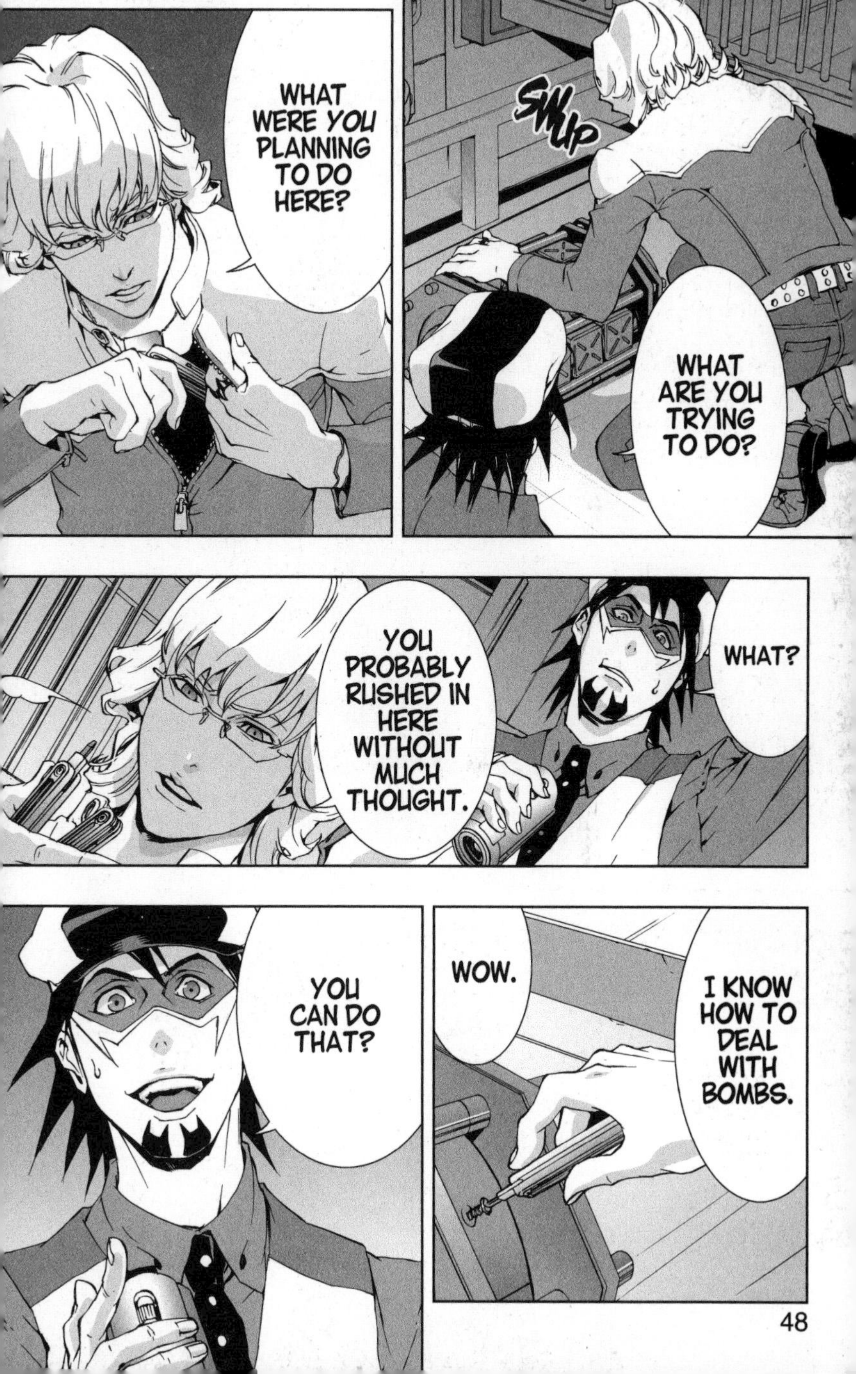
SWUP
WHAT ARE YOU TRYING TO DO?
WHAT WERE YOU PLANNING TO DO HERE?
WHAT?
YOU PROBABLY RUSHED IN HERE WITHOUT MUCH THOUGHT.
I KNOW HOW TO DEAL WITH BOMBS.
WOW.
YOU CAN DO THAT?

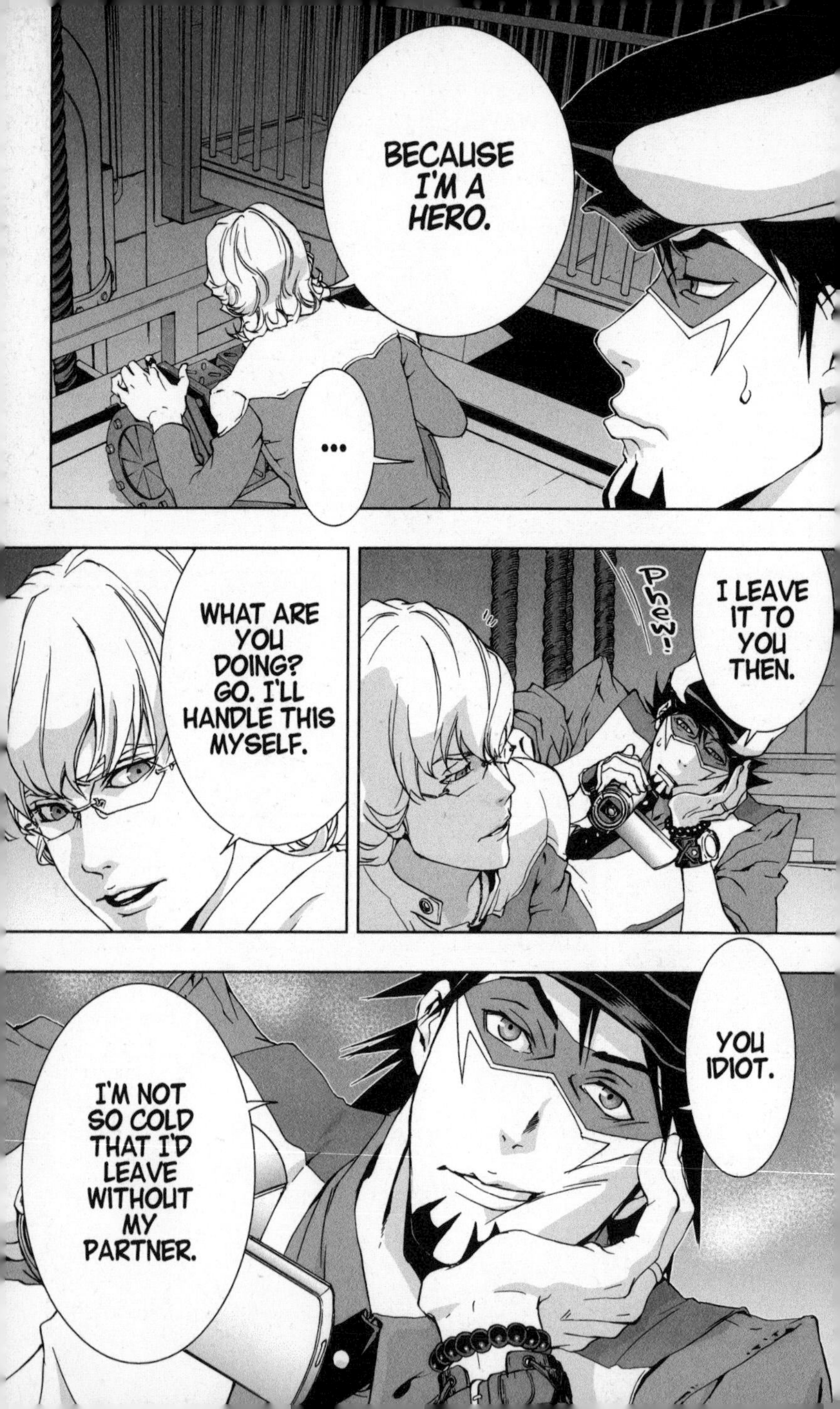
BECAUSE I'M A HERO.
...
I LEAVE IT TO YOU THEN.
Phew!
WHAT ARE YOU DOING? GO. I'LL HANDLE THIS MYSELF.
YOU IDIOT.
I'M NOT SO COLD THAT I'D LEAVE WITHOUT MY PARTNER.

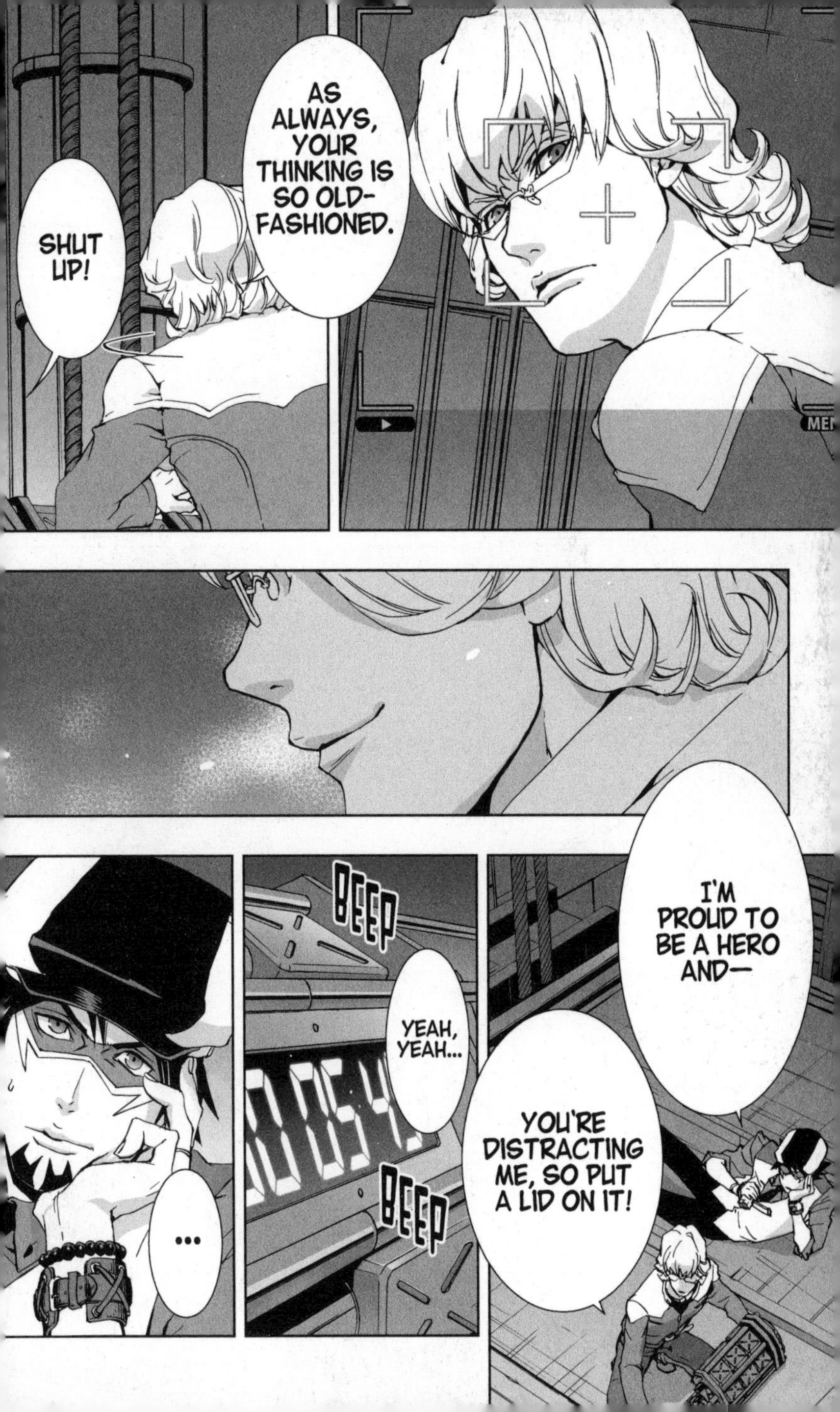
AS ALWAYS, YOUR THINKING IS SO OLD-FASHIONED.
SHUT UP!
I'M PROUD TO BE A HERO AND—
YOU'RE DISTRACTING ME, SO PUT A LID ON IT!
BEEP
YEAH, YEAH...
BEEP
...

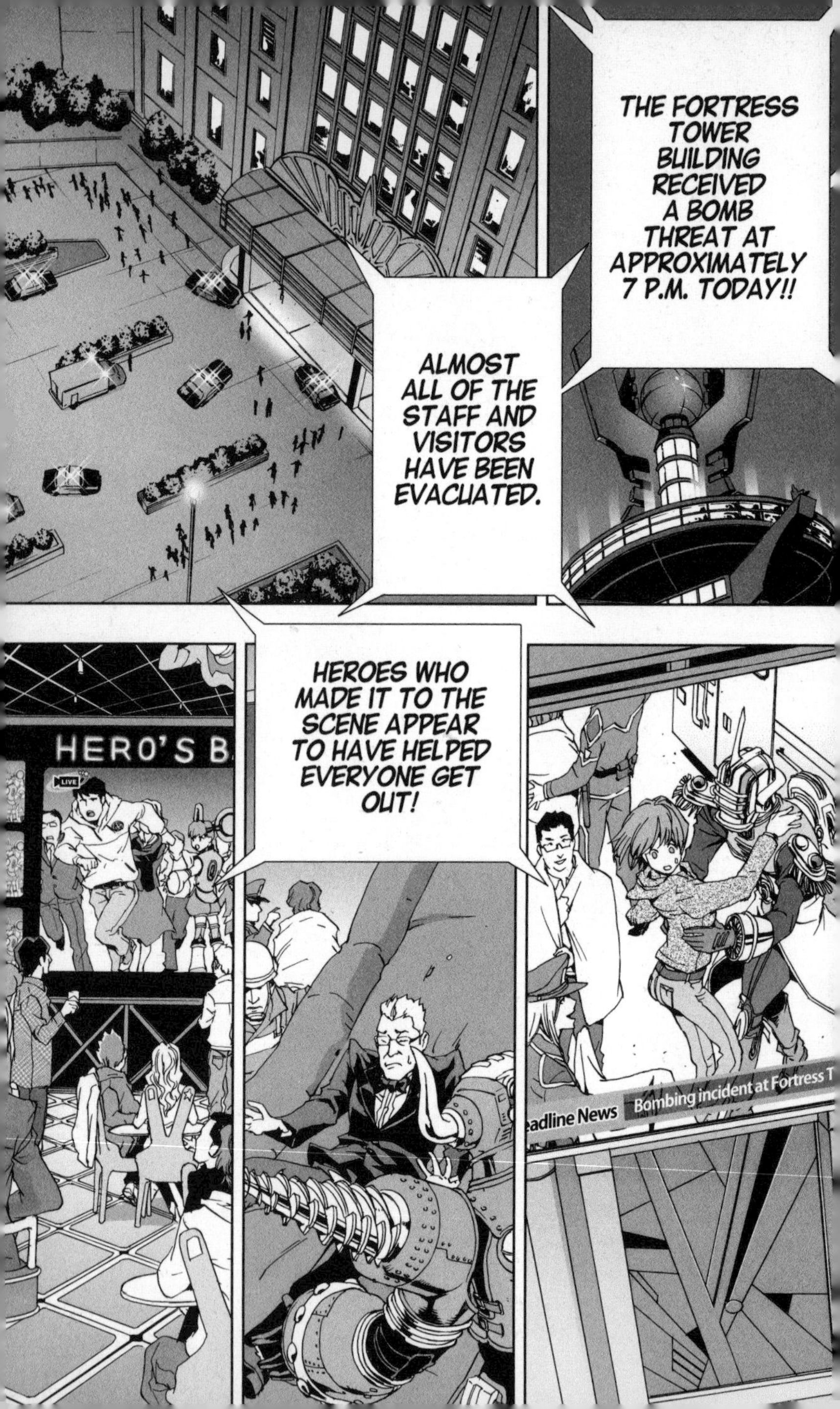
THE FORTRESS TOWER BUILDING RECEIVED A BOMB THREAT AT APPROXIMATELY 7 P.M. TODAY!!
ALMOST ALL OF THE STAFF AND VISITORS HAVE BEEN EVACUATED.
eadline News
Bombing incident at Fortress T
HEROES WHO MADE IT TO THE SCENE APPEAR TO HAVE HELPED EVERYONE GET OUT!
HERO'S B
LIVE

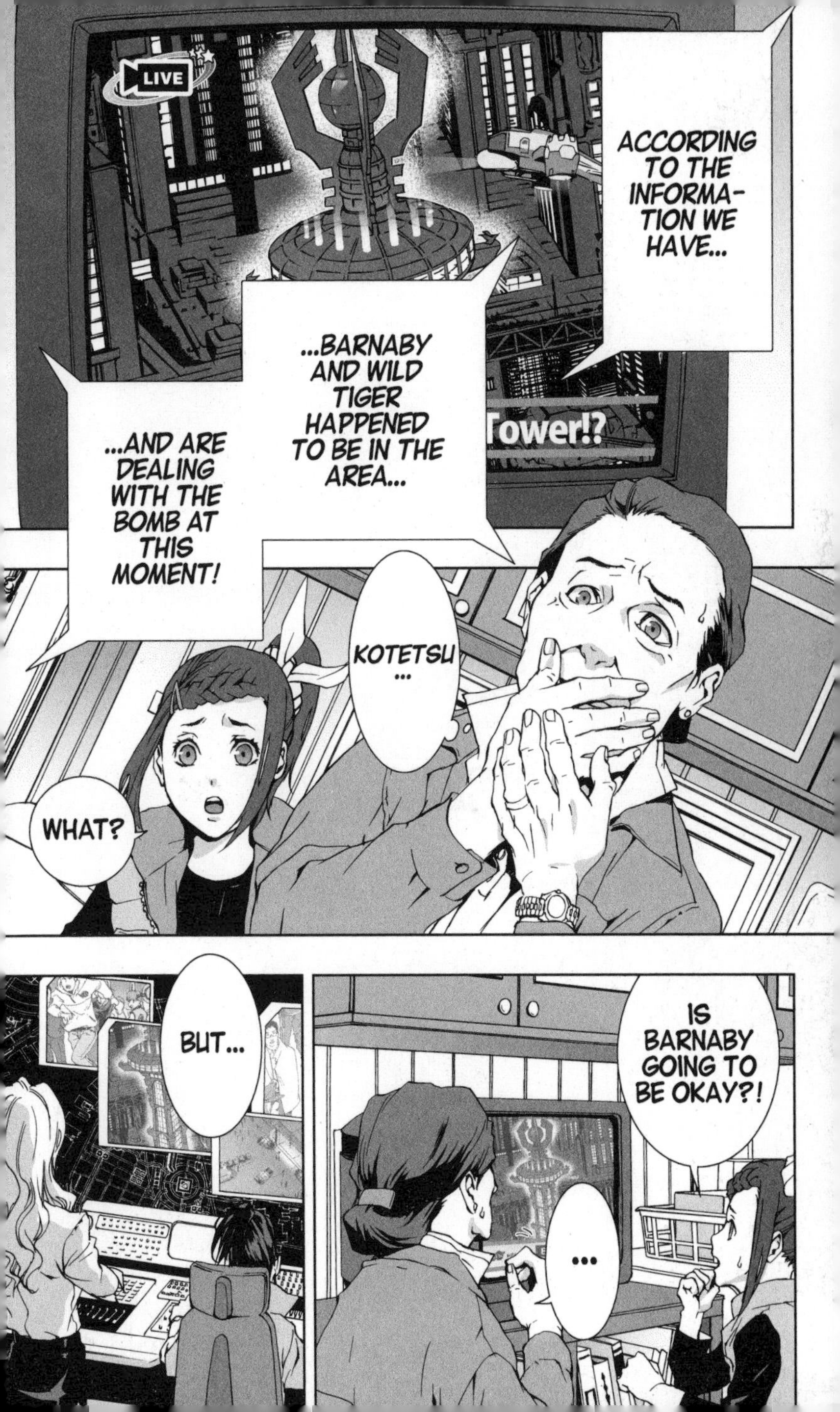
LIVE
ACCORDING TO THE INFORMATION WE HAVE...
...BARNABY AND WILD TIGER HAPPENED TO BE IN THE AREA...
...AND ARE DEALING WITH THE BOMB AT THIS MOMENT!
Tower!?
KOTETSU...
WHAT?
IS BARNABY GOING TO BE OKAY?!
...
BUT...

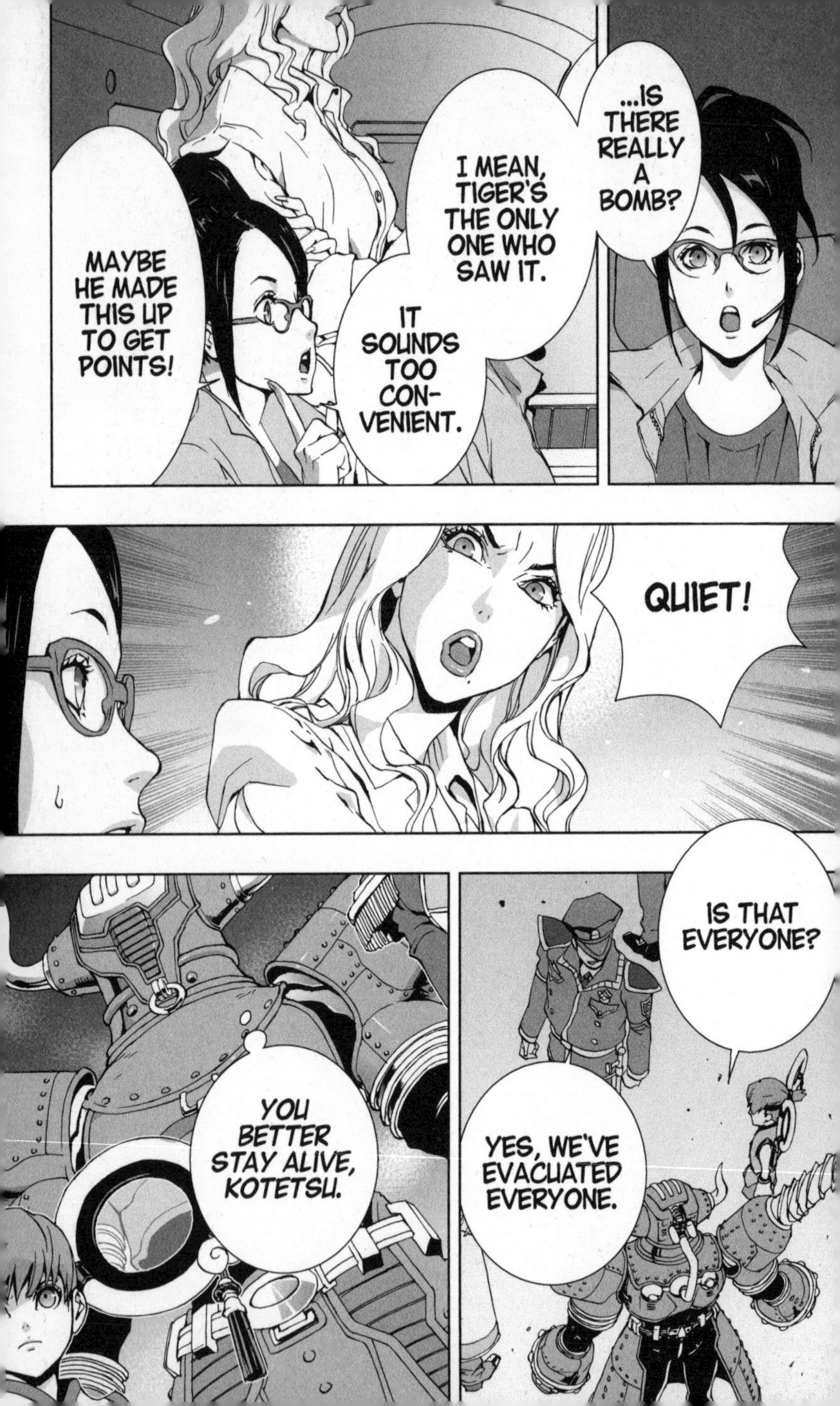

...IS THERE REALLY A BOMB?
I MEAN, TIGER'S THE ONLY ONE WHO SAW IT.
IT SOUNDS TOO CON-VENIENT.
MAYBE HE MADE THIS UP TO GET POINTS!
QUIET!
IS THAT EVERYONE?
YES, WE'VE EVACUATED EVERYONE.
YOU BETTER STAY ALIVE, KOTETSU.

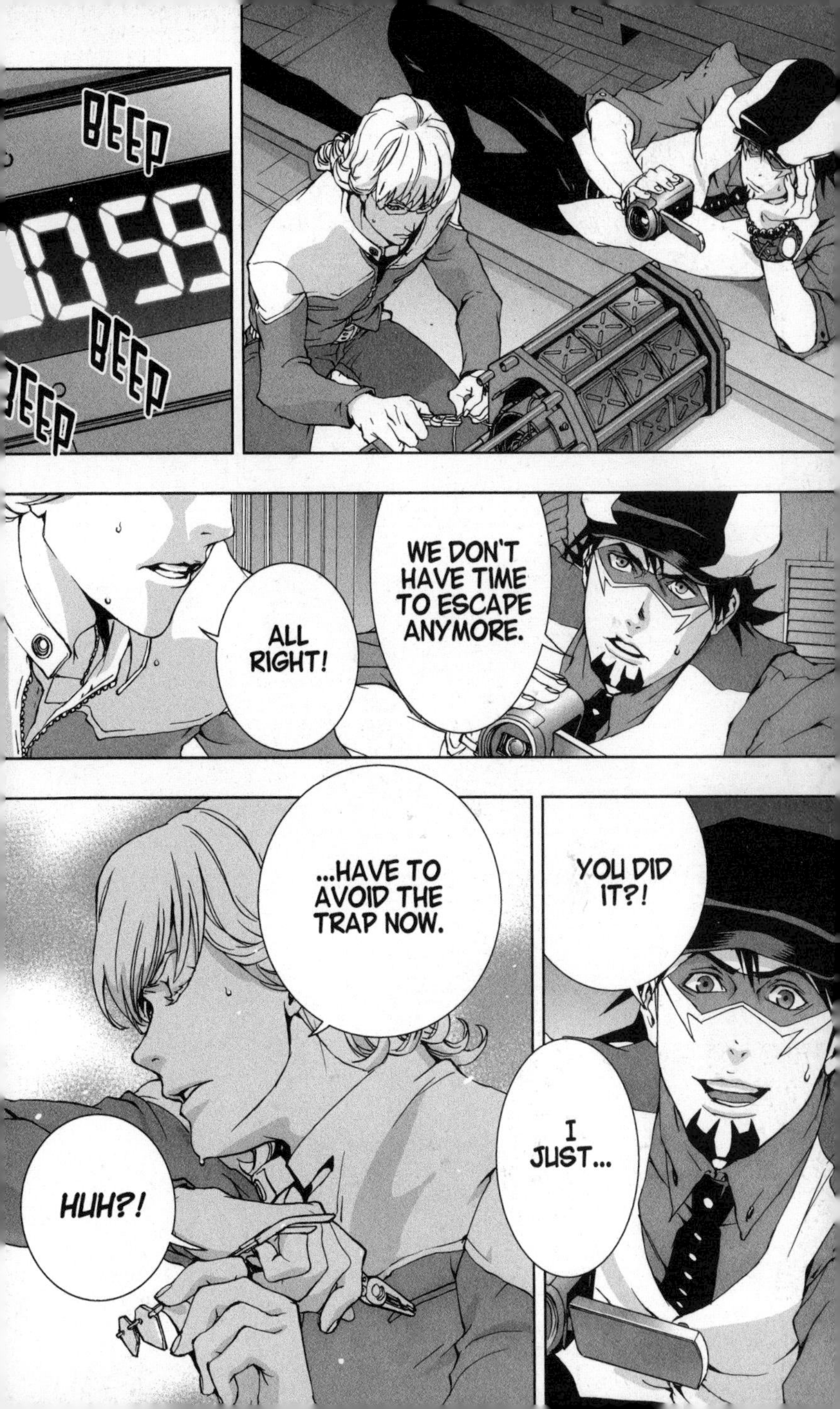
BEEP
BEEP
WE DON'T HAVE TIME TO ESCAPE ANYMORE.
ALL RIGHT!
YOU DID IT?!
I JUST...
...HAVE TO AVOID THE TRAP NOW.
HUH?!

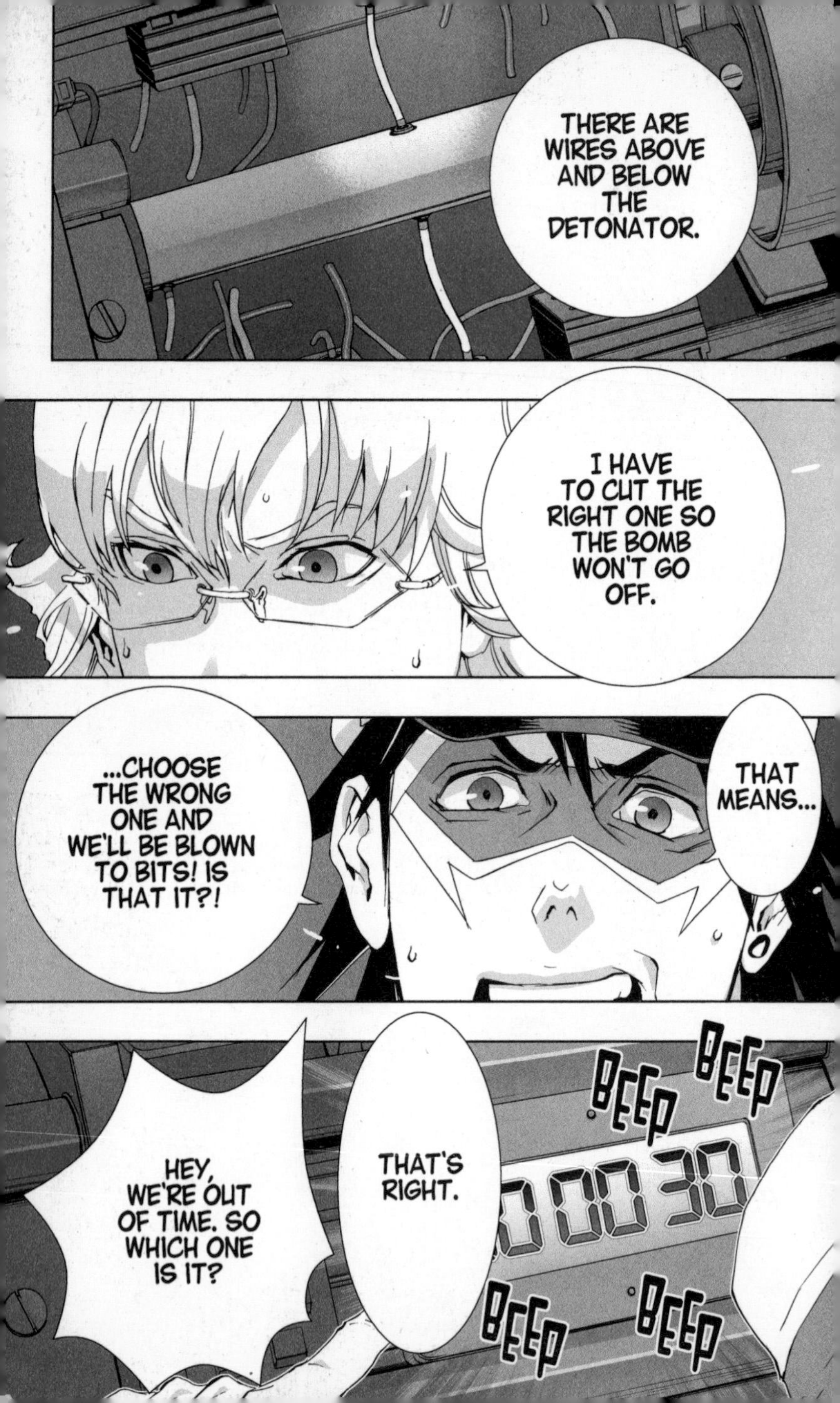
THERE ARE WIRES ABOVE AND BELOW THE DETONATOR.
I HAVE TO CUT THE RIGHT ONE SO THE BOMB WON'T GO OFF.
THAT MEANS...
...CHOOSE THE WRONG ONE AND WE'LL BE BLOWN TO BITS! IS THAT IT?!
BEEP
BEEP
THAT'S RIGHT.
HEY, WE'RE OUT OF TIME. SO WHICH ONE IS IT?
BEEP
BEEP

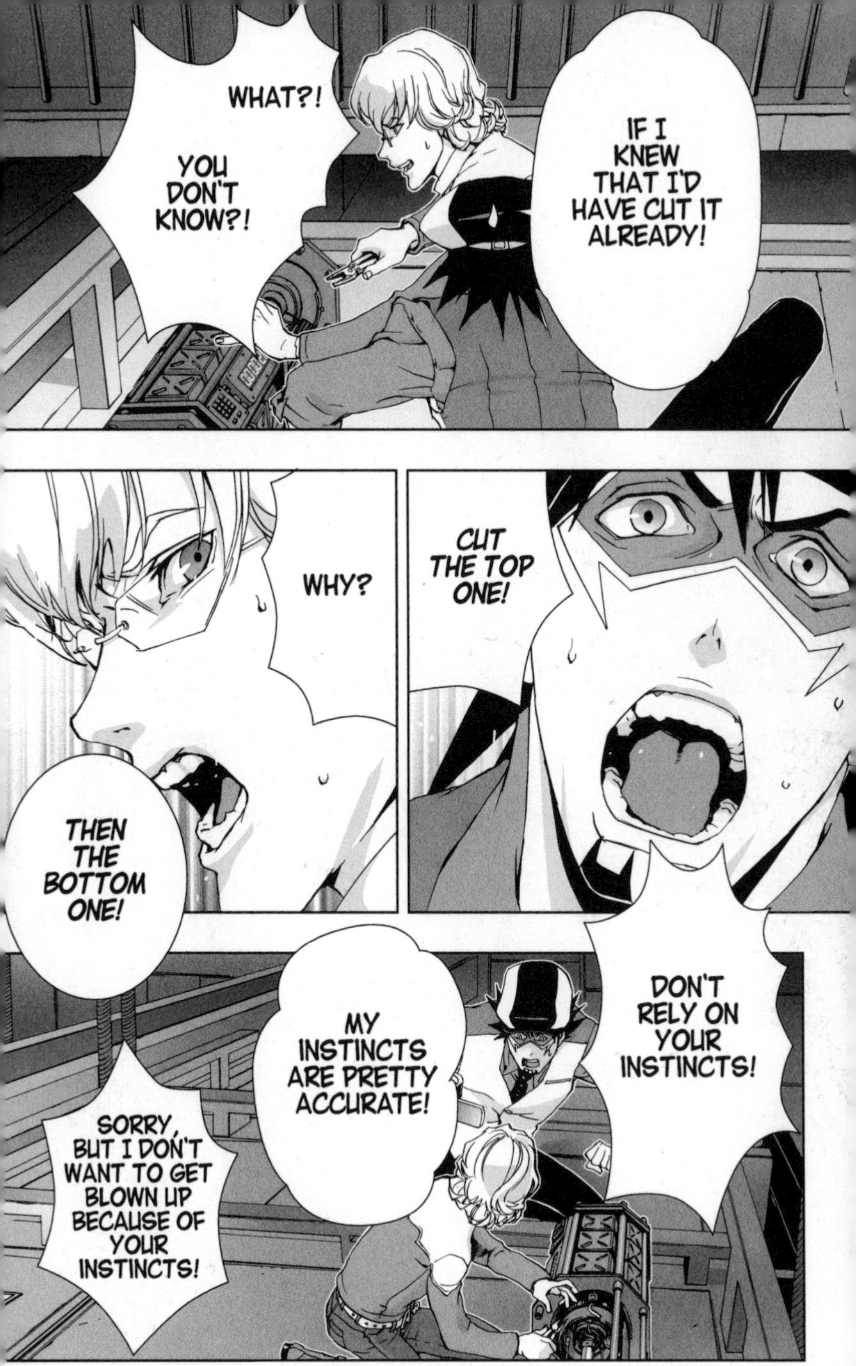
WHAT?!
YOU DON'T KNOW?!
IF I KNEW THAT I'D HAVE CUT IT ALREADY!
CUT THE TOP ONE!
WHY?
THEN THE BOTTOM ONE!
DON'T RELY ON YOUR INSTINCTS!
MY INSTINCTS ARE PRETTY ACCURATE!
SORRY, BUT I DON'T WANT TO GET BLOWN UP BECAUSE OF YOUR INSTINCTS!

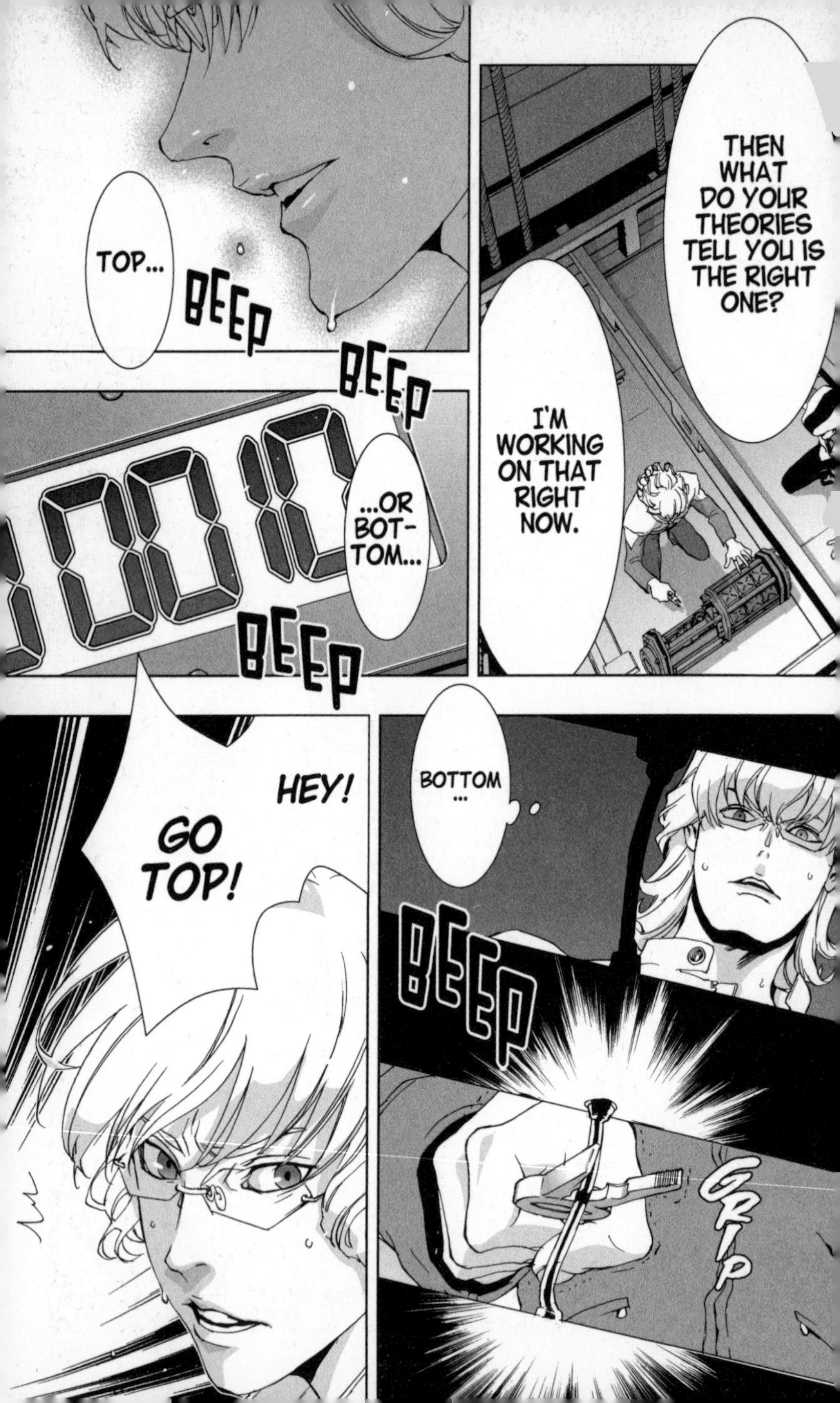
THEN WHAT DO YOUR THEORIES TELL YOU IS THE RIGHT ONE?
I'M WORKING ON THAT RIGHT NOW.
TOP...
BEEP
BEEP
...OR BOT-TOM...
BEEP
BOTTOM...
BEEP
GRIP
HEY!
GO TOP!

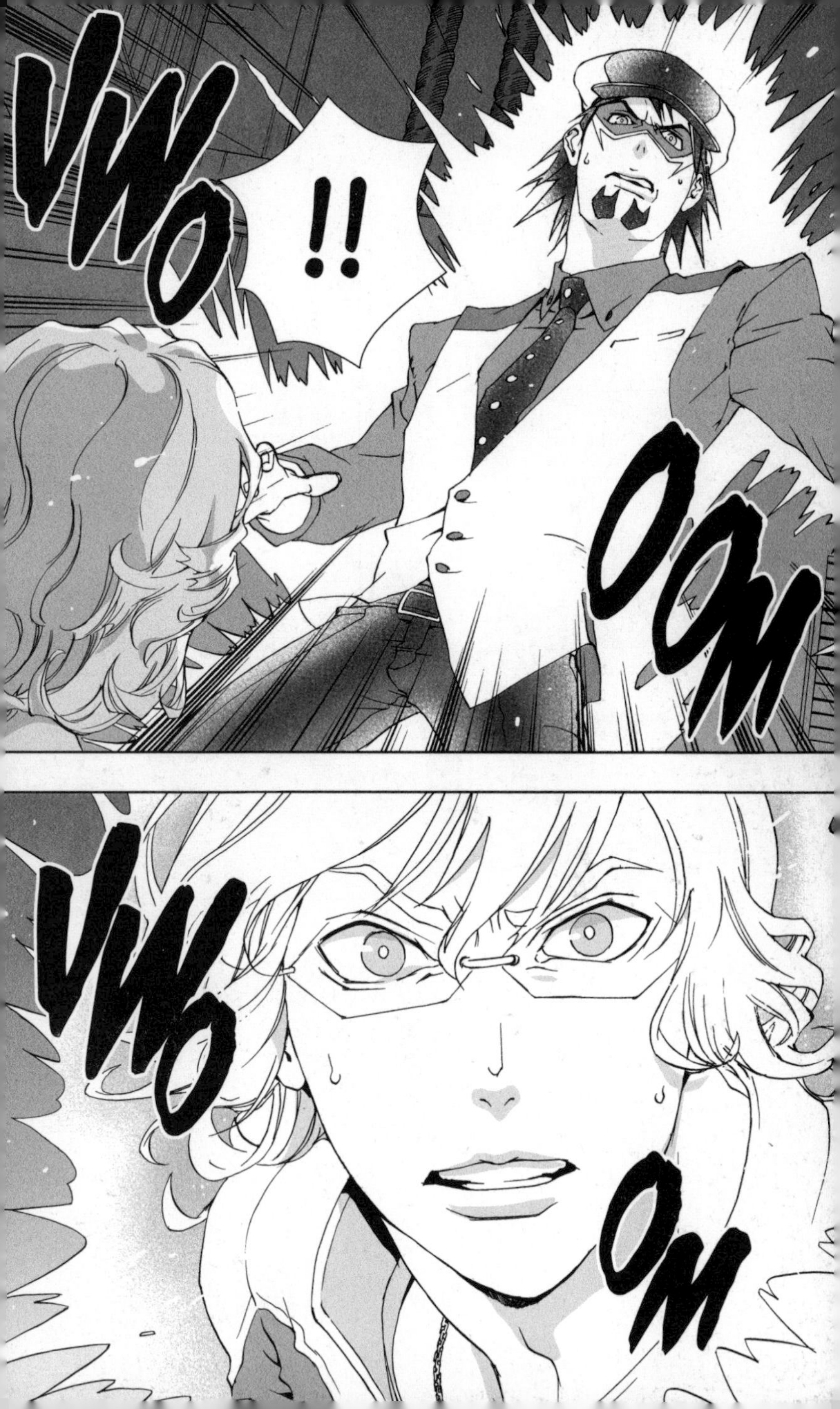
VWO
!!
OOM
VWO
OM

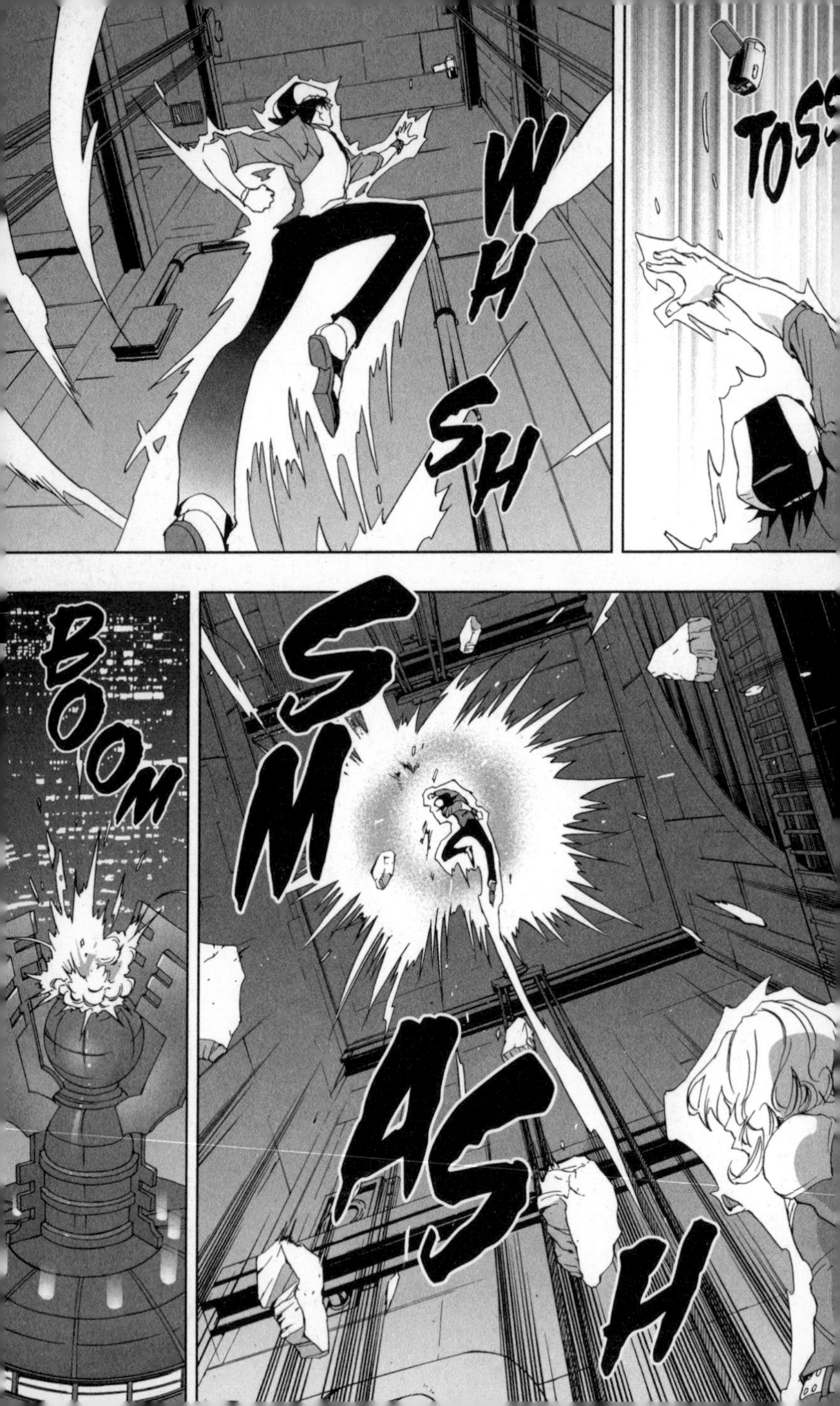
TOSS
WHSH
SMASH
BOOM

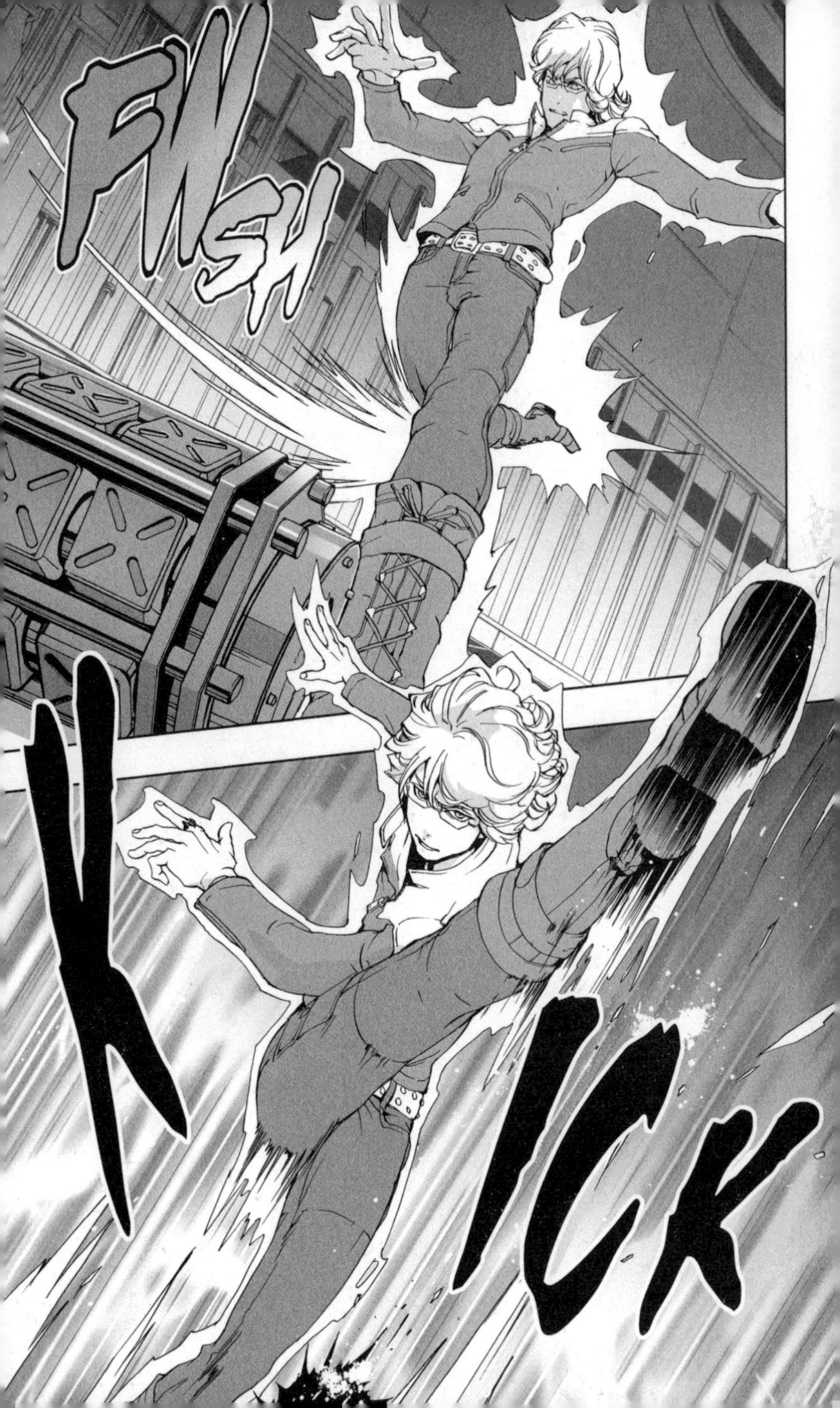
FWSH
KICK

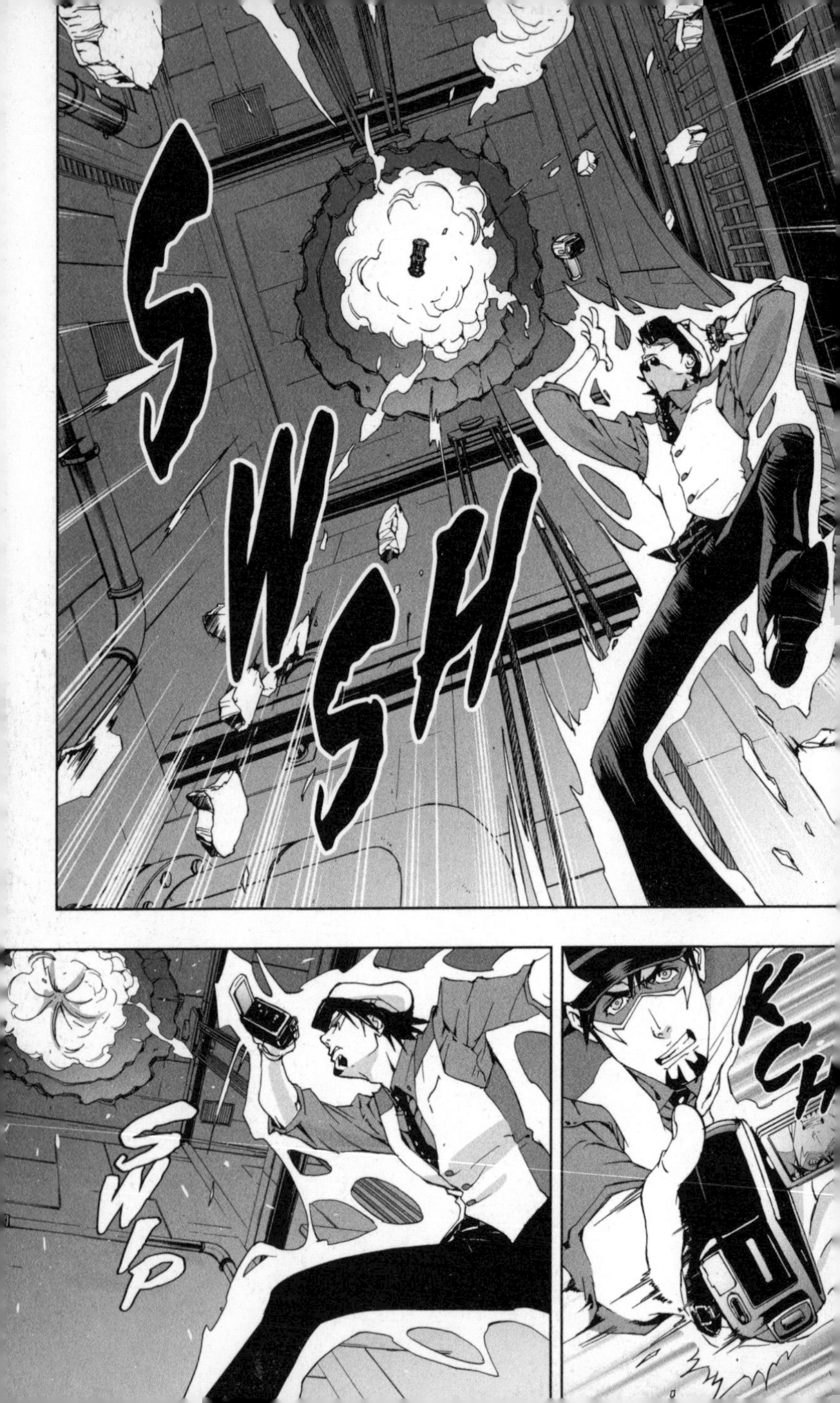
SWSH
KCH
SWIP

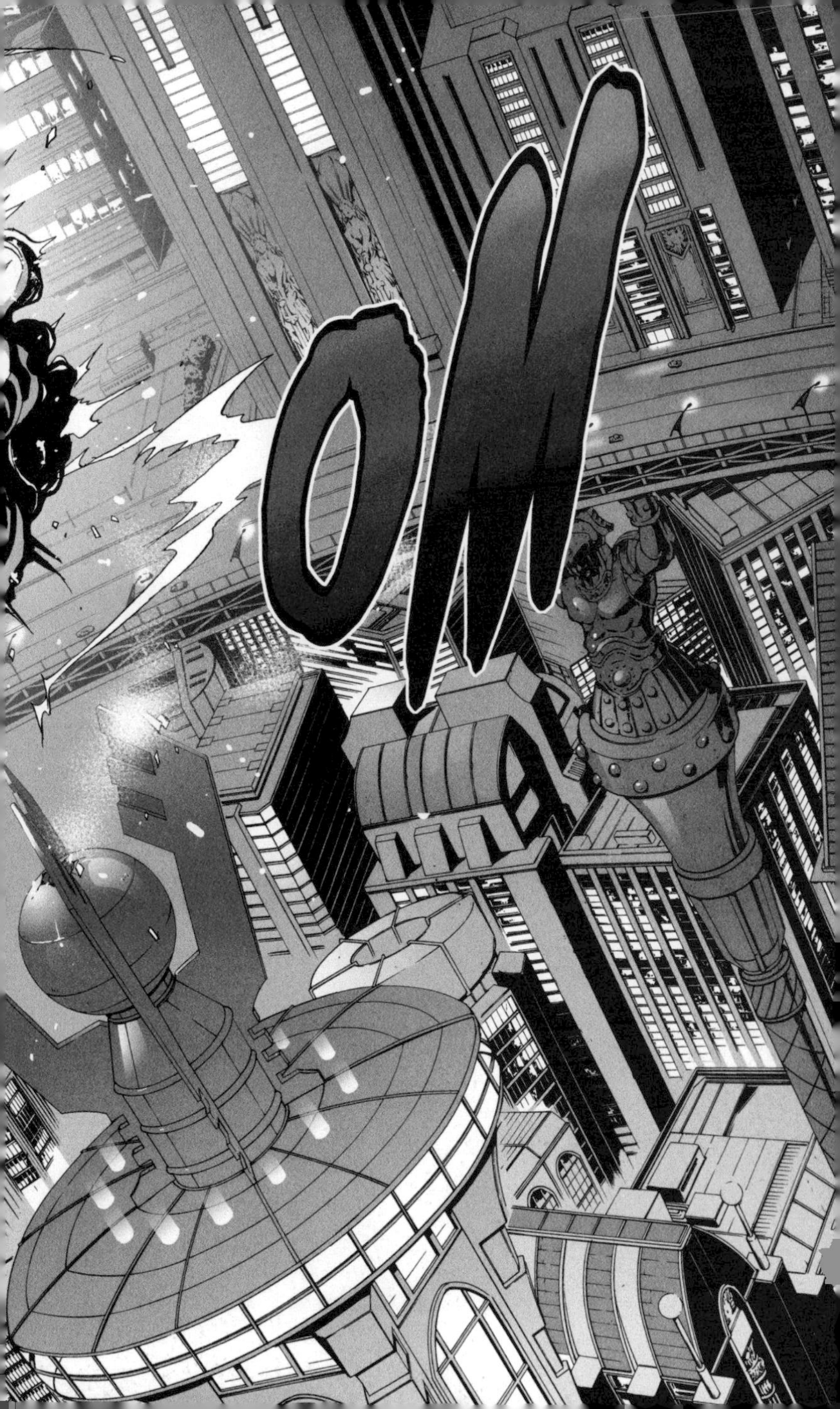
OM

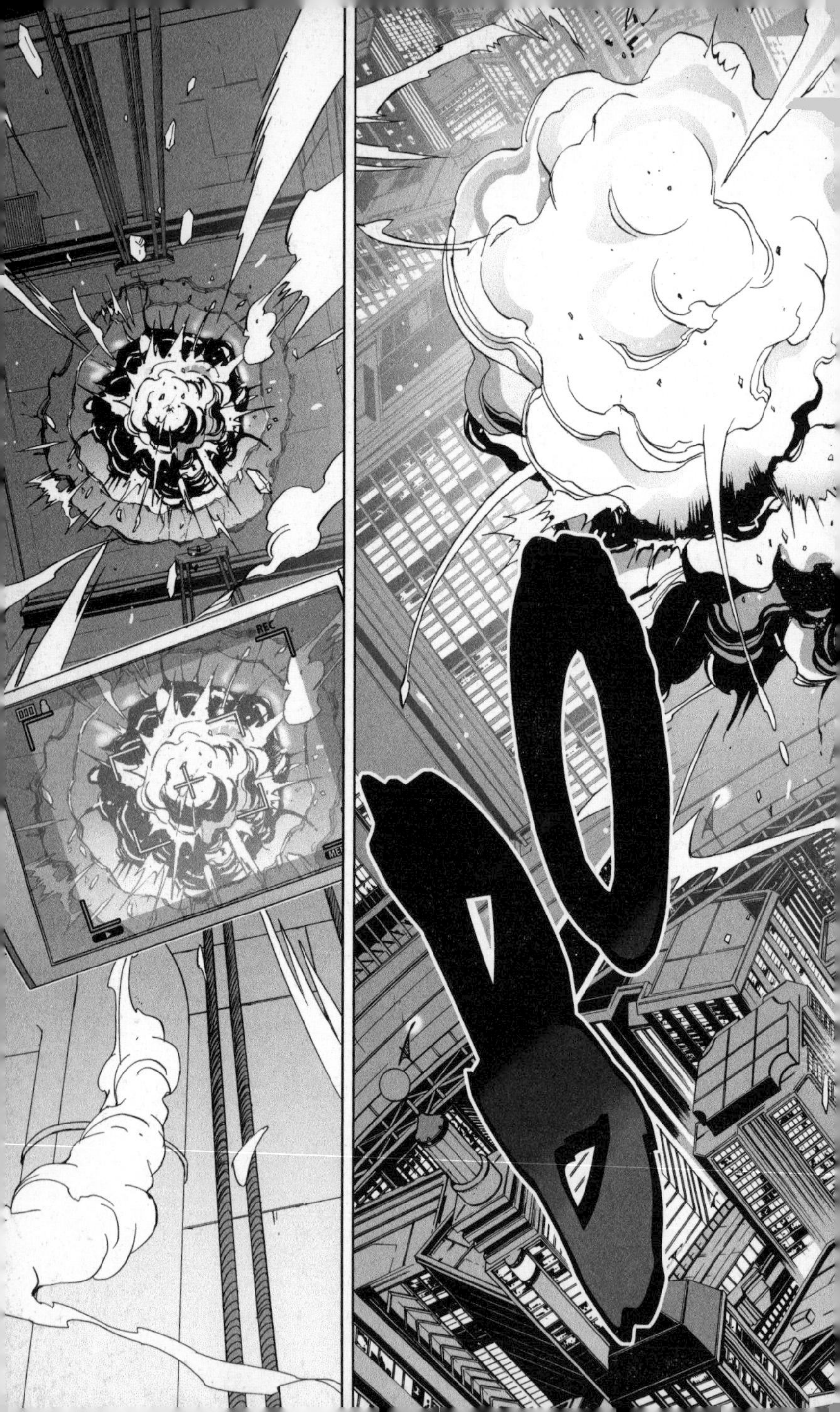
REC

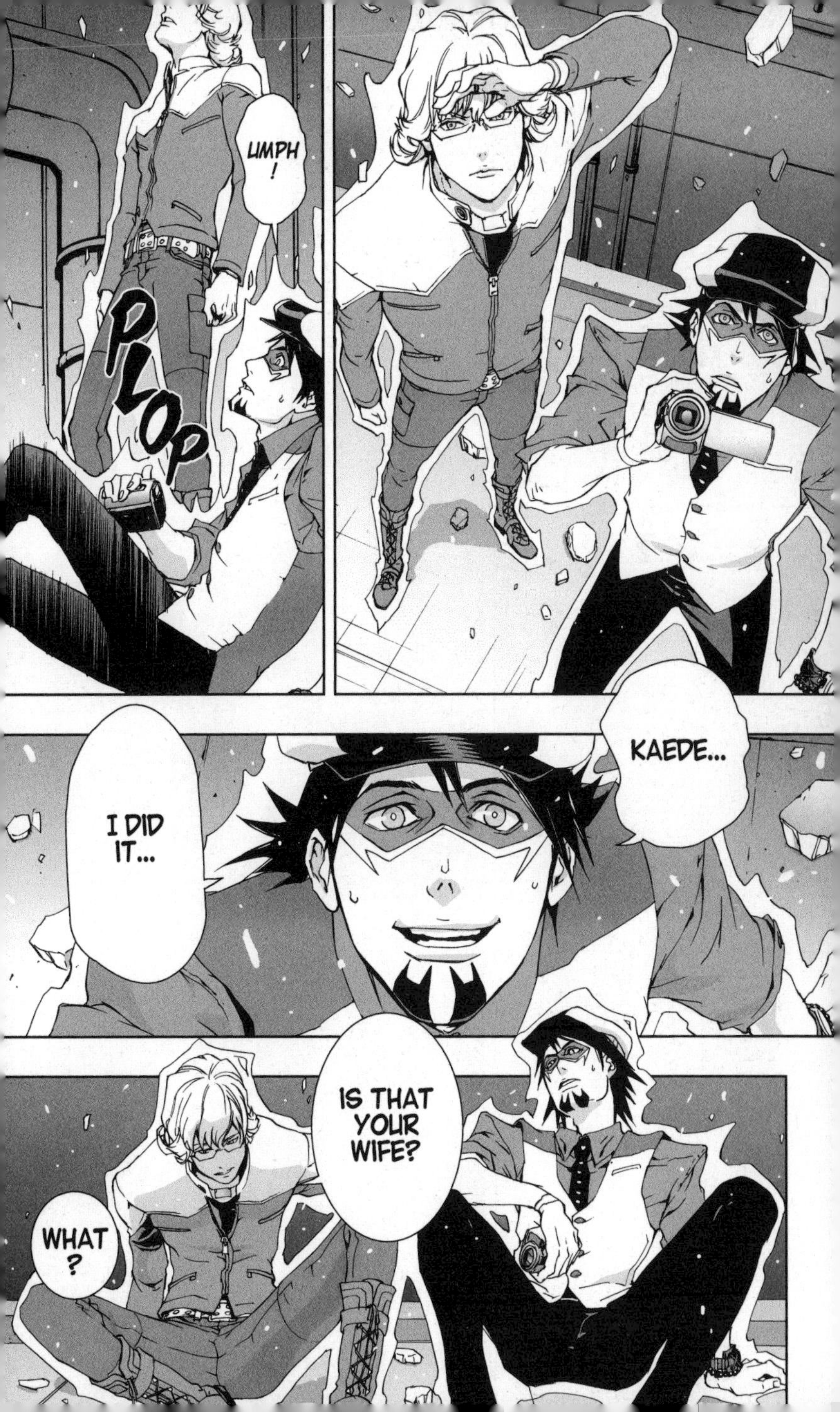
UMPH!
PLOP
KAEDE...
I DID IT...
IS THAT YOUR WIFE?
WHAT?

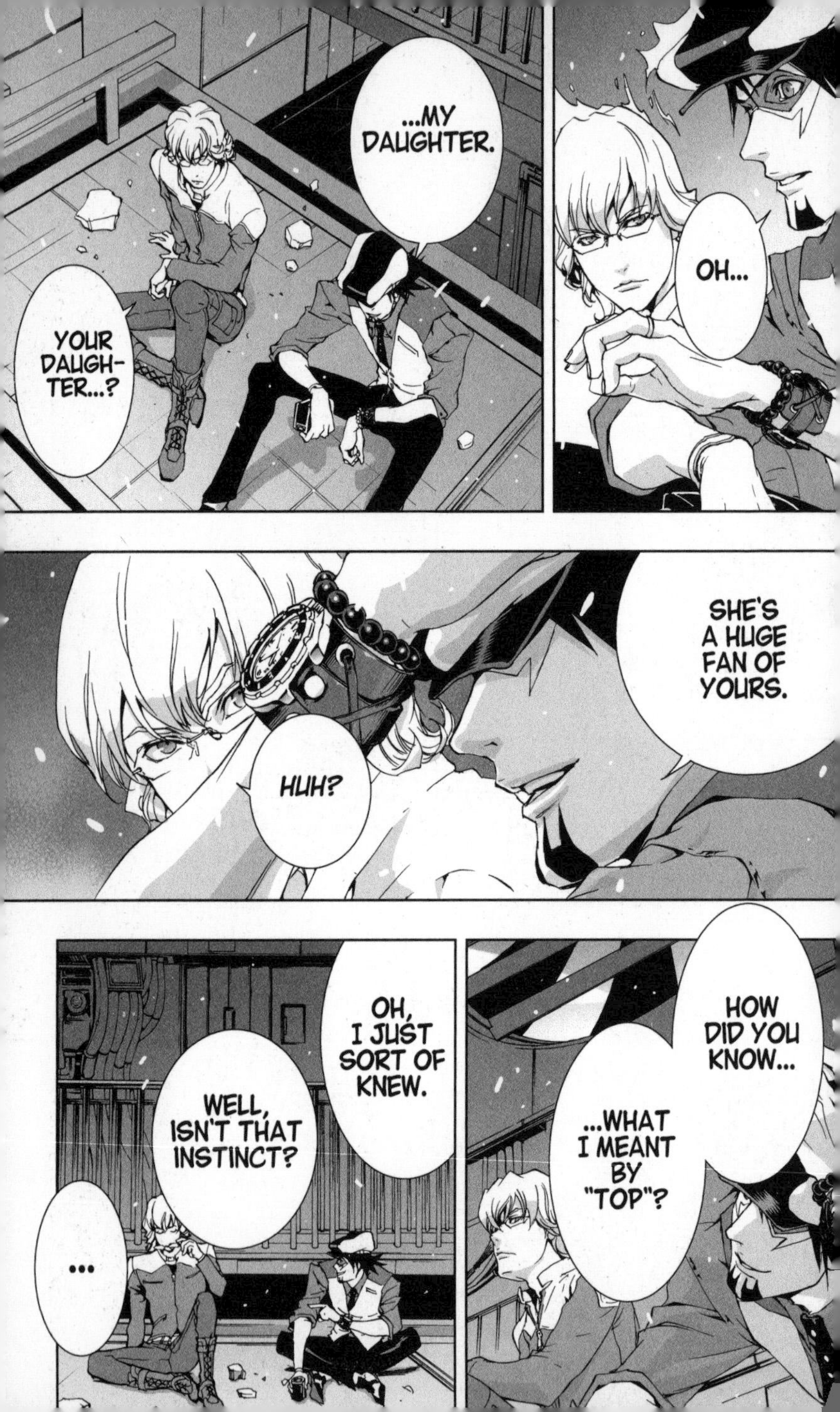
OH...
...MY DAUGHTER.
YOUR DAUGHTER-TER...?
SHE'S A HUGE FAN OF YOURS.
HUH?
HOW DID YOU KNOW...
...WHAT I MEANT BY "TOP"?
OH, I JUST SORT OF KNEW.
WELL, ISN'T THAT INSTINCT?
...

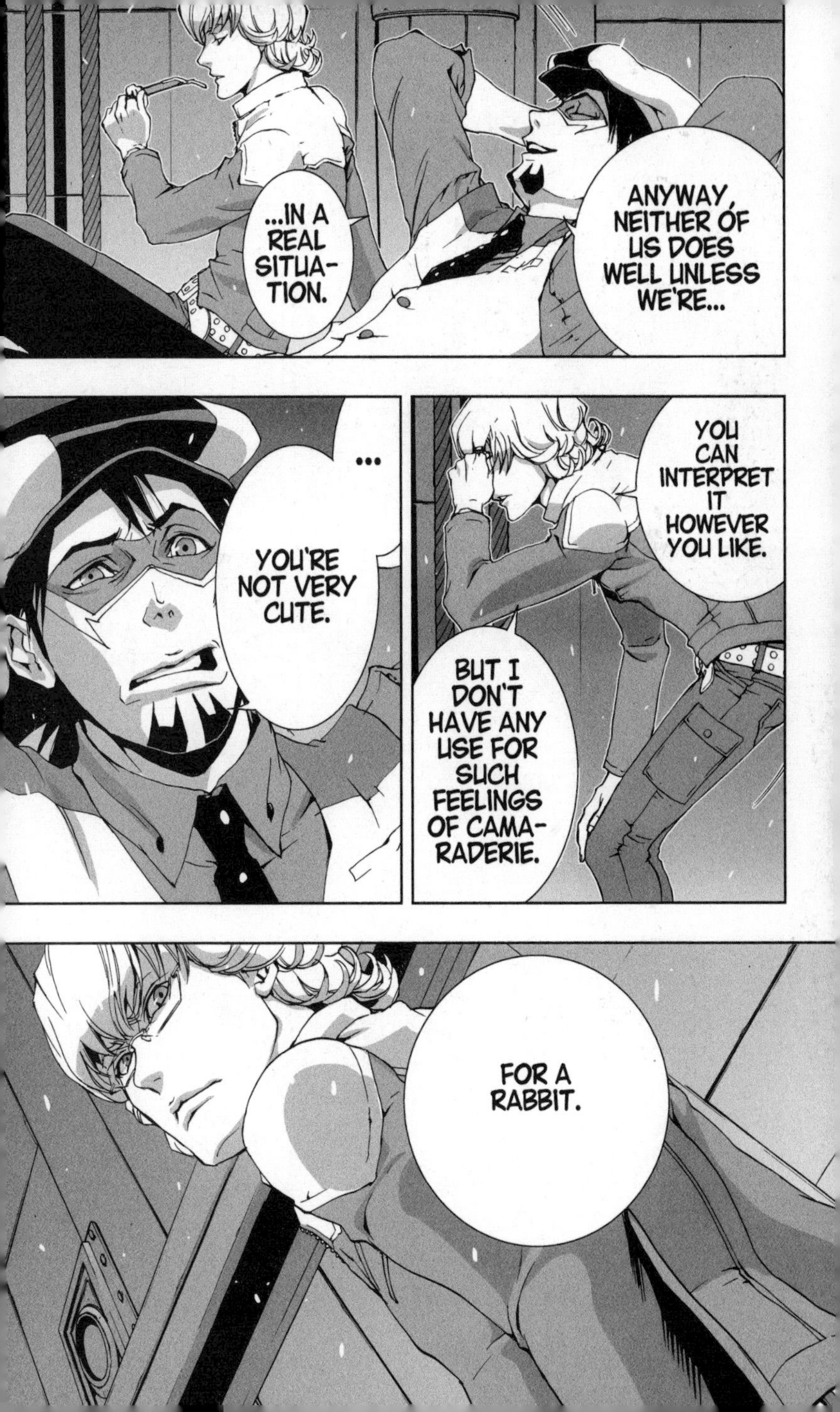
ANYWAY, NEITHER OF US DOES WELL UNLESS WE'RE...
...IN A REAL SITUATION.
YOU CAN INTERPRET IT HOWEVER YOU LIKE.
BUT I DON'T HAVE ANY USE FOR SUCH FEELINGS OF CAMARADERIE.
...
YOU'RE NOT VERY CUTE.
FOR A RABBIT.

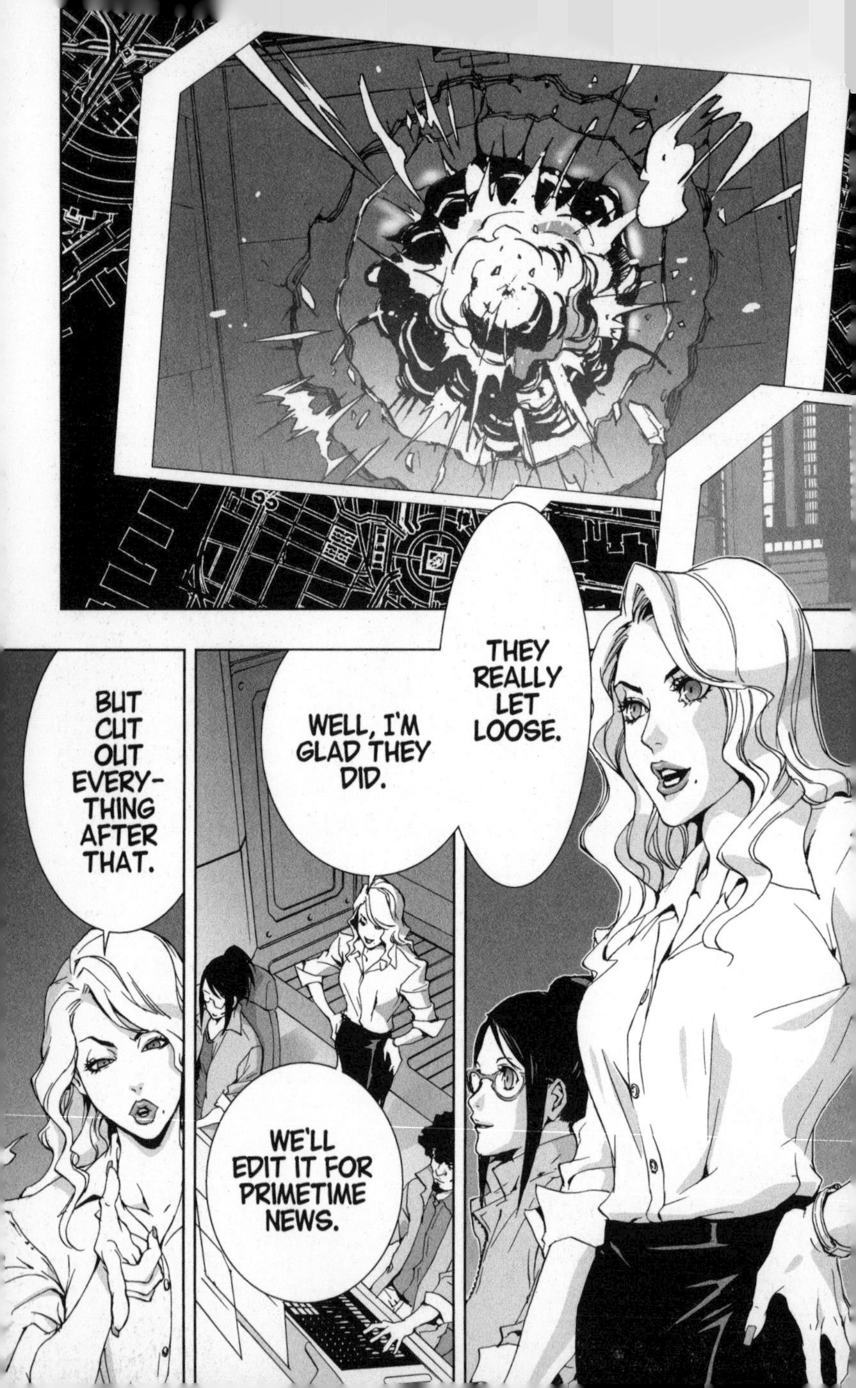
THEY REALLY LET LOOSE.
WELL, I'M GLAD THEY DID.
WE'LL EDIT IT FOR PRIMETIME NEWS.
BUT CUT OUT EVERYTHING AFTER THAT.

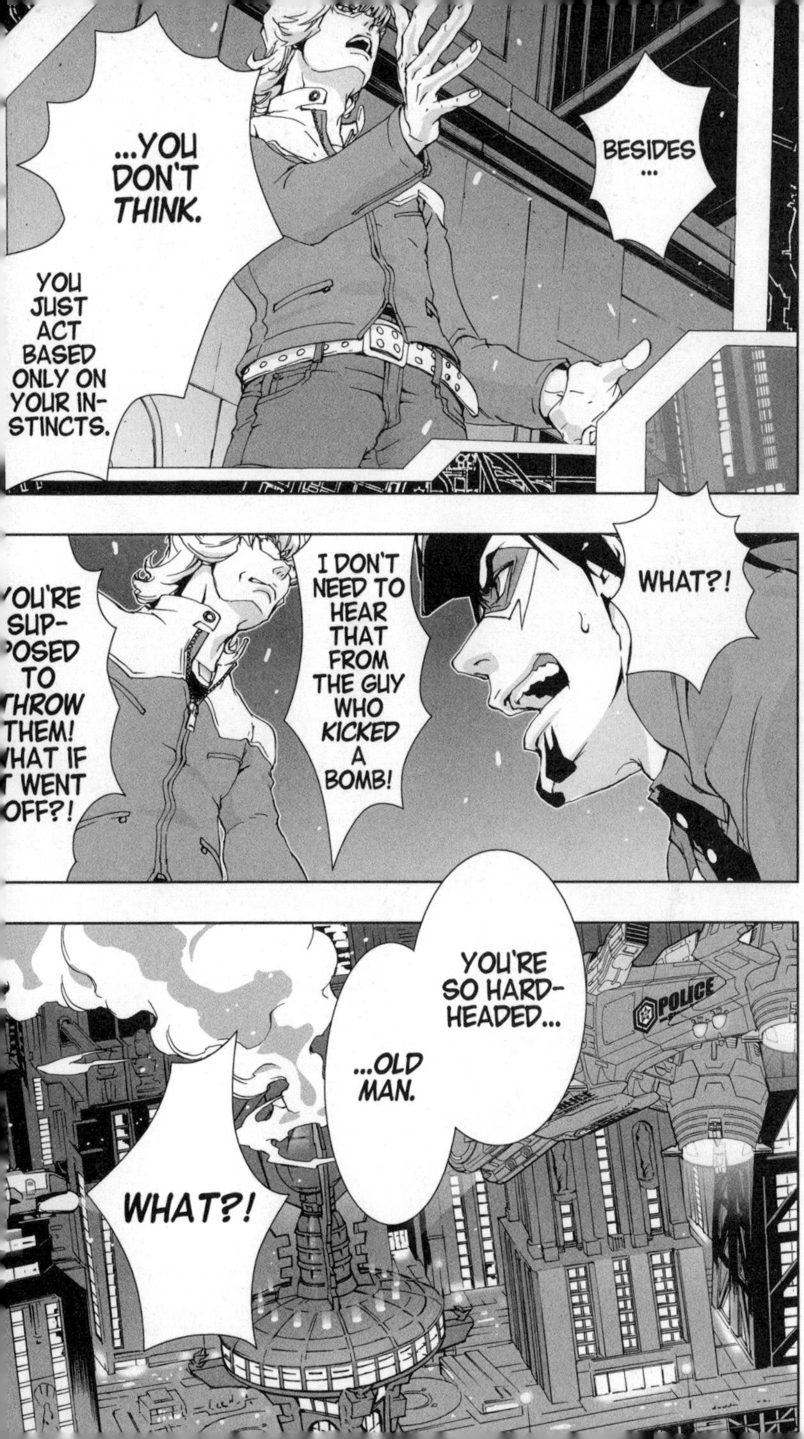
BESIDES ...
...YOU DON'T THINK.
YOU JUST ACT BASED ONLY ON YOUR IN-STINCTS.
WHAT?!
I DON'T NEED TO HEAR THAT FROM THE GUY WHO KICKED A BOMB!
OU'RE SUP-OSED TO HROW THEM! HAT IF T WENT OFF?!
POLICE
YOU'RE SO HARD-HEADED...
...OLD MAN.
WHAT?!

#07 Go for Broke! Part 1

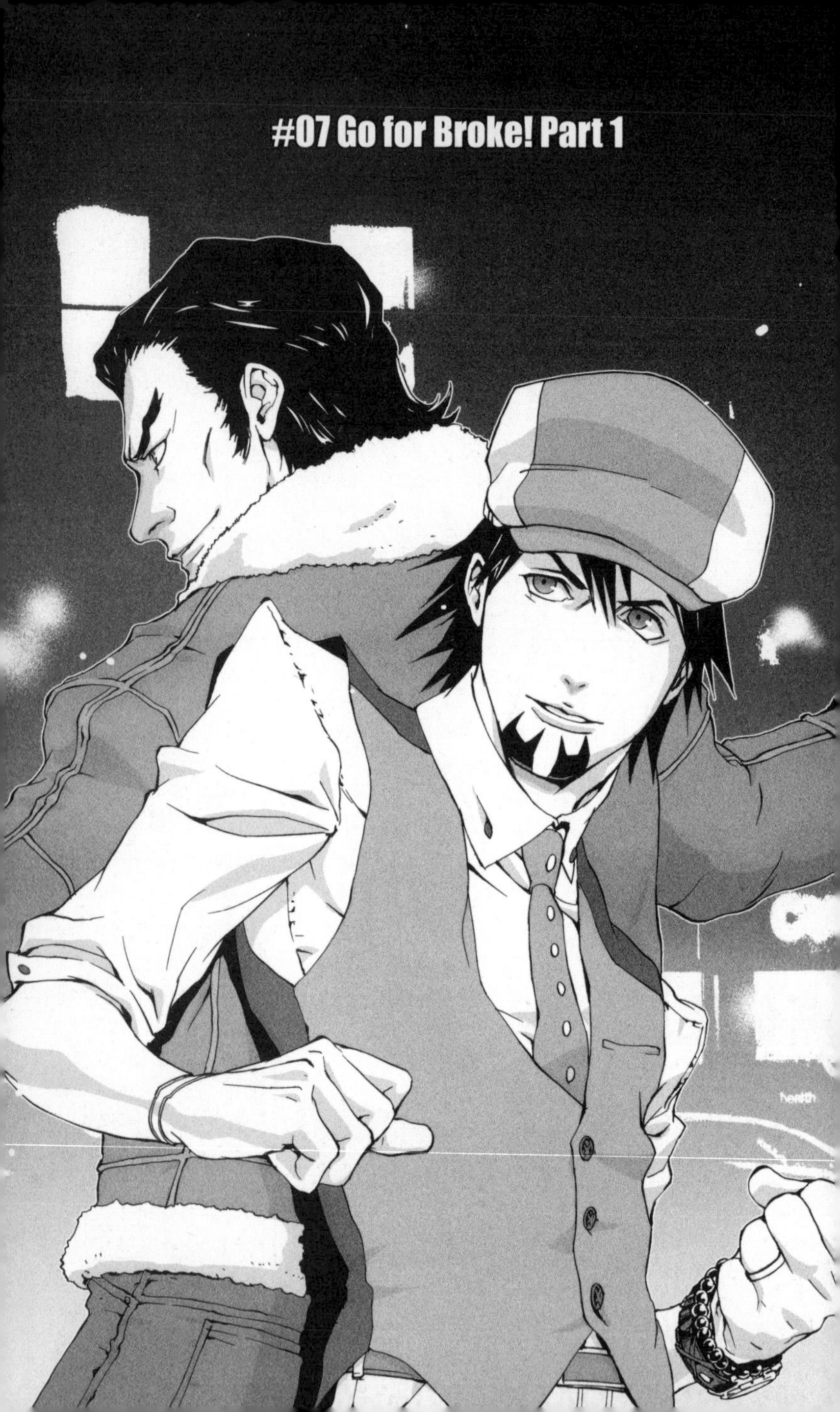
health

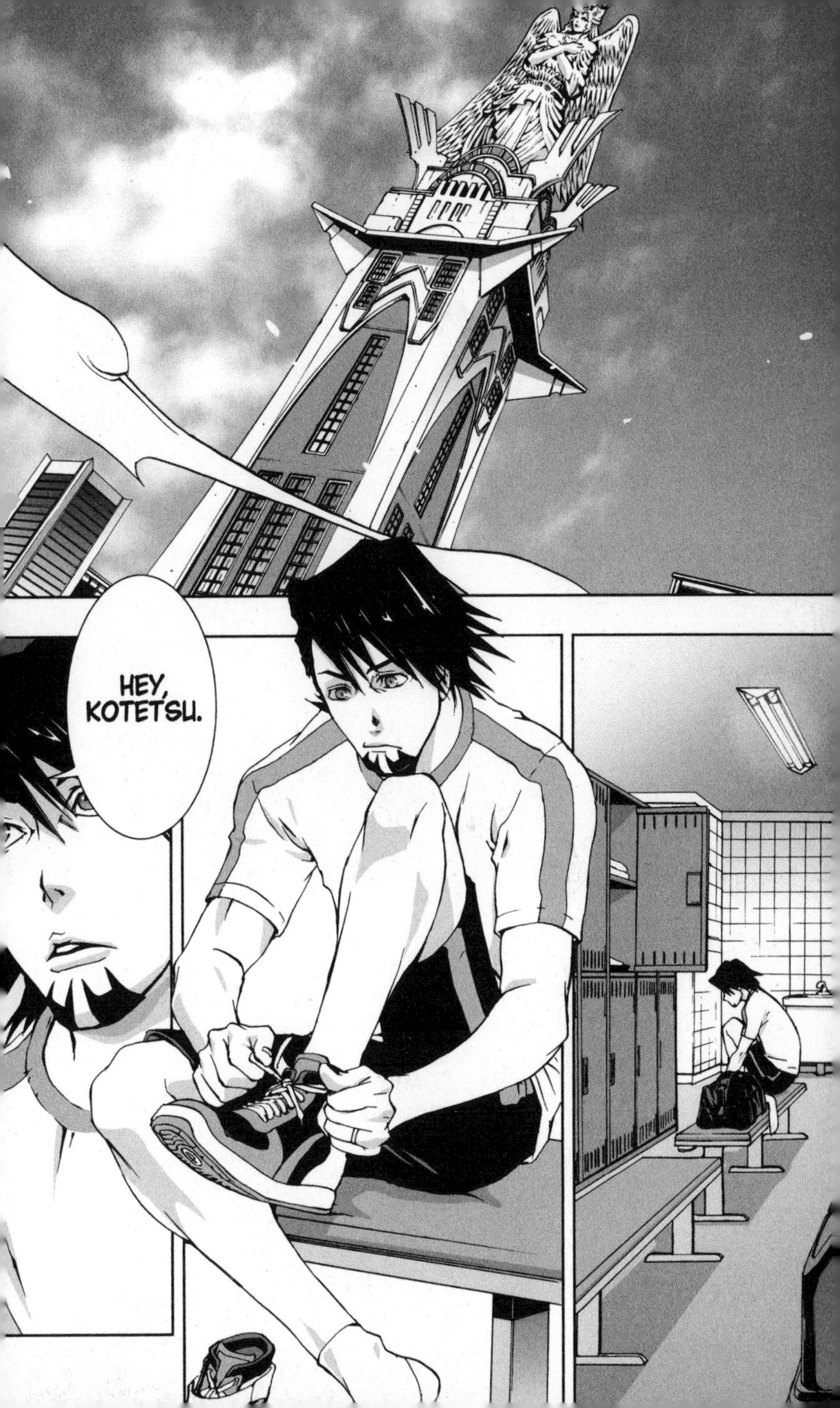
HEY, KOTETSU.

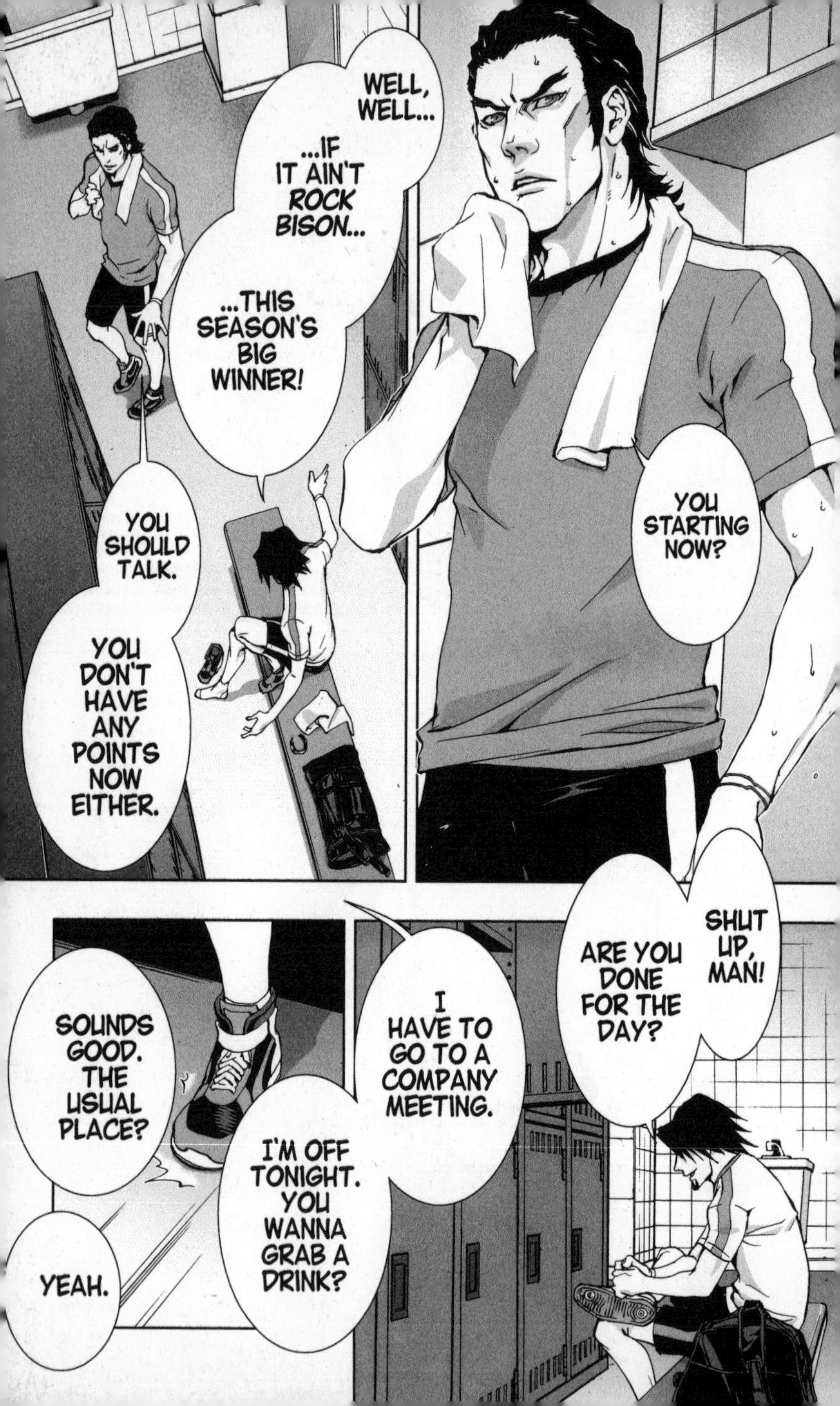
YOU STARTING NOW?
WELL, WELL...
...IF IT AIN'T ROCK BISON...
...THIS SEASON'S BIG WINNER!
YOU SHOULD TALK.
YOU DON'T HAVE ANY POINTS NOW EITHER.
SHUT UP, MAN!
ARE YOU DONE FOR THE DAY?
I HAVE TO GO TO A COMPANY MEETING.
I'M OFF TONIGHT. YOU WANNA GRAB A DRINK?
SOUNDS GOOD. THE USUAL PLACE?
YEAH.

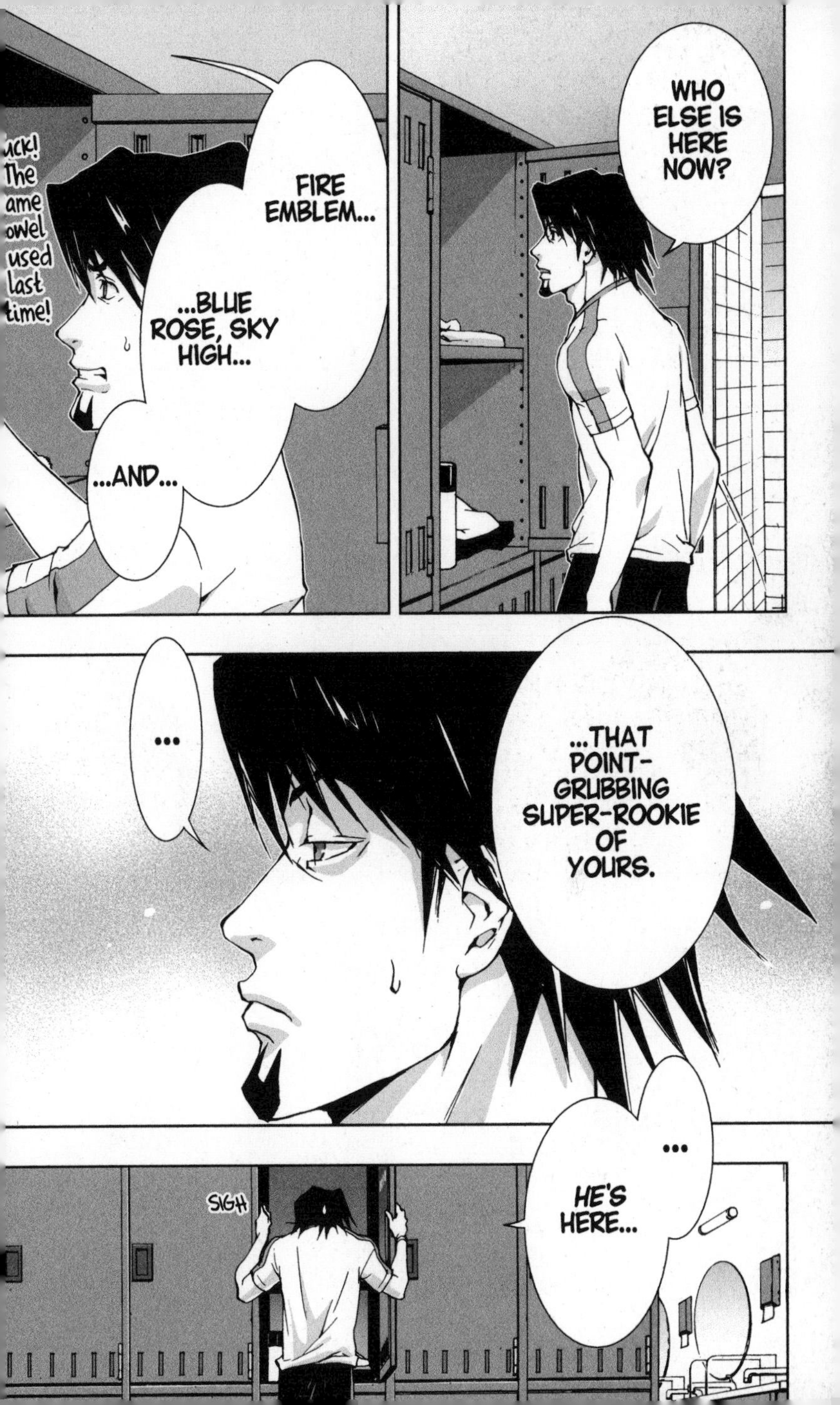
WHO ELSE IS HERE NOW?
FIRE EMBLEM...
...BLUE ROSE, SKY HIGH...
...AND...
ck! The ame owel used last time!
...THAT POINT-GRUBBING SUPER-ROOKIE OF YOURS.
...
...
HE'S HERE...
SIGH

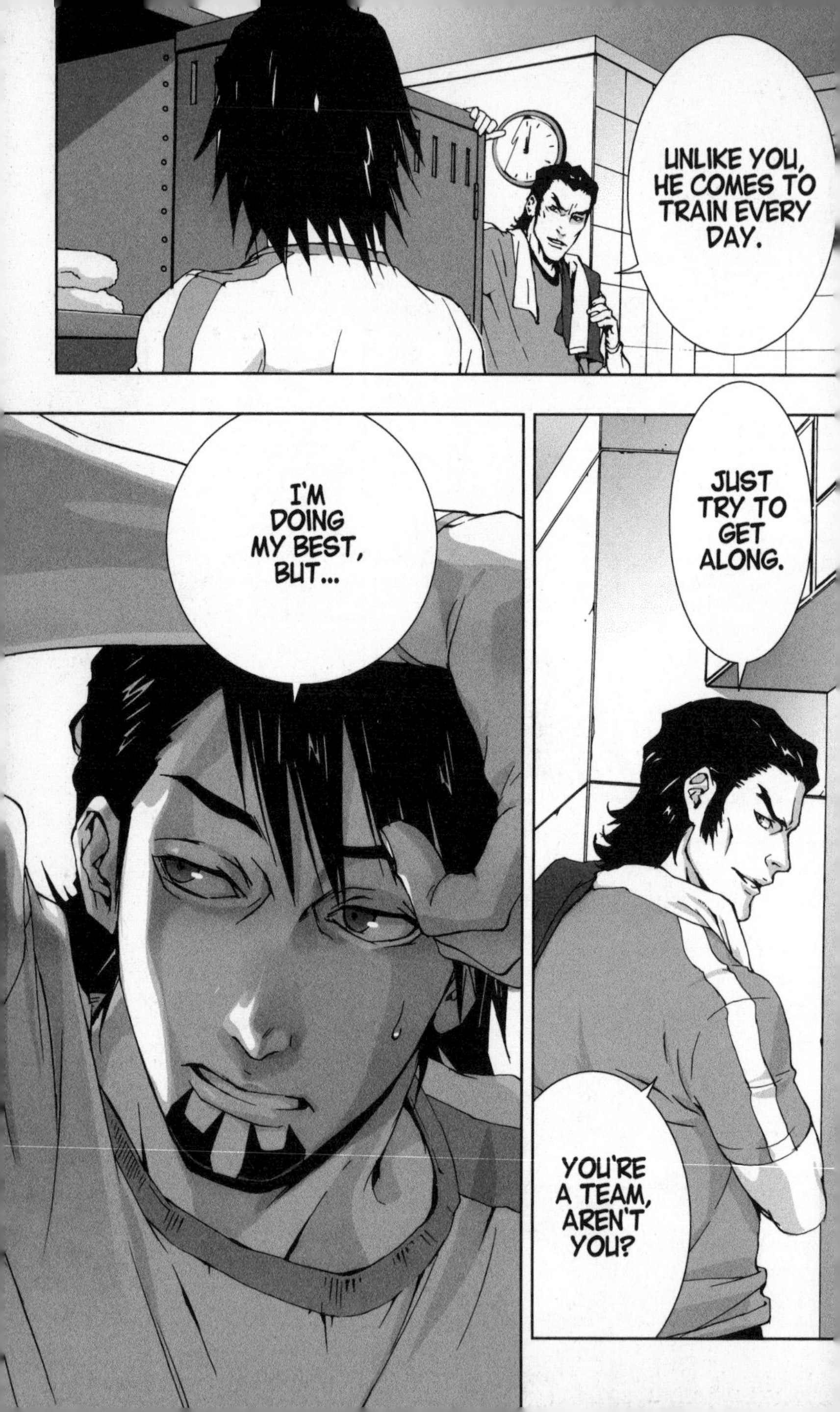
UNLIKE YOU, HE COMES TO TRAIN EVERY DAY.
JUST TRY TO GET ALONG.
YOU'RE A TEAM, AREN'T YOU?
I'M DOING MY BEST, BUT...

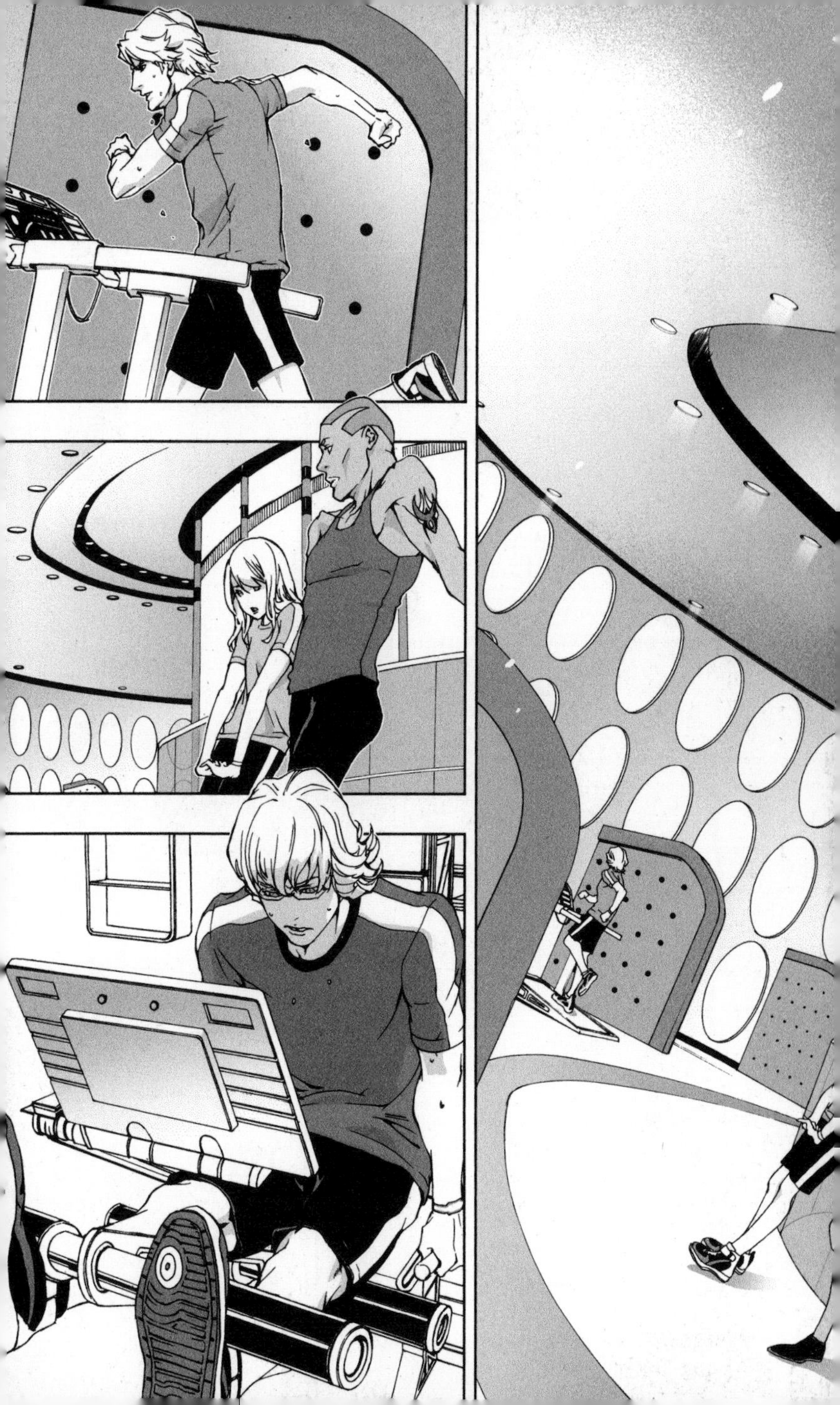

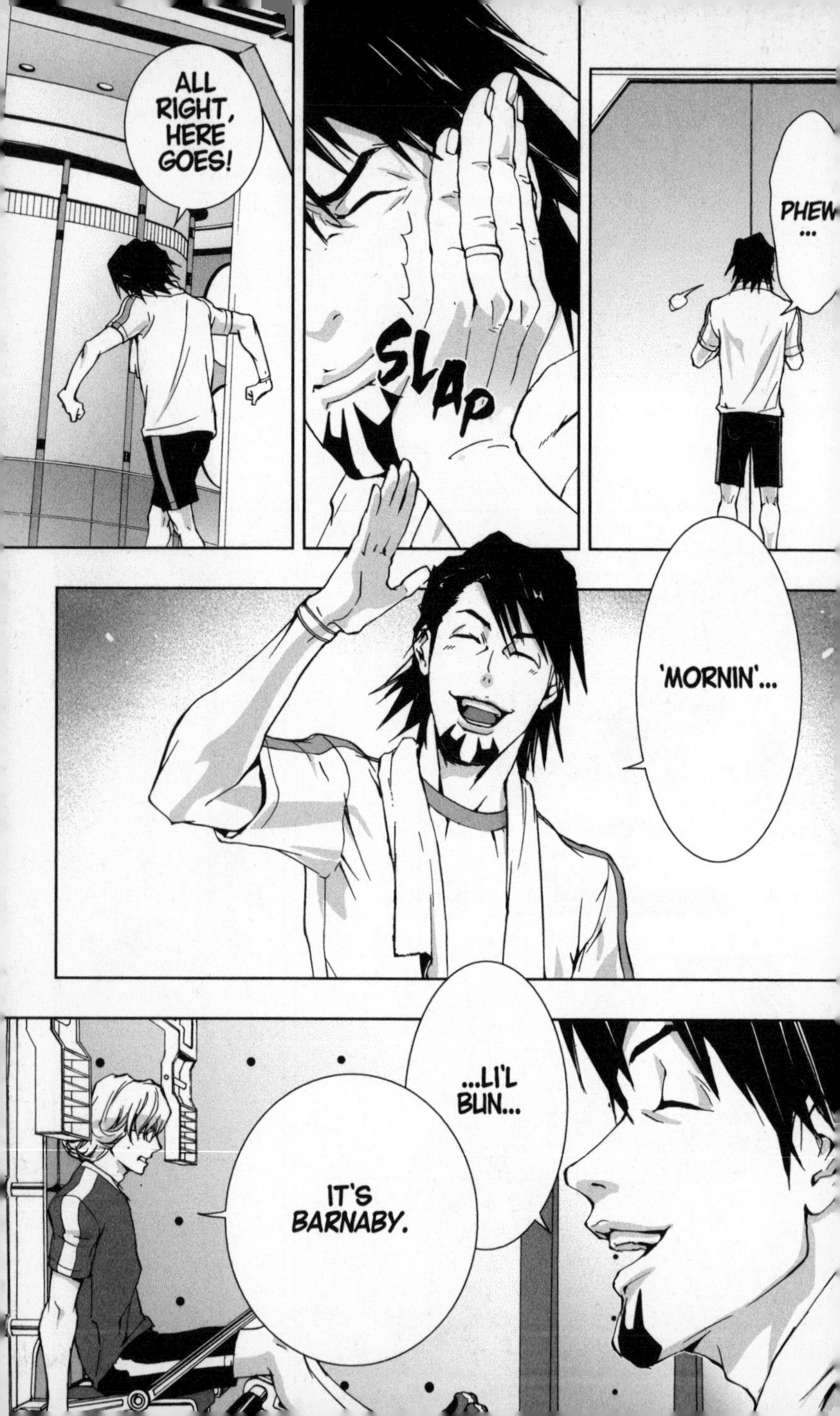
PHEW...
SLAP
ALL RIGHT, HERE GOES!
'MORNIN'...
...LI'L BUN...
IT'S BARNABY.

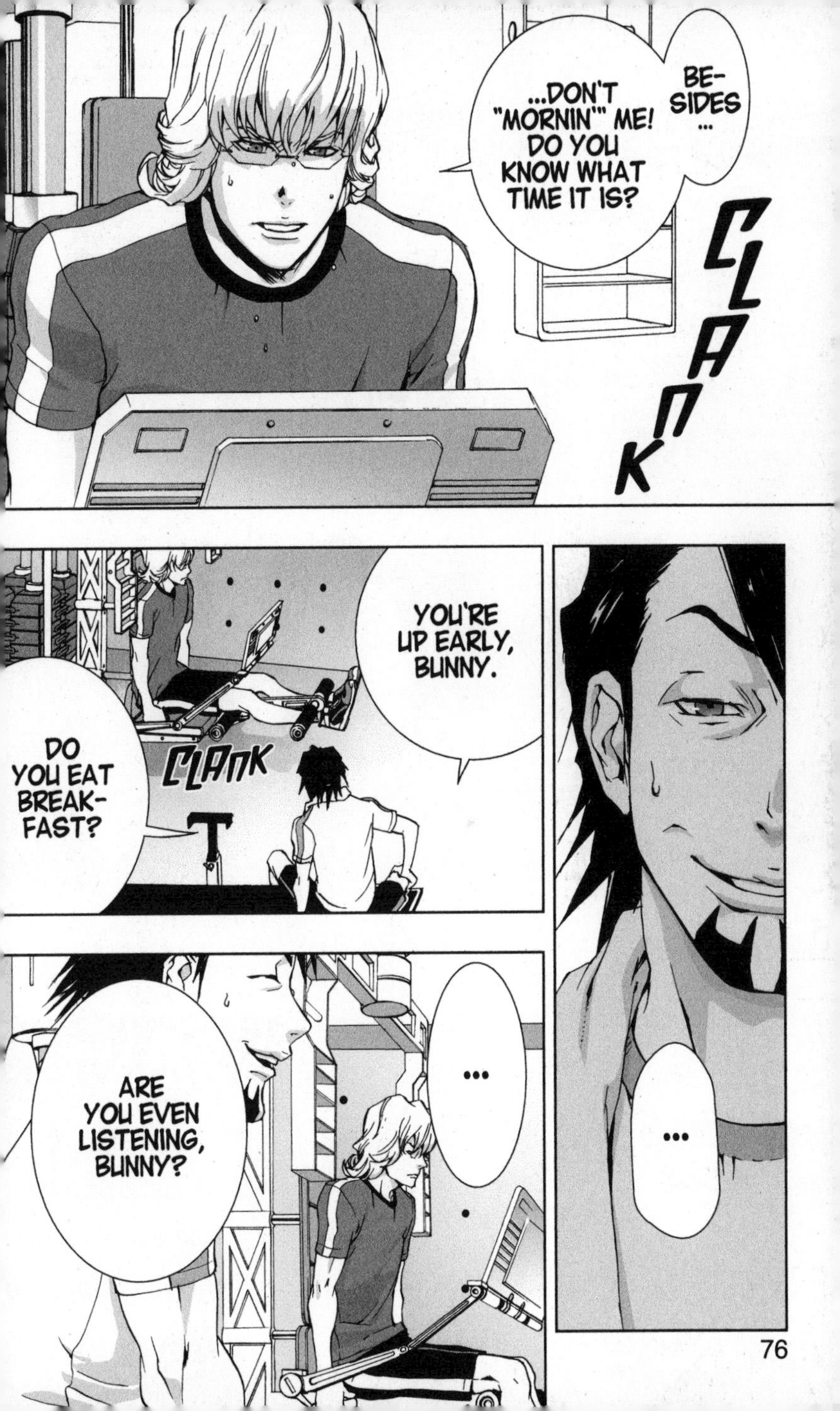
BE-SIDES...
...DON'T "MORNIN'" ME! DO YOU KNOW WHAT TIME IT IS?
CLANK
...
YOU'RE UP EARLY, BUNNY.
CLANK
DO YOU EAT BREAK-FAST?
...
ARE YOU EVEN LISTENING, BUNNY?

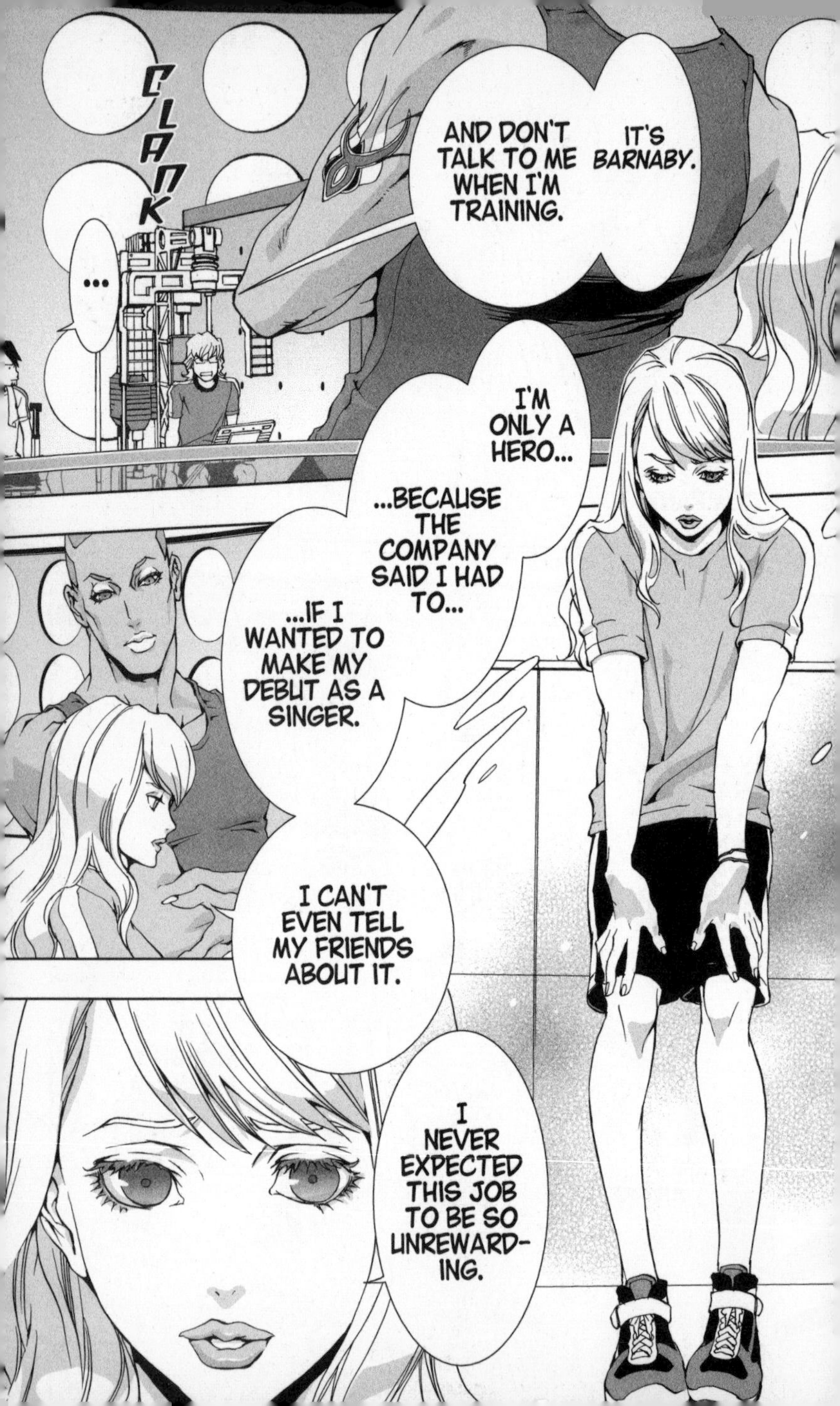
IT'S BARNABY.
AND DON'T TALK TO ME WHEN I'M TRAINING.
CLANK
...
I'M ONLY A HERO...
...BECAUSE THE COMPANY SAID I HAD TO...
...IF I WANTED TO MAKE MY DEBUT AS A SINGER.
I CAN'T EVEN TELL MY FRIENDS ABOUT IT.
I NEVER EXPECTED THIS JOB TO BE SO UNREWARDING.

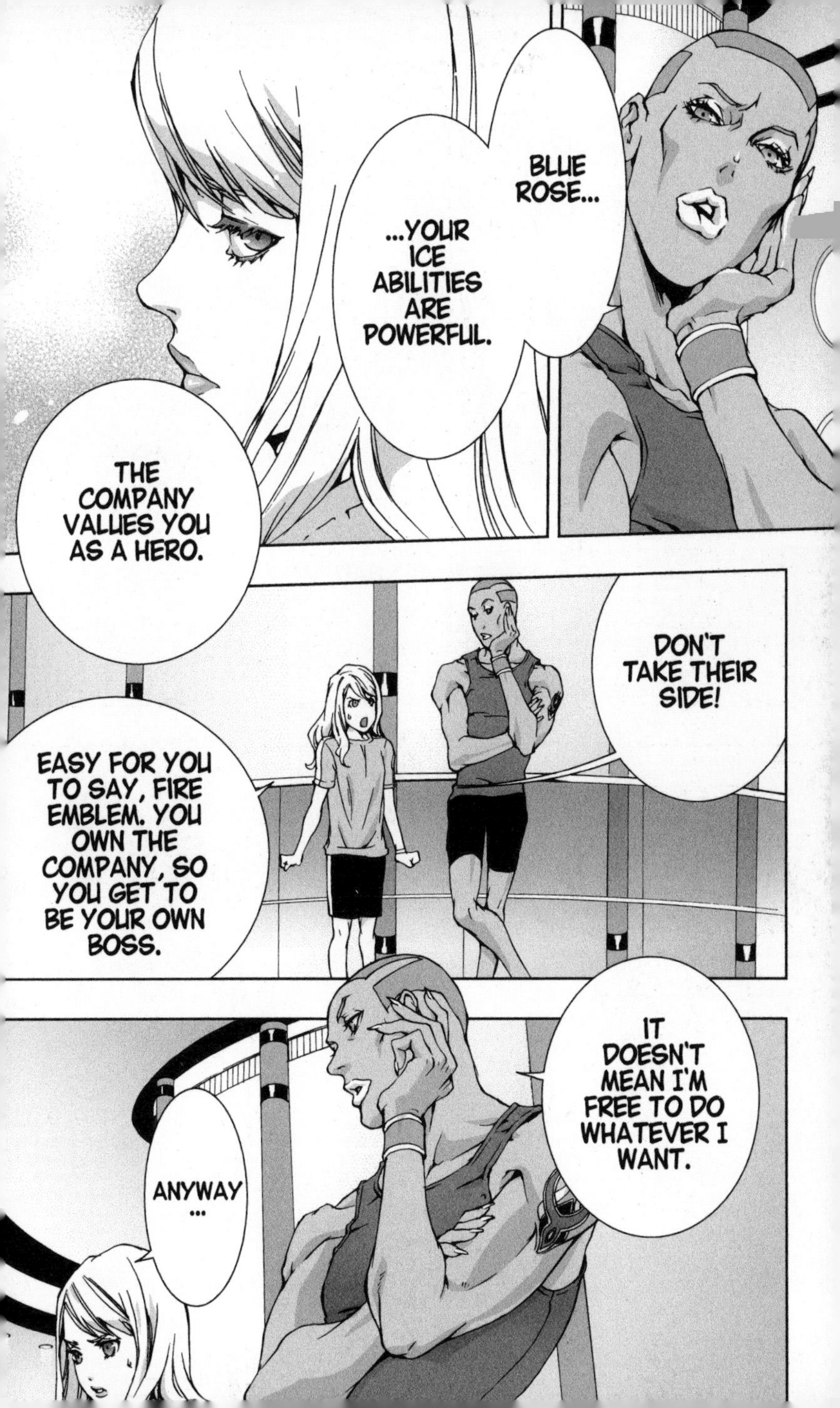
BLUE ROSE...
...YOUR ICE ABILITIES ARE POWERFUL.
THE COMPANY VALUES YOU AS A HERO.
DON'T TAKE THEIR SIDE!
EASY FOR YOU TO SAY, FIRE EMBLEM. YOU OWN THE COMPANY, SO YOU GET TO BE YOUR OWN BOSS.
IT DOESN'T MEAN I'M FREE TO DO WHATEVER I WANT.
ANYWAY...

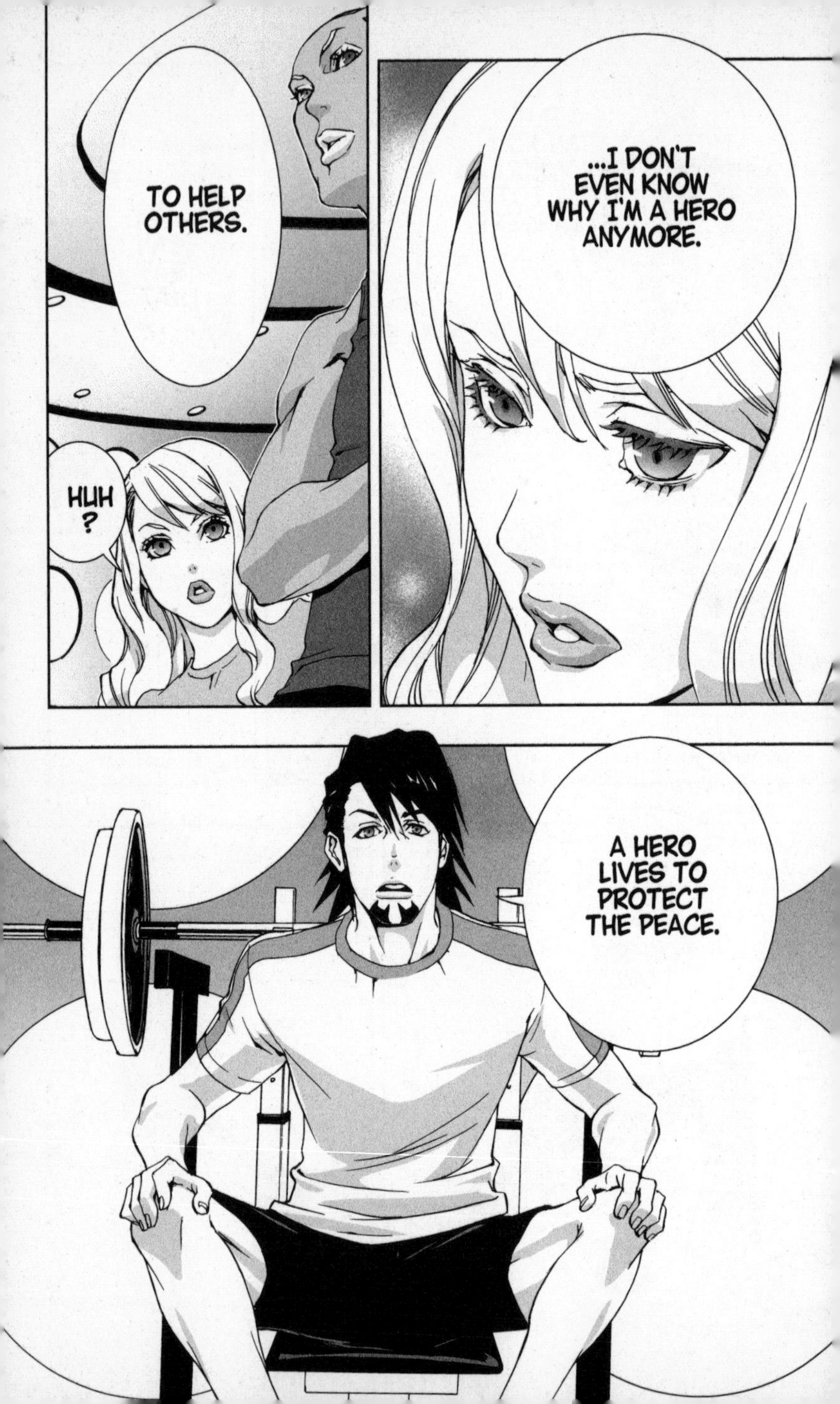
...I DON'T EVEN KNOW WHY I'M A HERO ANYMORE.
TO HELP OTHERS.
HUH?
A HERO LIVES TO PROTECT THE PEACE.

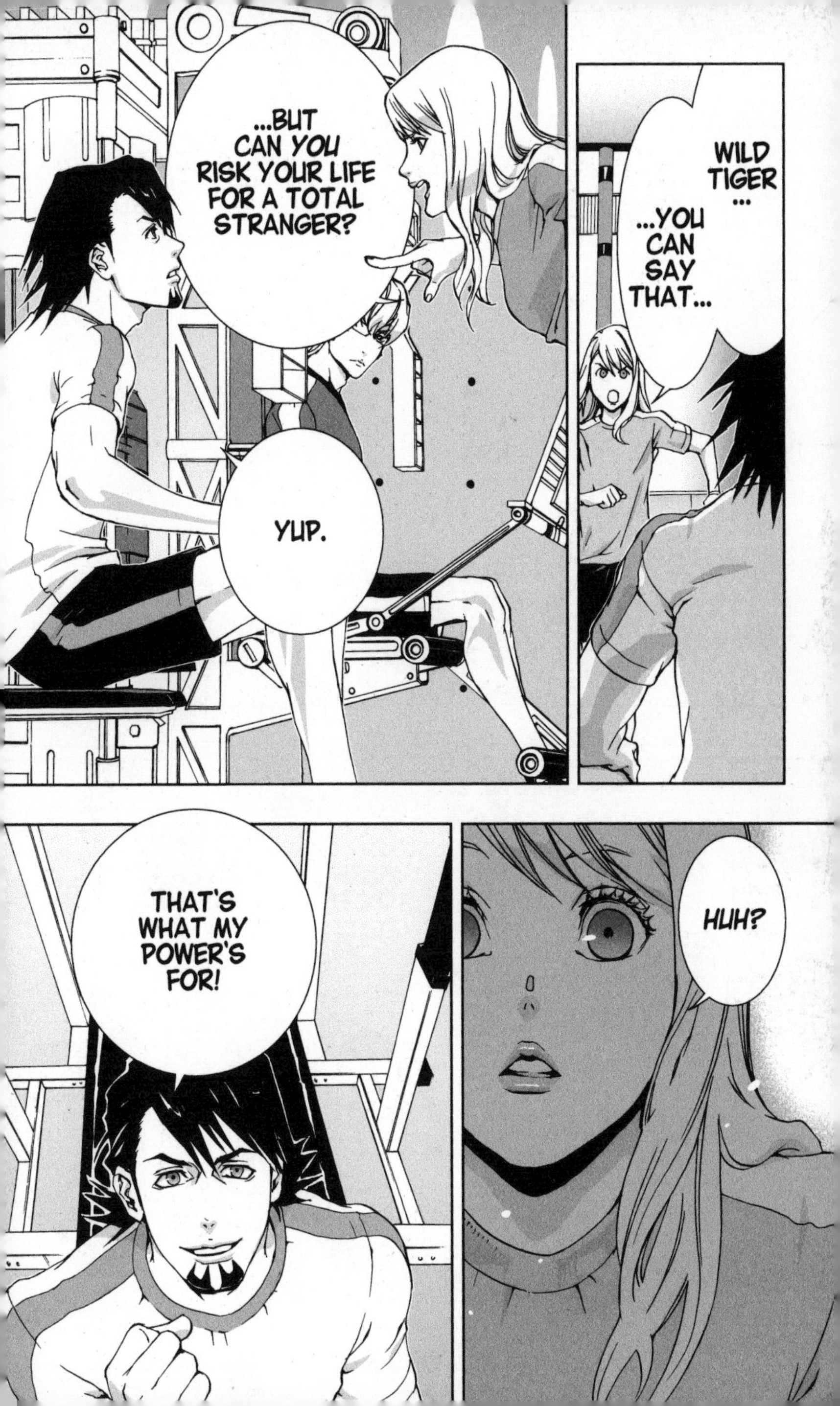
WILD TIGER ... ...YOU CAN SAY THAT...
...BUT CAN YOU RISK YOUR LIFE FOR A TOTAL STRANGER?
YUP.
HUH?
THAT'S WHAT MY POWER'S FOR!

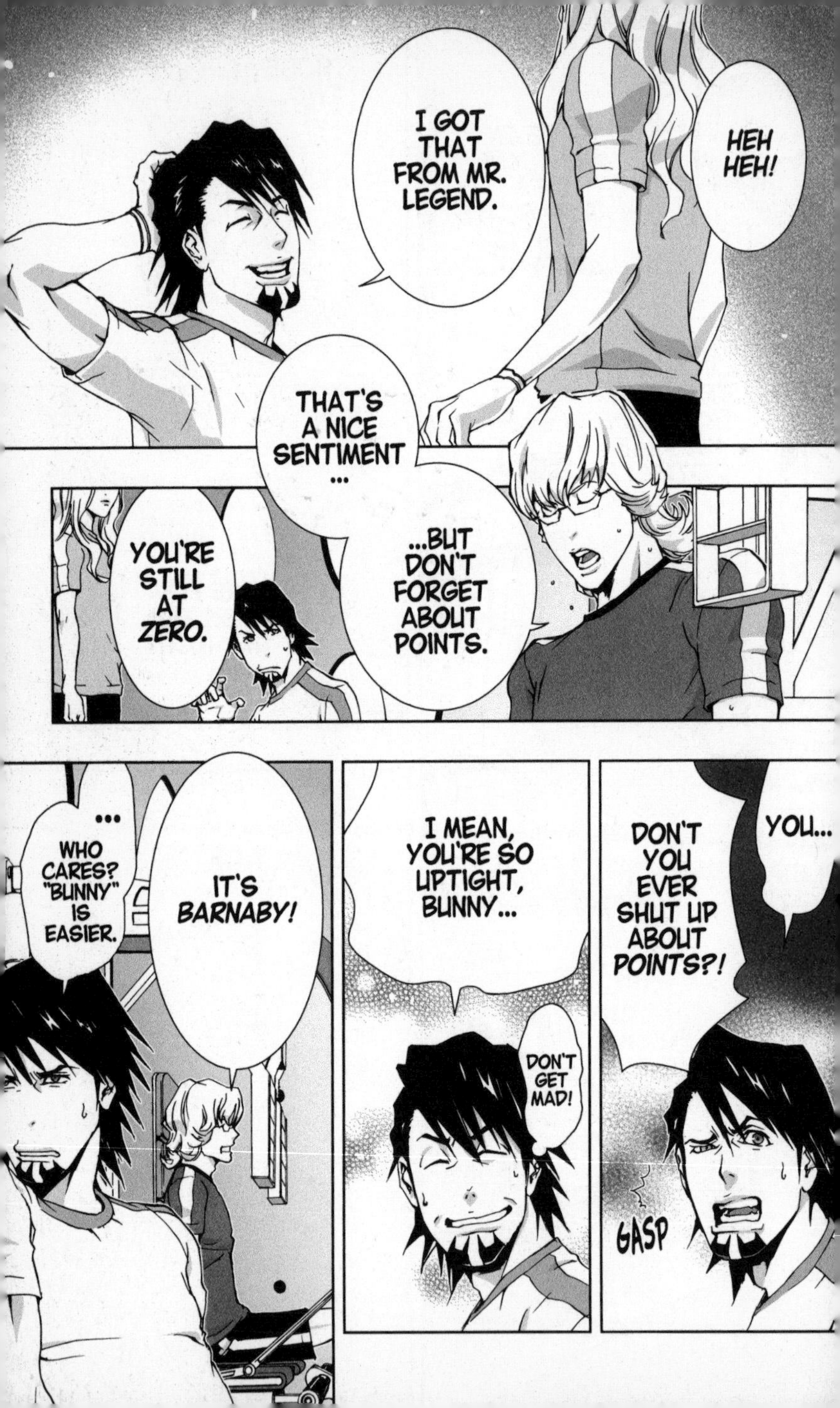
HEH HEH!
I GOT THAT FROM MR. LEGEND.
THAT'S A NICE SENTIMENT...
...BUT DON'T FORGET ABOUT POINTS.
YOU'RE STILL AT ZERO.
YOU...
DON'T YOU EVER SHUT UP ABOUT POINTS?!
GASP
I MEAN, YOU'RE SO UPTIGHT, BUNNY...
DON'T GET MAD!
IT'S BARNABY!
... WHO CARES? "BUNNY" IS EASIER.

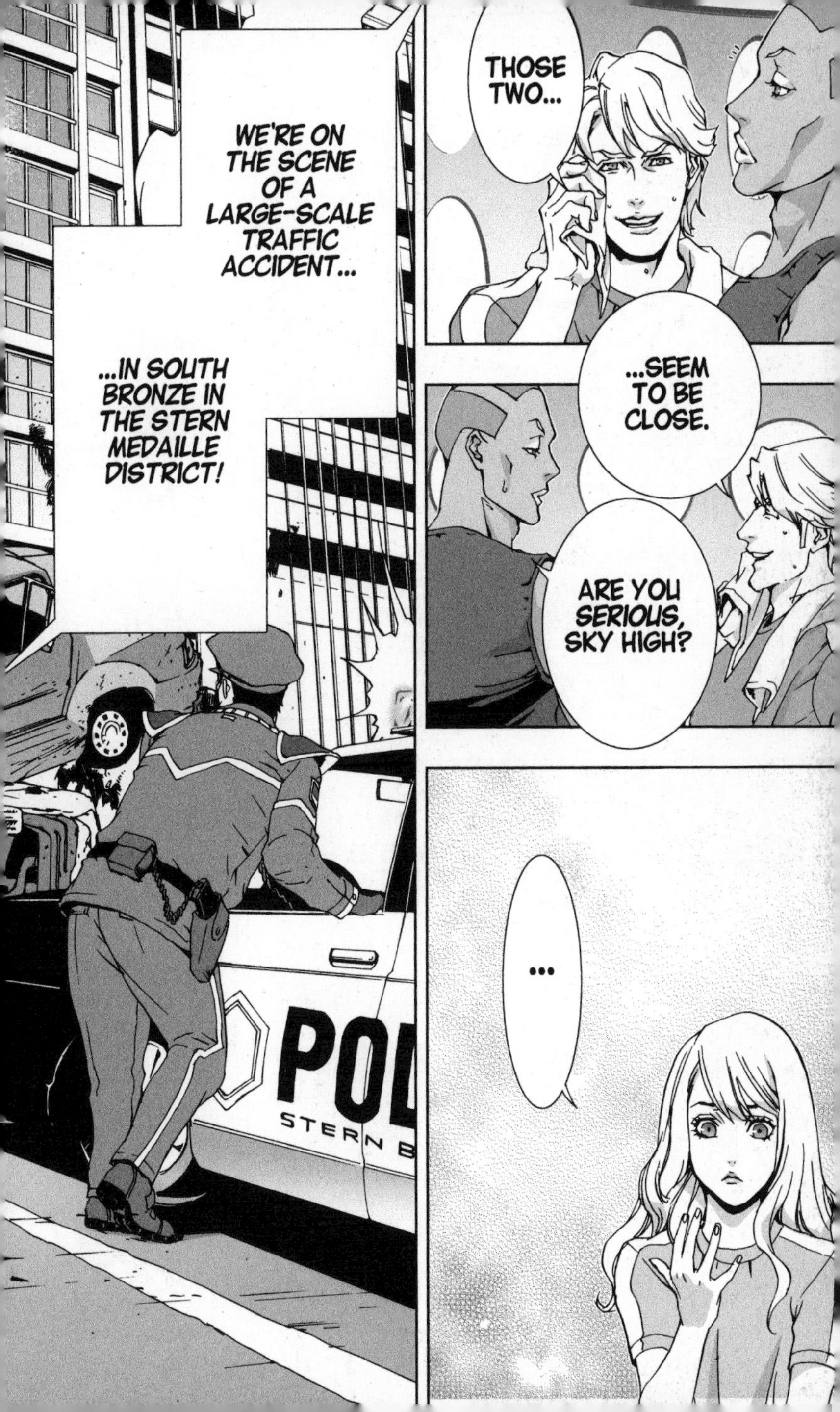
THOSE TWO...
...SEEM TO BE CLOSE.
ARE YOU SERIOUS, SKY HIGH?
...
WE'RE ON THE SCENE OF A LARGE-SCALE TRAFFIC ACCIDENT...
...IN SOUTH BRONZE IN THE STERN MEDAILLE DISTRICT!

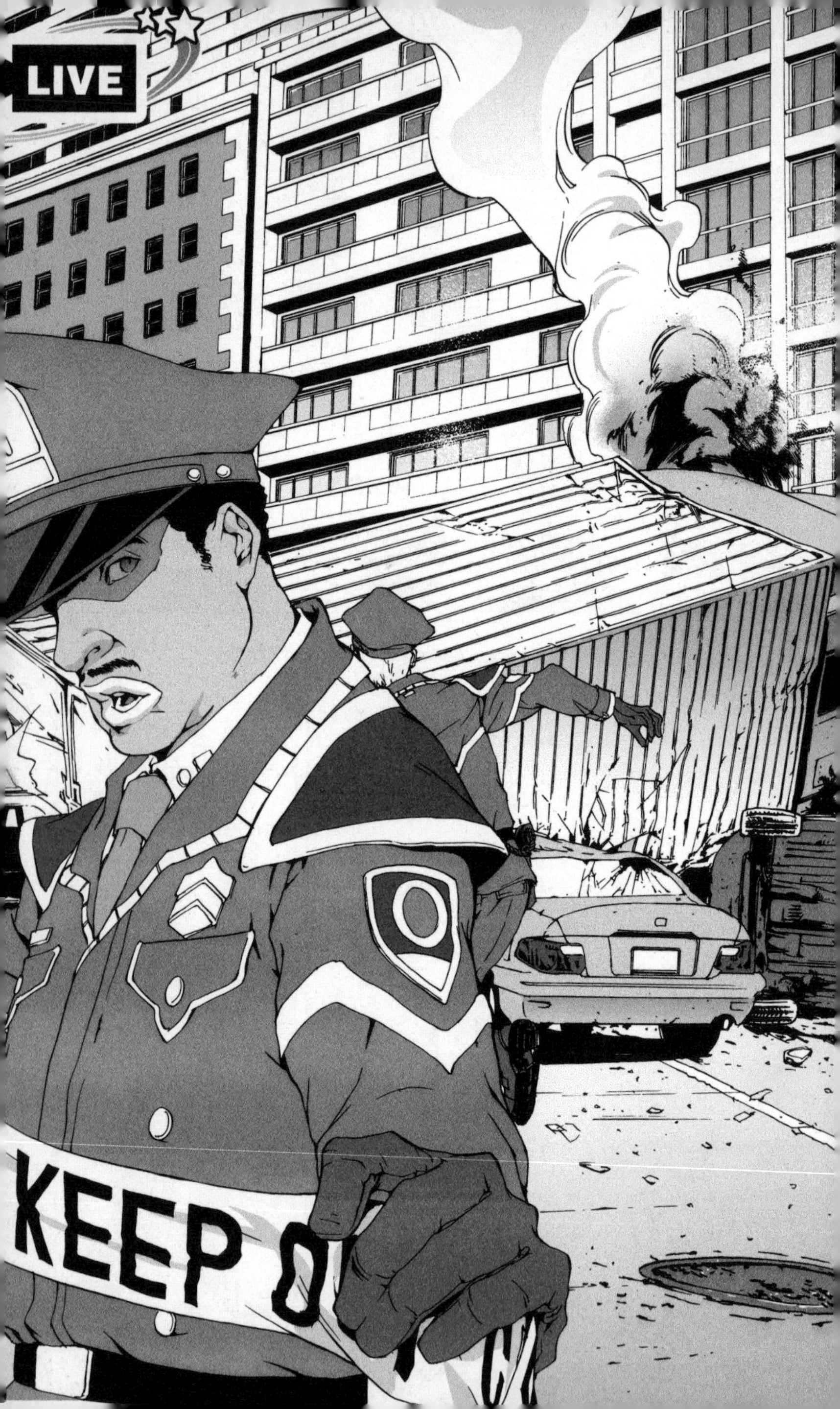

LIVE
KEEP O

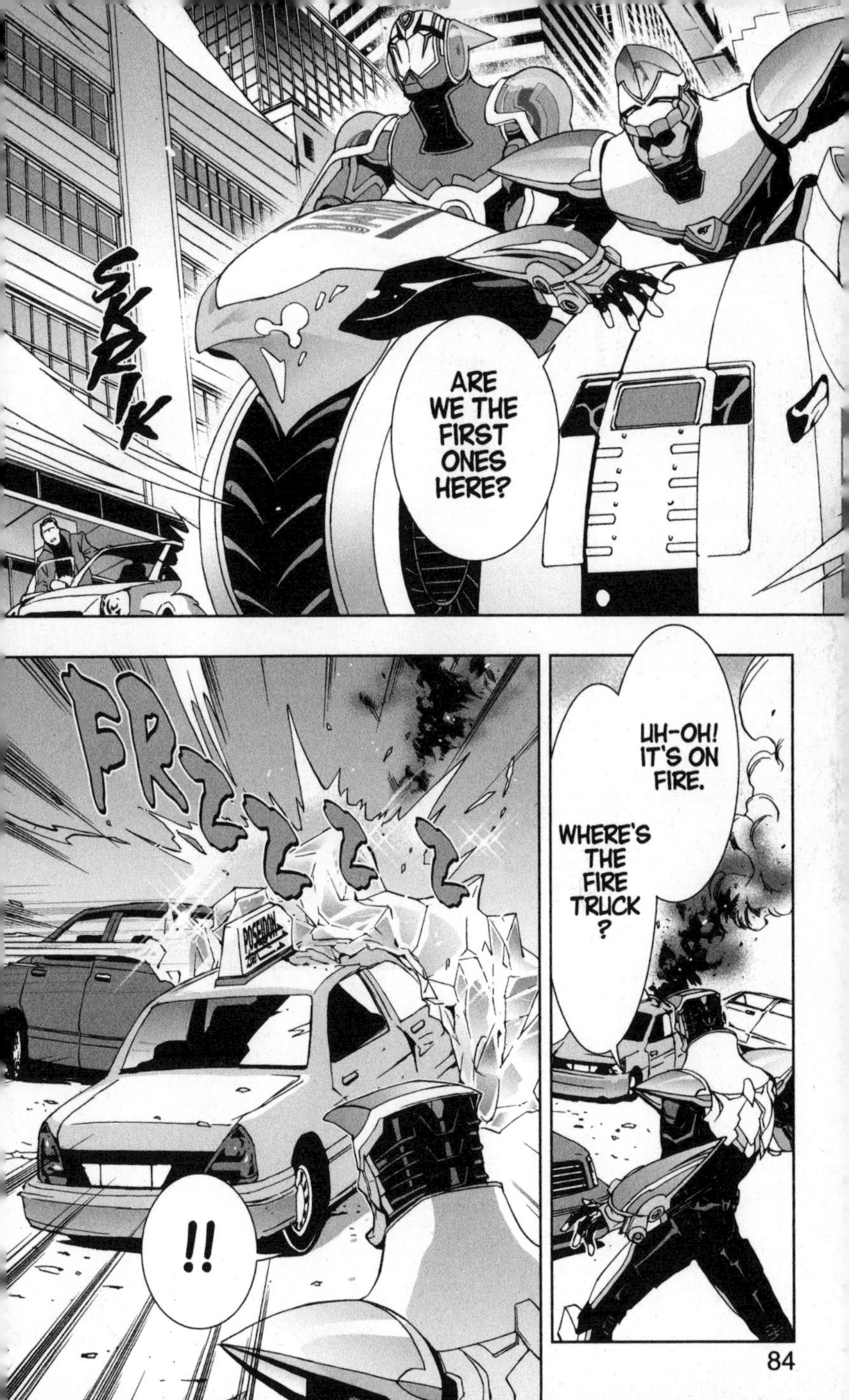
SKRIK
ARE WE THE FIRST ONES HERE?
UH-OH! IT'S ON FIRE.
WHERE'S THE FIRE TRUCK?
FRZZZZ
POSEIDON
!!

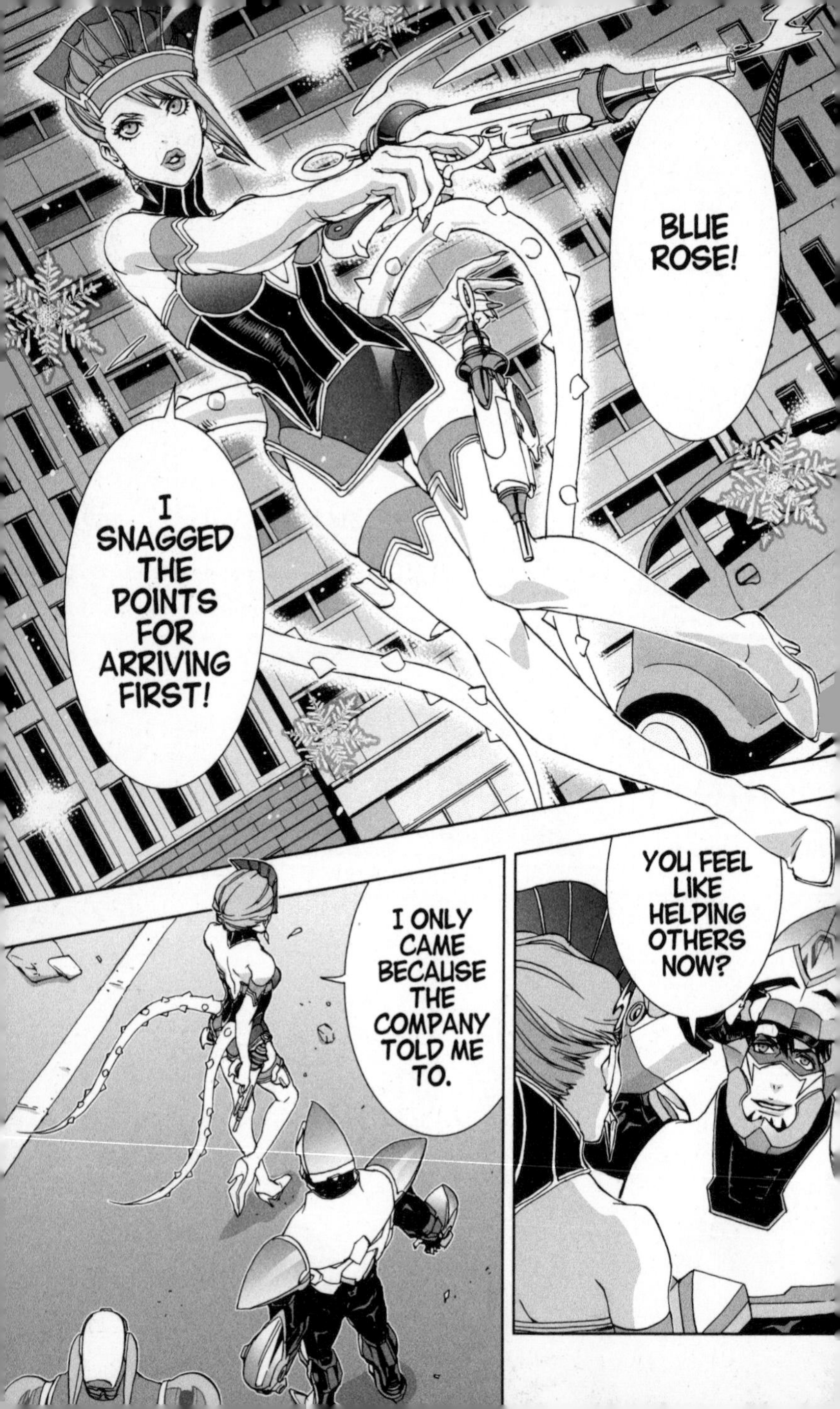
BLUE ROSE!
I SNAGGED THE POINTS FOR ARRIVING FIRST!
YOU FEEL LIKE HELPING OTHERS NOW?
I ONLY CAME BECAUSE THE COMPANY TOLD ME TO.

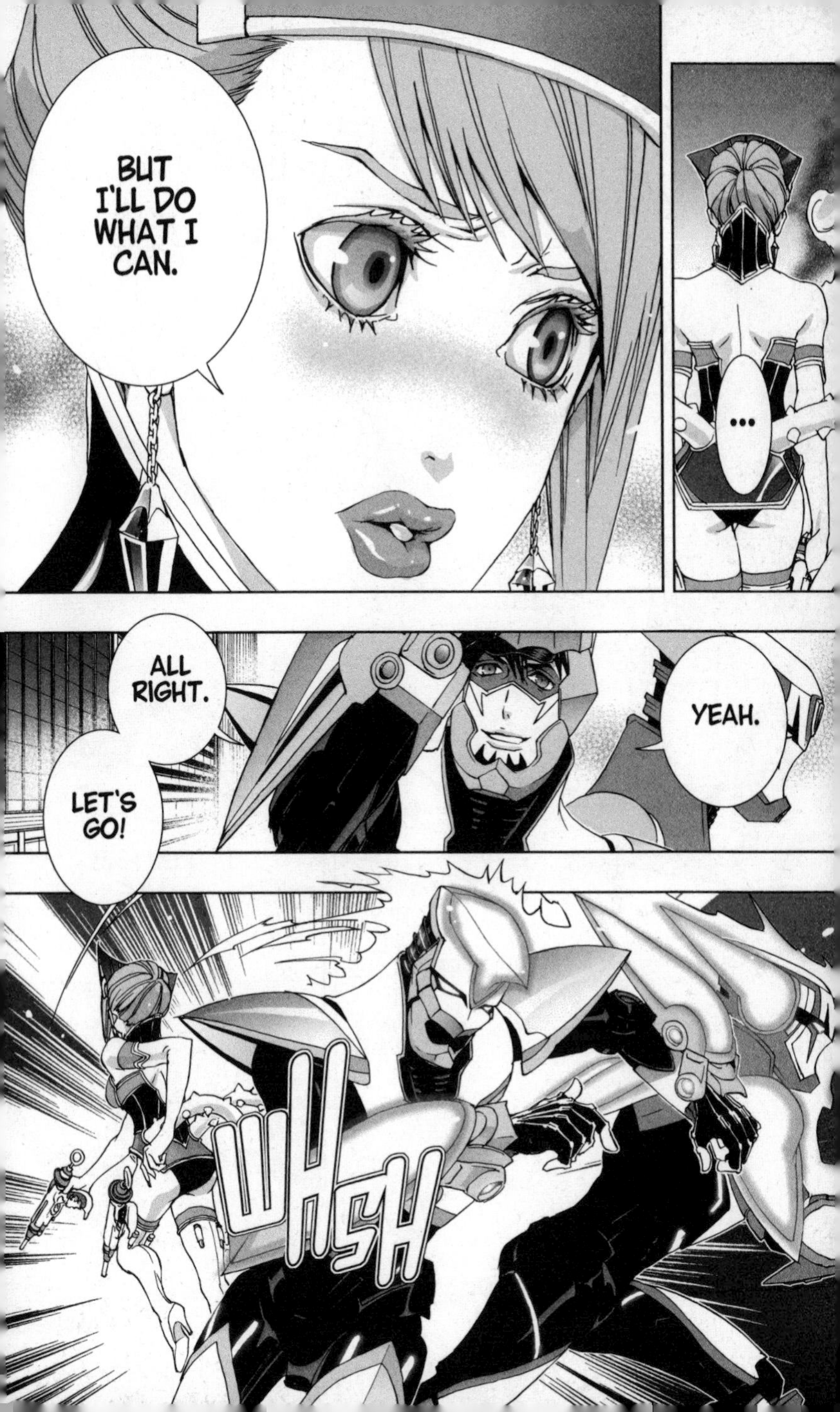
...
BUT I'LL DO WHAT I CAN.
YEAH.
ALL RIGHT.
LET'S GO!
WHSH

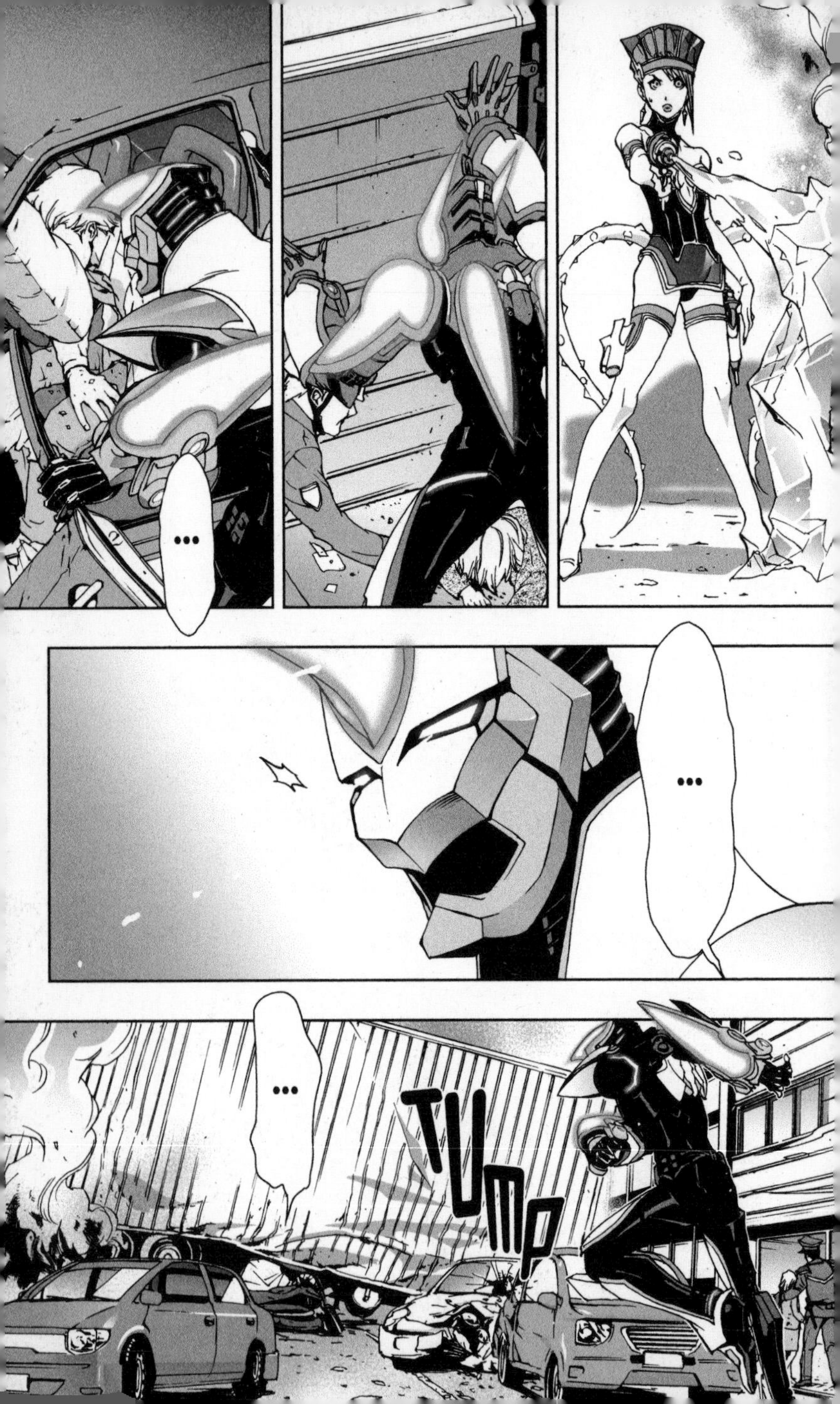
...
...
...
TUMP

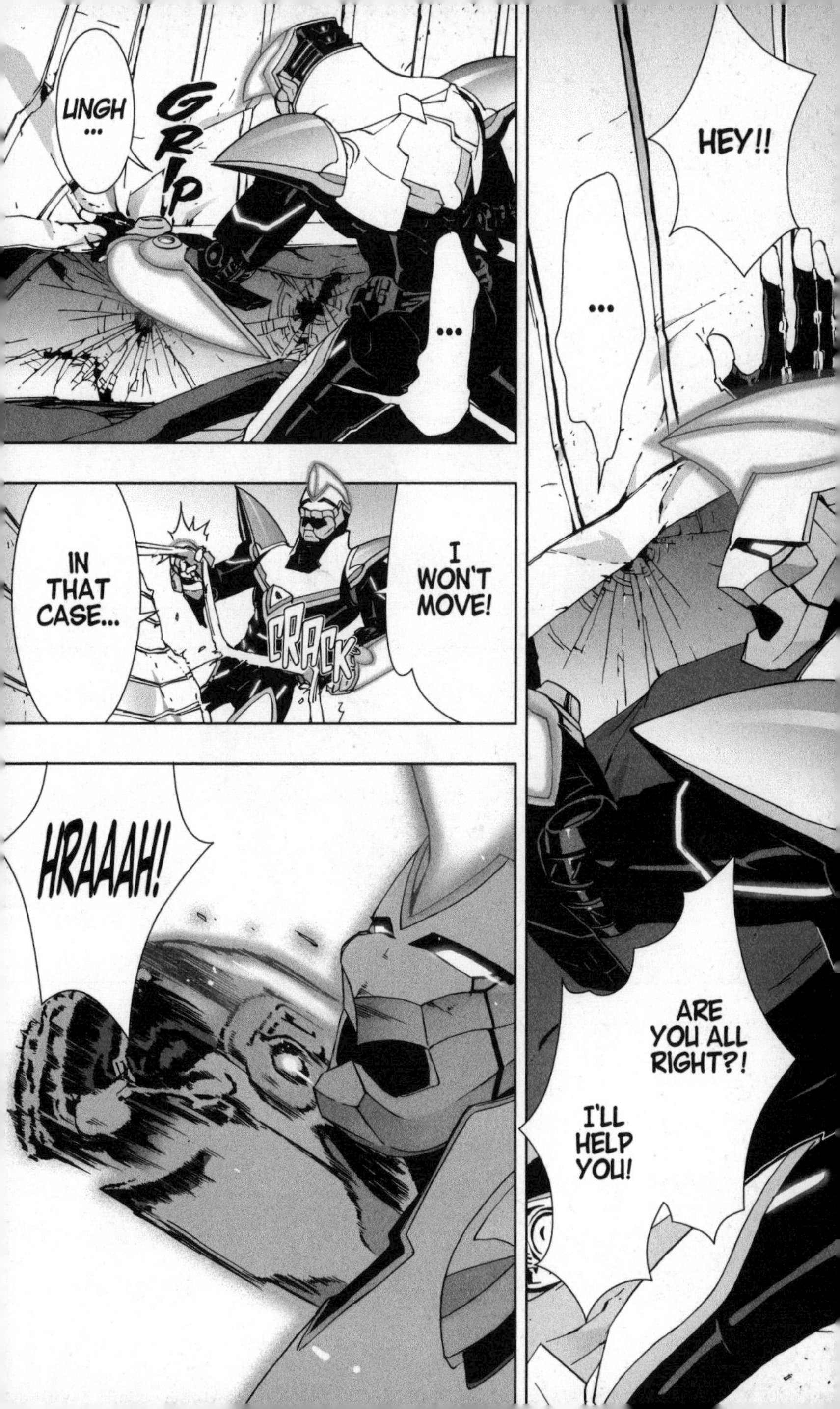
HEY!!
...
ARE YOU ALL RIGHT?!
I'LL HELP YOU!
...
GRIP
UNGH ...
I WON'T MOVE!
CRACK
IN THAT CASE...
HRAAAH!

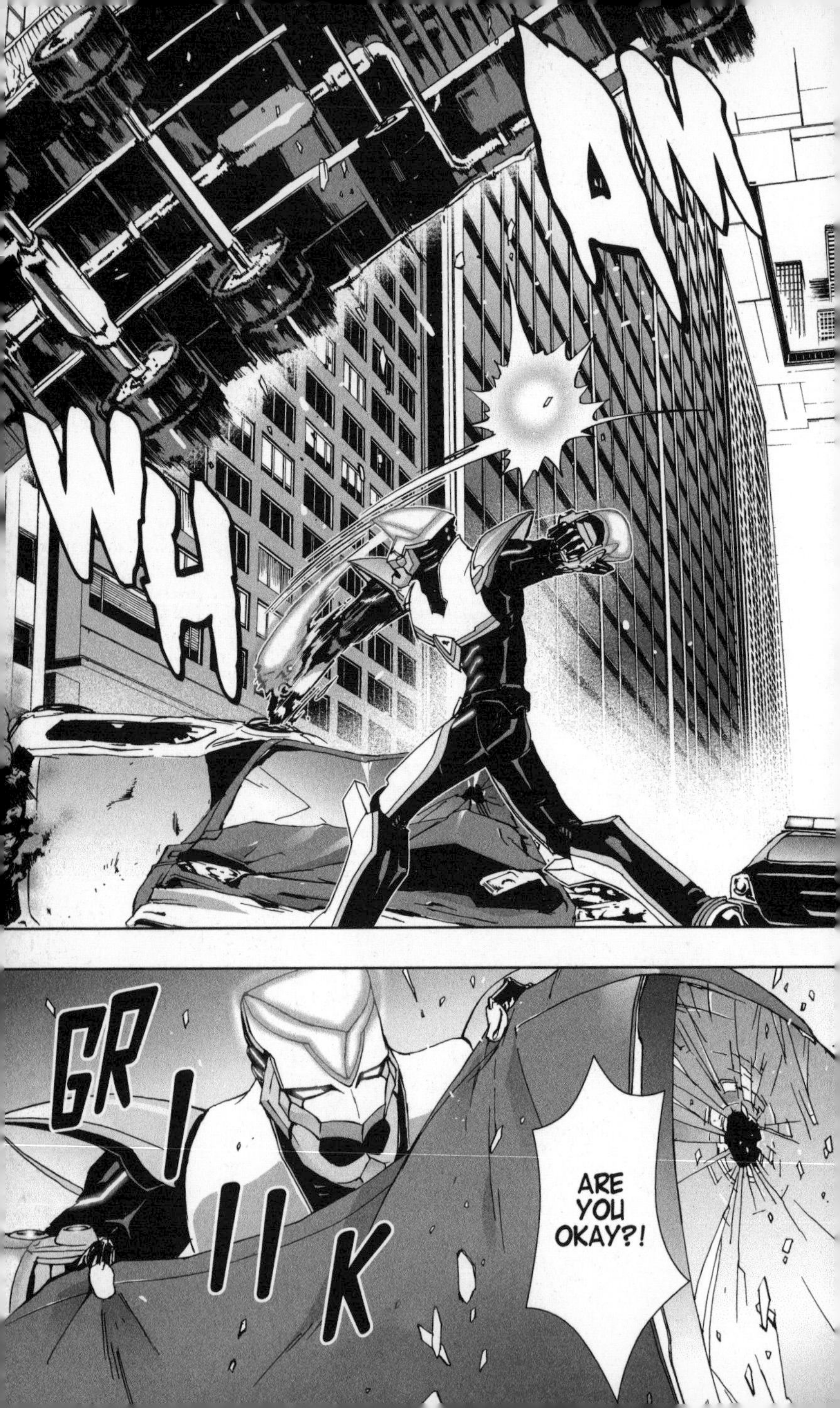
WHAM
GRIIIK
ARE YOU OKAY?!

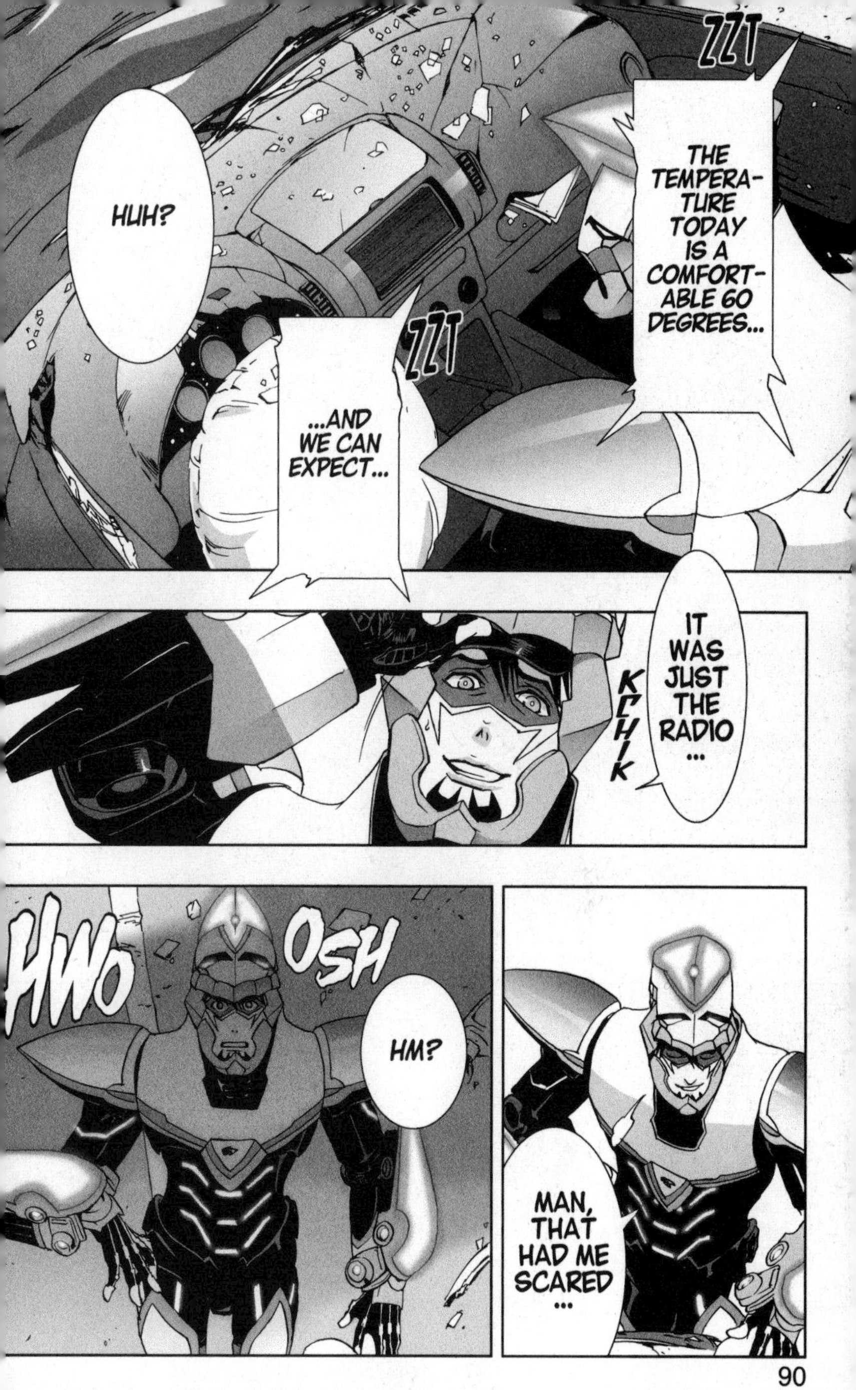
ZZT
THE TEMPERATURE TODAY IS A COMFORTABLE 60 DEGREES...
ZZT
...AND WE CAN EXPECT...
HUH?
KCHIK
IT WAS JUST THE RADIO...
MAN, THAT HAD ME SCARED...
HWOOSH
HM?

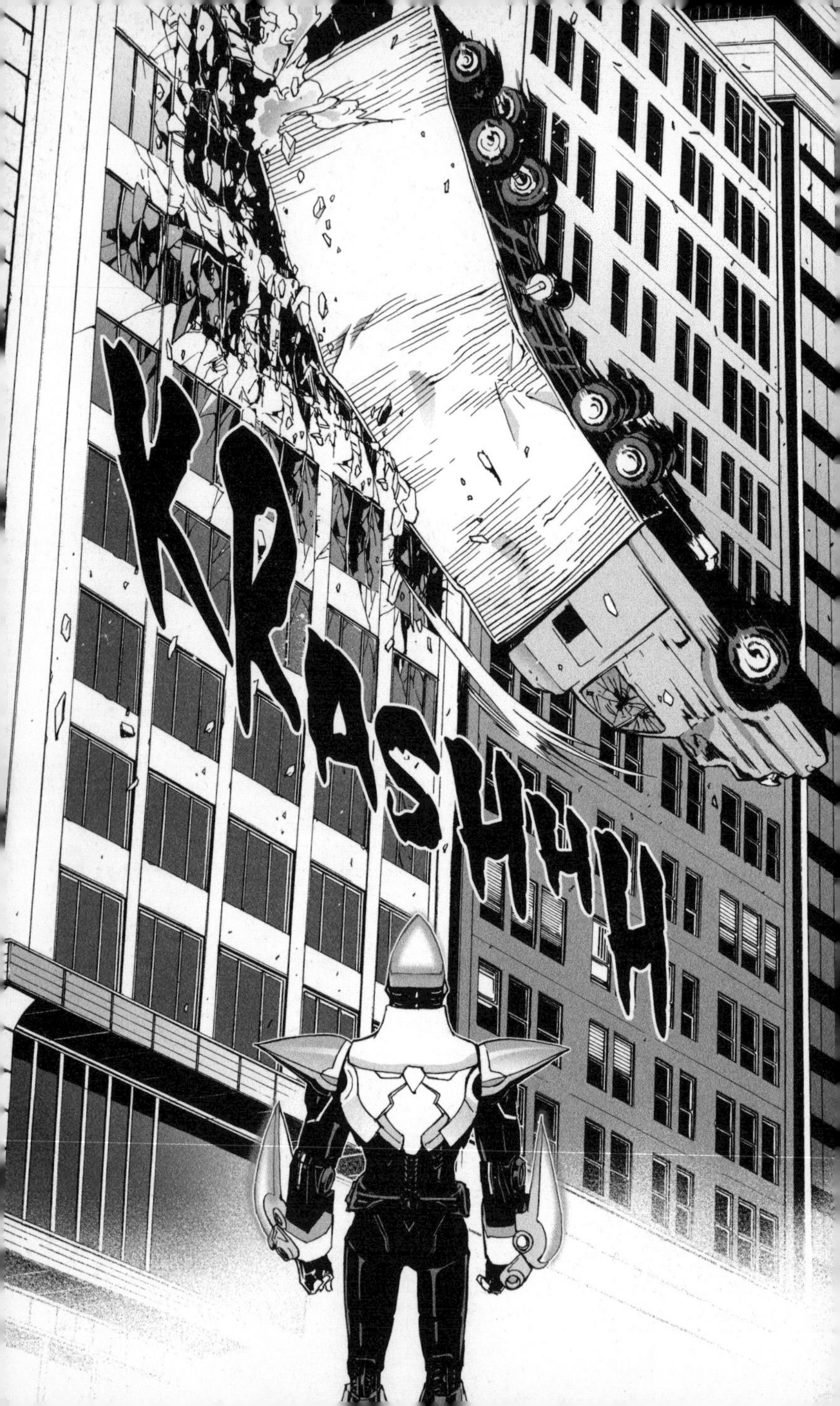
KRASHHHH

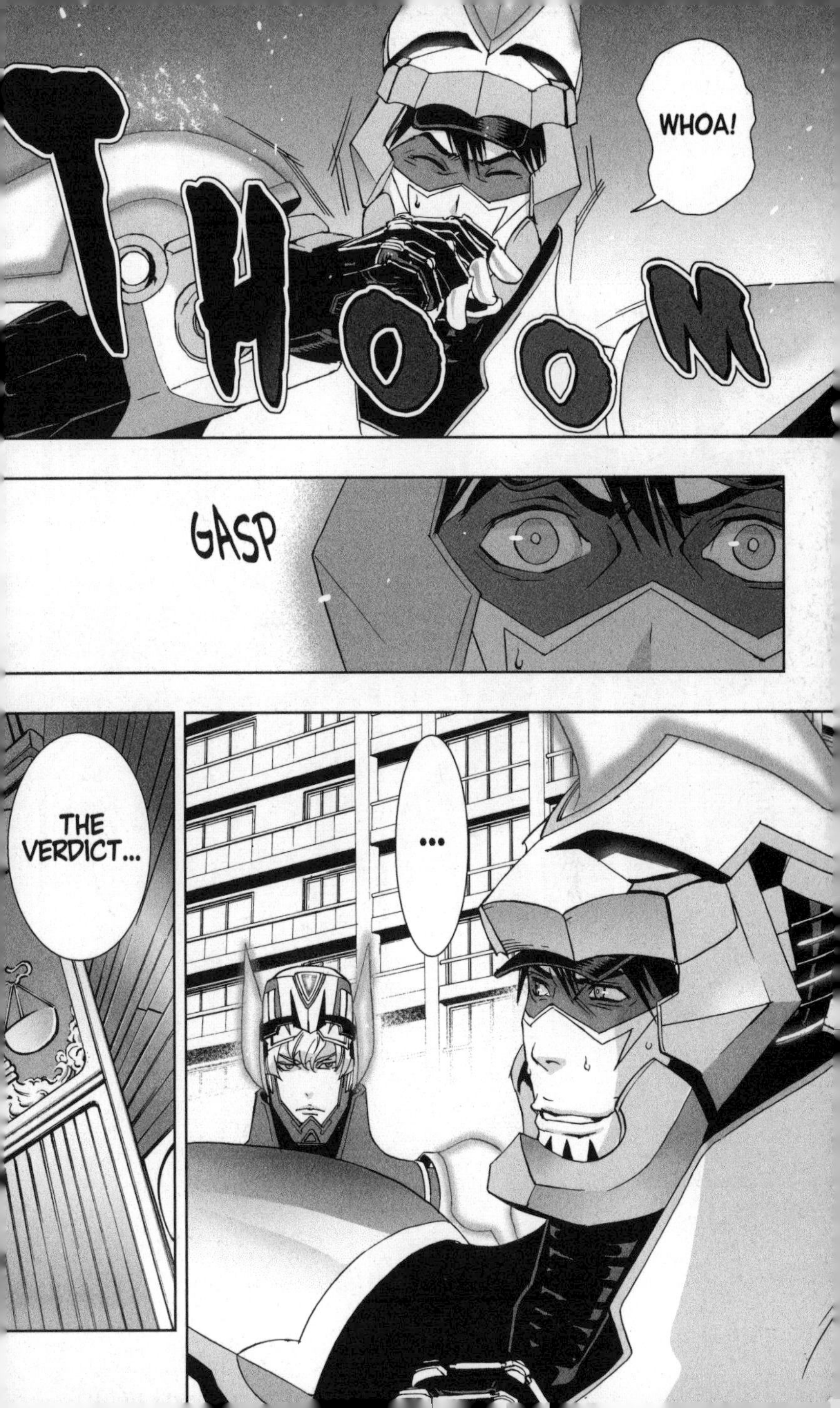
WHOA!
THOOM
GASP
...
THE VERDICT...

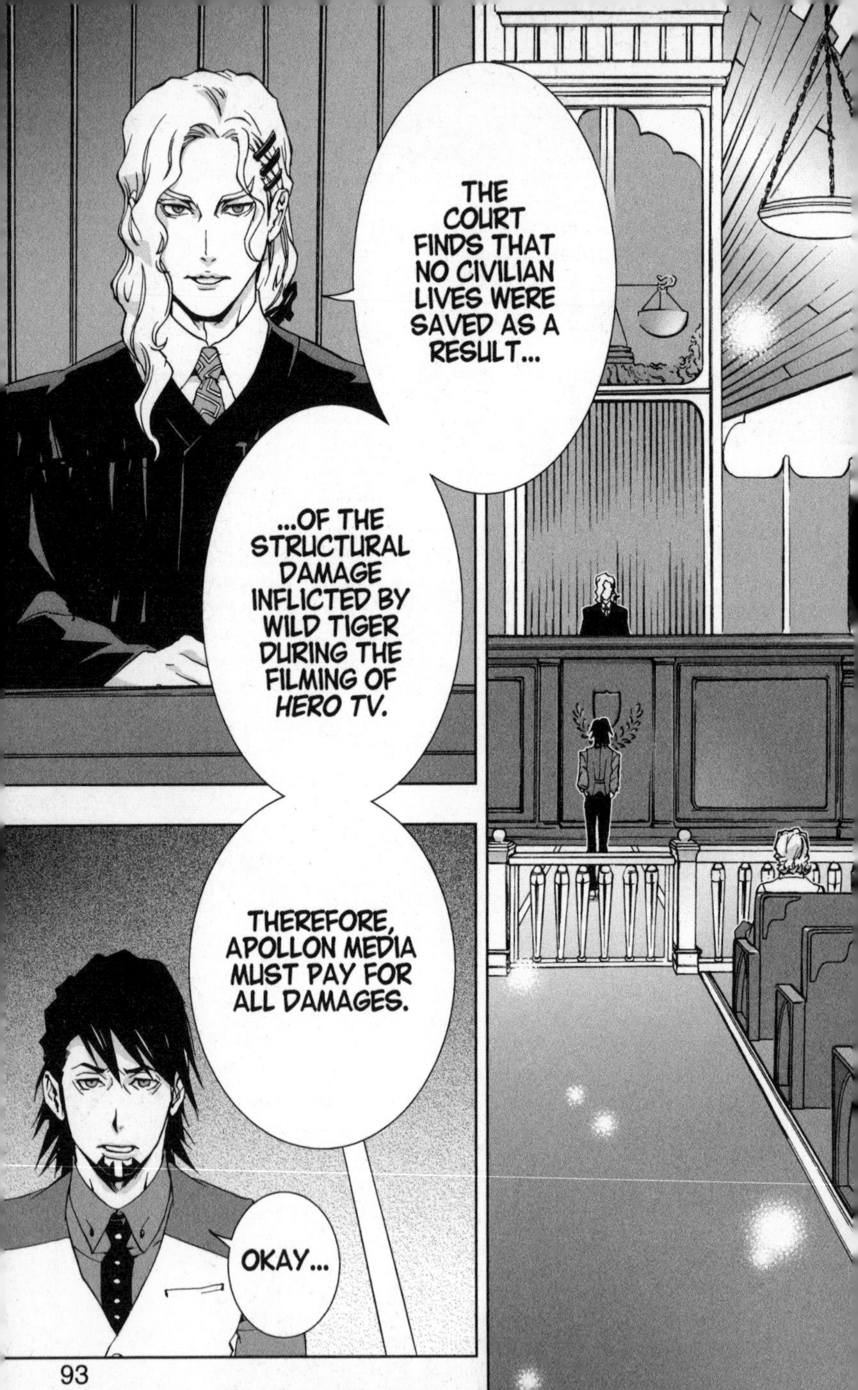
THE COURT FINDS THAT NO CIVILIAN LIVES WERE SAVED AS A RESULT...
...OF THE STRUCTURAL DAMAGE INFLICTED BY WILD TIGER DURING THE FILMING OF HERO TV.
THEREFORE, APOLLON MEDIA MUST PAY FOR ALL DAMAGES.
OKAY...

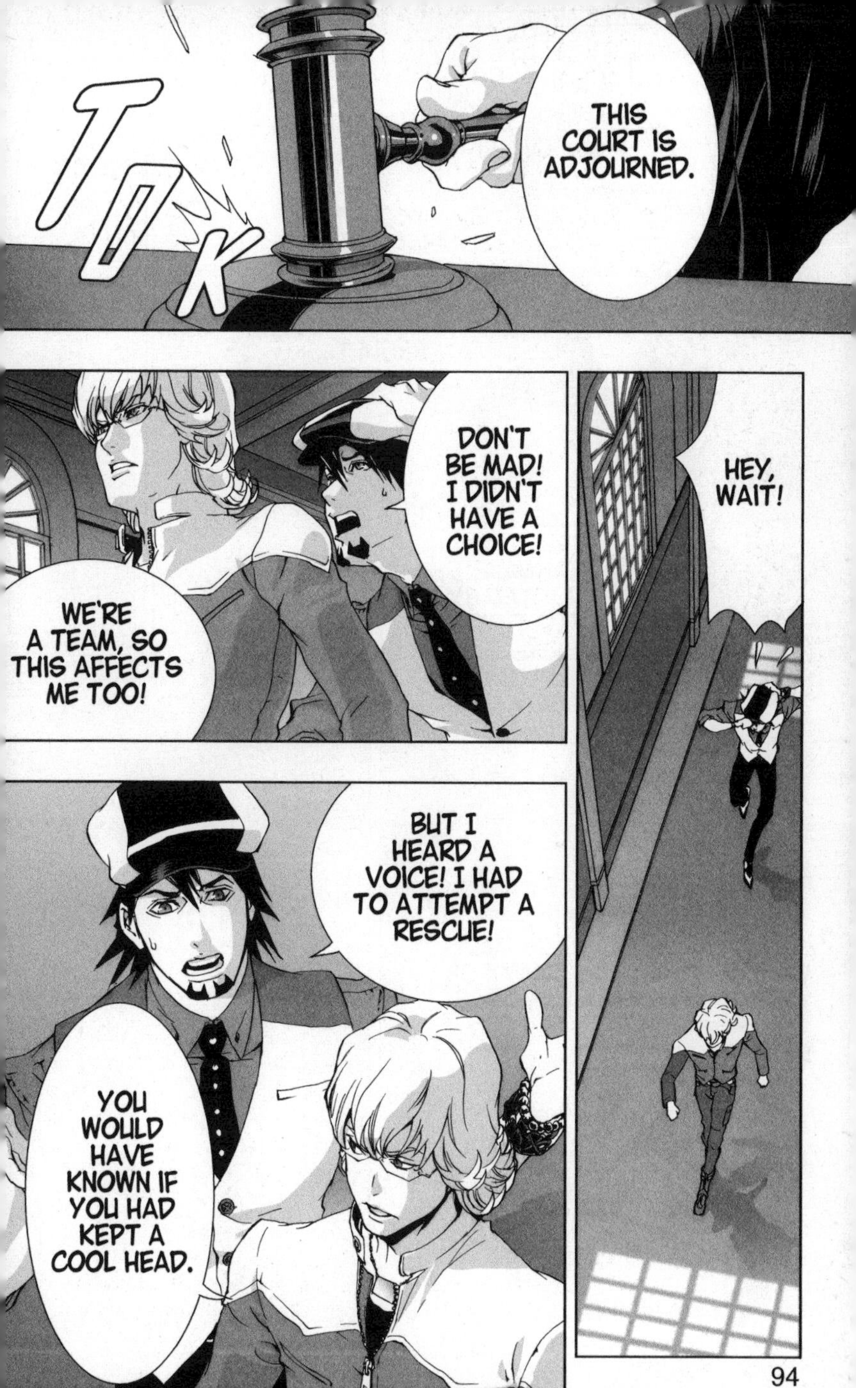
THIS COURT IS ADJOURNED.
TOK
HEY, WAIT!
DON'T BE MAD! I DIDN'T HAVE A CHOICE!
WE'RE A TEAM, SO THIS AFFECTS ME TOO!
BUT I HEARD A VOICE! I HAD TO ATTEMPT A RESCUE!
YOU WOULD HAVE KNOWN IF YOU HAD KEPT A COOL HEAD.

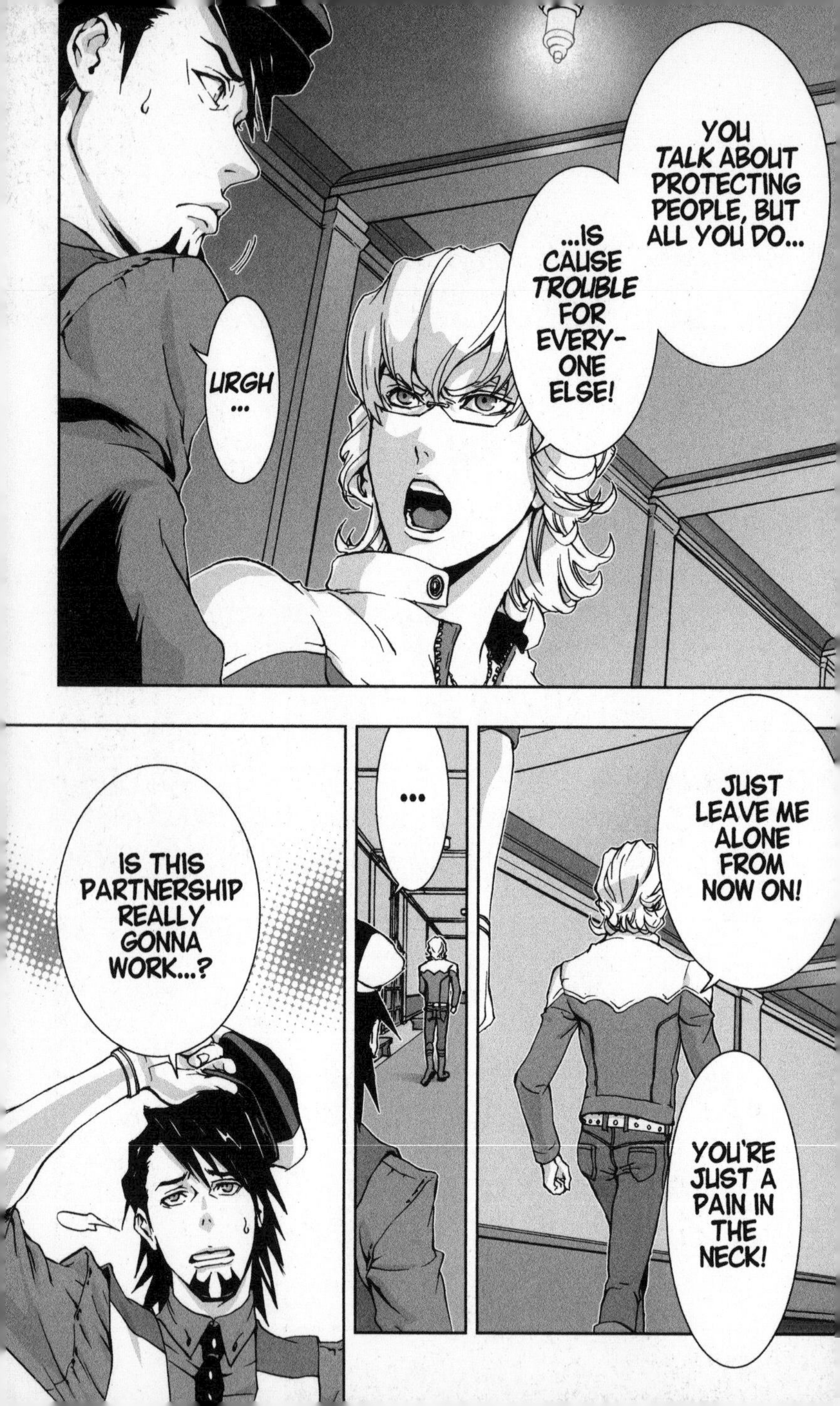
YOU TALK ABOUT PROTECTING PEOPLE, BUT ALL YOU DO...
...IS CAUSE TROUBLE FOR EVERY-ONE ELSE!
URGH...
JUST LEAVE ME ALONE FROM NOW ON!
YOU'RE JUST A PAIN IN THE NECK!
...
IS THIS PARTNERSHIP REALLY GONNA WORK...?

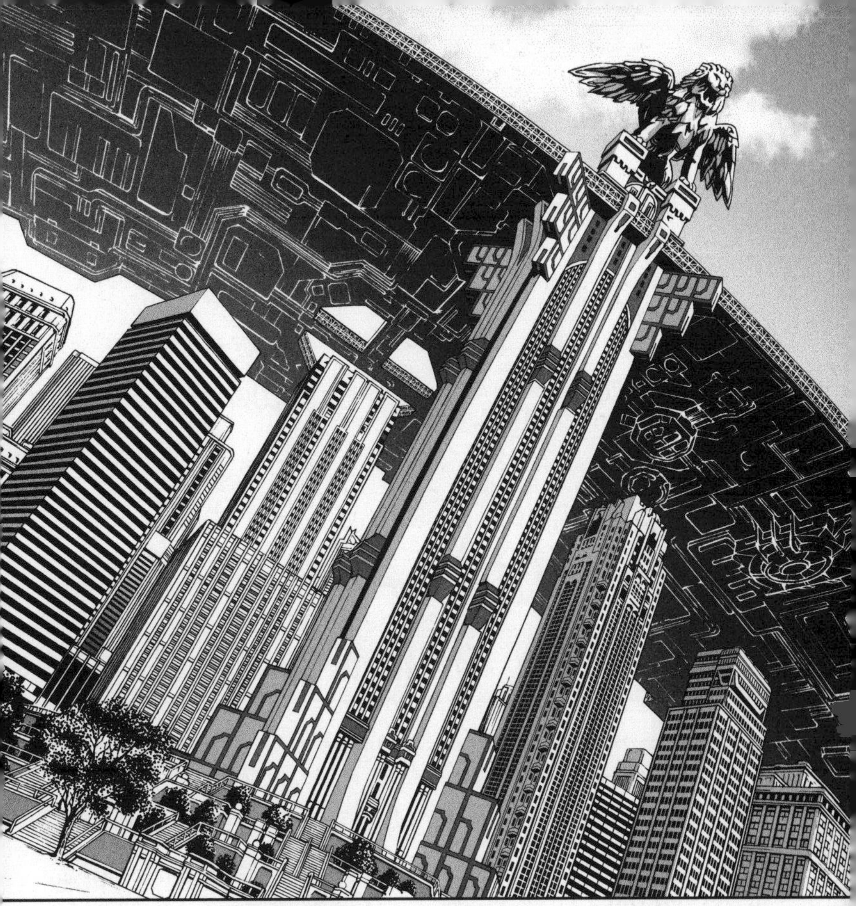

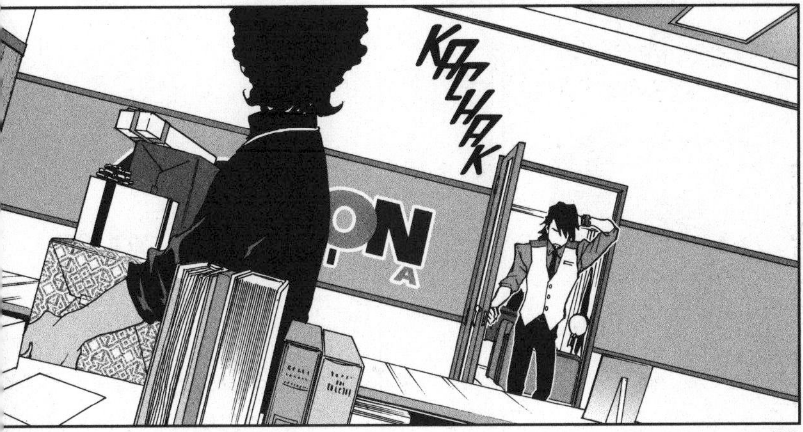
KACHAK

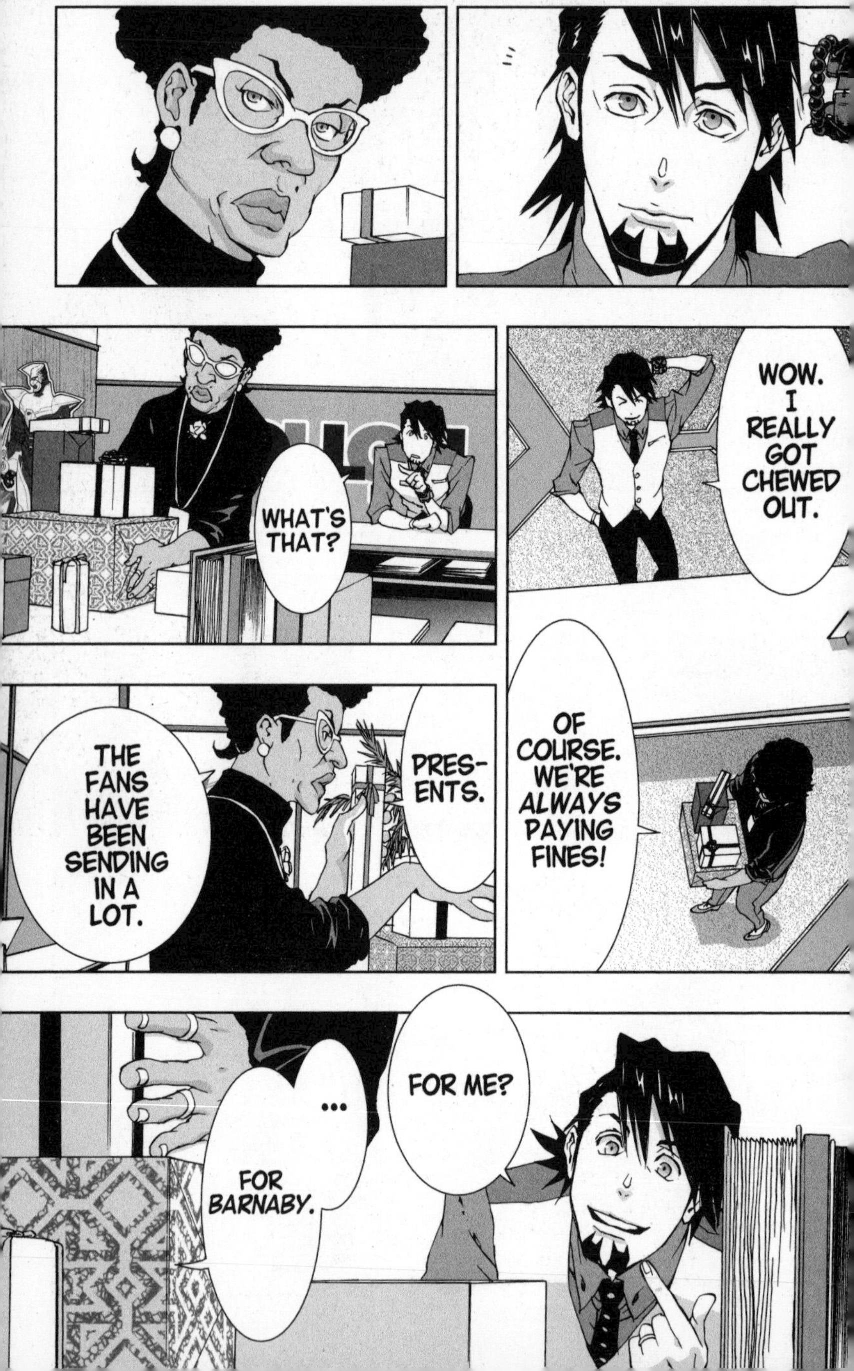
WOW. I REALLY GOT CHEWED OUT.
OF COURSE. WE'RE ALWAYS PAYING FINES!
WHAT'S THAT?
PRESENTS.
THE FANS HAVE BEEN SENDING IN A LOT.
FOR ME?
... FOR BARNABY.

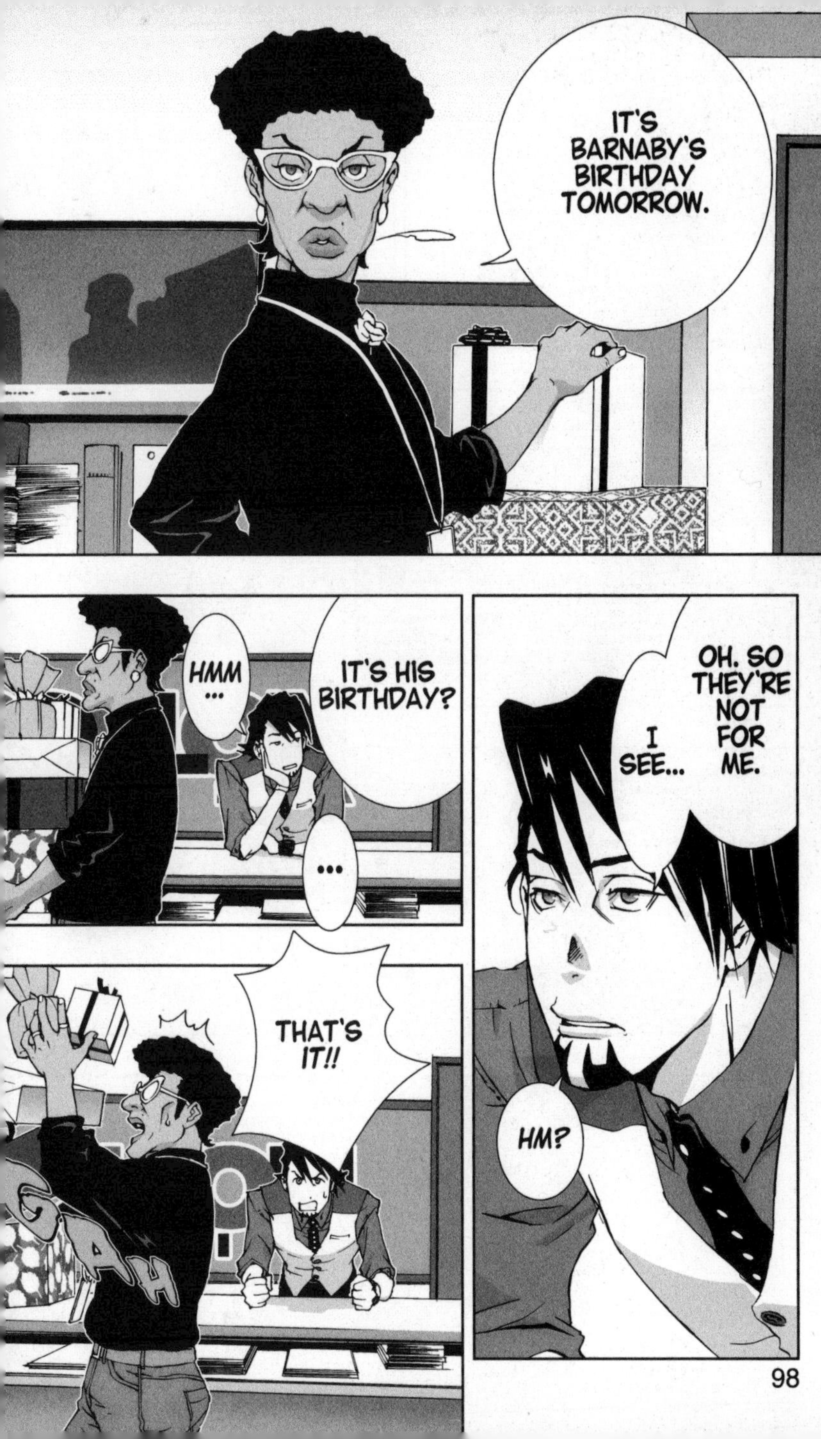
IT'S BARNABY'S BIRTHDAY TOMORROW.
OH. SO THEY'RE NOT FOR ME.
I SEE...
HM?
IT'S HIS BIRTHDAY?
HMM...
...
THAT'S IT!!

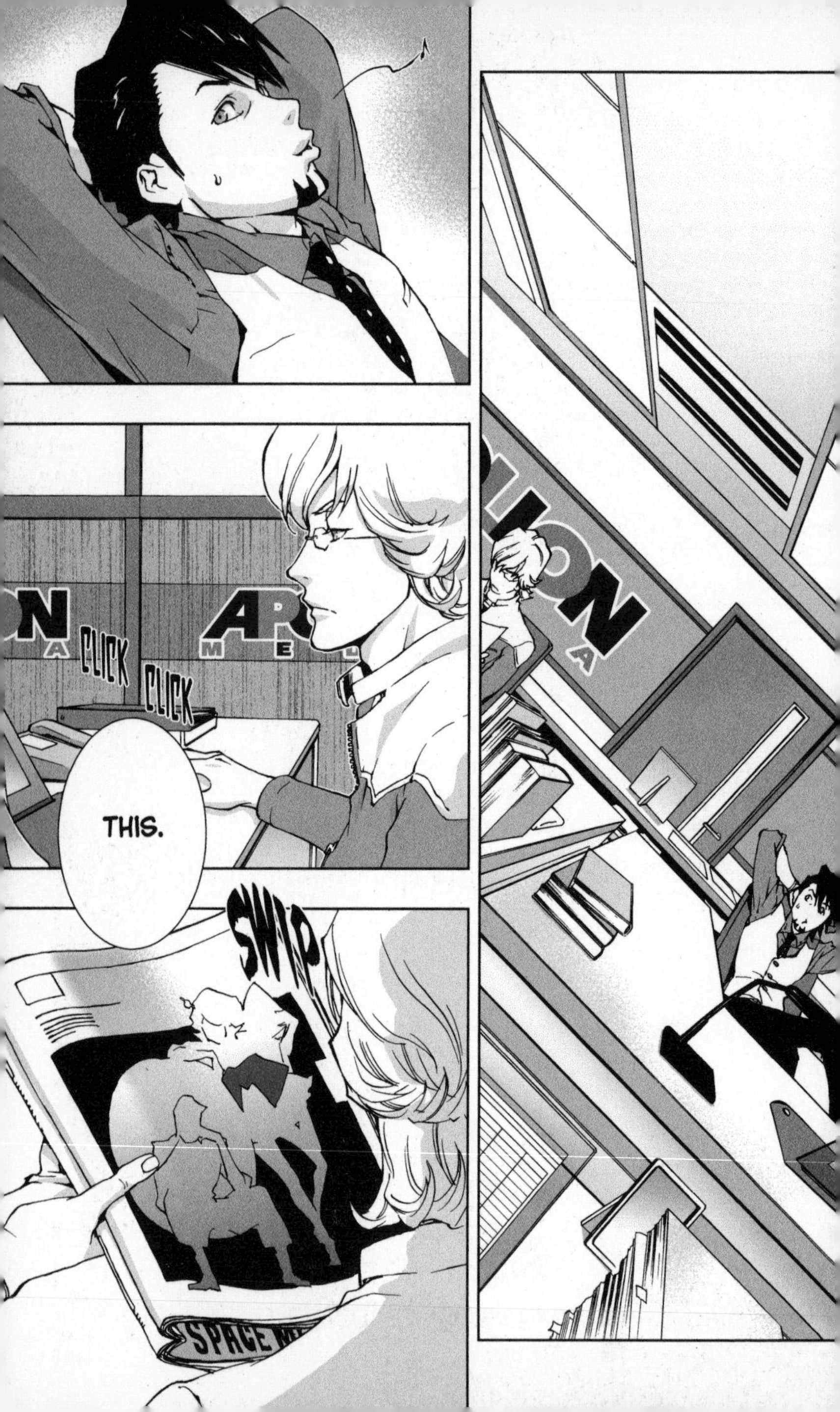
CLICK
CLICK
THIS.
SWIP

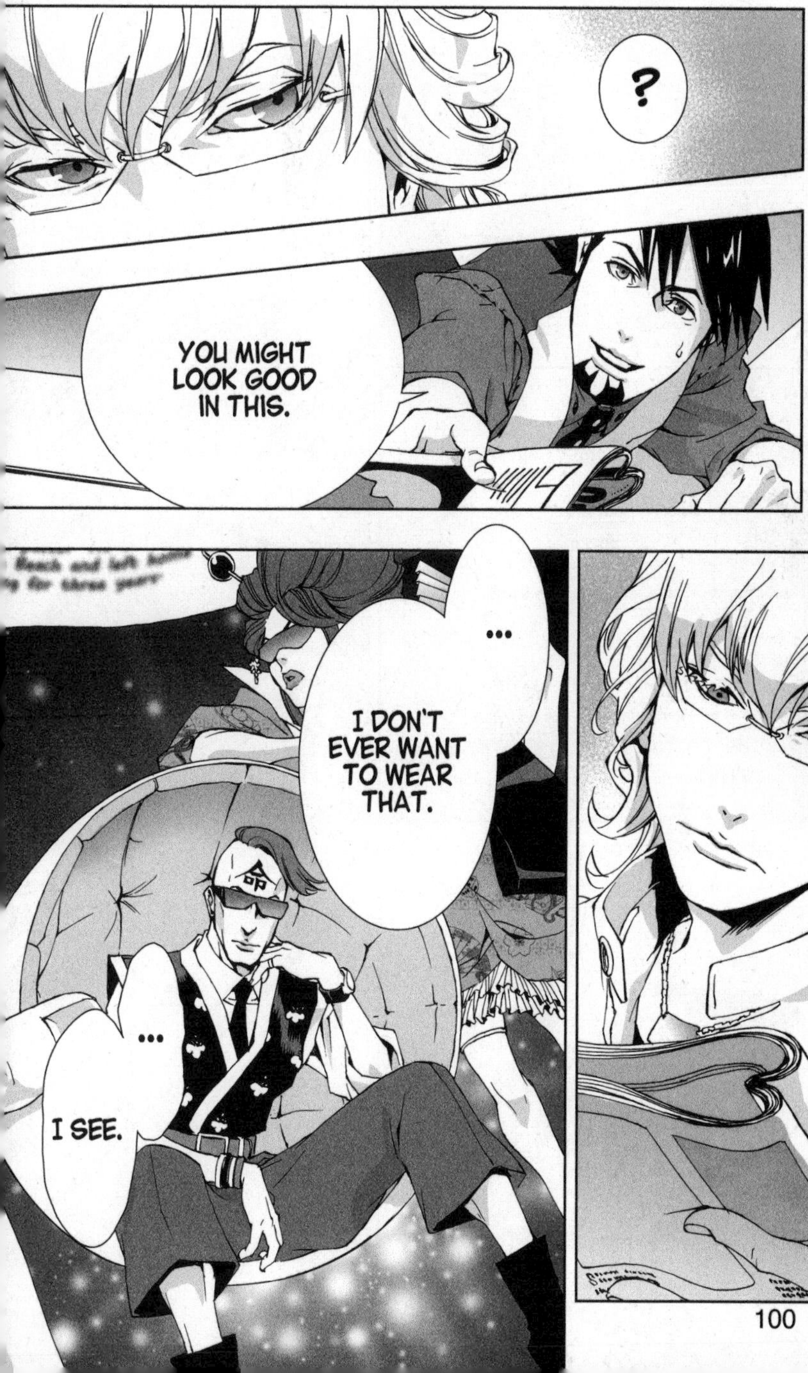
?
YOU MIGHT LOOK GOOD IN THIS.
... I DON'T EVER WANT TO WEAR THAT.
... I SEE.

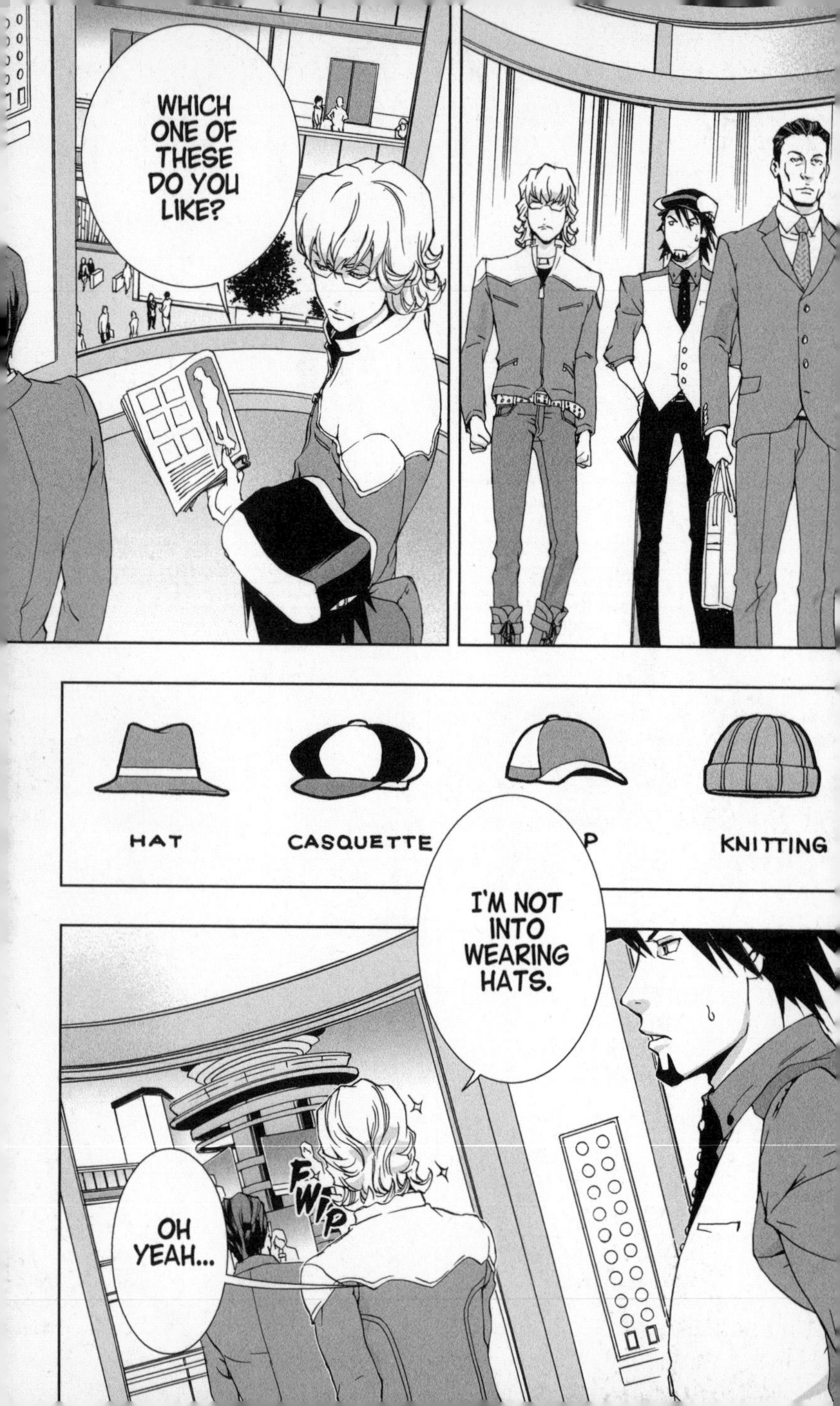
WHICH ONE OF THESE DO YOU LIKE?
HAT
CASQUETTE
KNITTING
I'M NOT INTO WEARING HATS.
FWIP
OH YEAH...

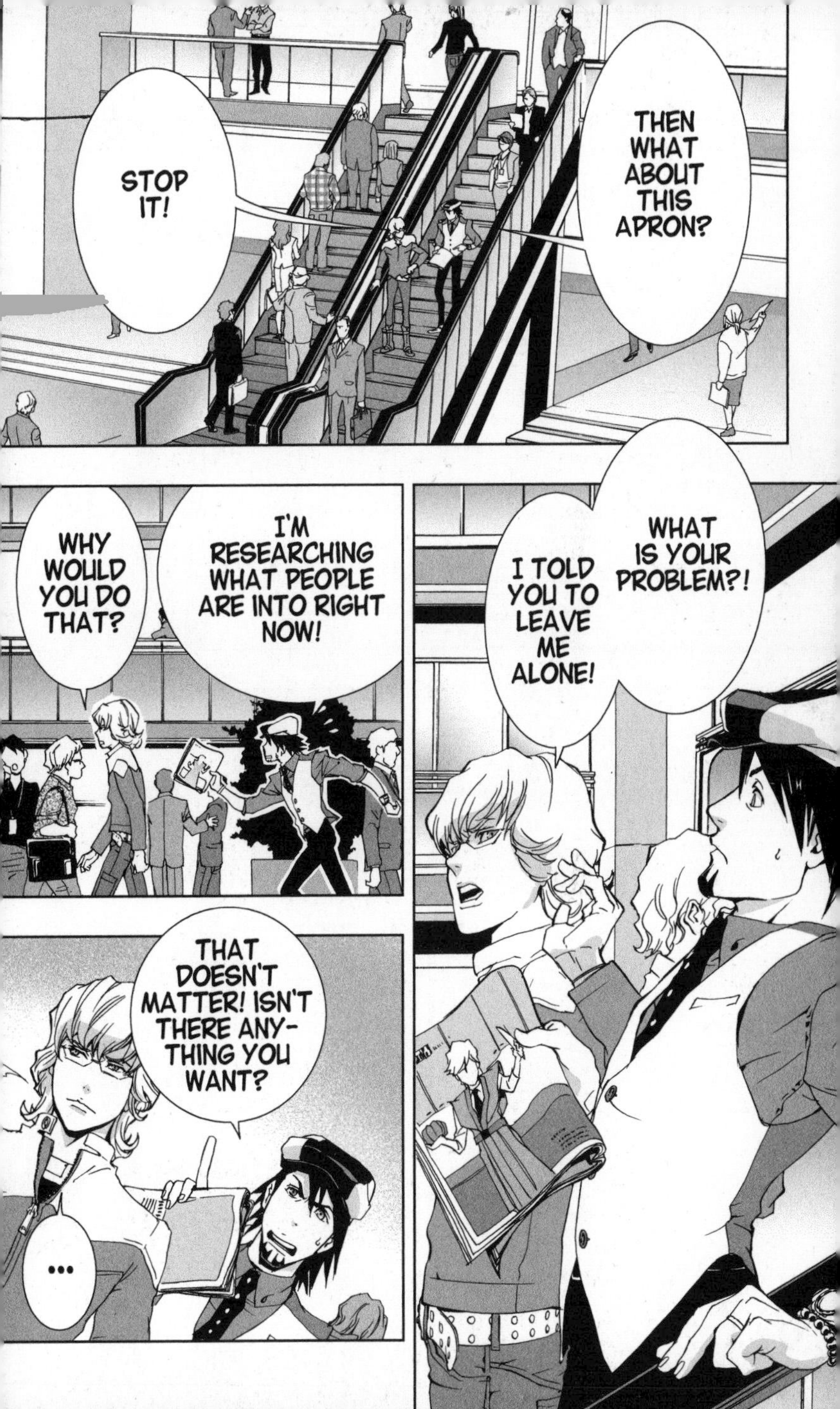
THEN WHAT ABOUT THIS APRON?
STOP IT!
WHAT IS YOUR PROBLEM?!
I TOLD YOU TO LEAVE ME ALONE!
I'M RESEARCHING WHAT PEOPLE ARE INTO RIGHT NOW!
WHY WOULD YOU DO THAT?
THAT DOESN'T MATTER! ISN'T THERE ANY-THING YOU WANT?
...

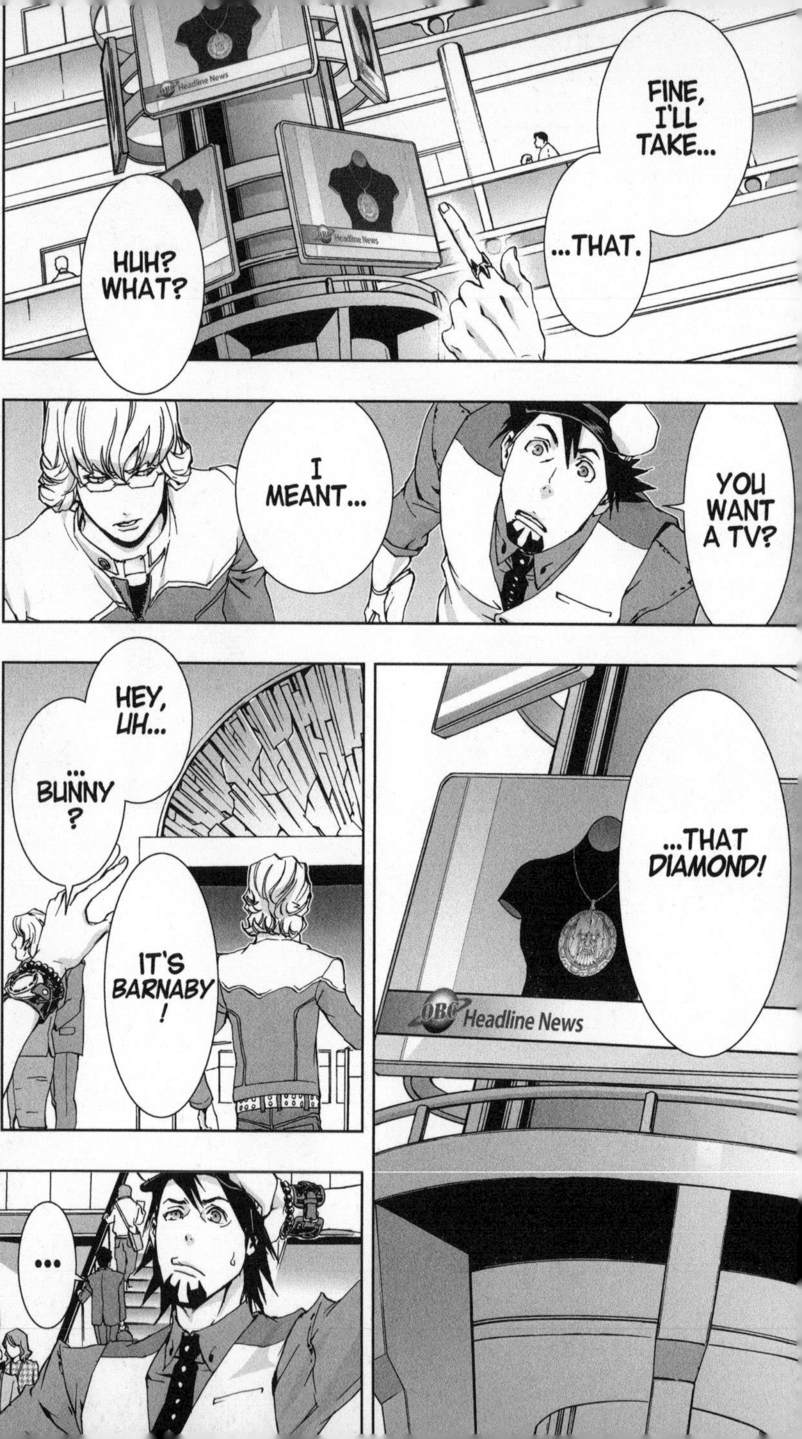
FINE, I'LL TAKE...
...THAT.
HUH? WHAT?
YOU WANT A TV?
I MEANT...
...THAT DIAMOND!
OBC Headline News
HEY, UH... ...BUNNY?
IT'S BARNABY!
...

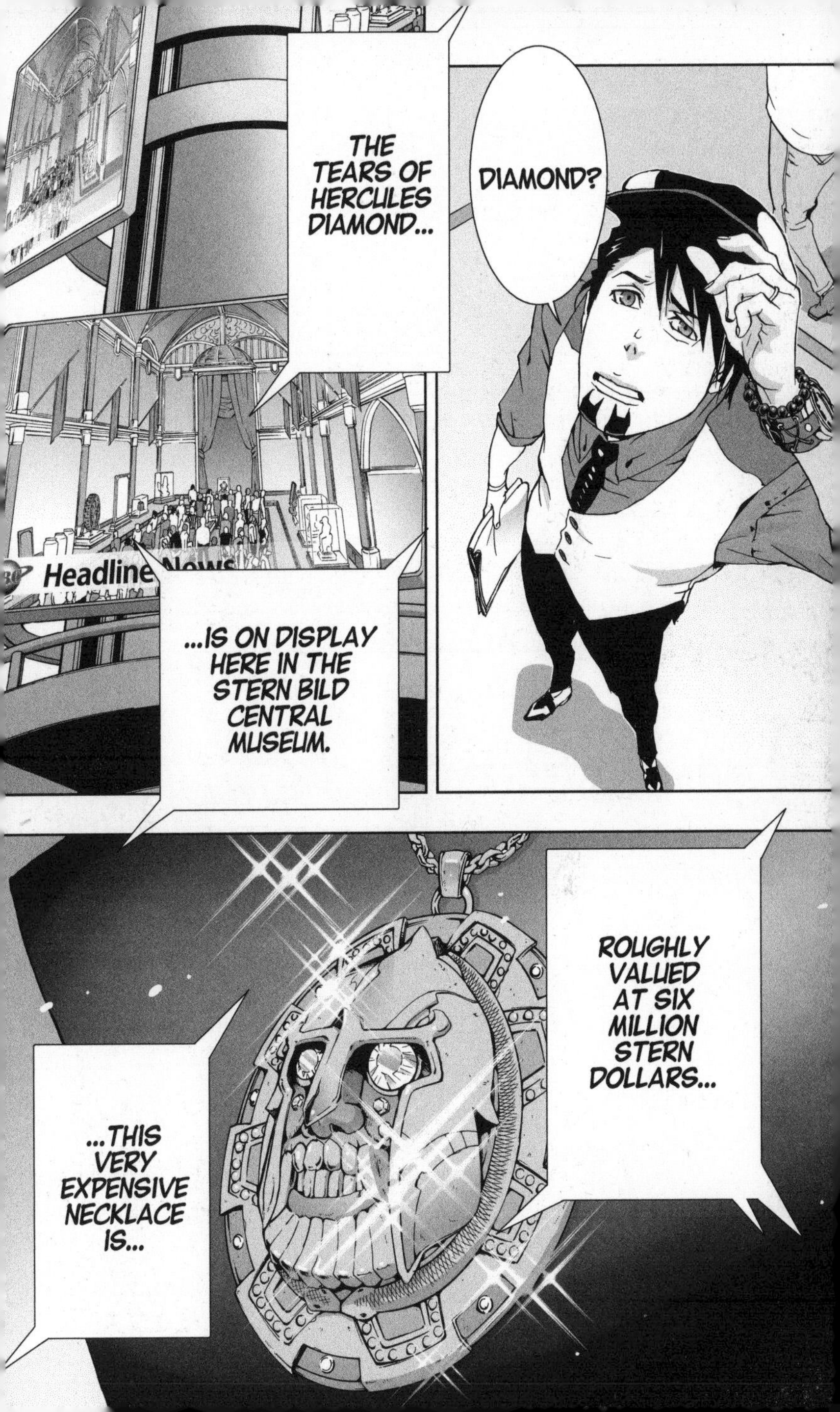
DIAMOND?
THE TEARS OF HERCULES DIAMOND...
Headline News
...IS ON DISPLAY HERE IN THE STERN BILD CENTRAL MUSEUM.
ROUGHLY VALUED AT SIX MILLION STERN DOLLARS...
...THIS VERY EXPENSIVE NECKLACE IS...

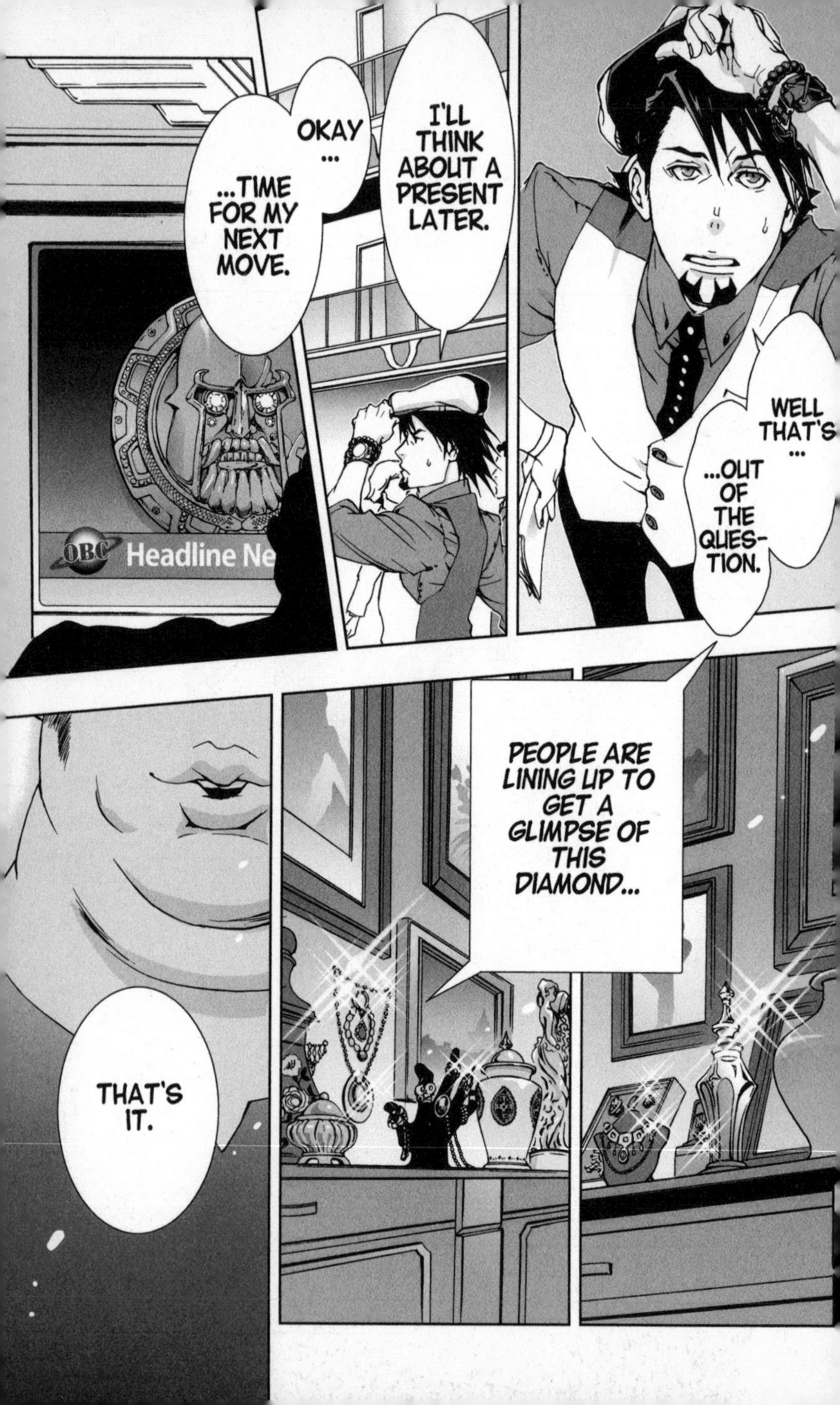
WELL THAT'S ...
...OUT OF THE QUES-TION.
I'LL THINK ABOUT A PRESENT LATER.
OKAY ...
...TIME FOR MY NEXT MOVE.
OBC Headline Ne
PEOPLE ARE LINING UP TO GET A GLIMPSE OF THIS DIAMOND...
THAT'S IT.

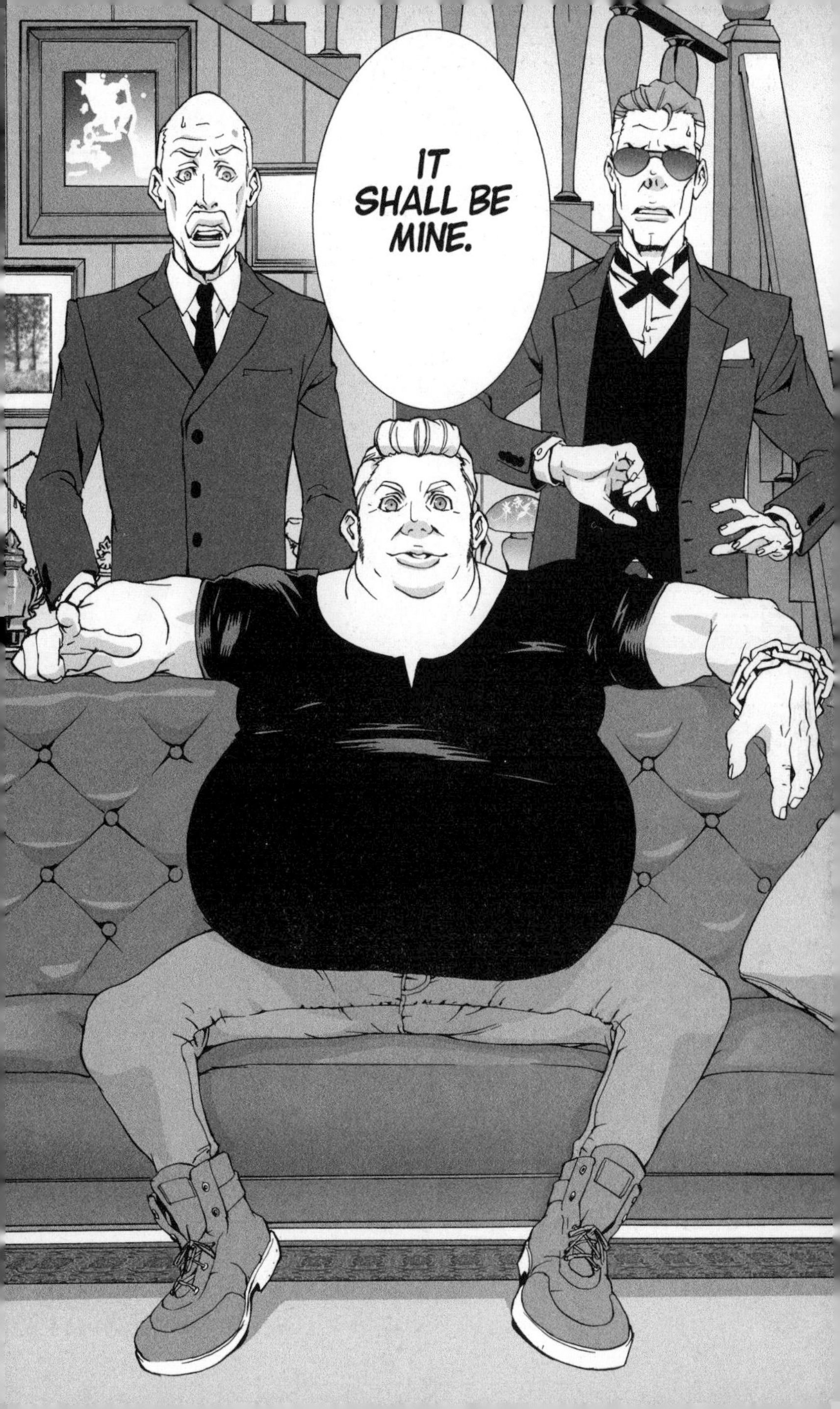
IT SHALL BE MINE.

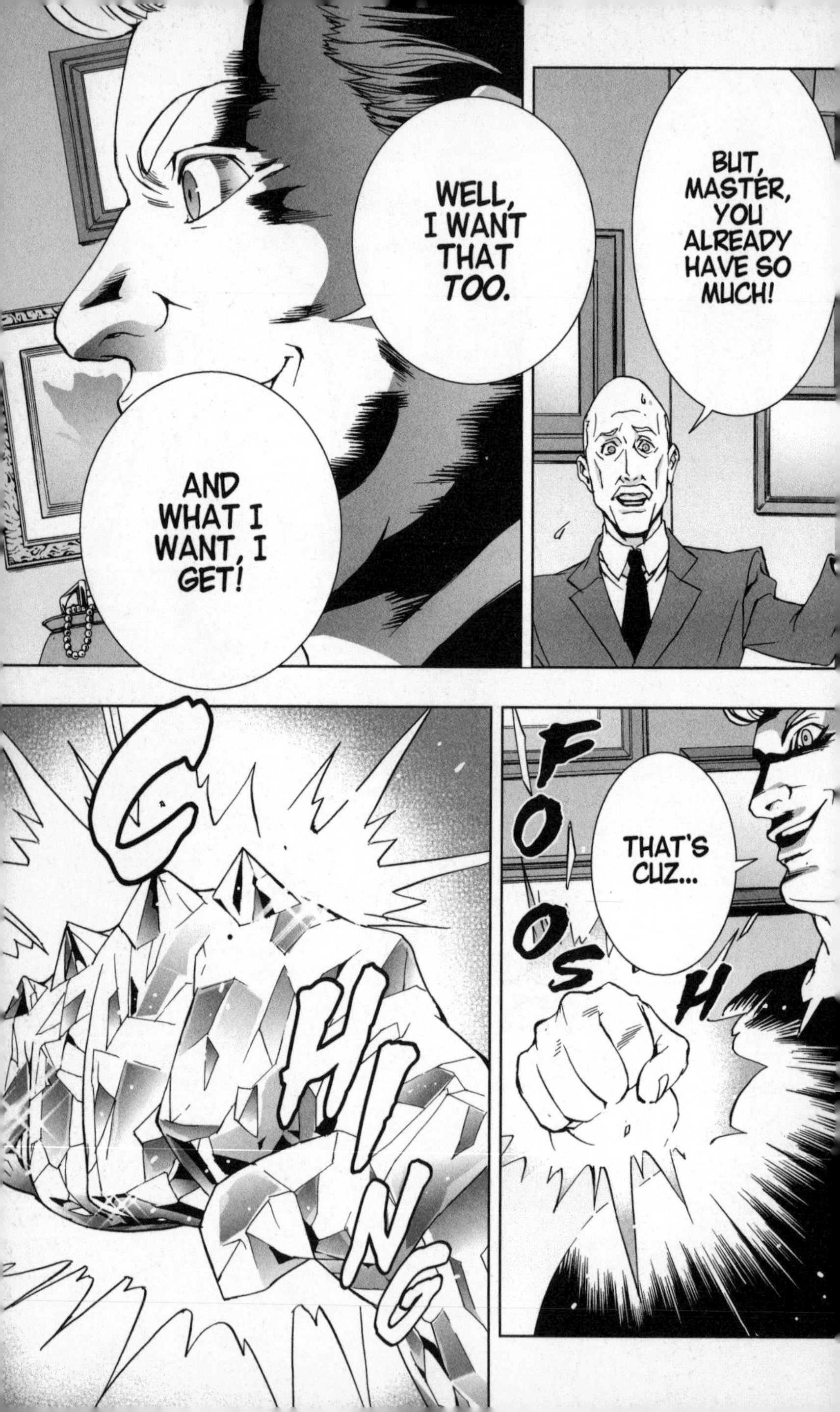
BUT, MASTER, YOU ALREADY HAVE SO MUCH!
WELL, I WANT THAT TOO.
AND WHAT I WANT, I GET!
FOOOSH
THAT'S CUZ...
CHING

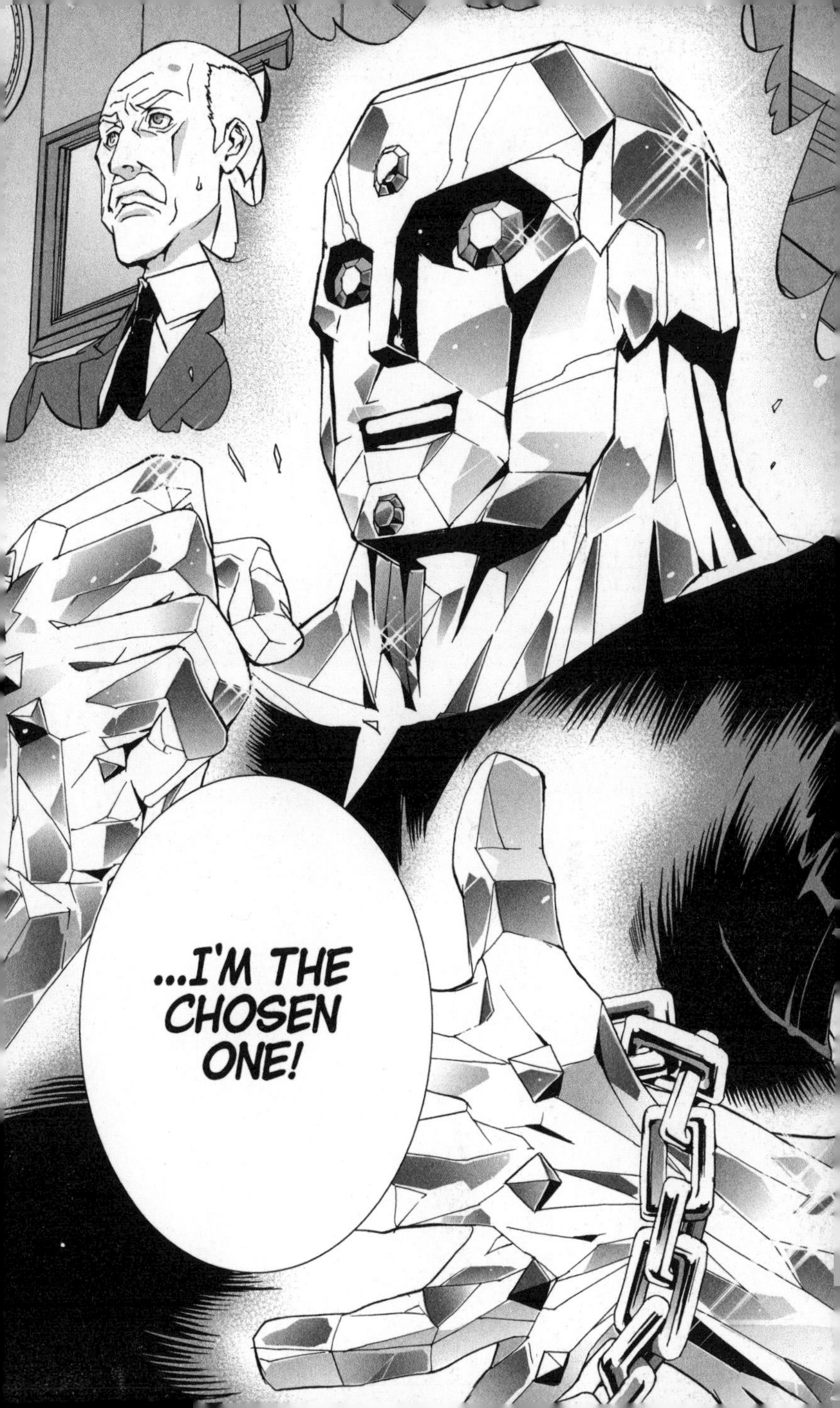
...I'M THE CHOSEN ONE!

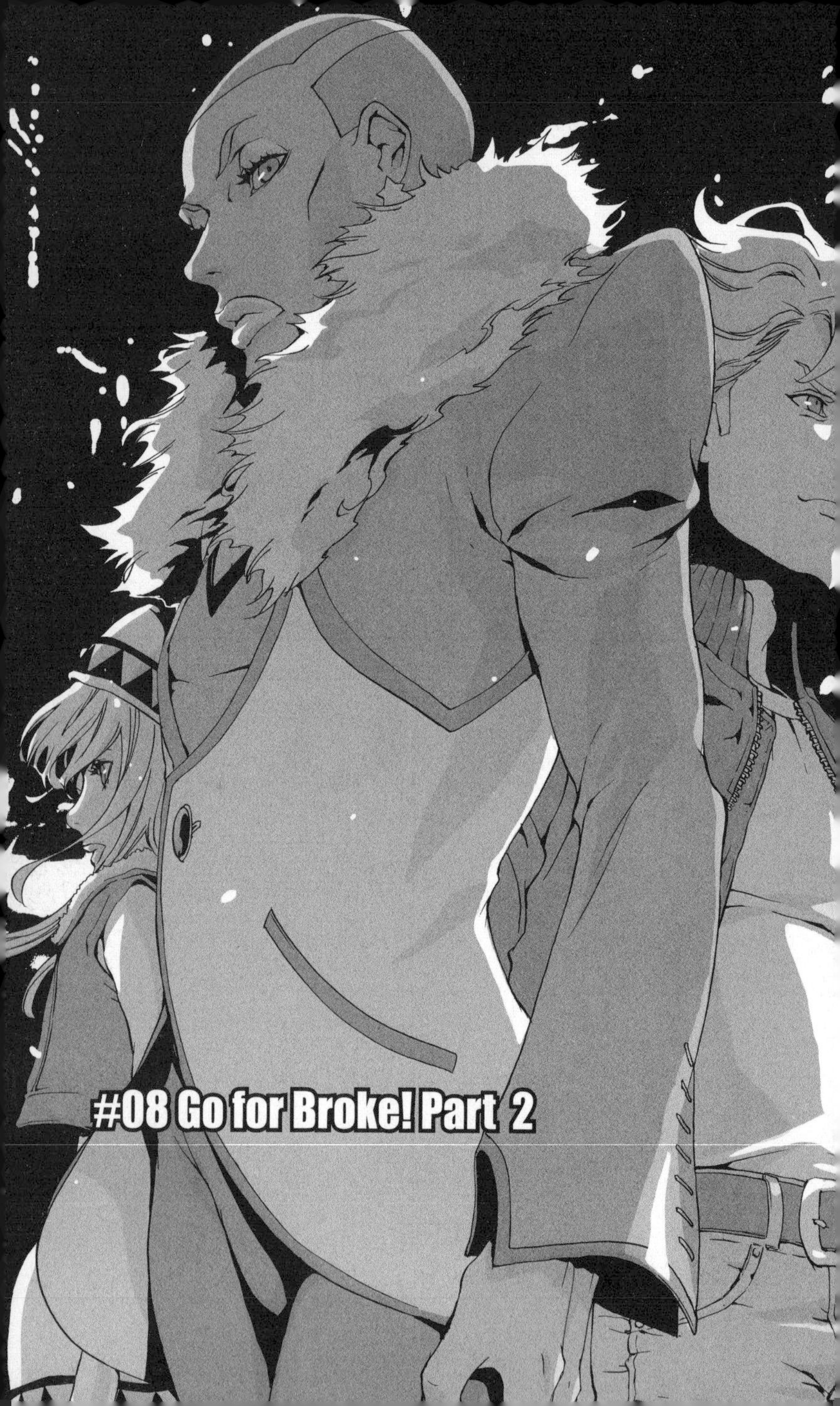
#08 Go for Broke! Part 2

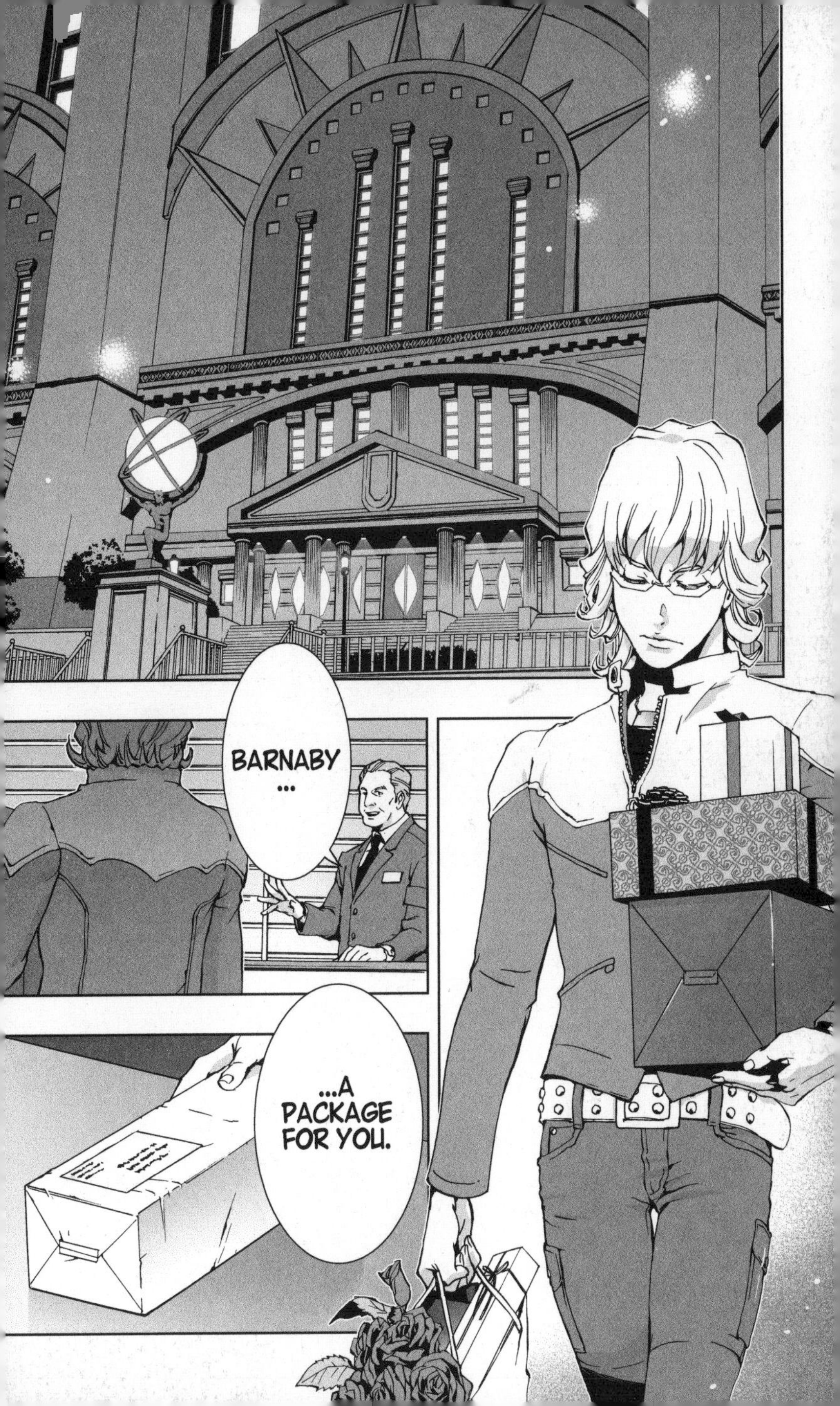
BARNABY ...
...A PACKAGE FOR YOU.

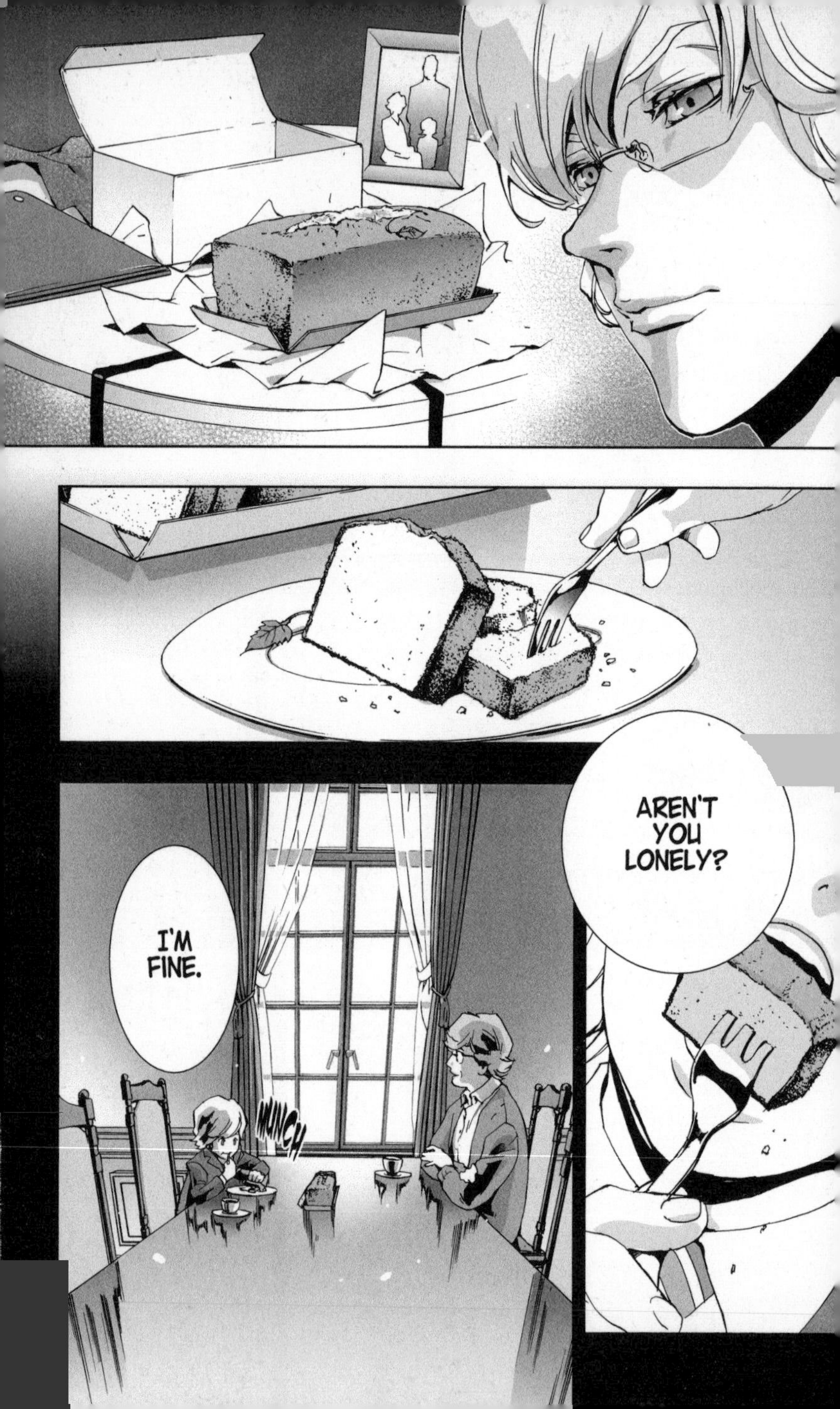
AREN'T YOU LONELY?
I'M FINE.
MUNCH

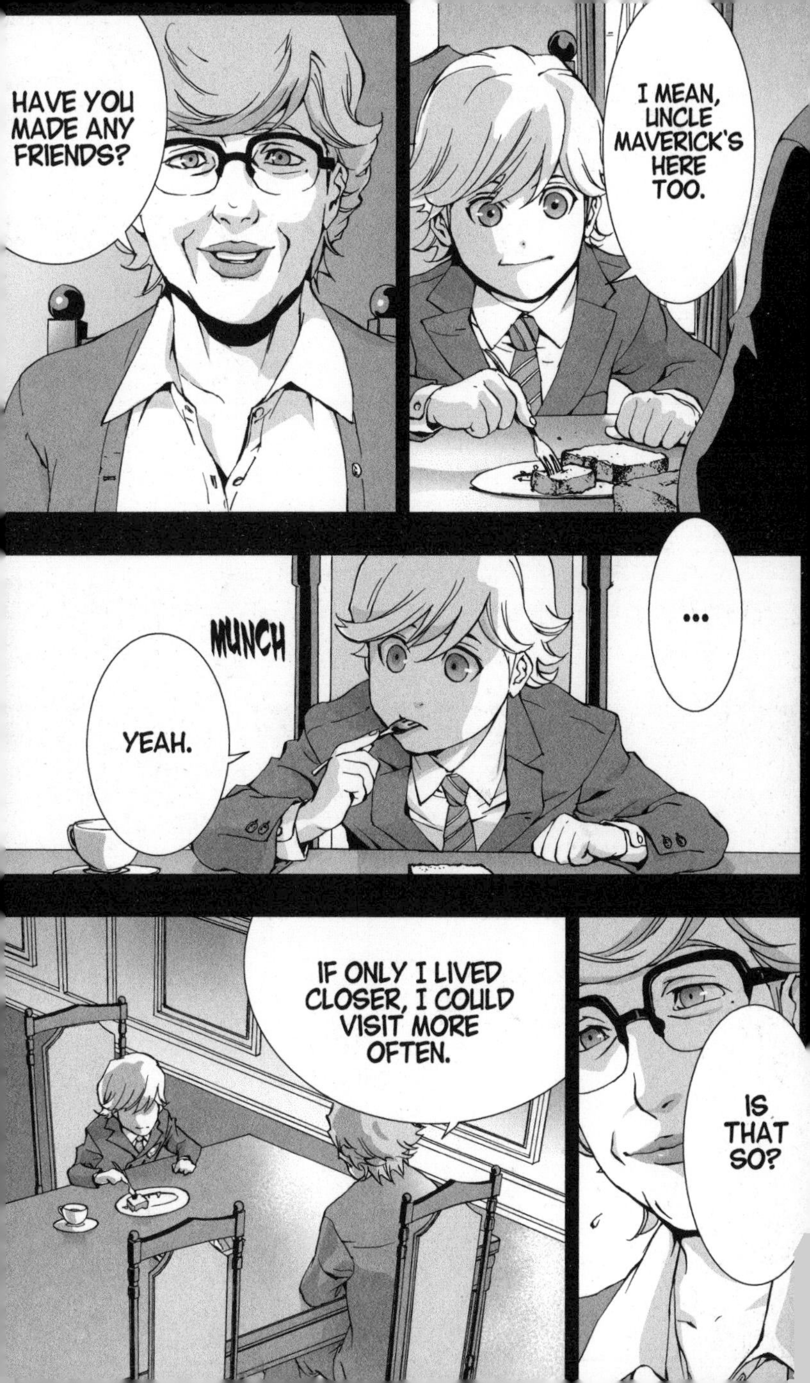
I MEAN, UNCLE MAVERICK'S HERE TOO.
HAVE YOU MADE ANY FRIENDS?
...
MUNCH
YEAH.
IS THAT SO?
IF ONLY I LIVED CLOSER, I COULD VISIT MORE OFTEN.

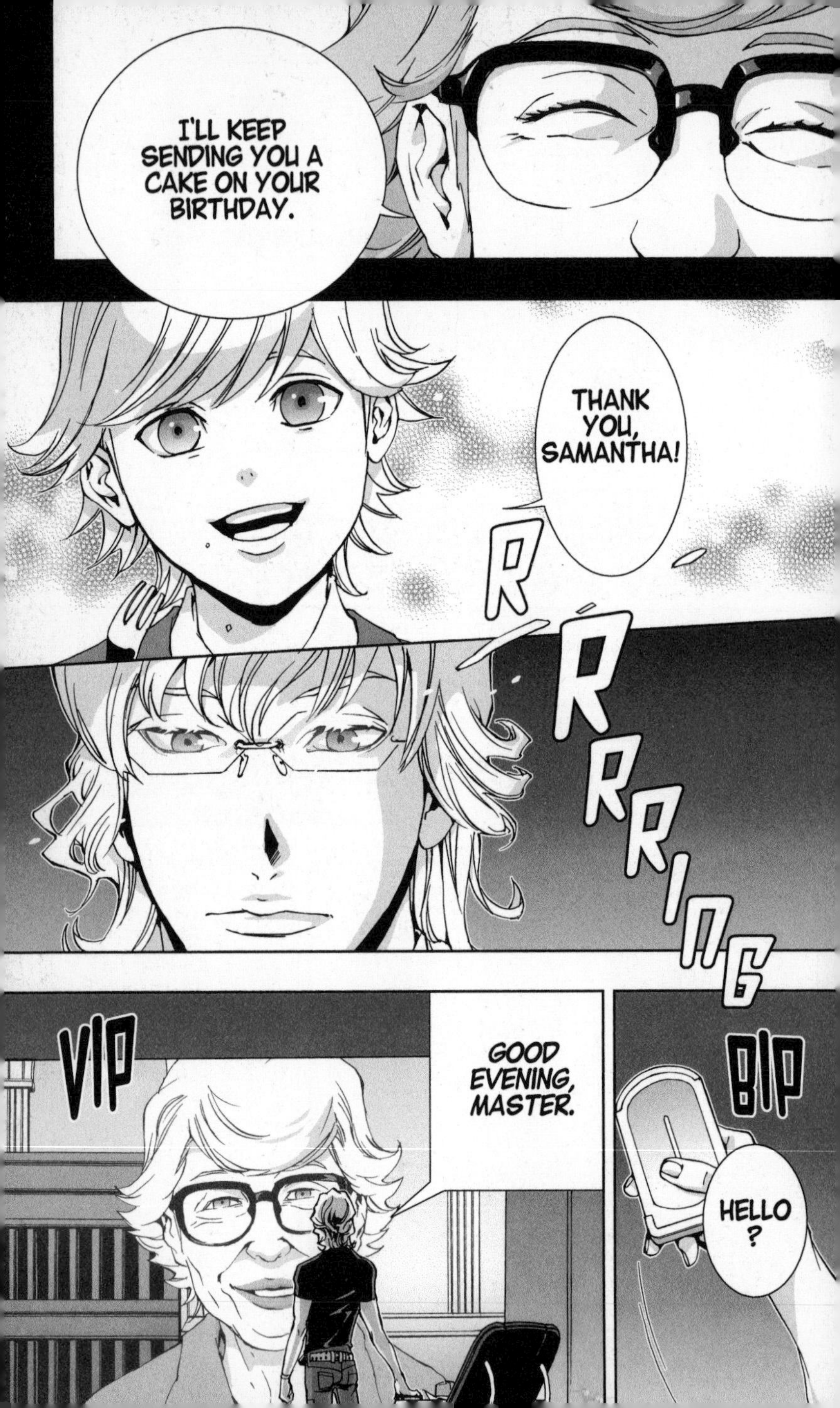
I'LL KEEP SENDING YOU A CAKE ON YOUR BIRTHDAY.
THANK YOU, SAMANTHA!
RRRRING
BIP
HELLO?
VIP
GOOD EVENING, MASTER.

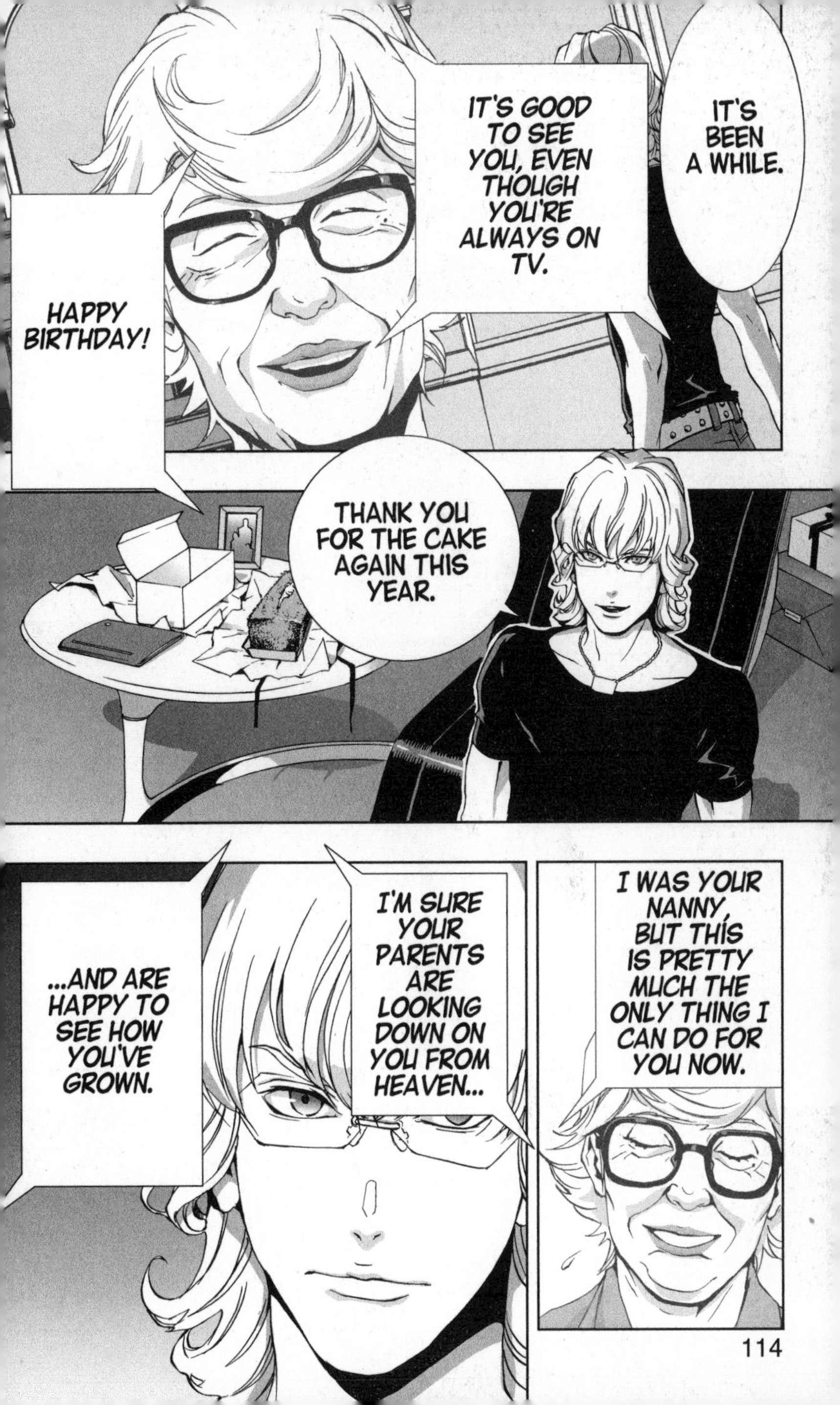
IT'S BEEN A WHILE.
IT'S GOOD TO SEE YOU, EVEN THOUGH YOU'RE ALWAYS ON TV.
HAPPY BIRTHDAY!
THANK YOU FOR THE CAKE AGAIN THIS YEAR.
I WAS YOUR NANNY, BUT THIS IS PRETTY MUCH THE ONLY THING I CAN DO FOR YOU NOW.
I'M SURE YOUR PARENTS ARE LOOKING DOWN ON YOU FROM HEAVEN...
...AND ARE HAPPY TO SEE HOW YOU'VE GROWN.

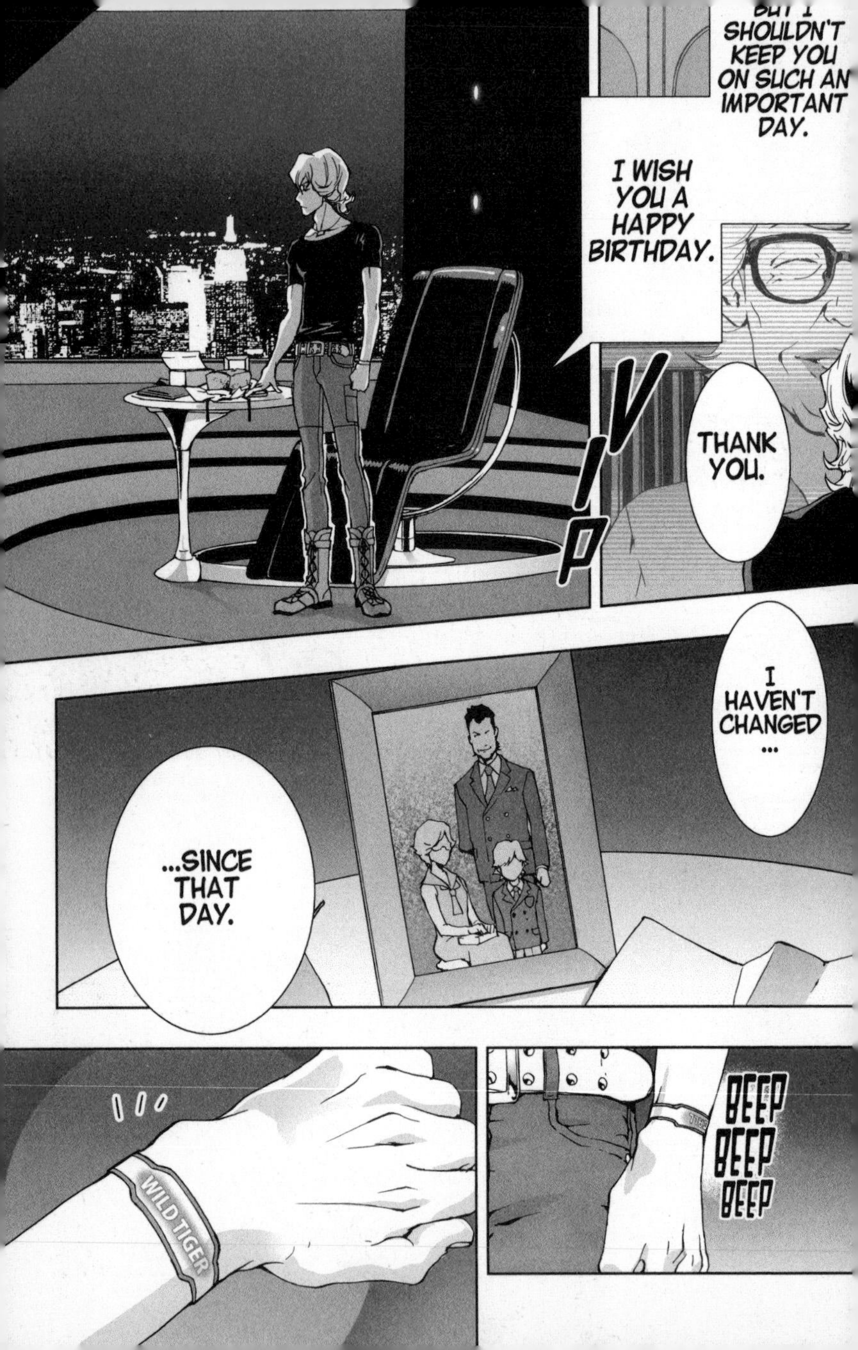

SHOULDN'T KEEP YOU ON SUCH AN IMPORTANT DAY.
I WISH YOU A HAPPY BIRTHDAY.
VIP
THANK YOU.
I HAVEN'T CHANGED...
...SINCE THAT DAY.
BEEP BEEP BEEP
WILD TIGER

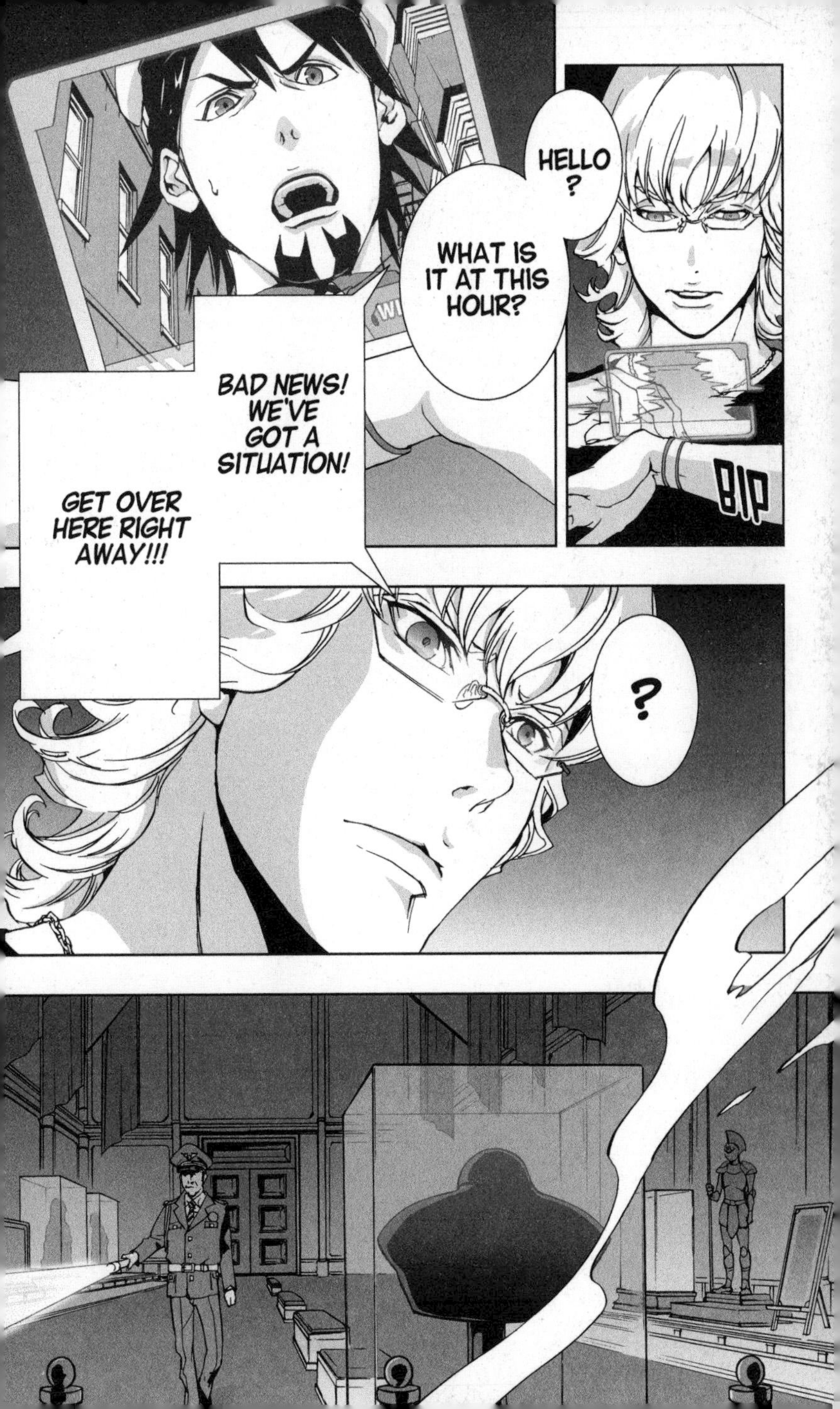
HELLO?
WHAT IS IT AT THIS HOUR?
BIP
BAD NEWS! WE'VE GOT A SITUATION!
GET OVER HERE RIGHT AWAY!!!
?

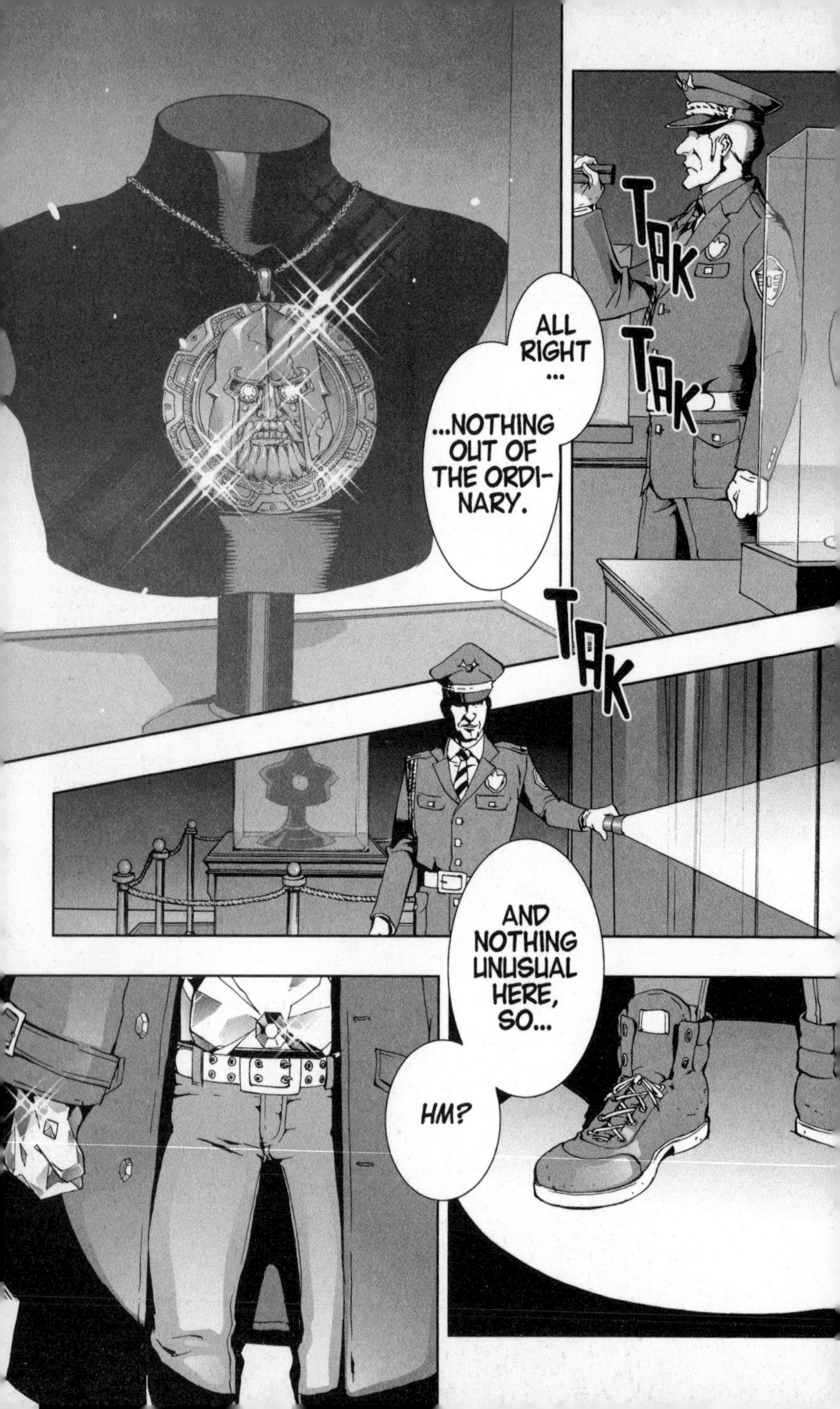
TAK
TAK
ALL RIGHT...
...NOTHING OUT OF THE ORDINARY.
TAK
AND NOTHING UNUSUAL HERE, SO...
HM?

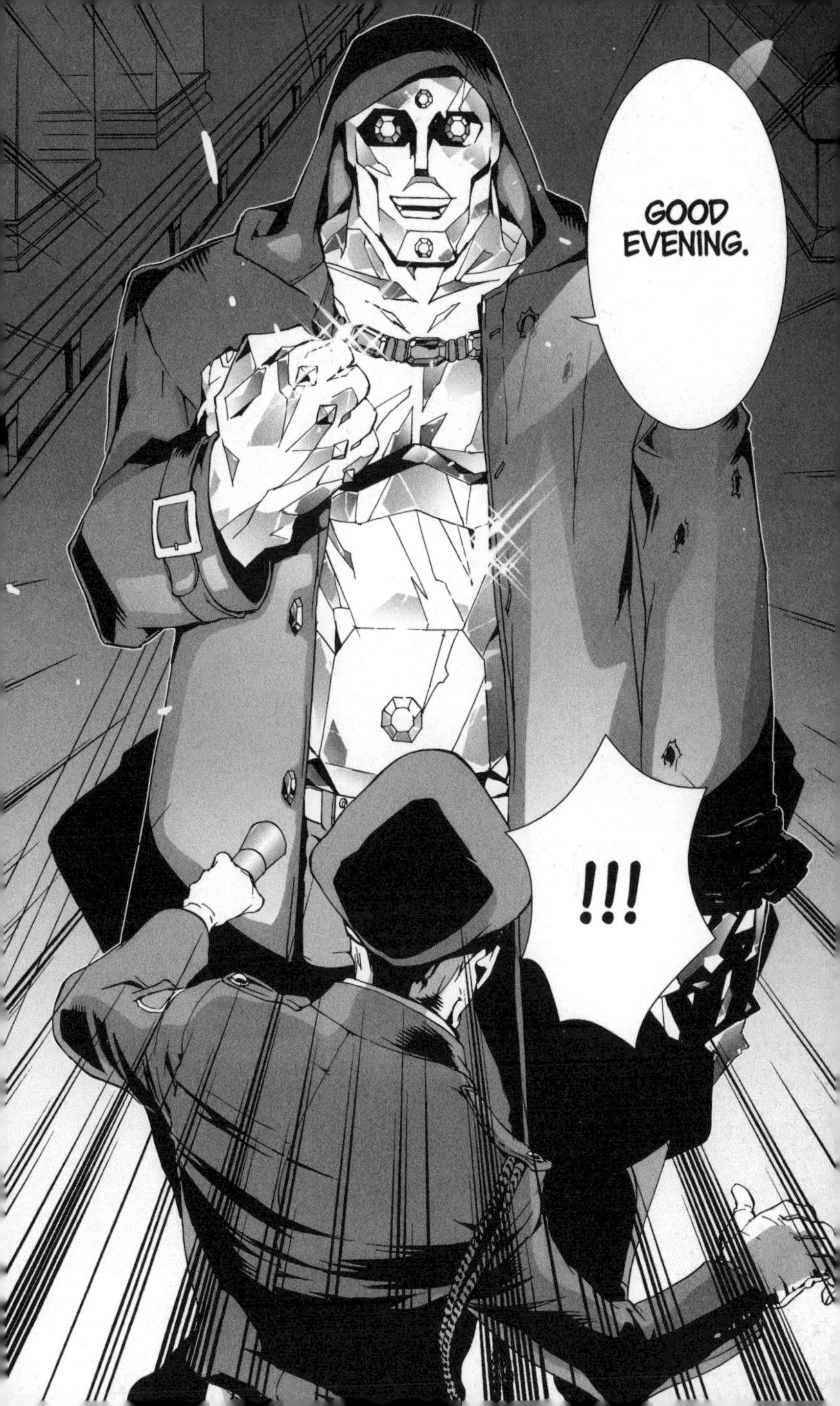
GOOD EVENING.
!!!

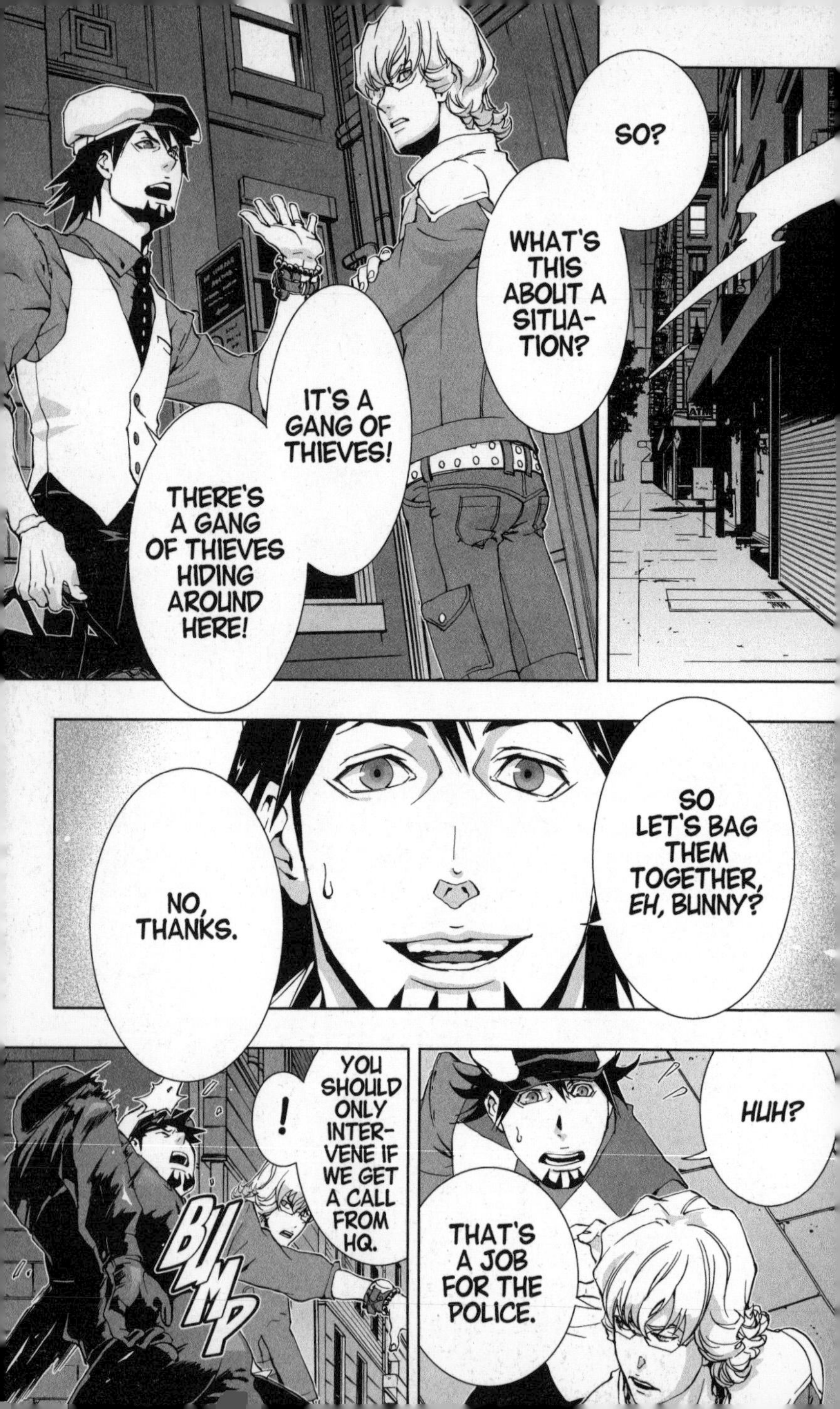
SO?
WHAT'S THIS ABOUT A SITUATION?
IT'S A GANG OF THIEVES!
THERE'S A GANG OF THIEVES HIDING AROUND HERE!
SO LET'S BAG THEM TOGETHER, EH, BUNNY?
NO, THANKS.
HUH?
THAT'S A JOB FOR THE POLICE.
YOU SHOULD ONLY INTERVENE IF WE GET A CALL FROM HQ.
!
BUMP

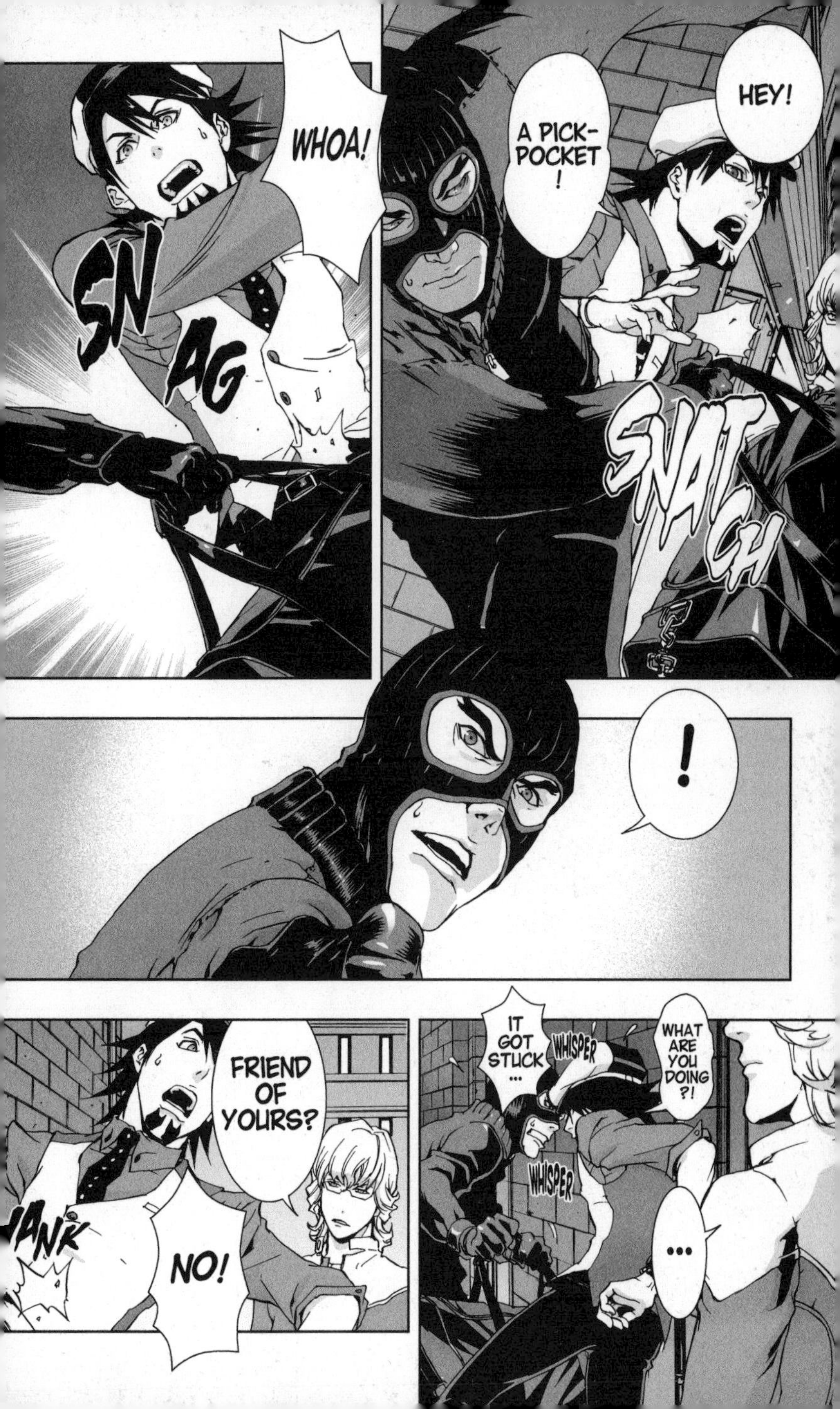
HEY!
A PICK-POCKET!
SNATCH
WHOA!
SNAG
!
WHAT ARE YOU DOING?!
IT GOT STUCK...
WHISPER
WHISPER
...
FRIEND OF YOURS?
NO!

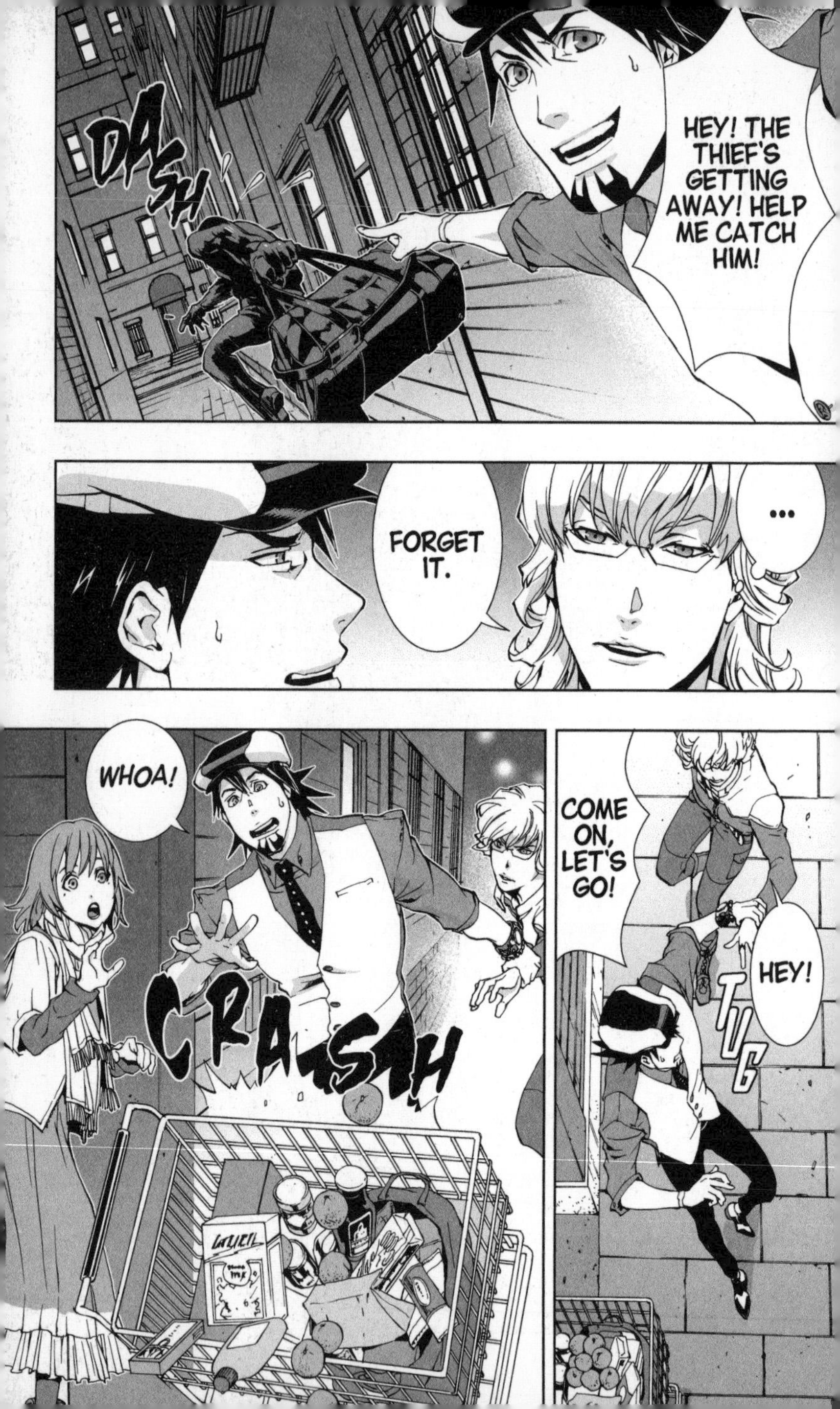
HEY! THE THIEF'S GETTING AWAY! HELP ME CATCH HIM!
DASH
...
FORGET IT.
COME ON, LET'S GO!
HEY!
TUG
WHOA!
CRASH

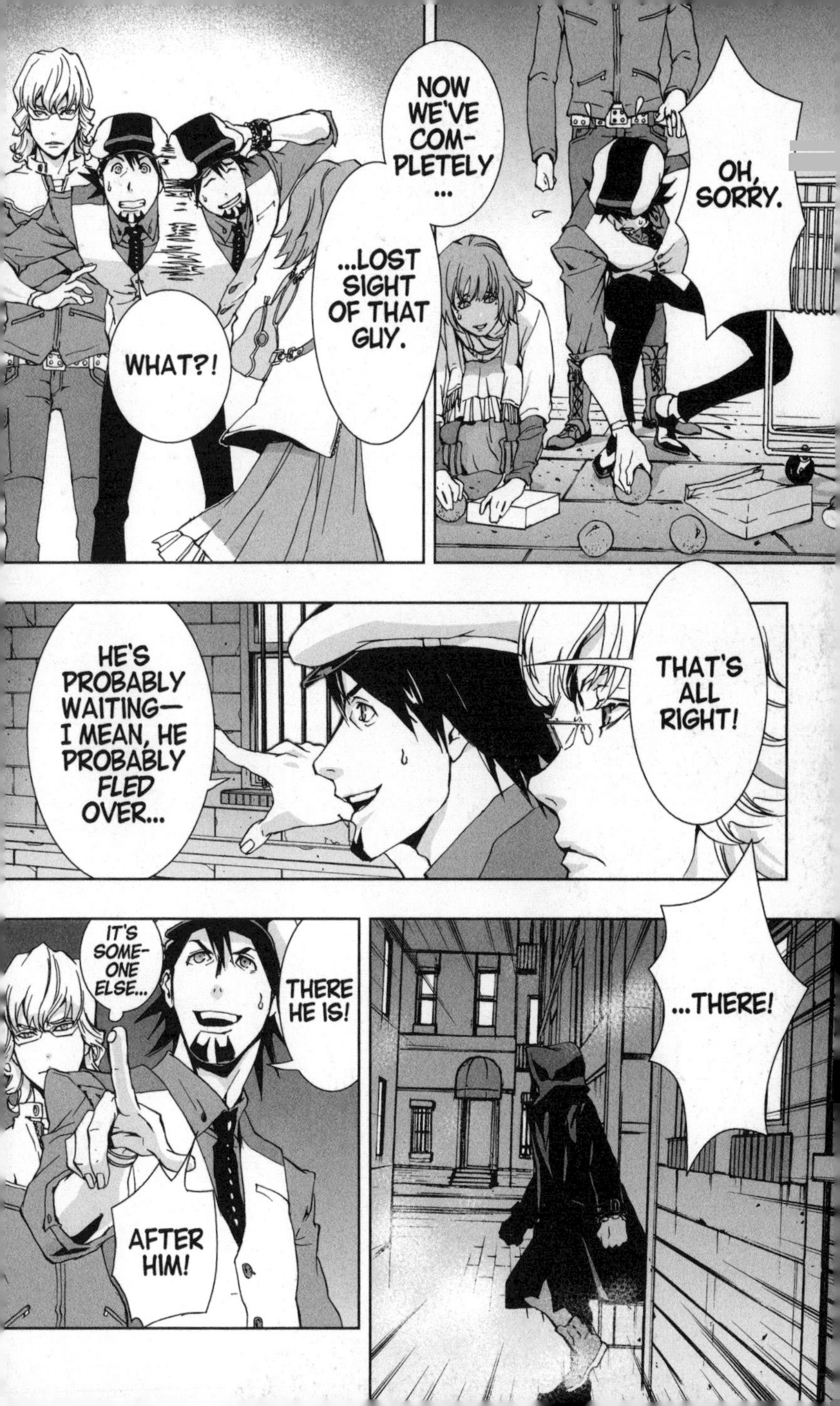
OH, SORRY.
NOW WE'VE COMPLETELY...
...LOST SIGHT OF THAT GUY.
WHAT?!
THAT'S ALL RIGHT!
HE'S PROBABLY WAITING— I MEAN, HE PROBABLY FLED OVER...
...THERE!
THERE HE IS!
IT'S SOMEONE ELSE...
AFTER HIM!

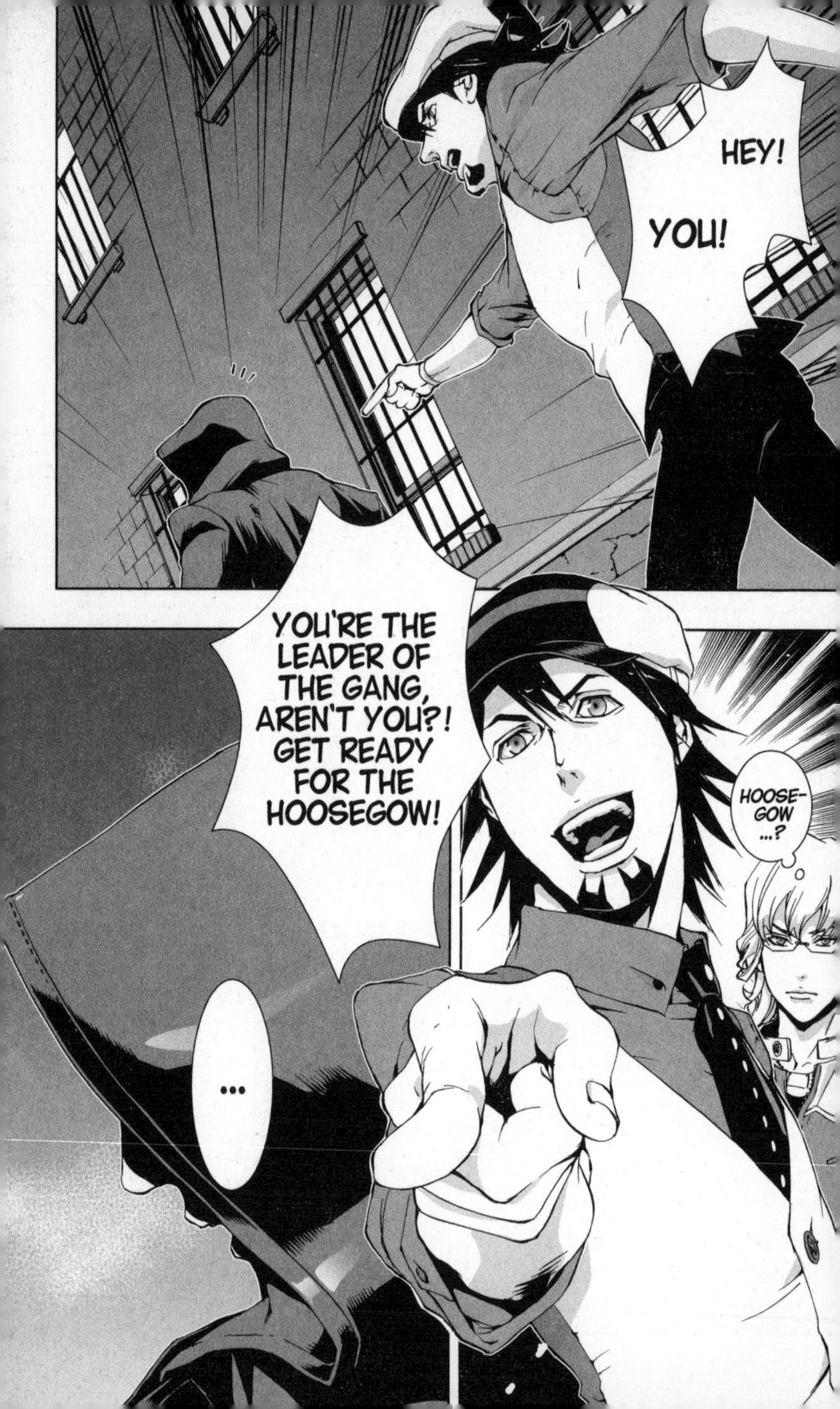
HEY!
YOU!
YOU'RE THE LEADER OF THE GANG, AREN'T YOU?! GET READY FOR THE HOOSEGOW!
HOOSE-GOW ...?
...

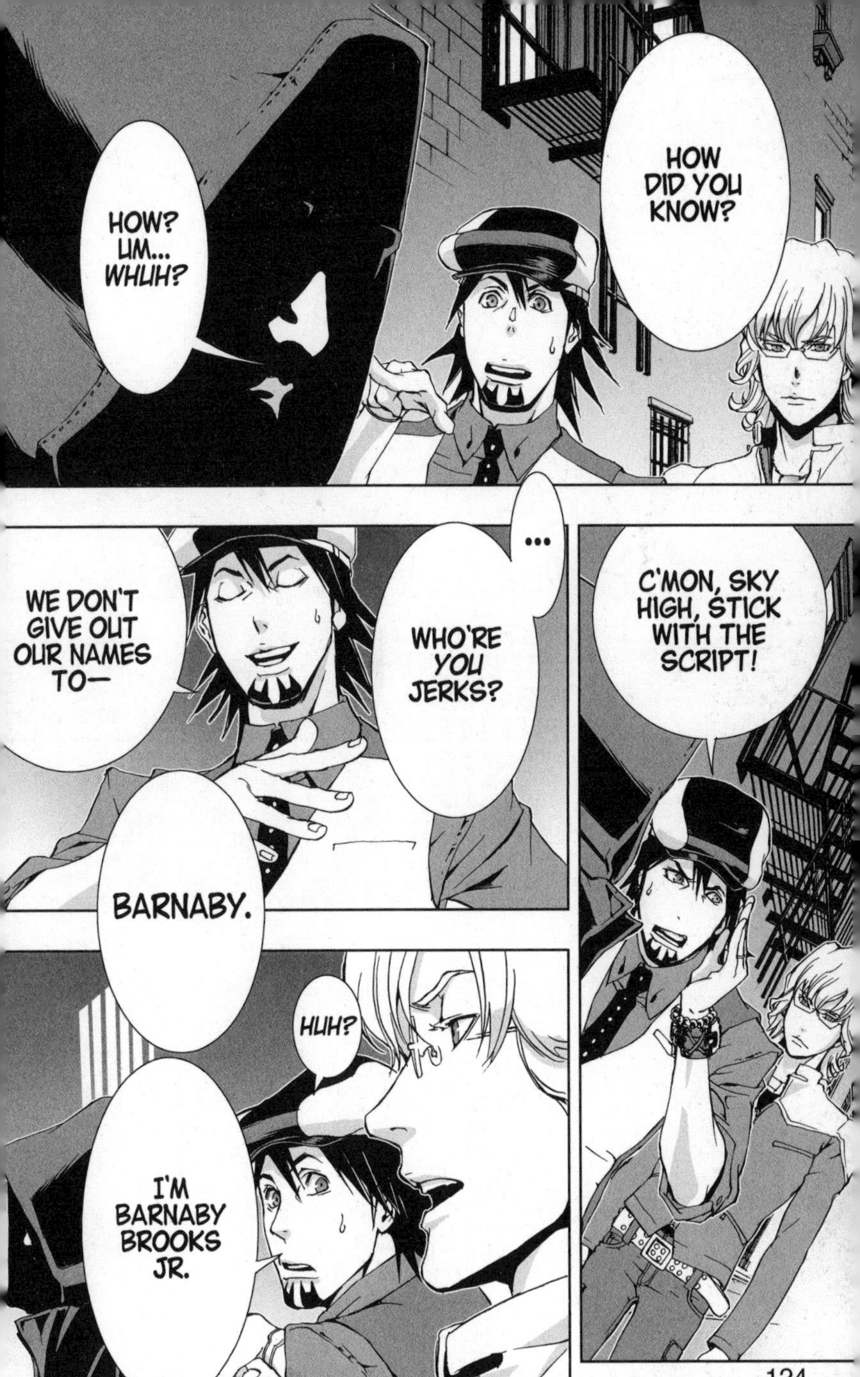

HOW DID YOU KNOW?
HOW? UM... WHUH?
C'MON, SKY HIGH, STICK WITH THE SCRIPT!
...
WHO'RE YOU JERKS?
WE DON'T GIVE OUT OUR NAMES TO—
BARNABY.
HUH?
I'M BARNABY BROOKS JR.

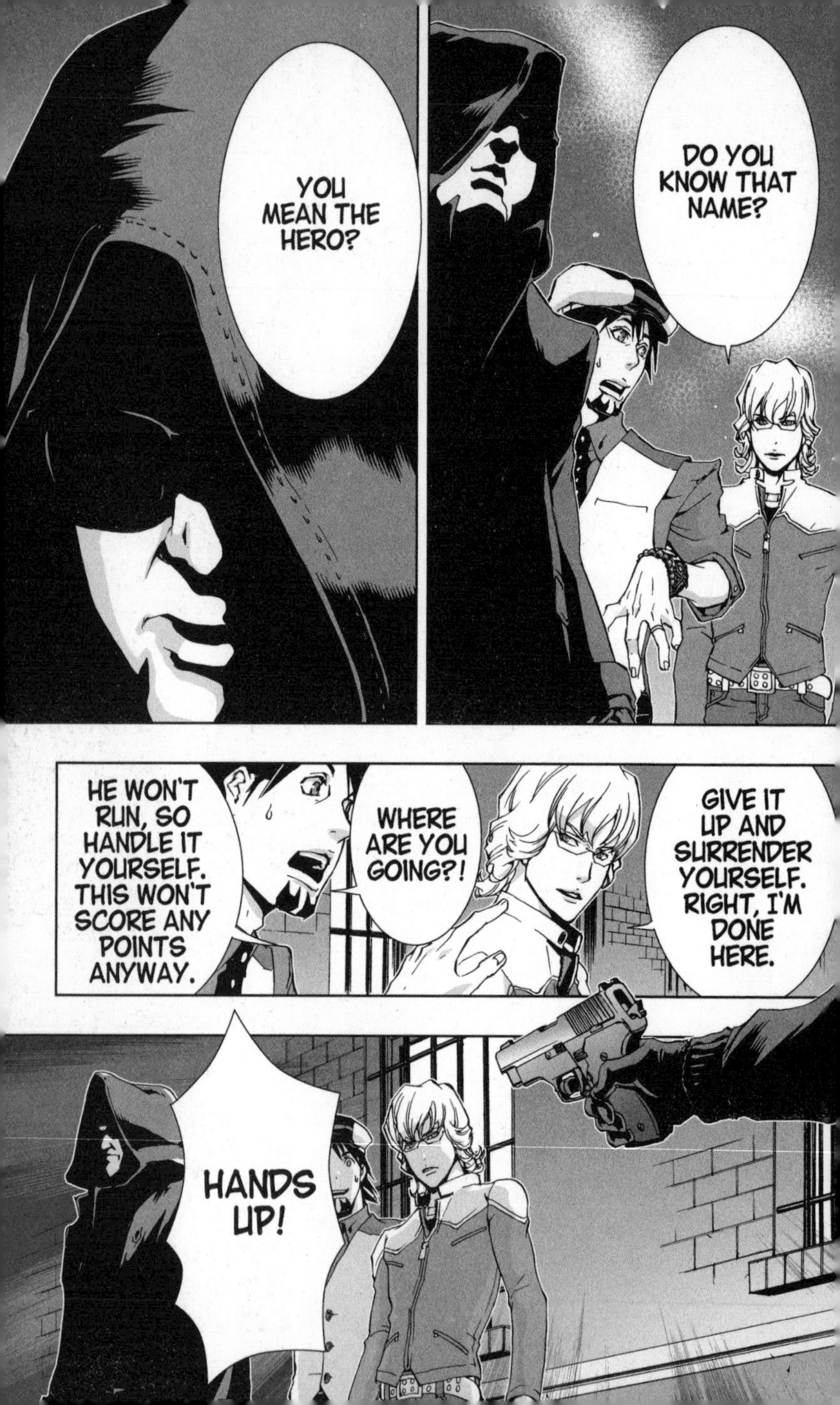
DO YOU KNOW THAT NAME?
YOU MEAN THE HERO?
GIVE IT UP AND SURRENDER YOURSELF. RIGHT, I'M DONE HERE.
WHERE ARE YOU GOING?!
HE WON'T RUN, SO HANDLE IT YOURSELF. THIS WON'T SCORE ANY POINTS ANYWAY.
HANDS UP!

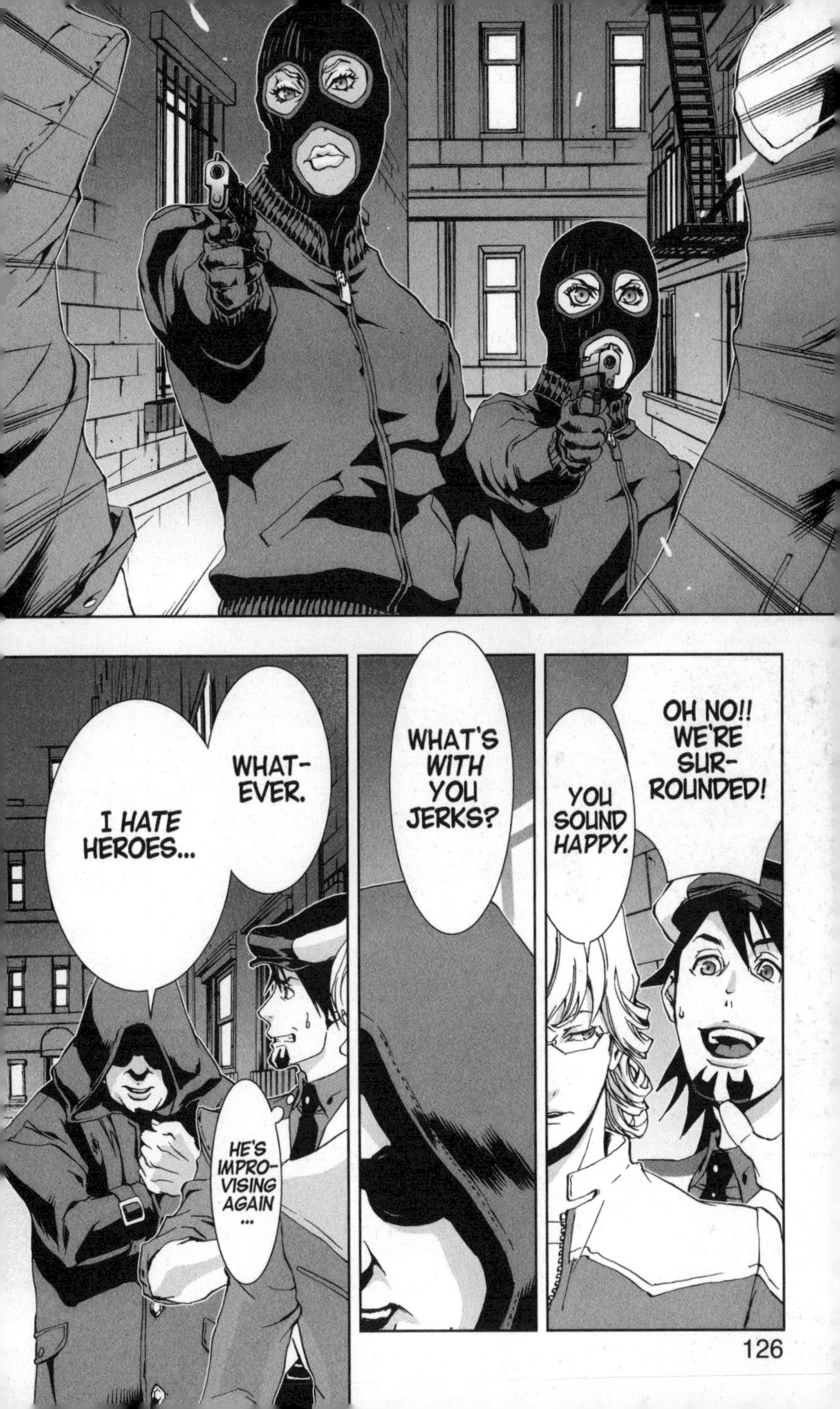
OH NO!! WE'RE SUR-ROUNDED!
YOU SOUND HAPPY.
WHAT'S WITH YOU JERKS?
WHAT-EVER.
I HATE HEROES...
HE'S IMPRO-VISING AGAIN...

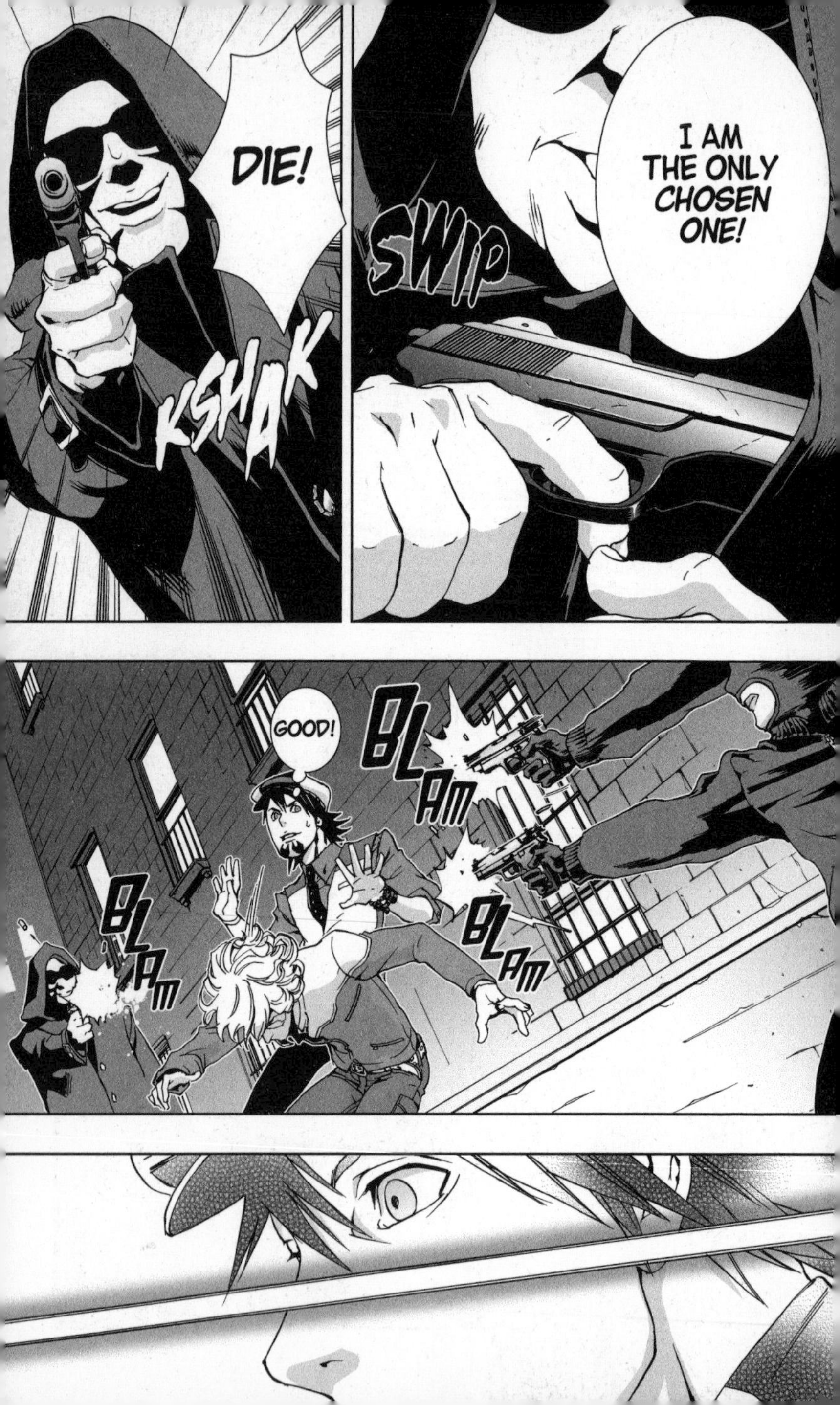
I AM THE ONLY CHOSEN ONE!
SWIP
DIE!
KSHAK
GOOD!
BLAM
BLAM
BLAM

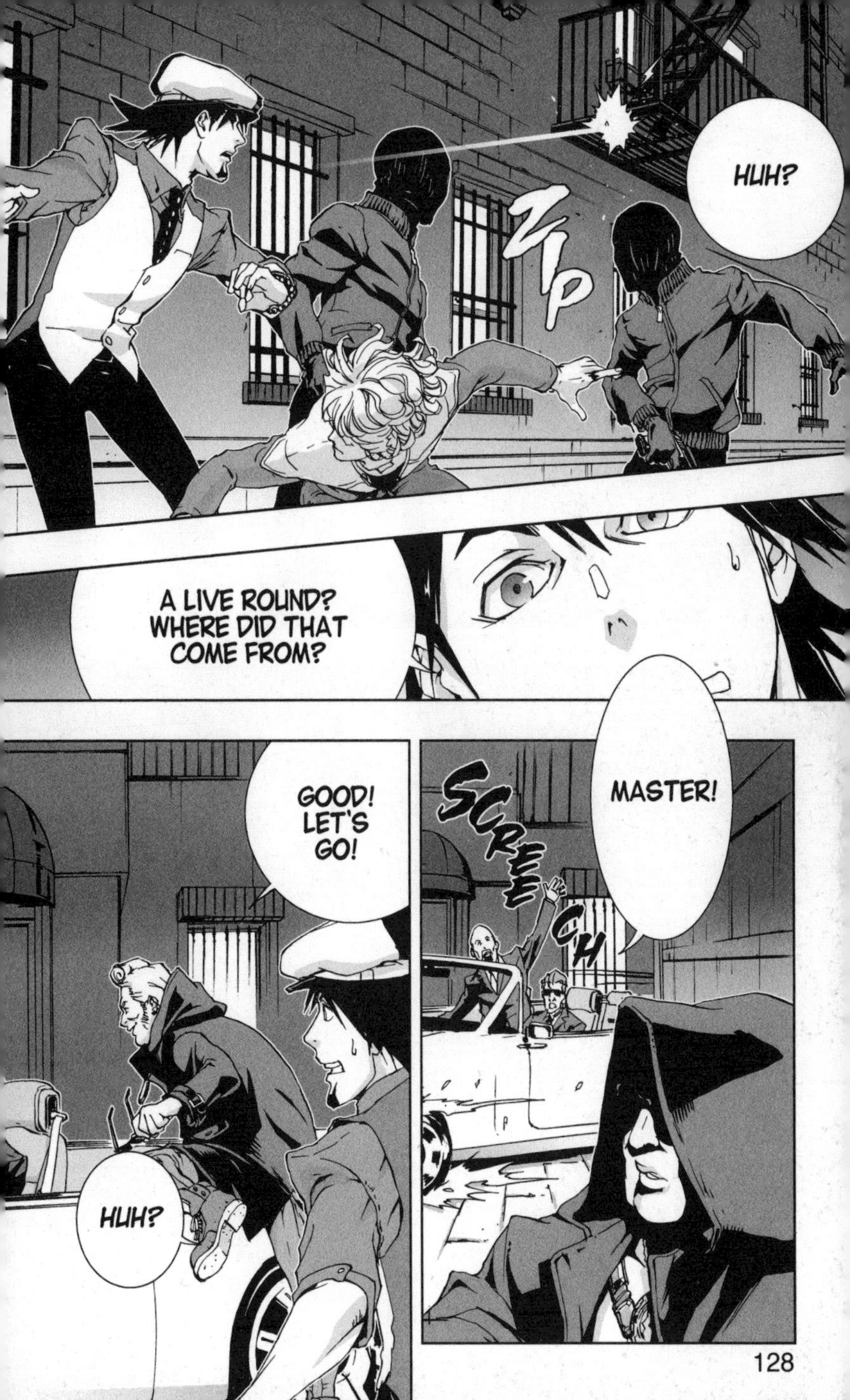
HUH?
ZIP
A LIVE ROUND? WHERE DID THAT COME FROM?
MASTER!
SCREECH
GOOD! LET'S GO!
HUH?

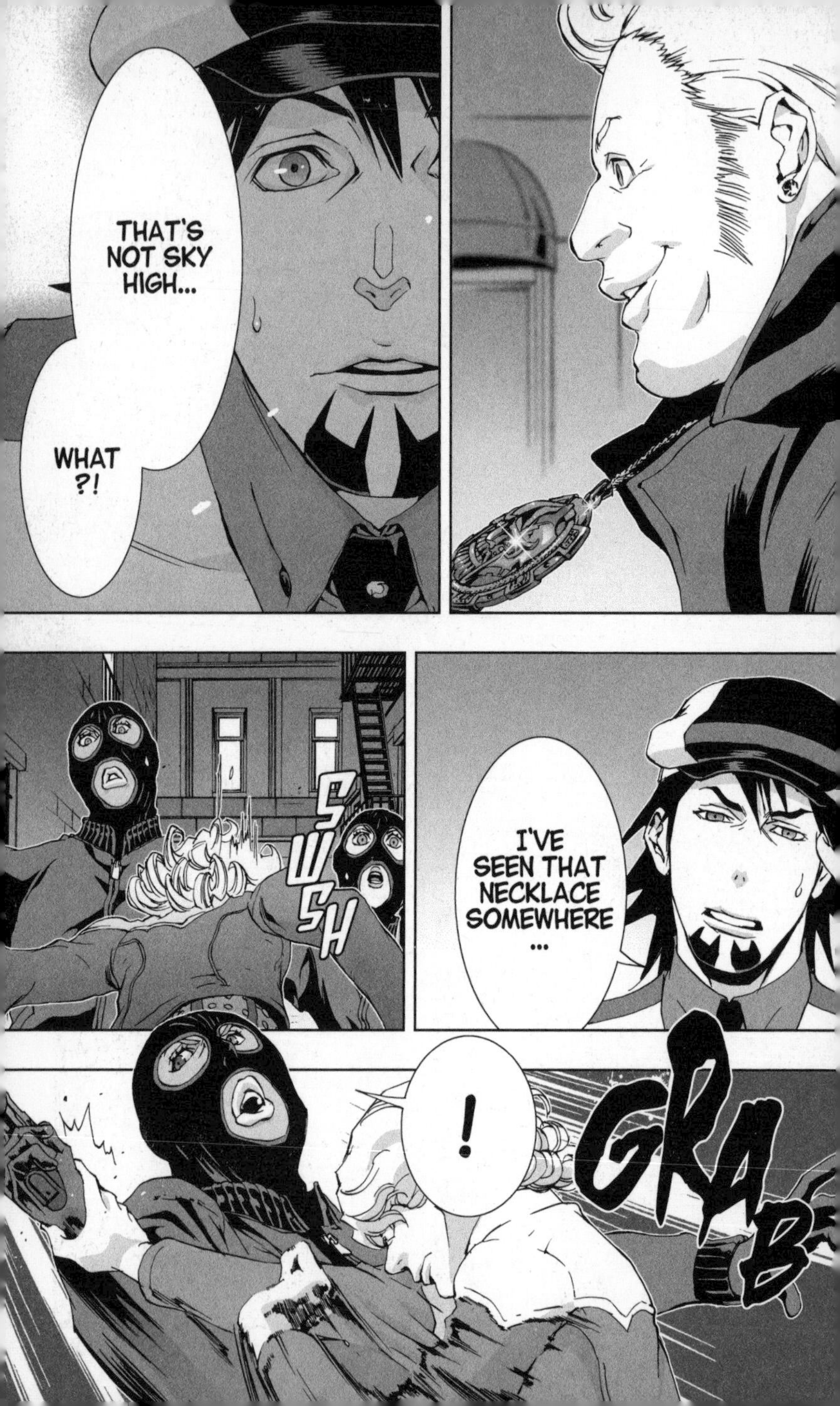
THAT'S NOT SKY HIGH...
WHAT?!
I'VE SEEN THAT NECKLACE SOMEWHERE ...
SWISH
GRAB
!

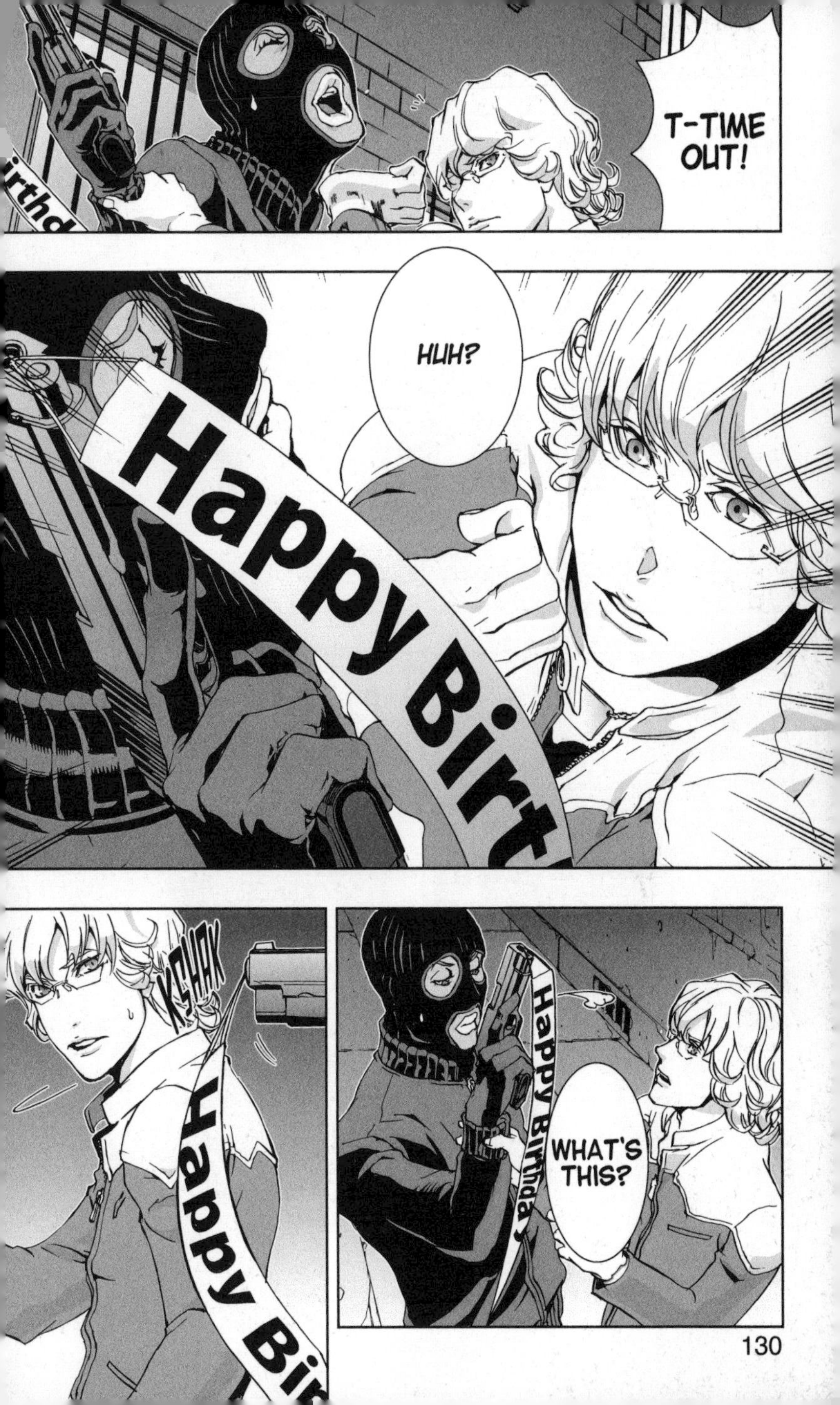
T-TIME OUT!
irthd
HUH?
Happy Birt
WHAT'S THIS?
Happy Birthday
KSHAK
Happy Bir

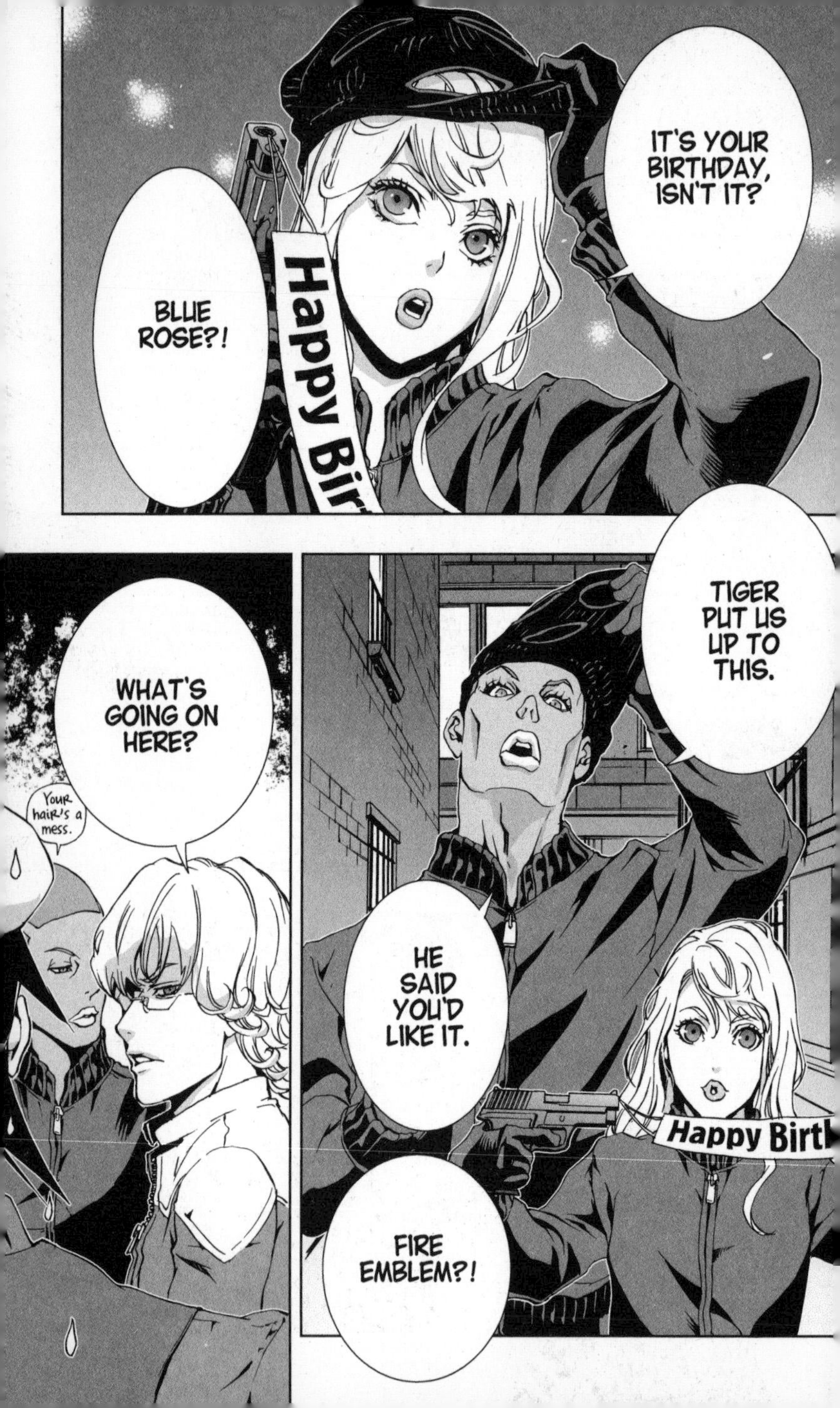
IT'S YOUR BIRTHDAY, ISN'T IT?
Happy Bir
BLUE ROSE?!
TIGER PUT US UP TO THIS.
HE SAID YOU'D LIKE IT.
Happy Birt
FIRE EMBLEM?!
WHAT'S GOING ON HERE?
Your hair's a mess.

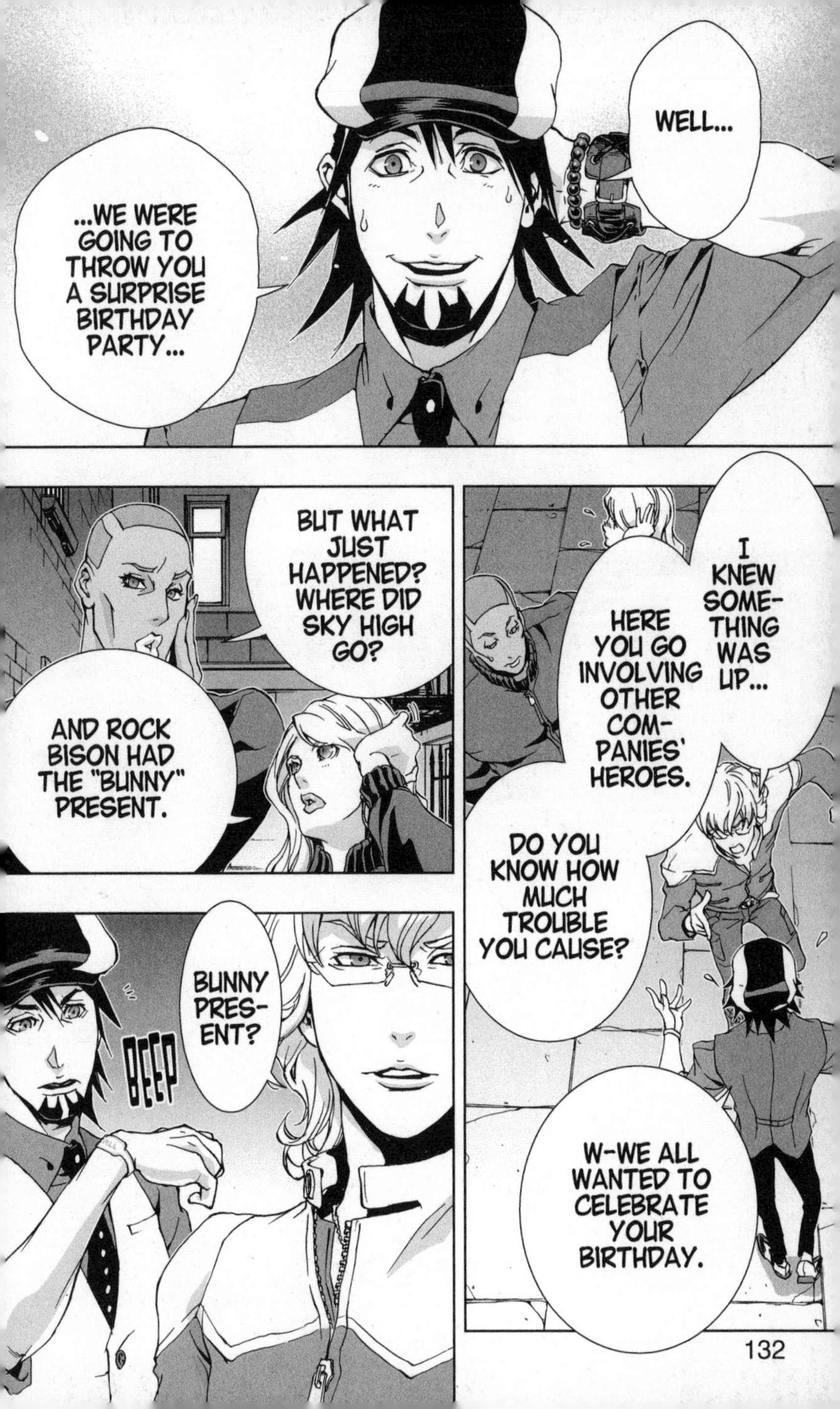
WELL...
...WE WERE GOING TO THROW YOU A SURPRISE BIRTHDAY PARTY...
I KNEW SOME-THING WAS UP...
HERE YOU GO INVOLVING OTHER COM-PANIES' HEROES.
DO YOU KNOW HOW MUCH TROUBLE YOU CAUSE?
W-WE ALL WANTED TO CELEBRATE YOUR BIRTHDAY.
BUT WHAT JUST HAPPENED? WHERE DID SKY HIGH GO?
AND ROCK BISON HAD THE "BUNNY" PRESENT.
BUNNY PRES-ENT?
BEEP

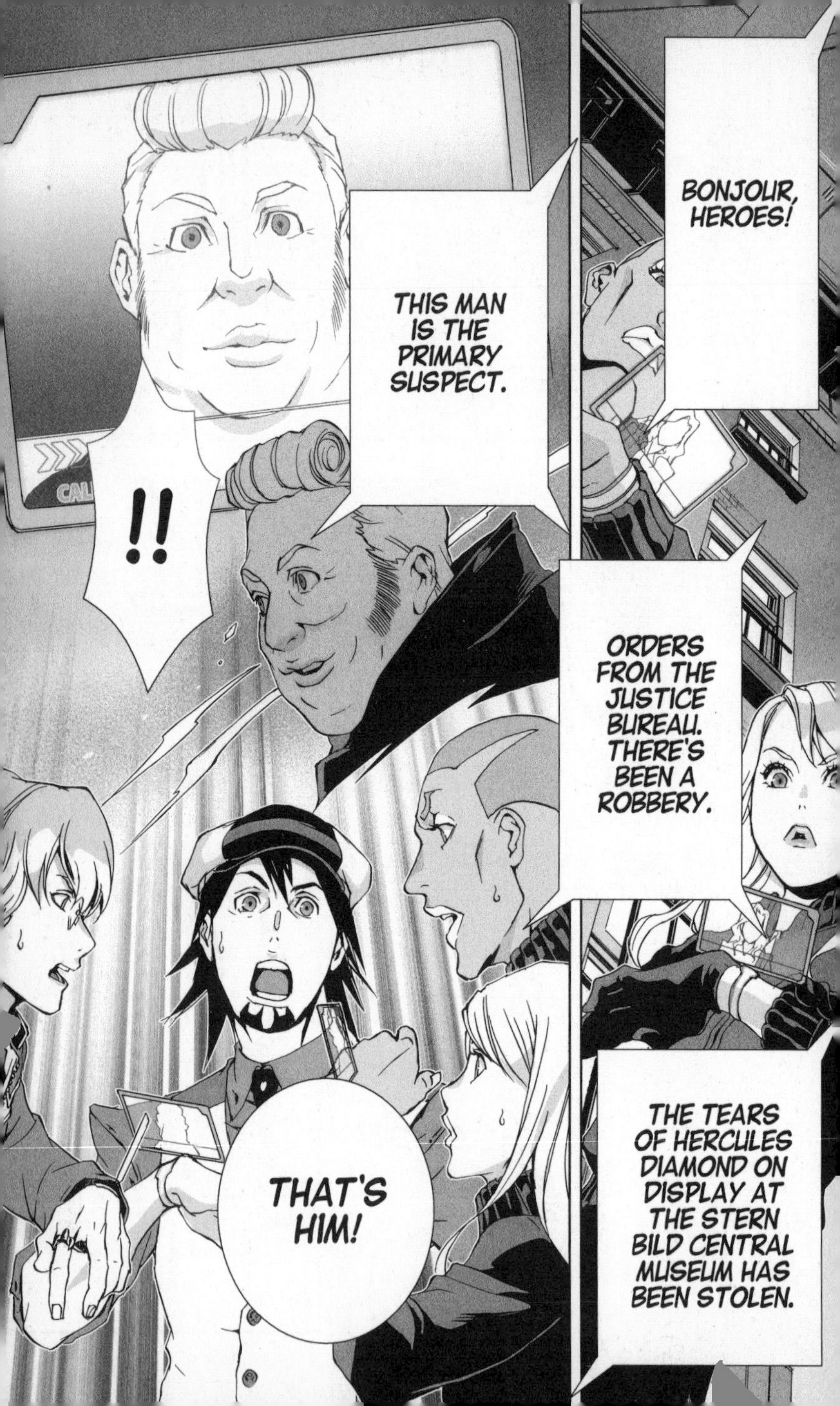
BONJOUR, HEROES!
ORDERS FROM THE JUSTICE BUREAU. THERE'S BEEN A ROBBERY.
THE TEARS OF HERCULES DIAMOND ON DISPLAY AT THE STERN BILD CENTRAL MUSEUM HAS BEEN STOLEN.
THIS MAN IS THE PRIMARY SUSPECT.
!!
THAT'S HIM!

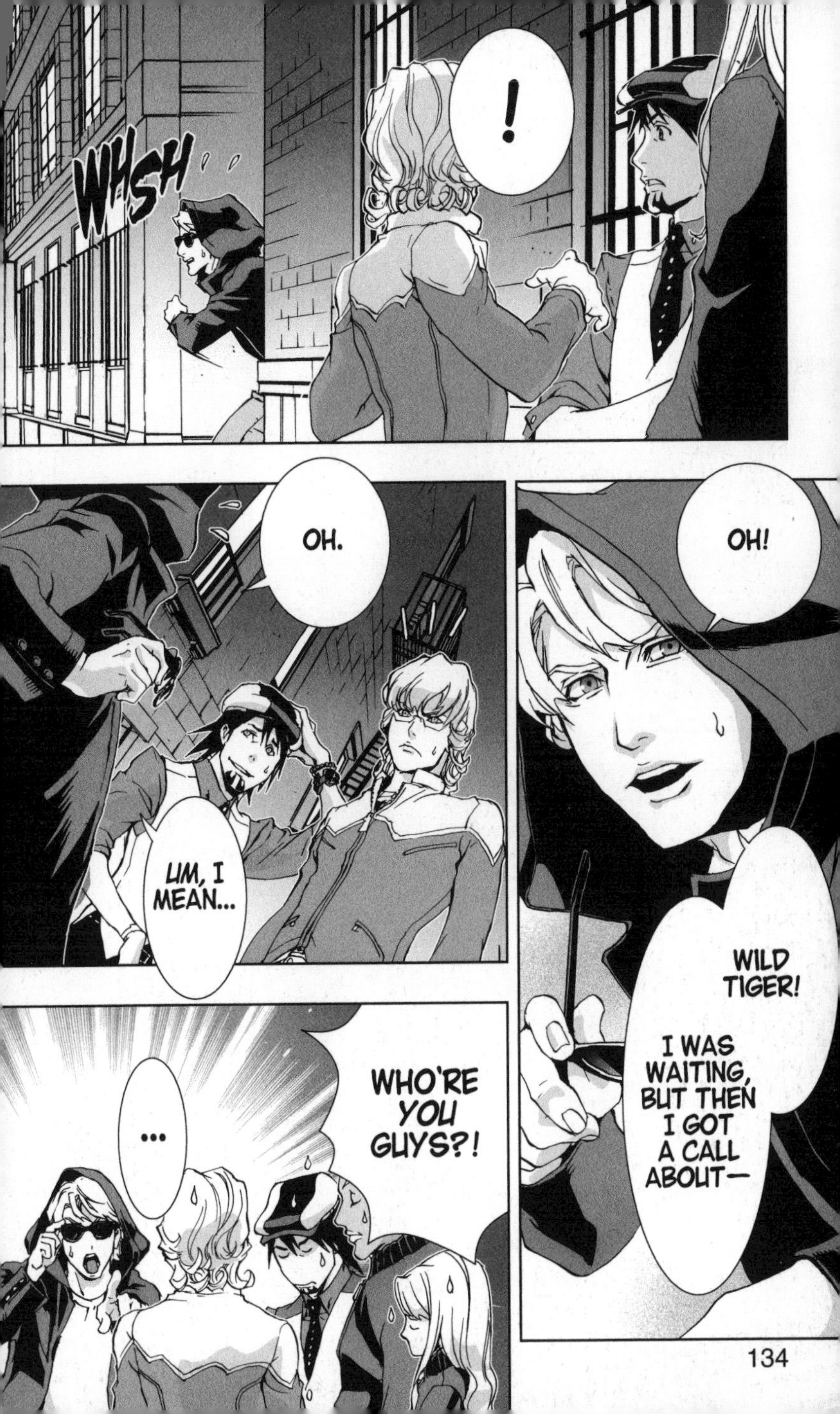
!
WHSH
OH!
WILD TIGER!
I WAS WAITING, BUT THEN I GOT A CALL ABOUT—
OH.
UM, I MEAN...
WHO'RE YOU GUYS?!
...

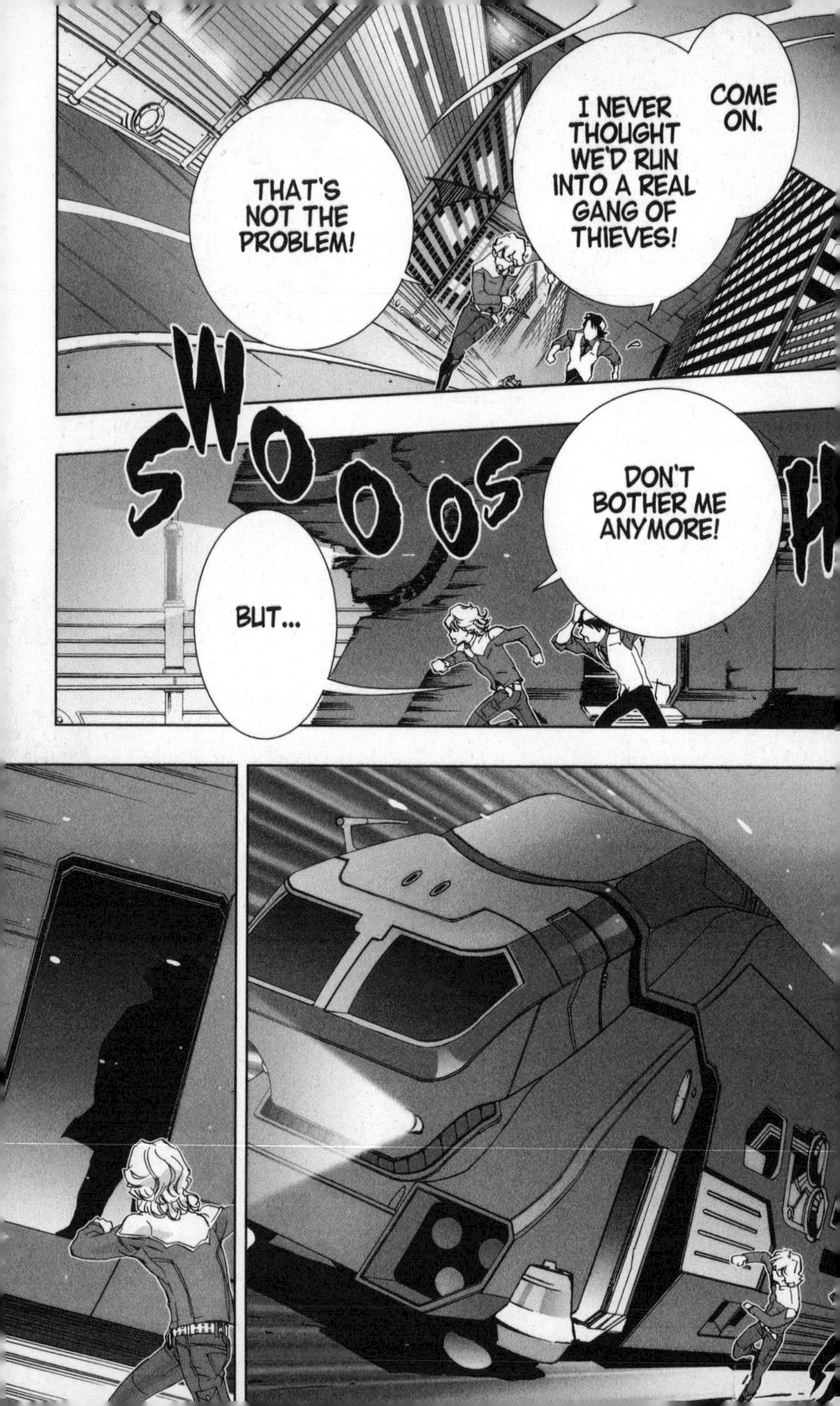
COME ON.
I NEVER THOUGHT WE'D RUN INTO A REAL GANG OF THIEVES!
THAT'S NOT THE PROBLEM!
SWOOOSH
DON'T BOTHER ME ANYMORE!
BUT...

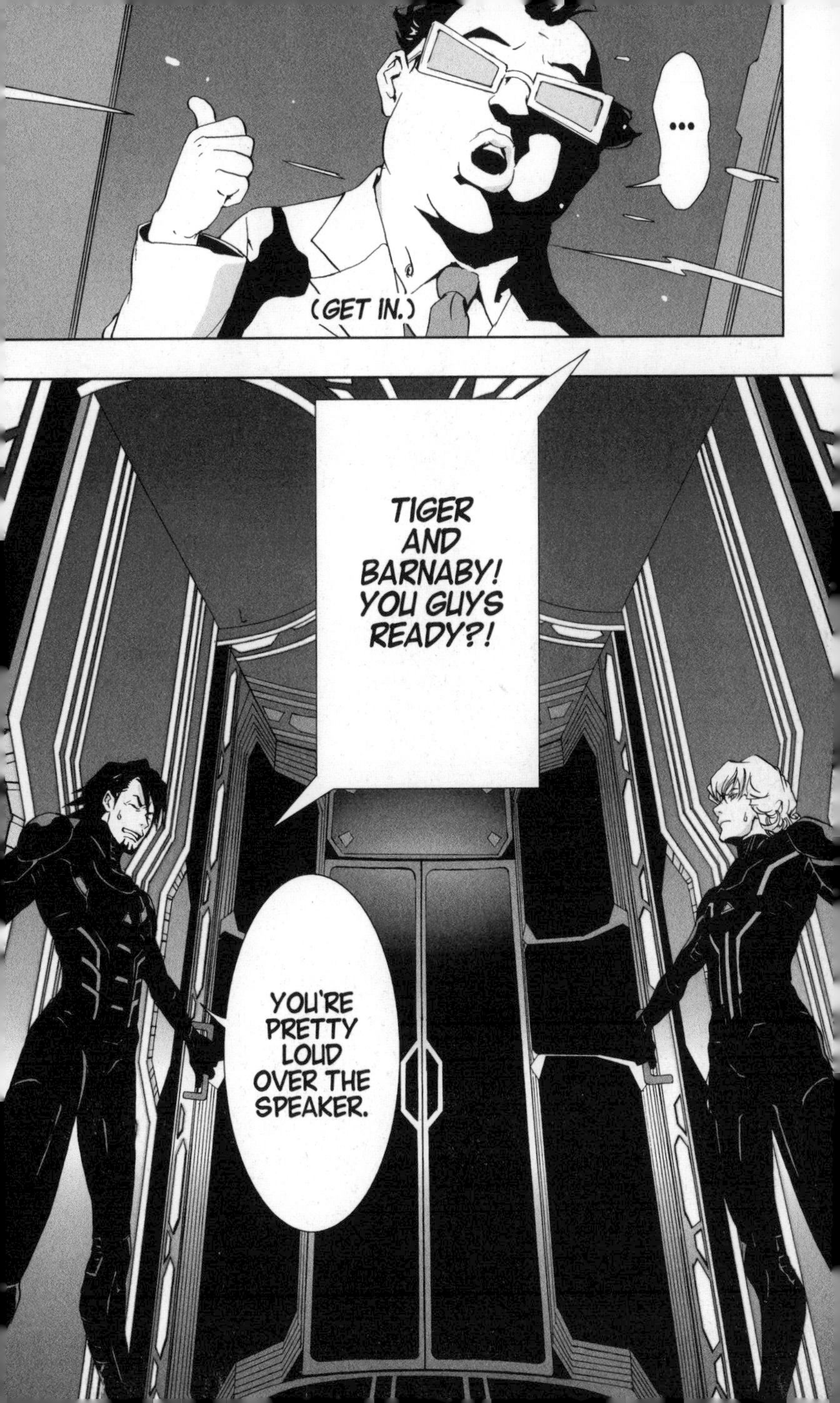
...
(GET IN.)
TIGER AND BARNABY! YOU GUYS READY?!
YOU'RE PRETTY LOUD OVER THE SPEAKER.

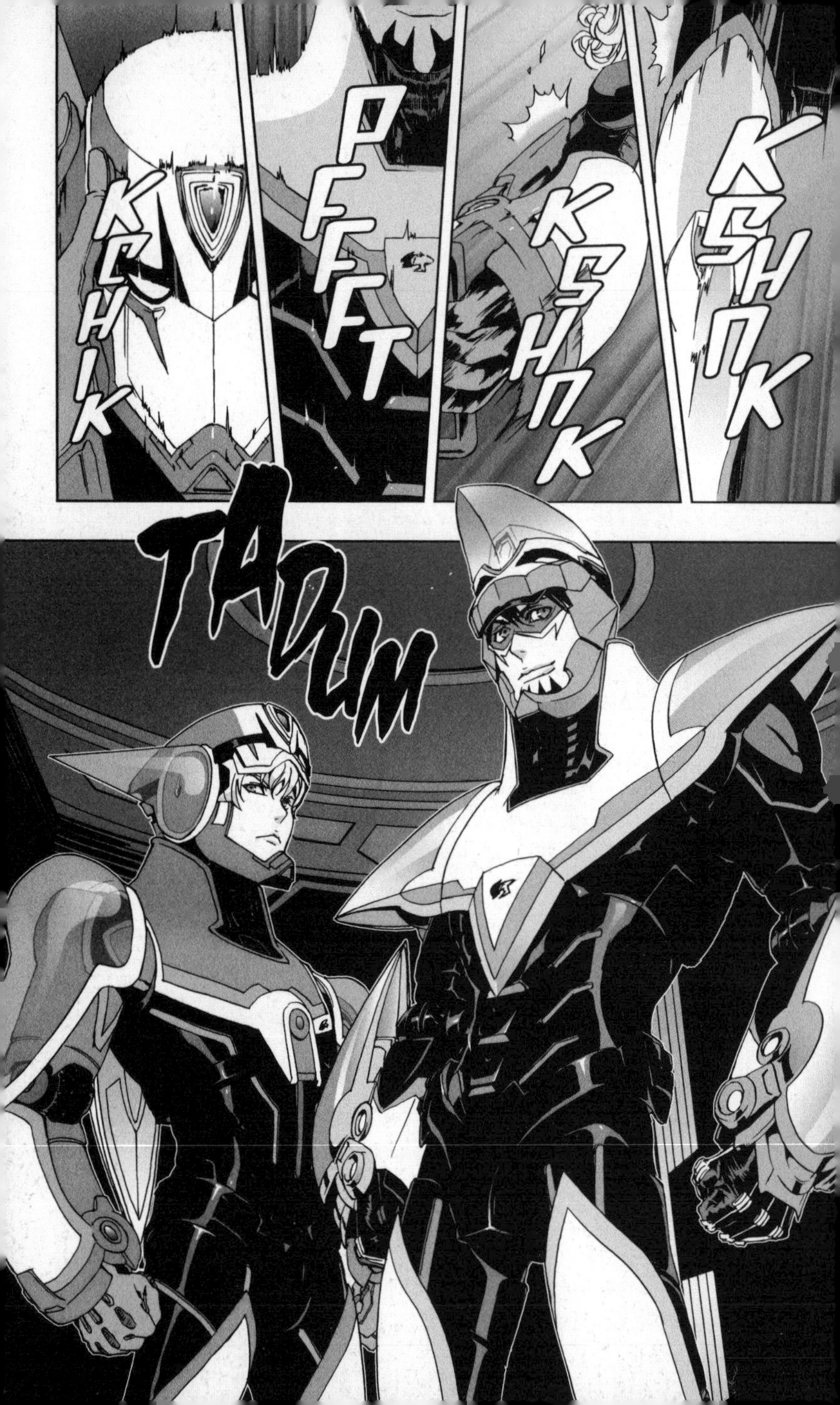
KSHNK
KSHNK
PFFFT
KCHIK
TADUM

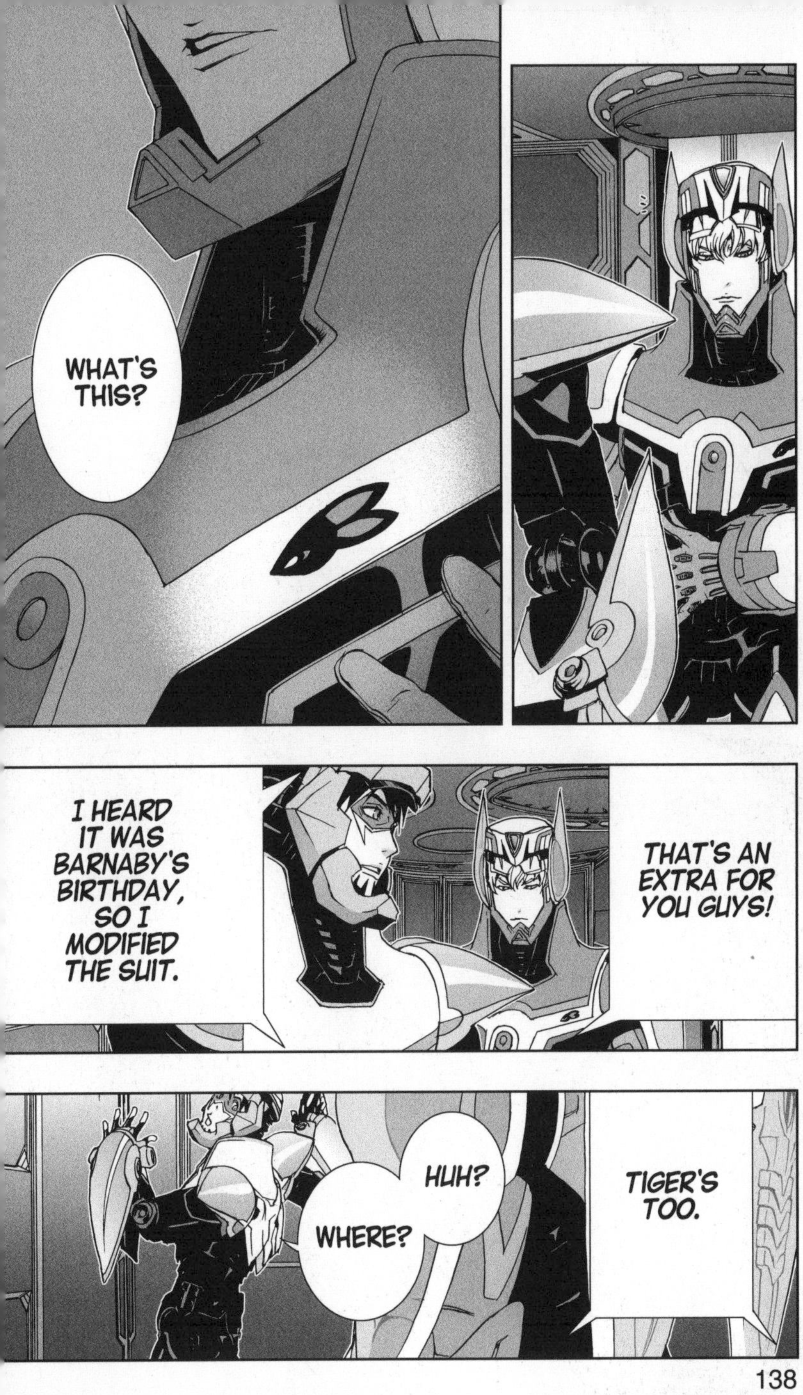
WHAT'S THIS?
THAT'S AN EXTRA FOR YOU GUYS!
I HEARD IT WAS BARNABY'S BIRTHDAY, SO I MODIFIED THE SUIT.
TIGER'S TOO.
HUH?
WHERE?

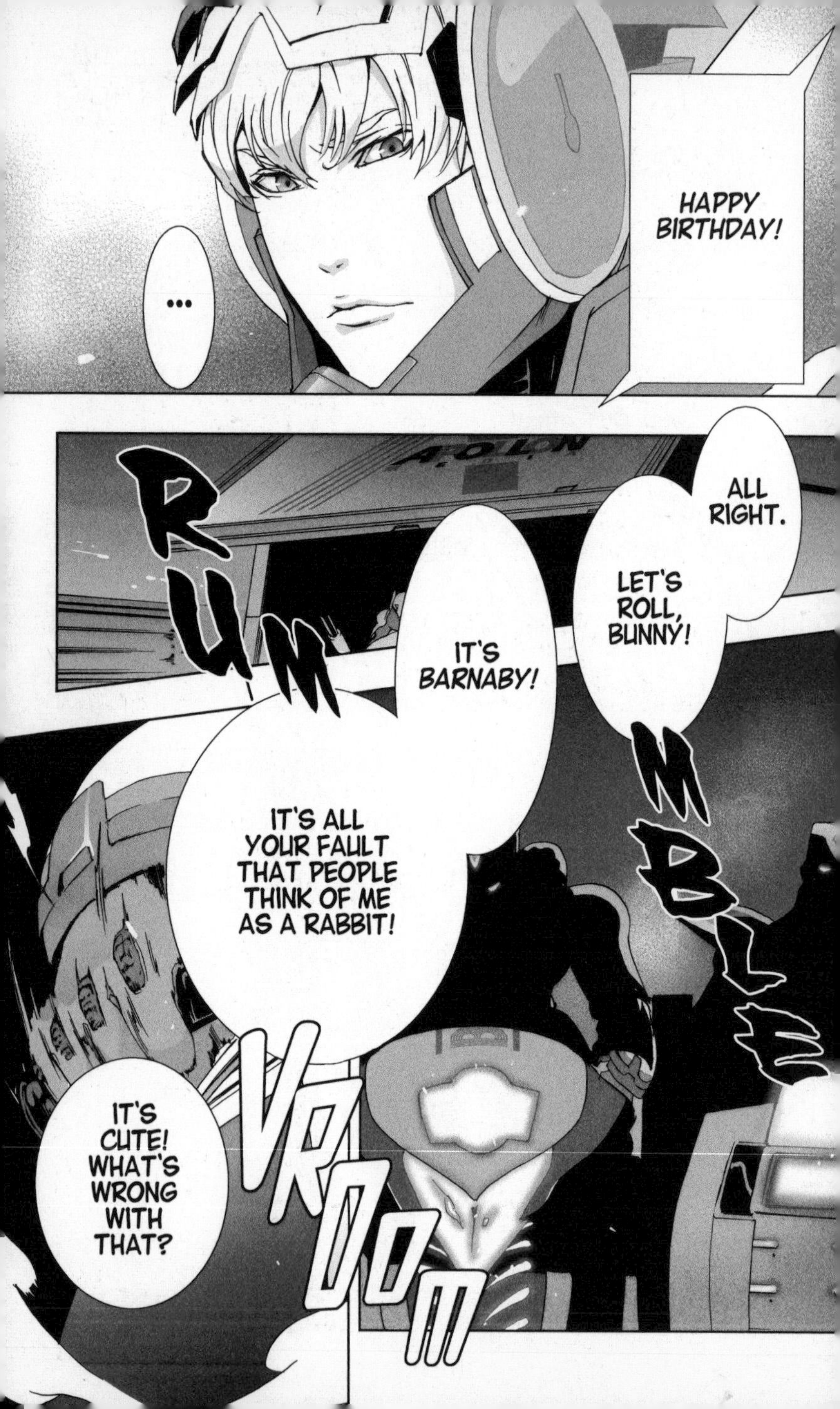
HAPPY BIRTHDAY!
...
ALL RIGHT.
LET'S ROLL, BUNNY!
IT'S BARNABY!
RUMMBLE
IT'S ALL YOUR FAULT THAT PEOPLE THINK OF ME AS A RABBIT!
VROOM
IT'S CUTE! WHAT'S WRONG WITH THAT?

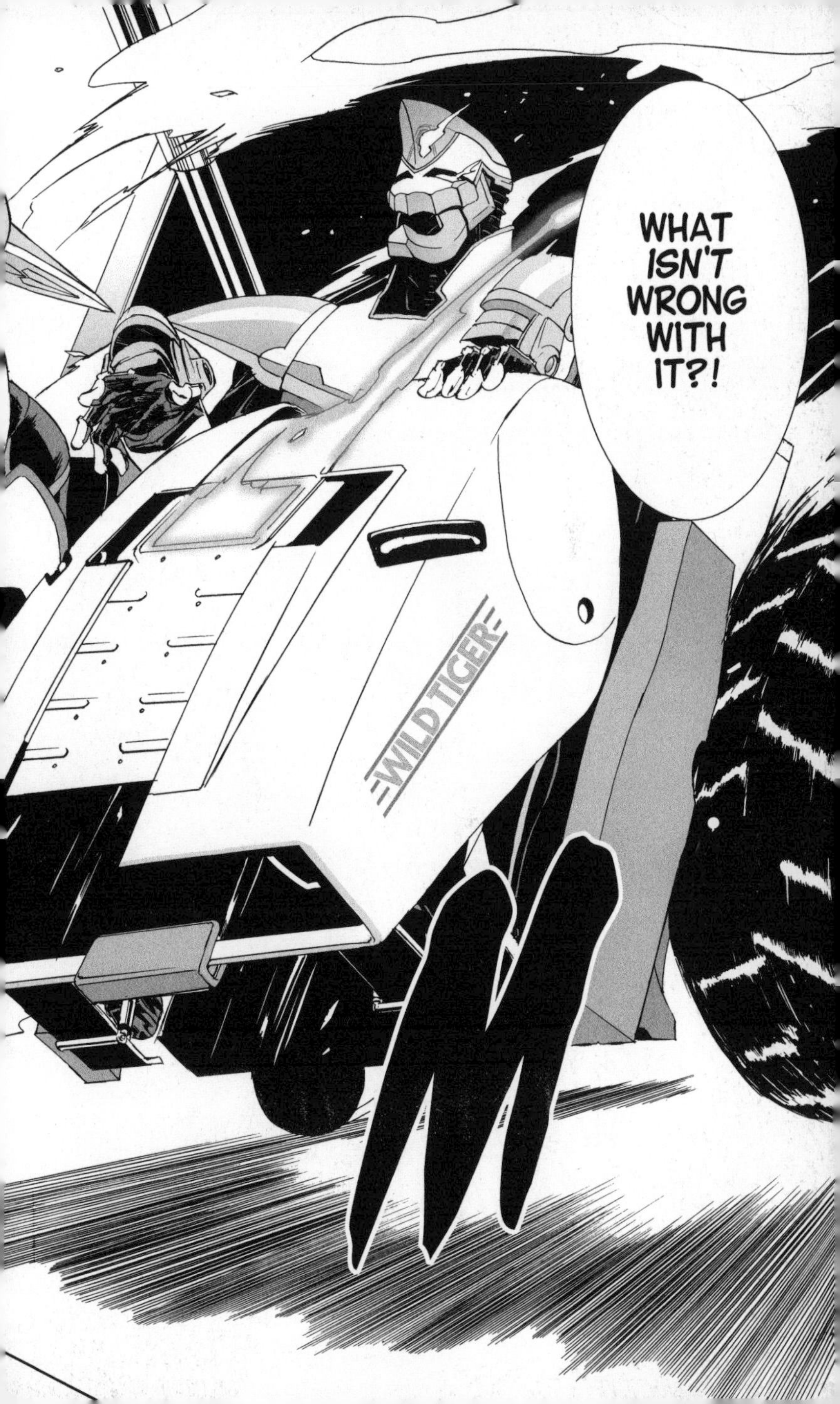
WHAT ISN'T WRONG WITH IT?!
WILD TIGER

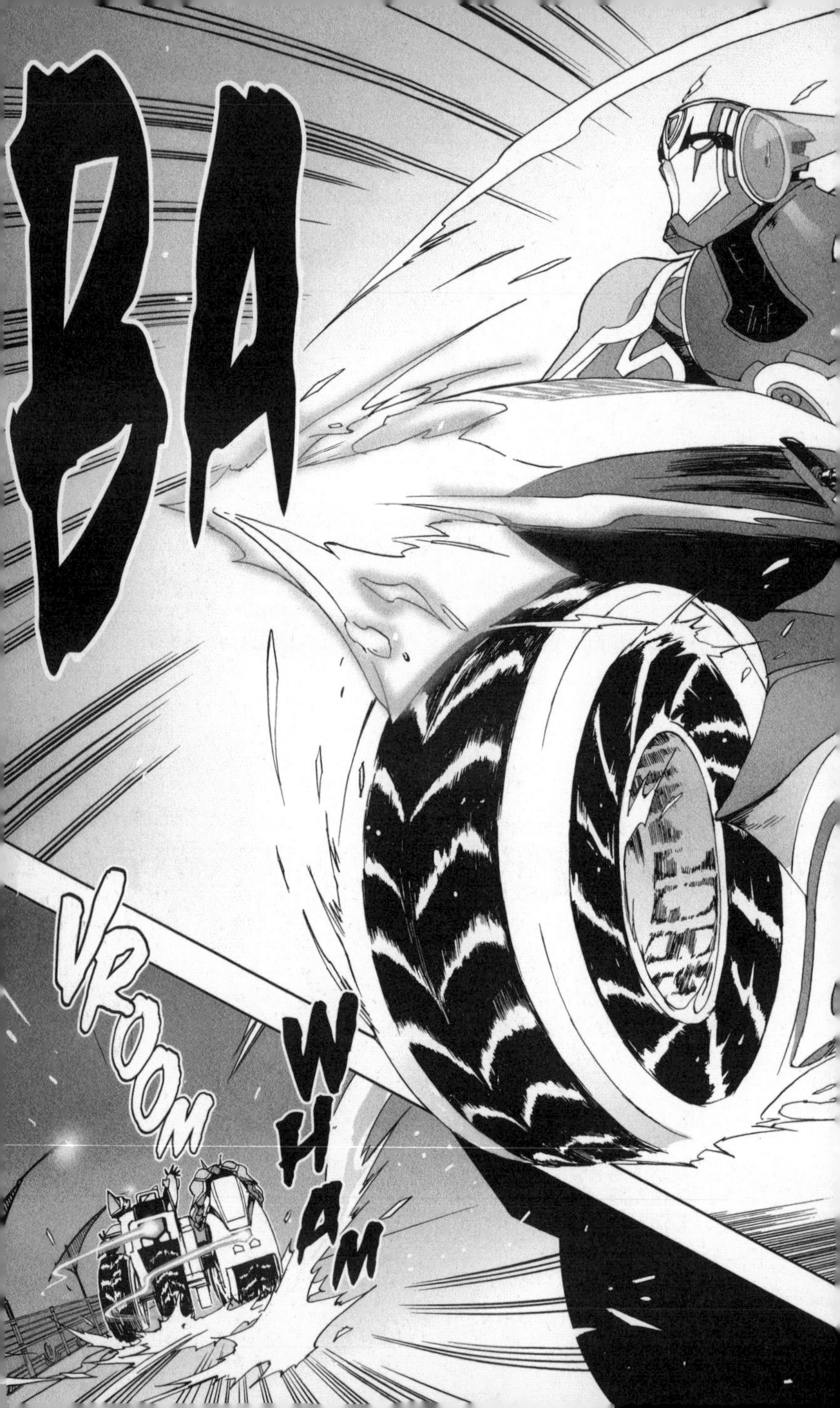
BA
WHAM
VROOM

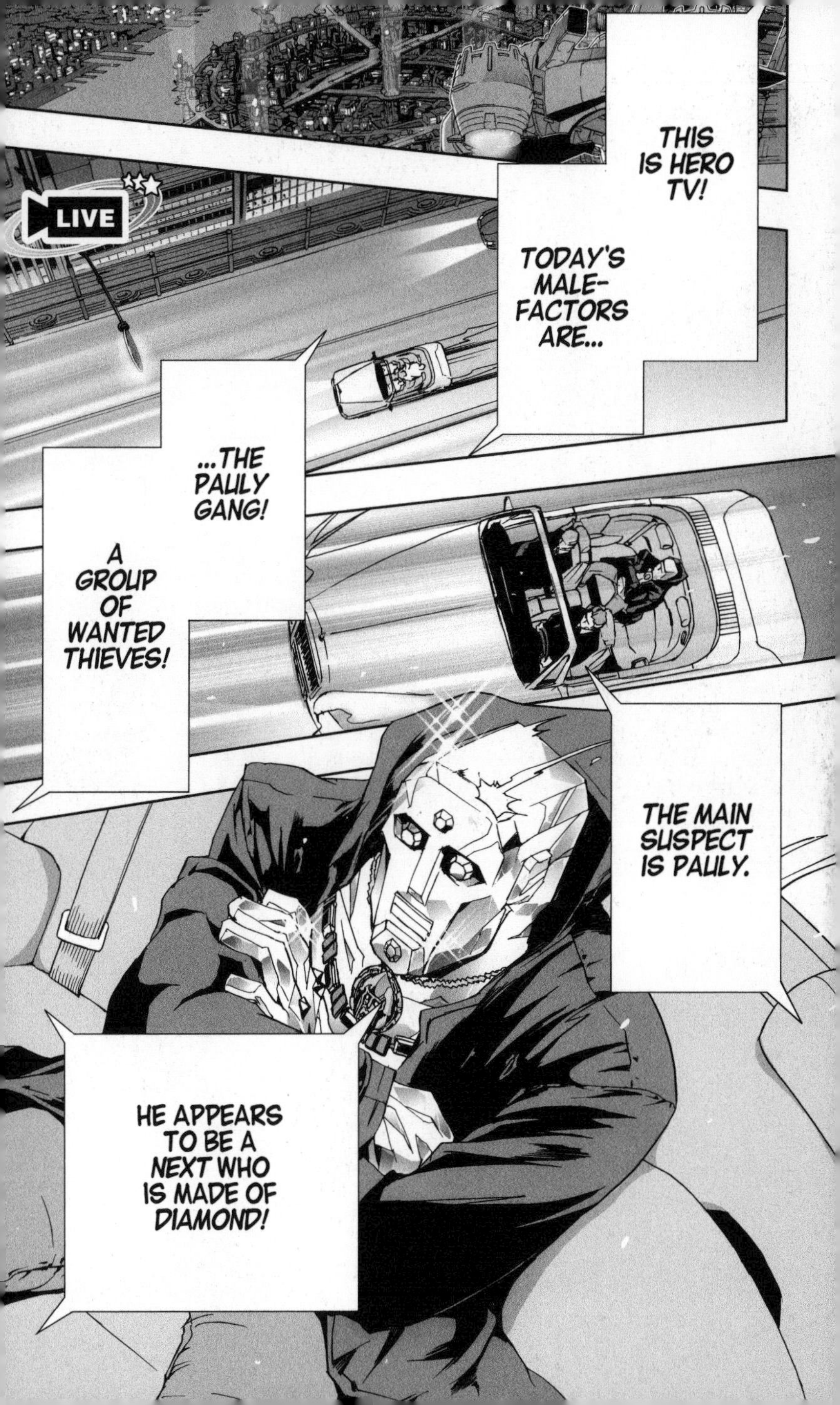

LIVE
THIS IS HERO TV!
TODAY'S MALE-FACTORS ARE...
...THE PAULY GANG!
A GROUP OF WANTED THIEVES!
THE MAIN SUSPECT IS PAULY.
HE APPEARS TO BE A NEXT WHO IS MADE OF DIAMOND!

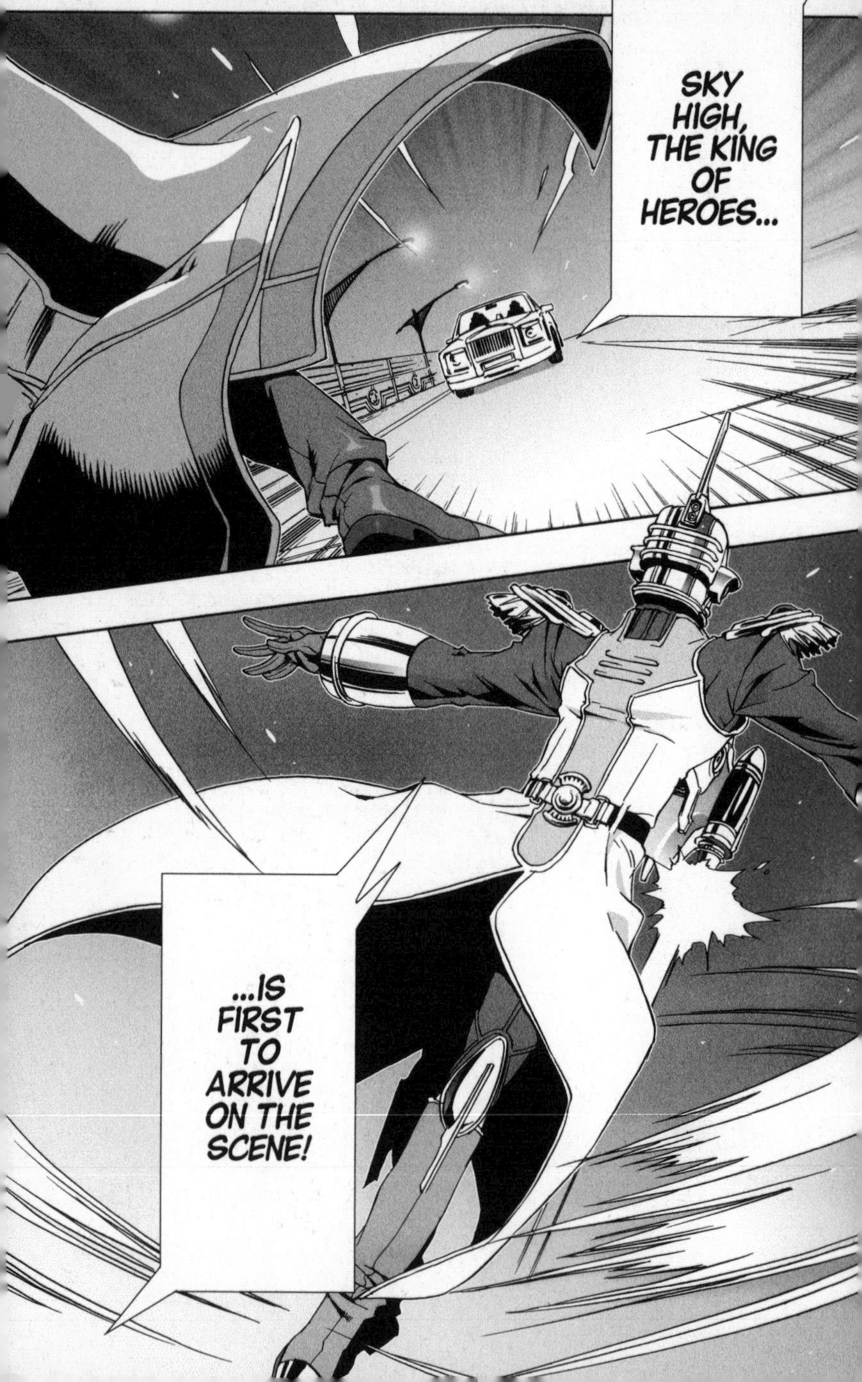
SKY HIGH, THE KING OF HEROES...
...IS FIRST TO ARRIVE ON THE SCENE!

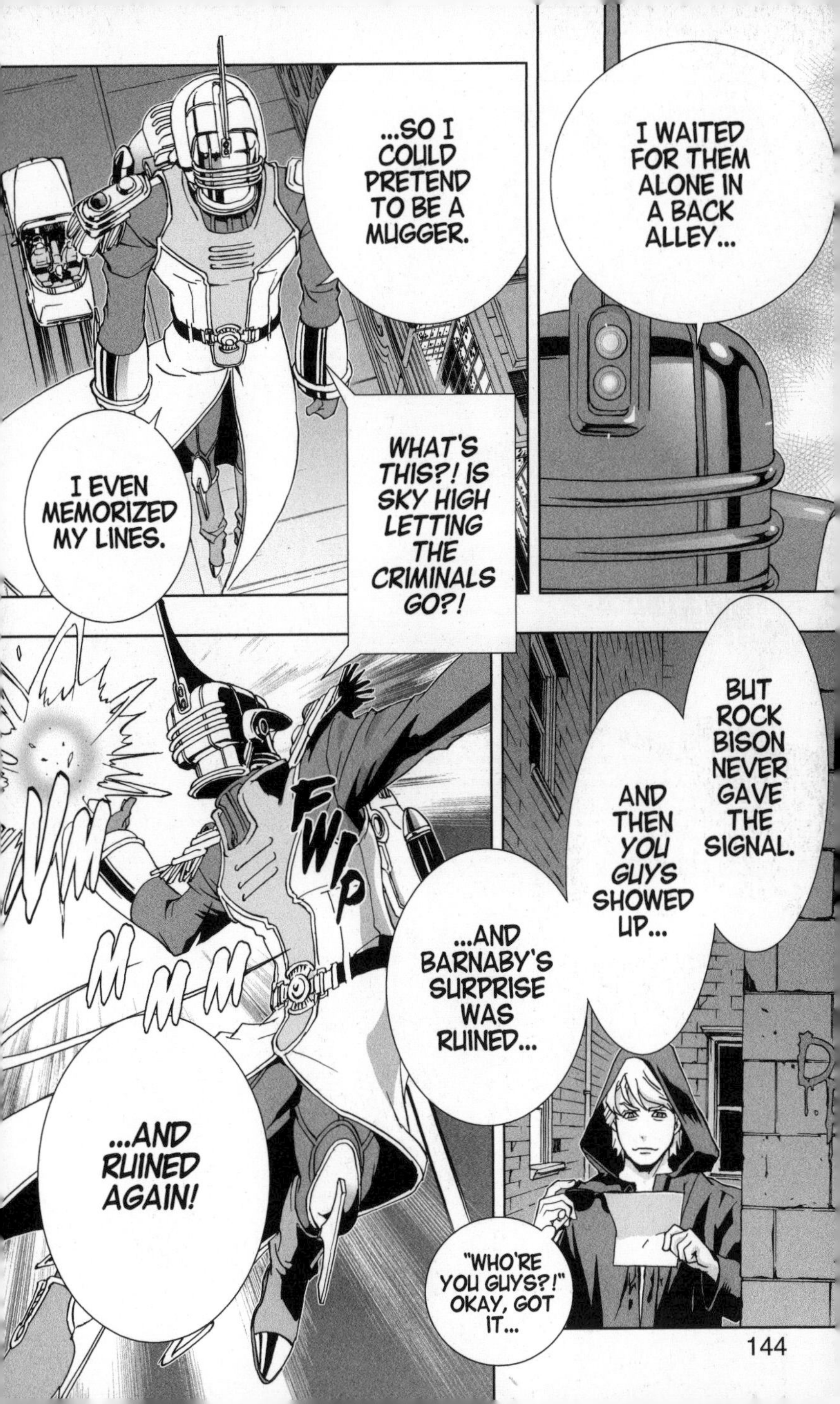
I WAITED FOR THEM ALONE IN A BACK ALLEY...
...SO I COULD PRETEND TO BE A MUGGER.
I EVEN MEMORIZED MY LINES.
BUT ROCK BISON NEVER GAVE THE SIGNAL.
AND THEN YOU GUYS SHOWED UP...
...AND BARNABY'S SURPRISE WAS RUINED...
"WHO'RE YOU GUYS?!" OKAY, GOT IT...
WHAT'S THIS?! IS SKY HIGH LETTING THE CRIMINALS GO?!
FWIP
VMMMM
...AND RUINED AGAIN!

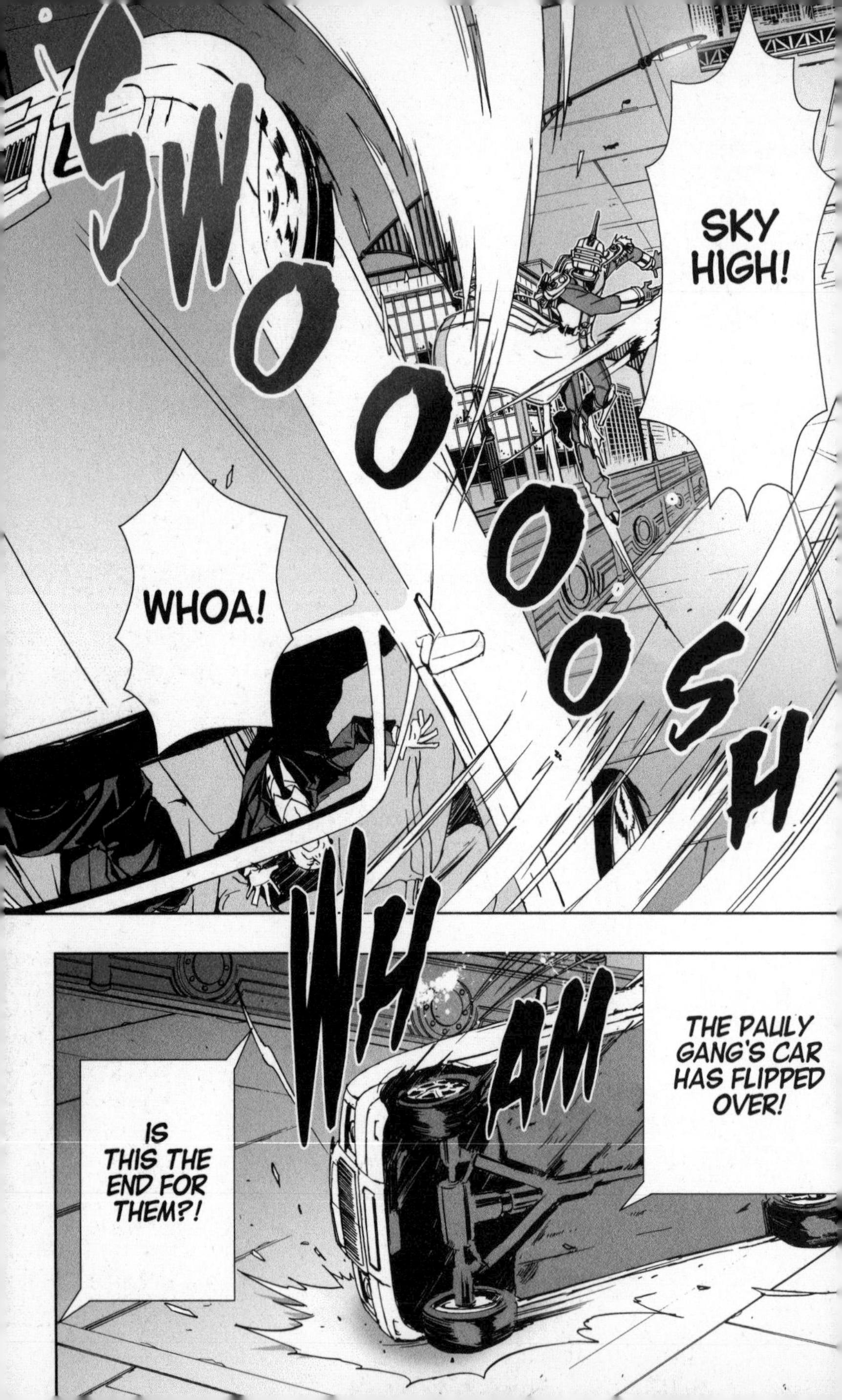
SKY HIGH!
SWOOOOOSH
WHOA!
THE PAULY GANG'S CAR HAS FLIPPED OVER!
WHAM
IS THIS THE END FOR THEM?!

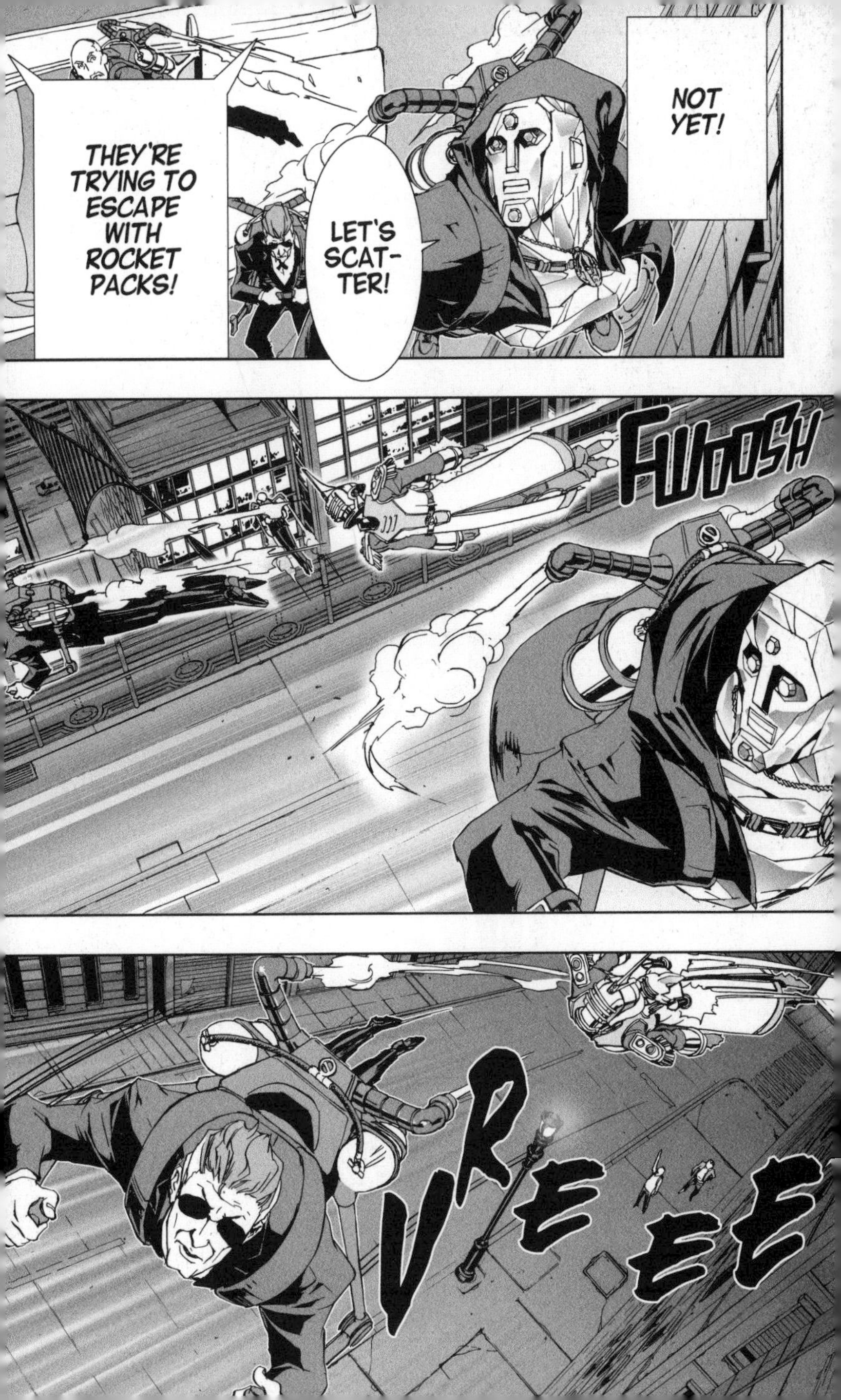
NOT YET!
THEY'RE TRYING TO ESCAPE WITH ROCKET PACKS!
LET'S SCAT-TER!
FWOOSH
VREEEE

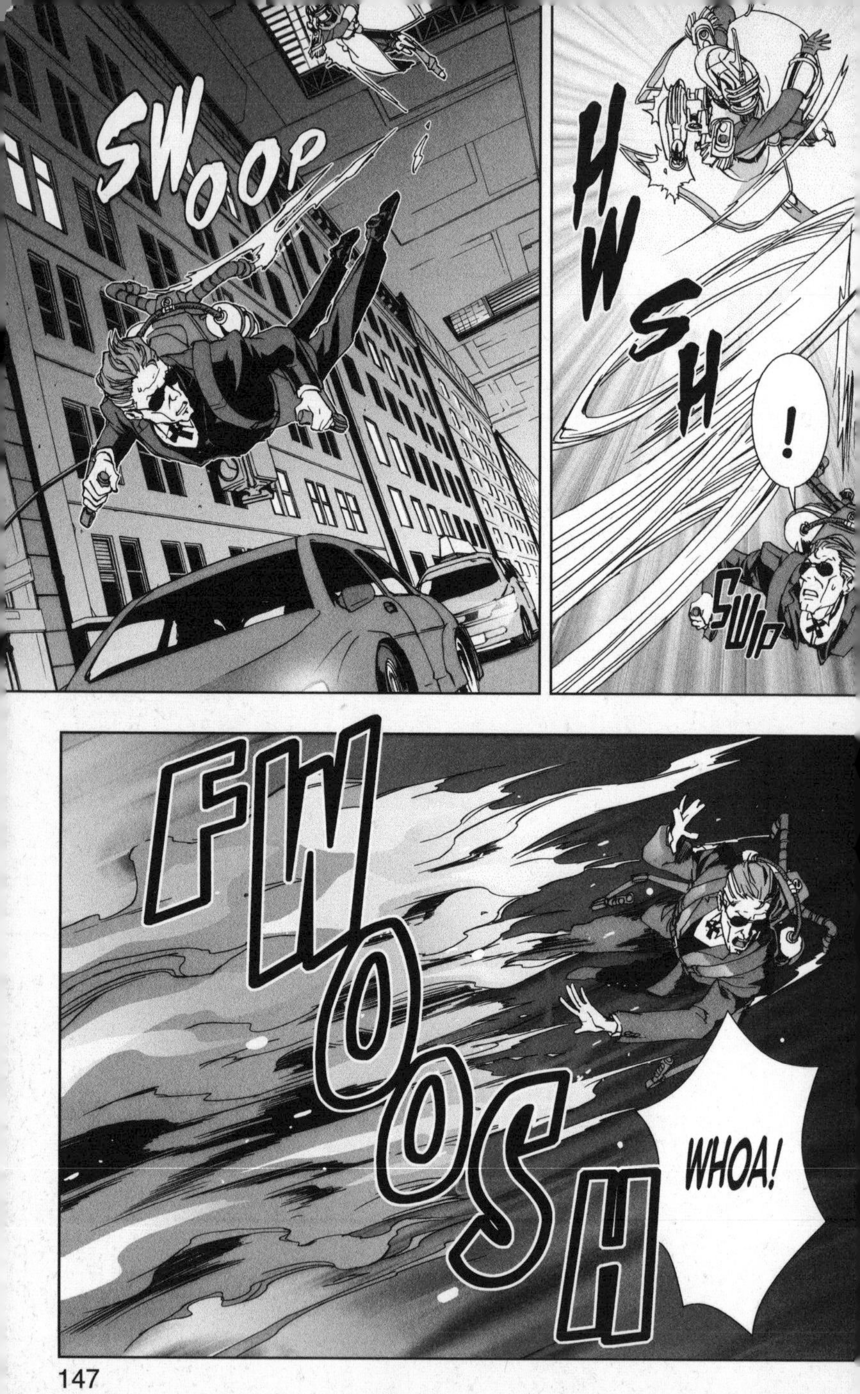
HWWSH
!
SWIP
SWOOP
FWOOOSH
WHOA!

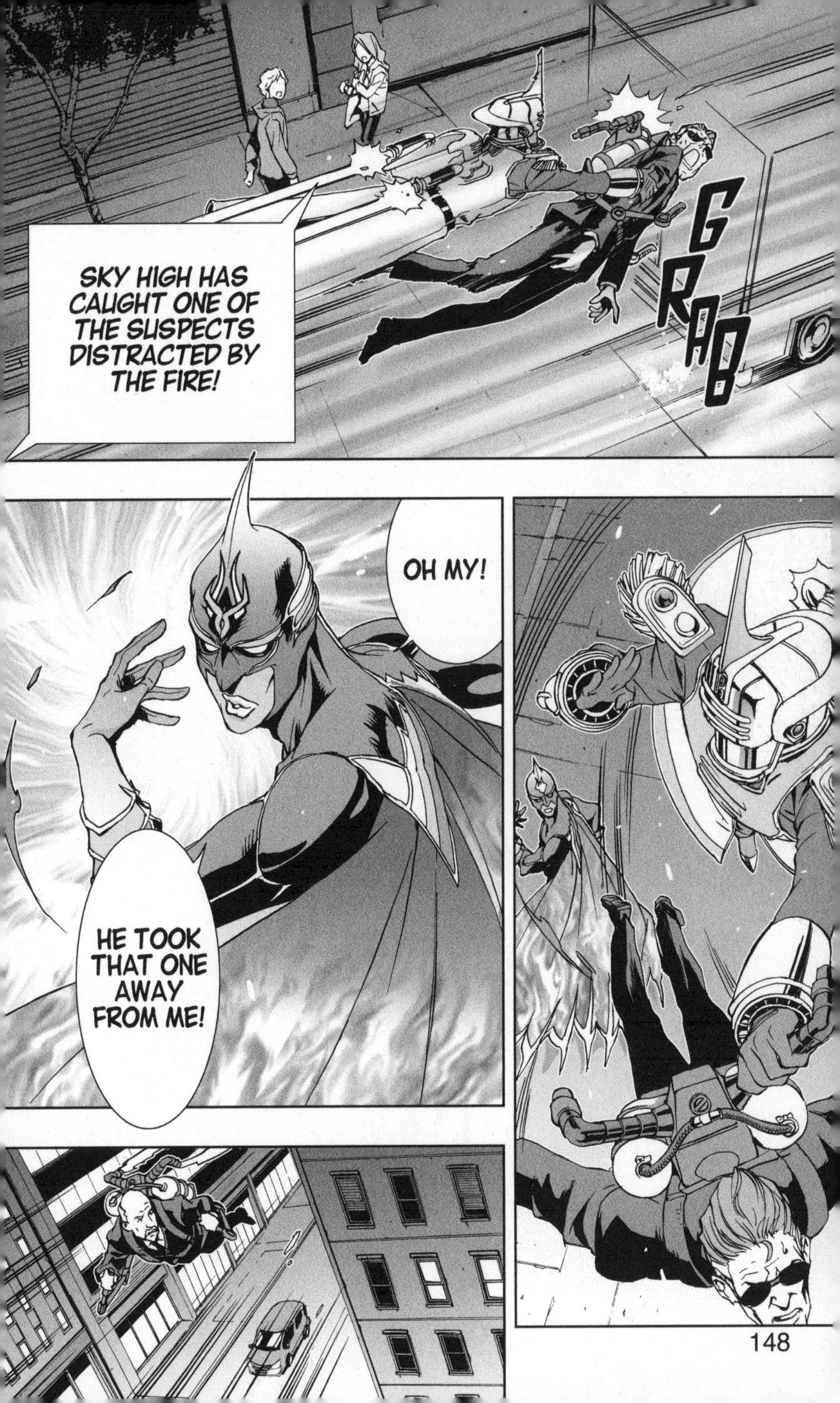
SKY HIGH HAS CAUGHT ONE OF THE SUSPECTS DISTRACTED BY THE FIRE!
GRAB
OH MY!
HE TOOK THAT ONE AWAY FROM ME!

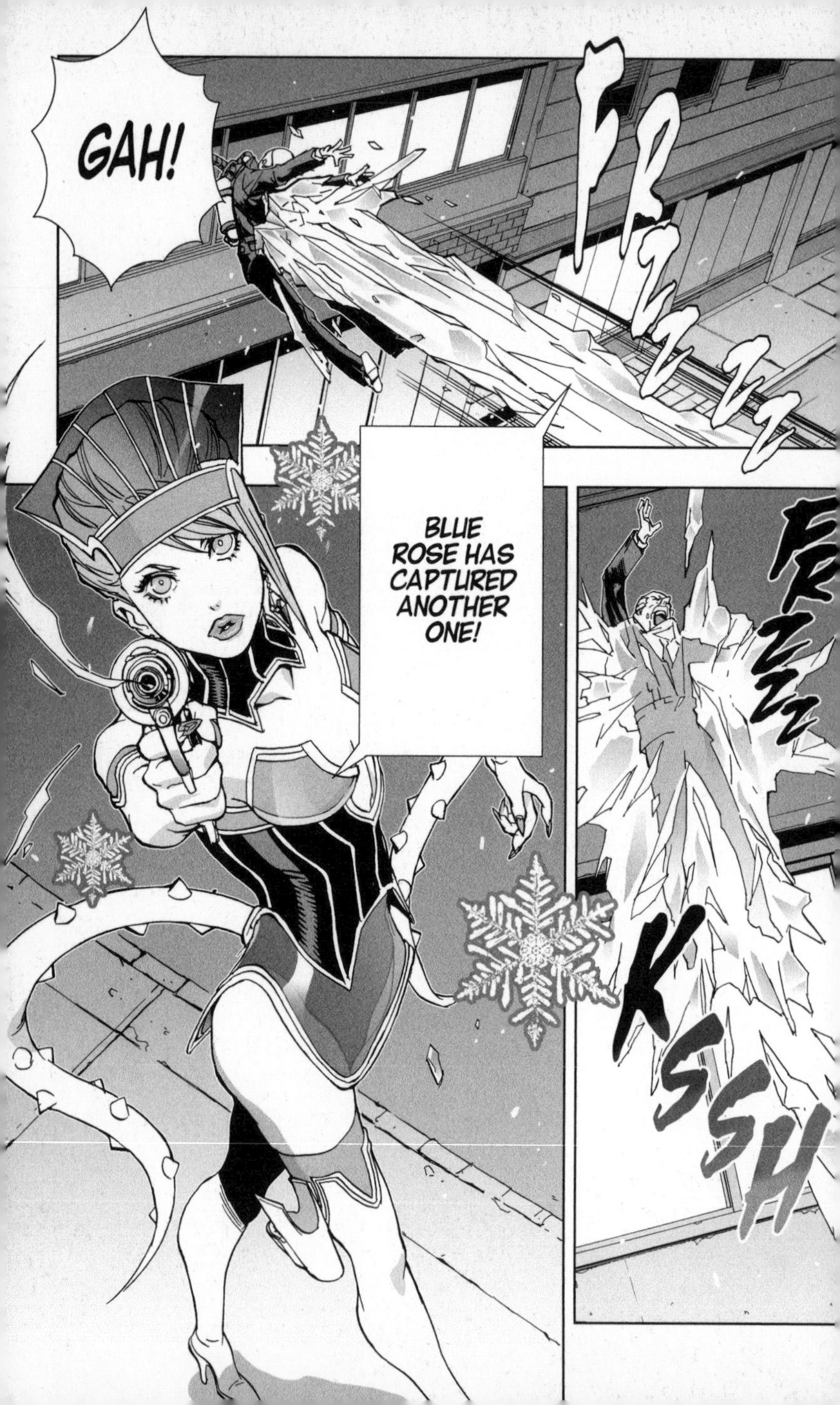
FRZZZZZZ
GAH!
FRZZZ
KSSH
BLUE ROSE HAS CAPTURED ANOTHER ONE!

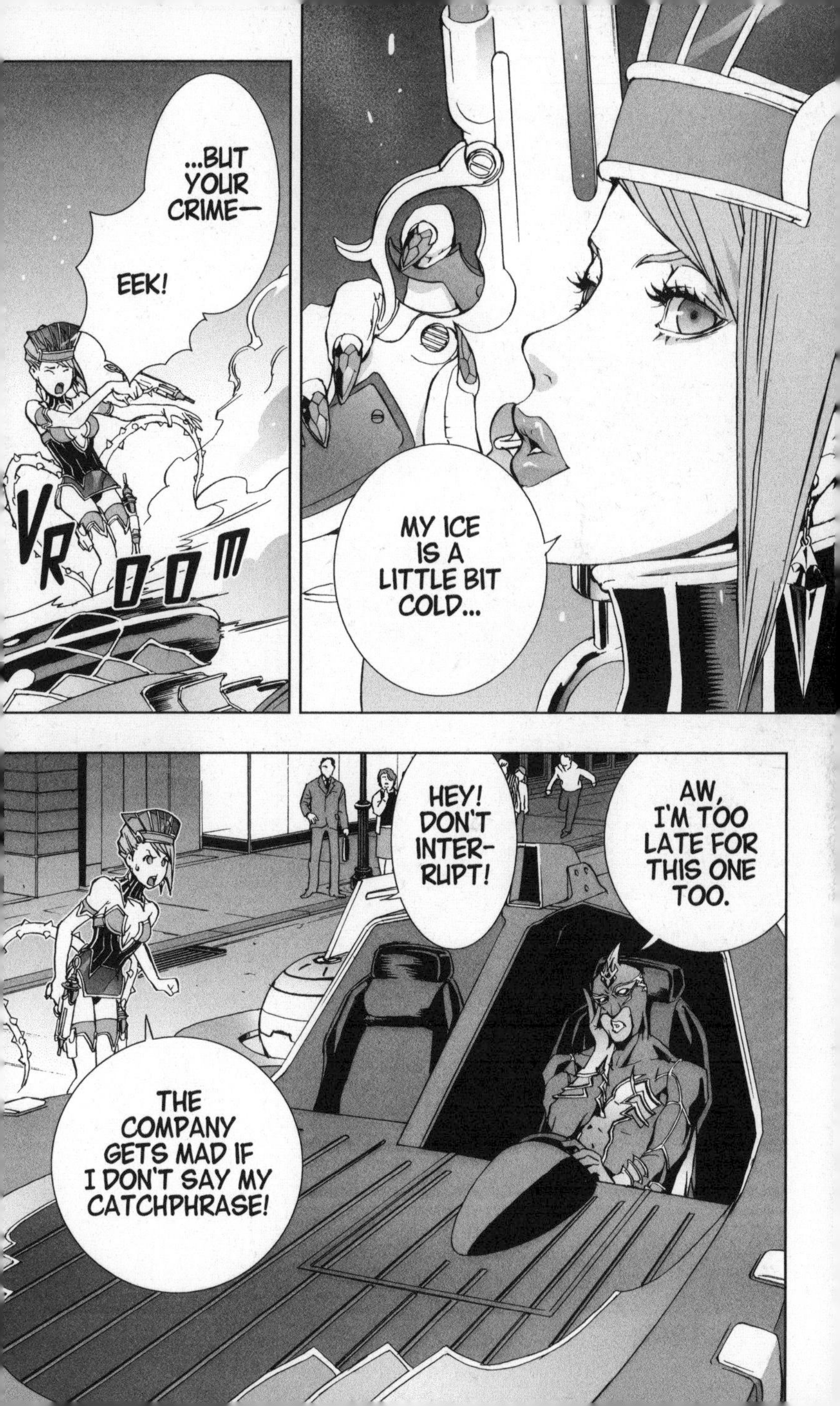
MY ICE IS A LITTLE BIT COLD...
...BUT YOUR CRIME—
EEK!
VROOM
AW, I'M TOO LATE FOR THIS ONE TOO.
HEY! DON'T INTER-RUPT!
THE COMPANY GETS MAD IF I DON'T SAY MY CATCHPHRASE!

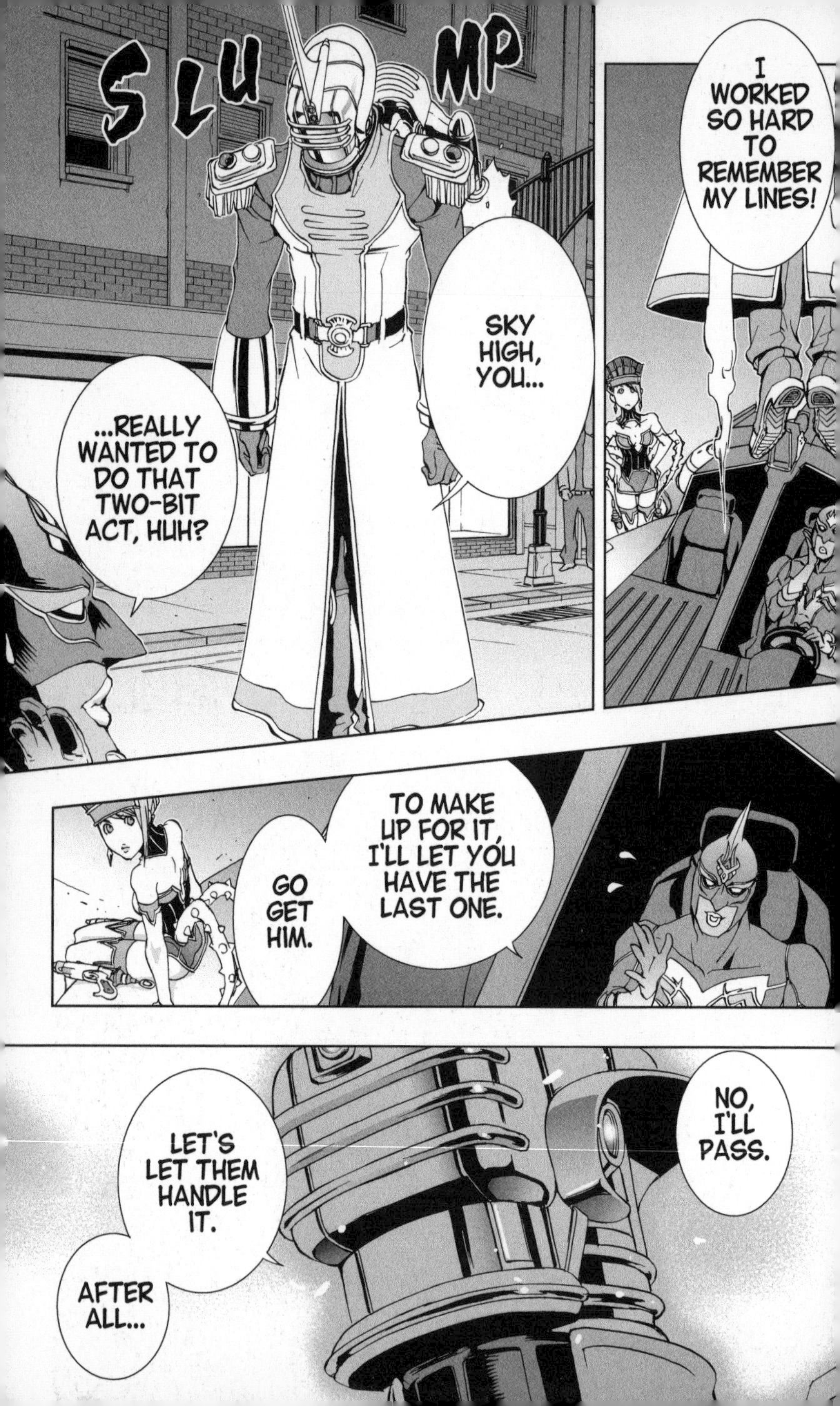
I WORKED SO HARD TO REMEMBER MY LINES!
SLUMP
SKY HIGH, YOU...
...REALLY WANTED TO DO THAT TWO-BIT ACT, HUH?
TO MAKE UP FOR IT, I'LL LET YOU HAVE THE LAST ONE.
GO GET HIM.
NO, I'LL PASS.
LET'S LET THEM HANDLE IT.
AFTER ALL...

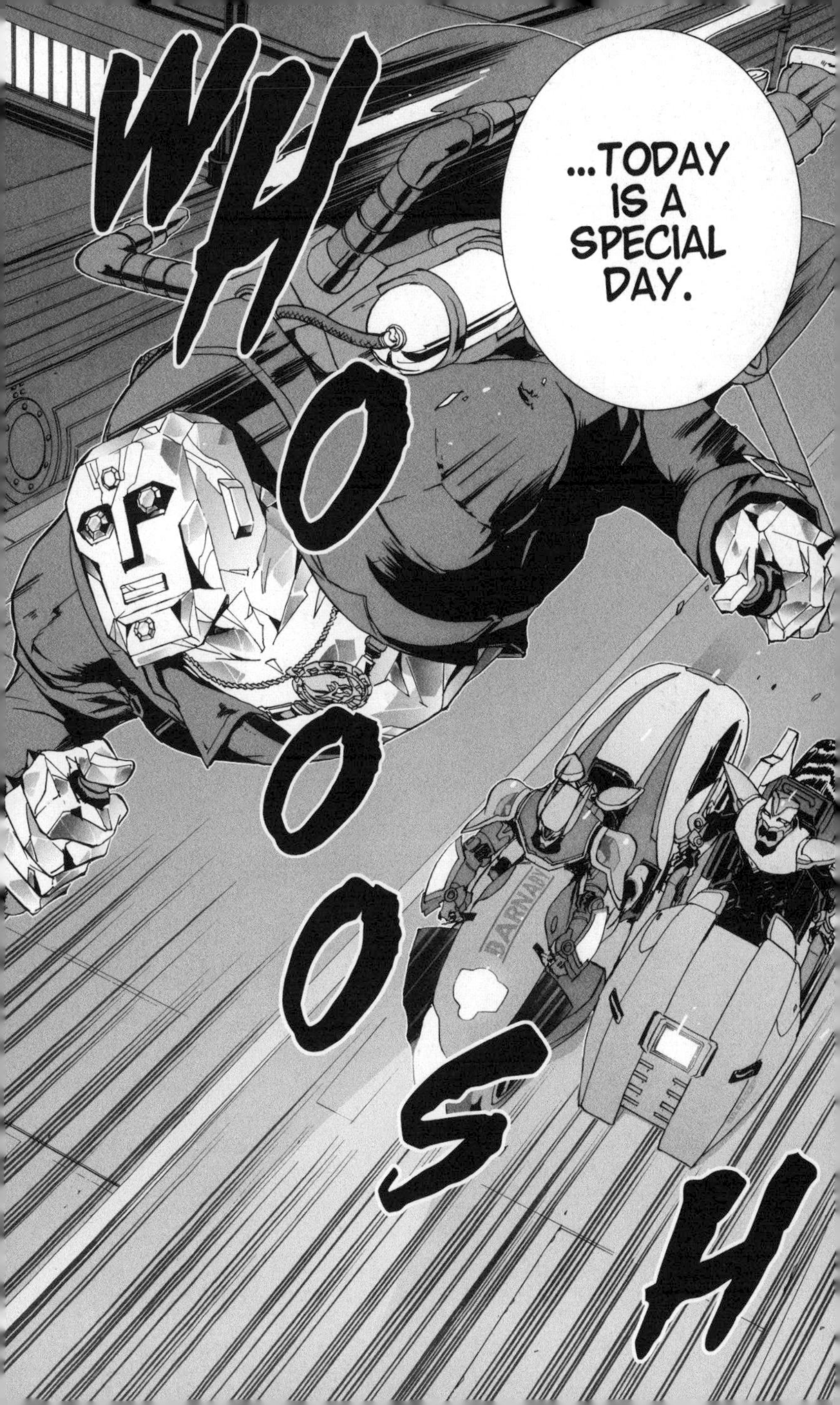
...TODAY IS A SPECIAL DAY.
WHOOOOSH
BARNABY

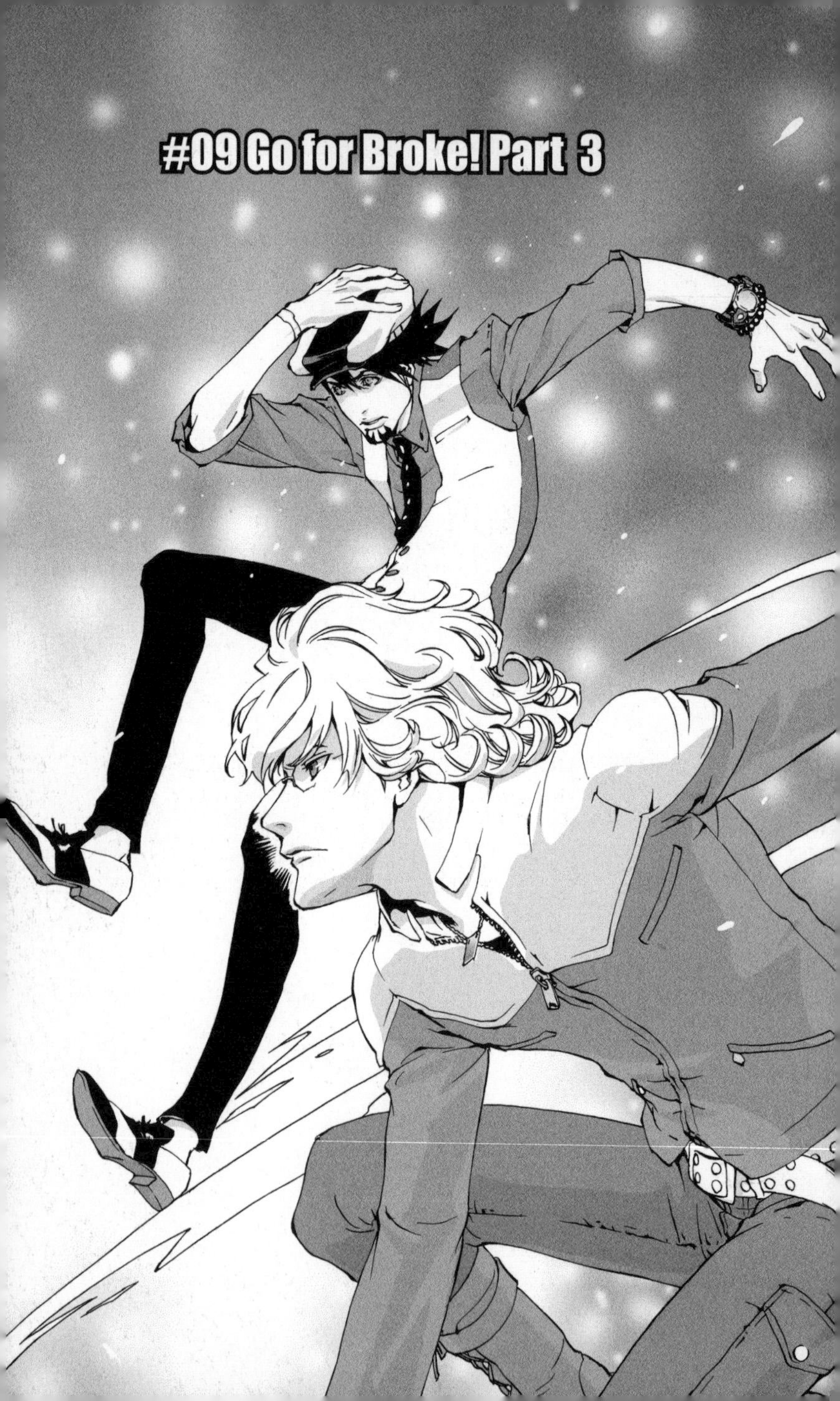
#09 Go for Broke! Part 3

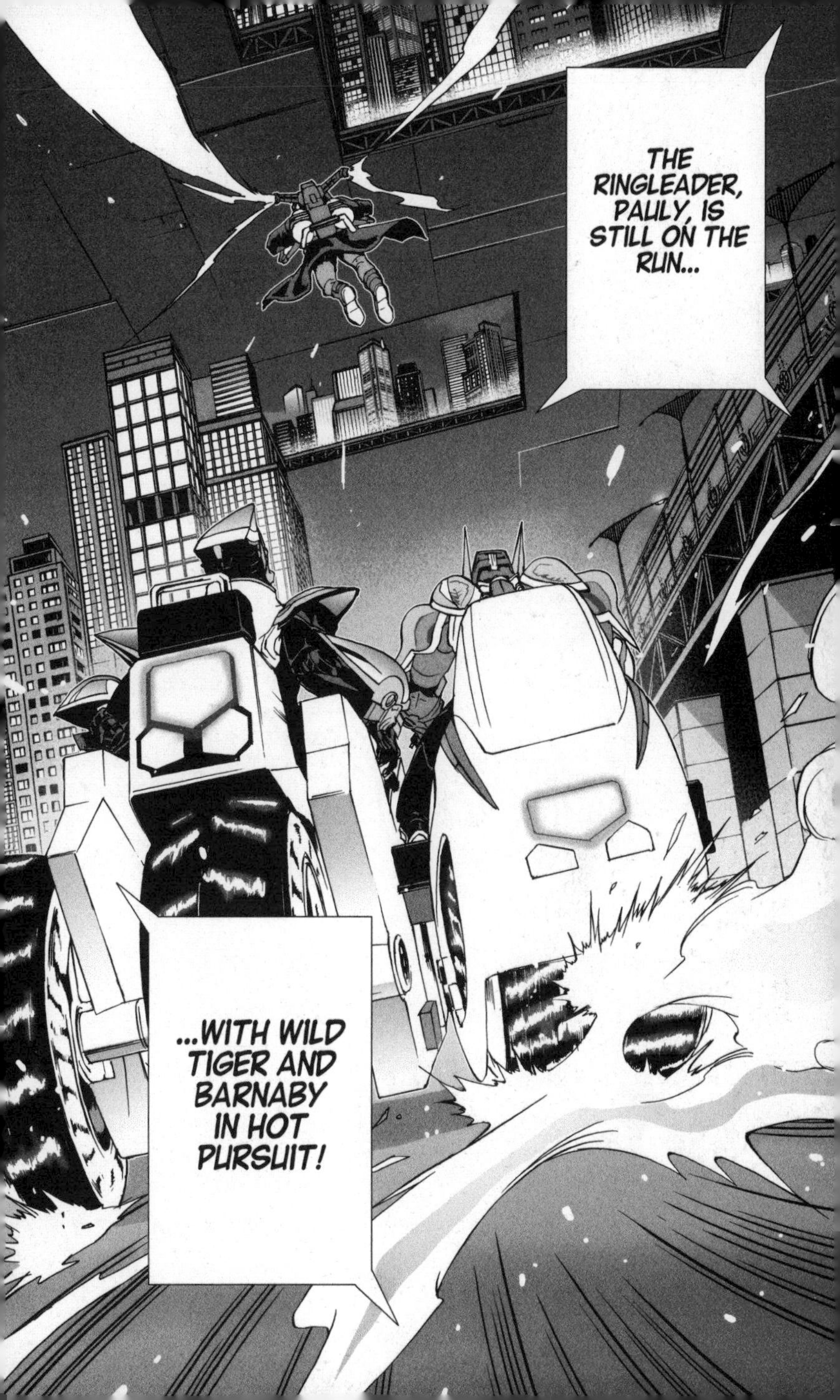
THE RINGLEADER, PAULY, IS STILL ON THE RUN...
...WITH WILD TIGER AND BARNABY IN HOT PURSUIT!

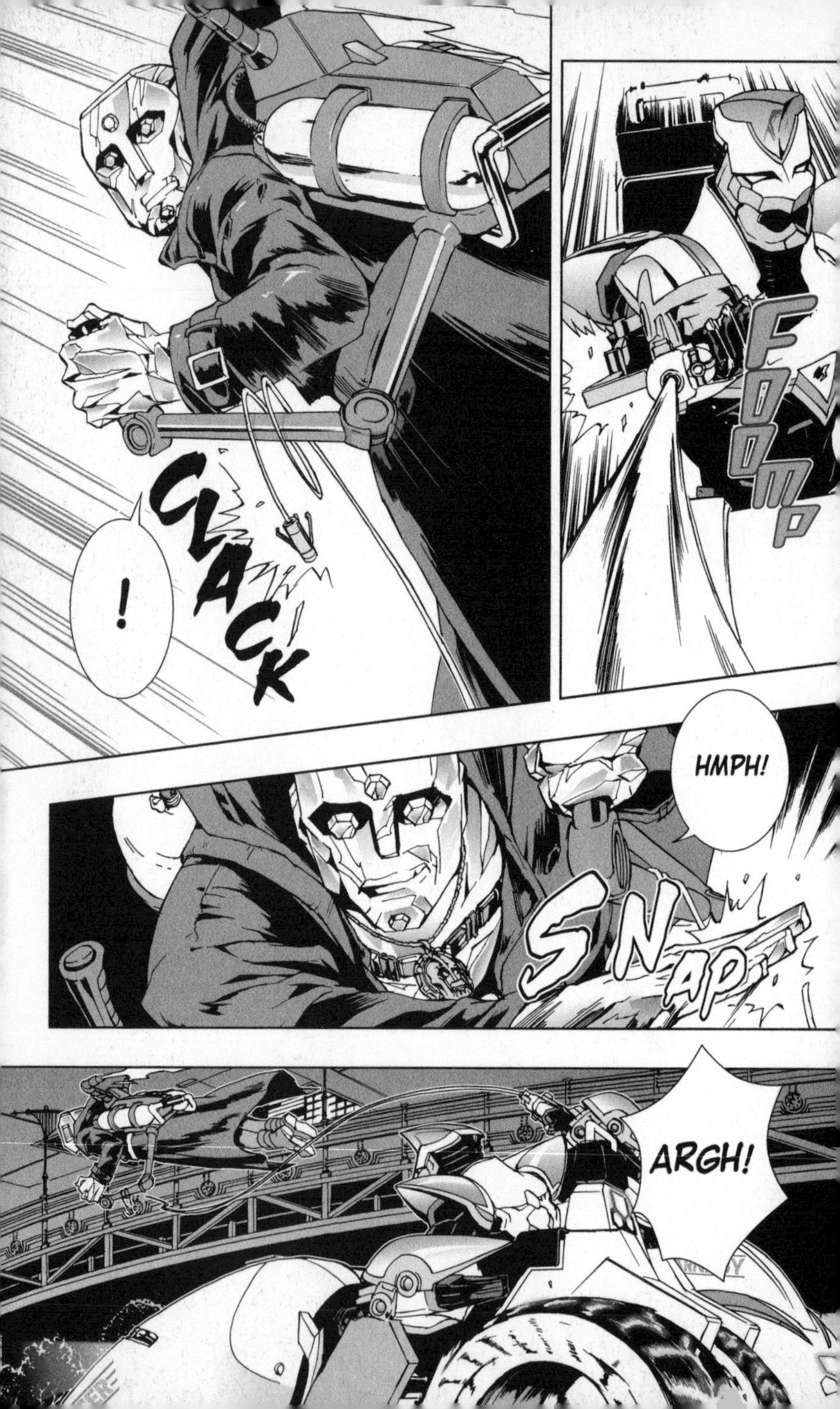
FDOMP
CLACK
!
HMPH!
SNAP
ARGH!

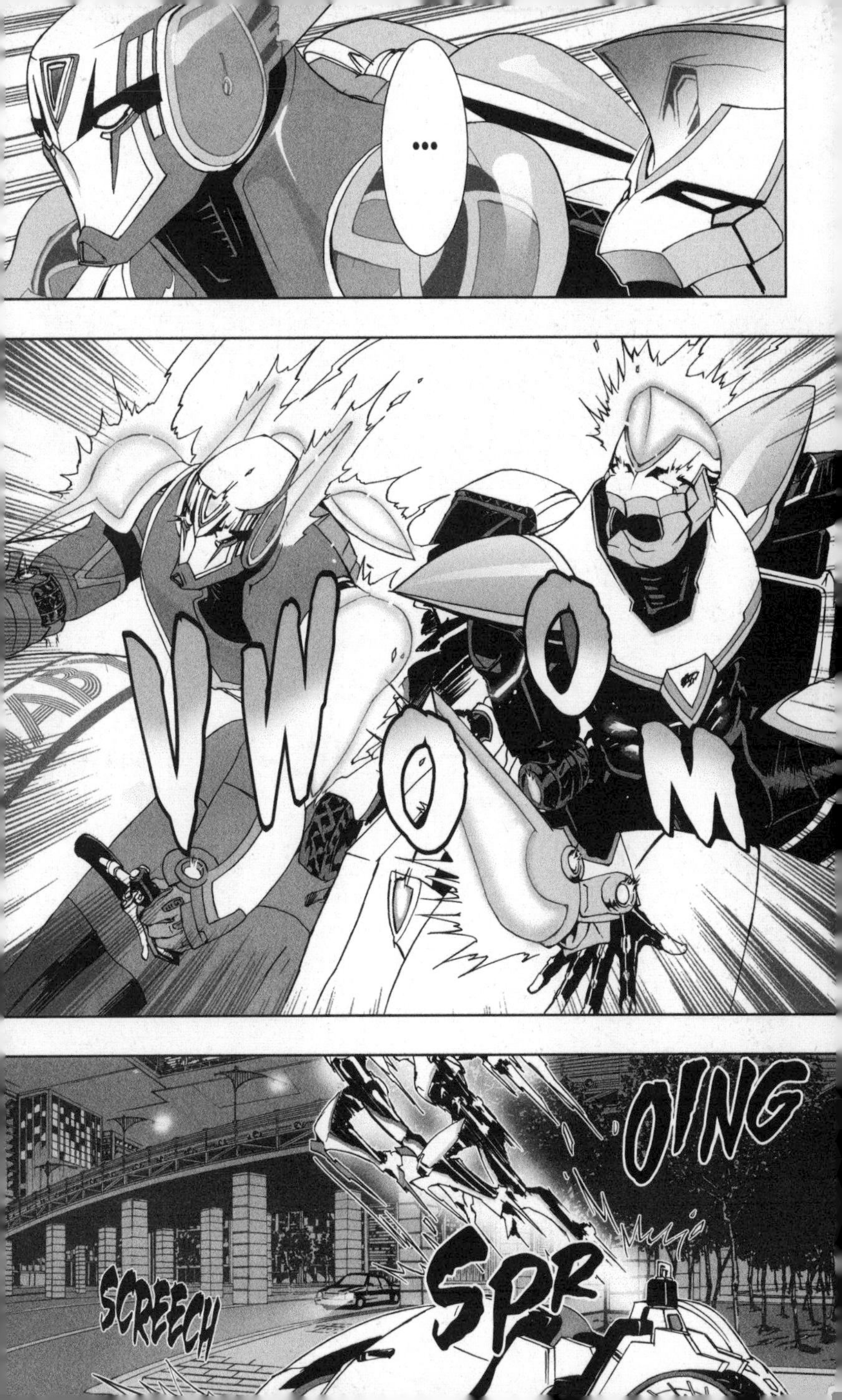
...
VWOOM
OING
SPR
SCREECH

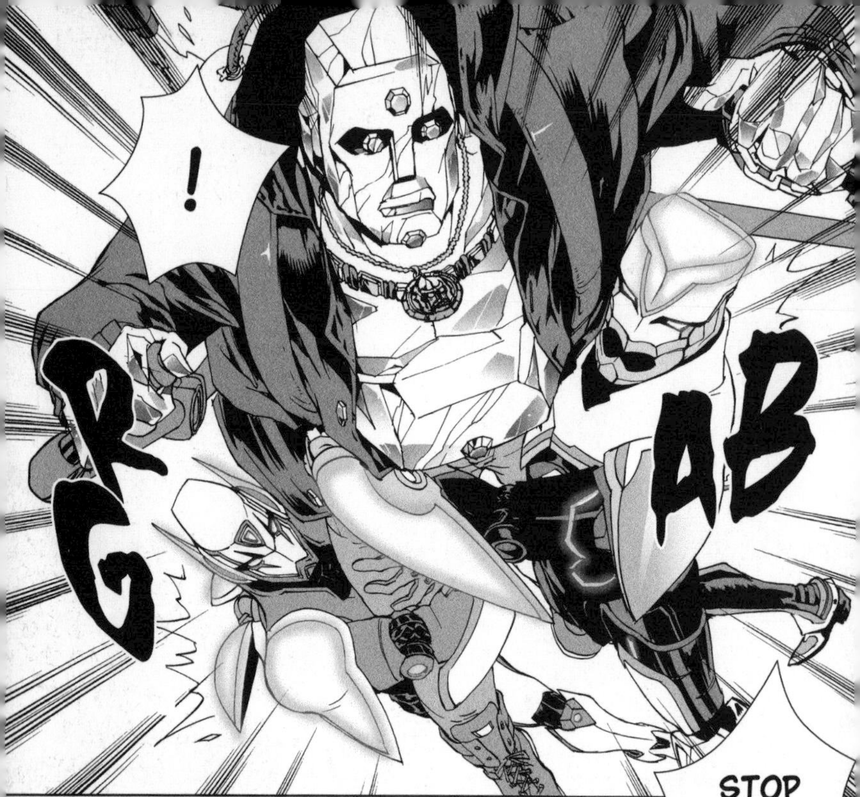
!
GRAB

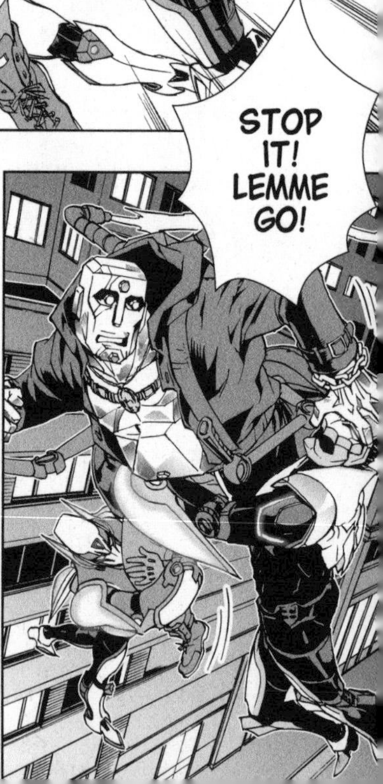
STOP IT! LEMME GO!

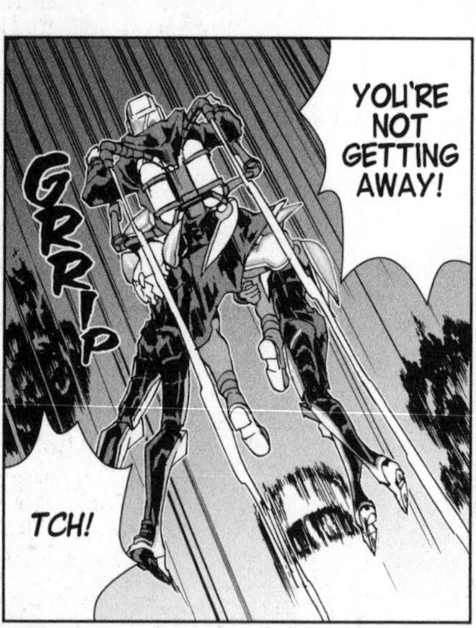
YOU'RE NOT GETTING AWAY!
GRRIP
TCH!

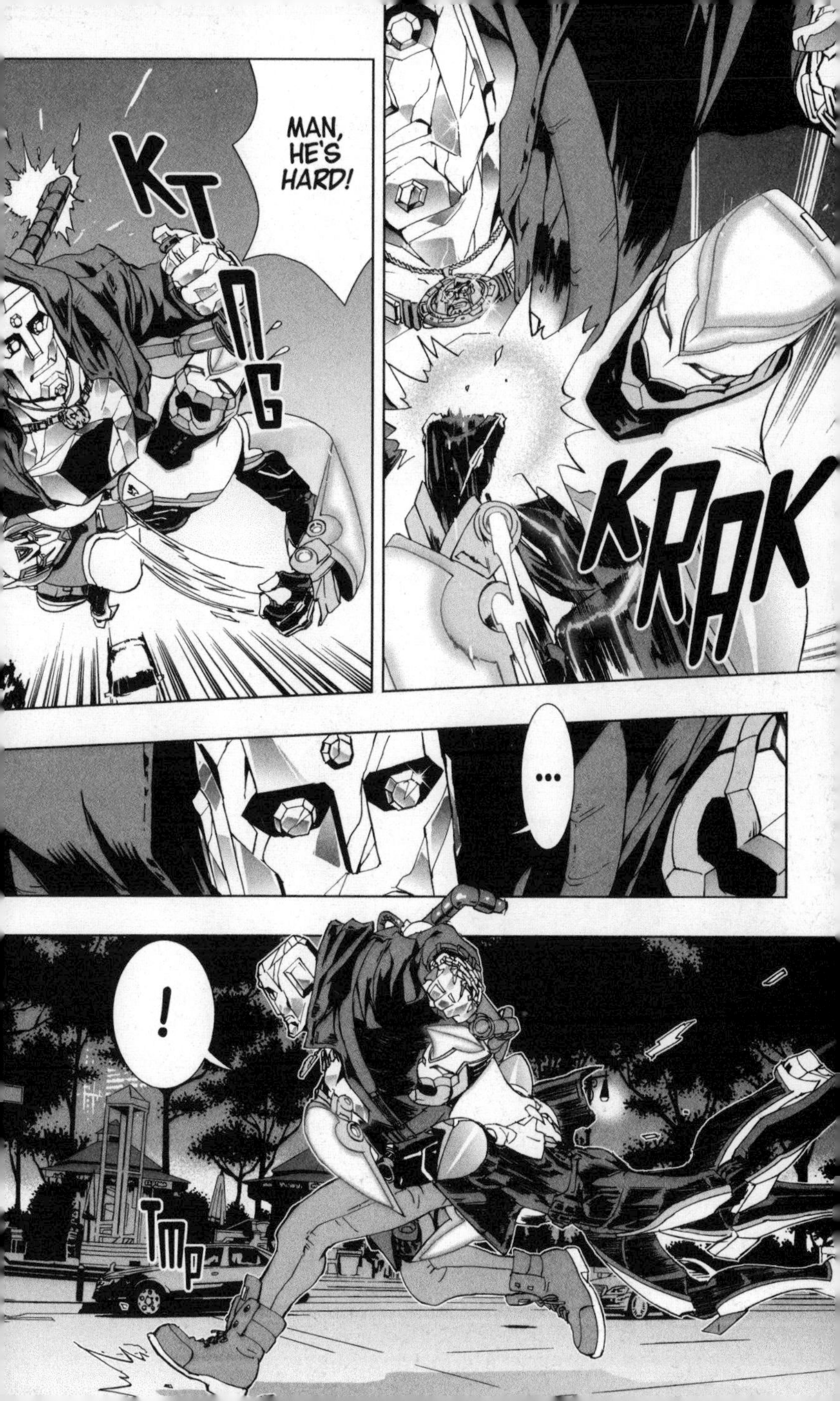
KRAK
KTNG
MAN, HE'S HARD!
...
!
TMP

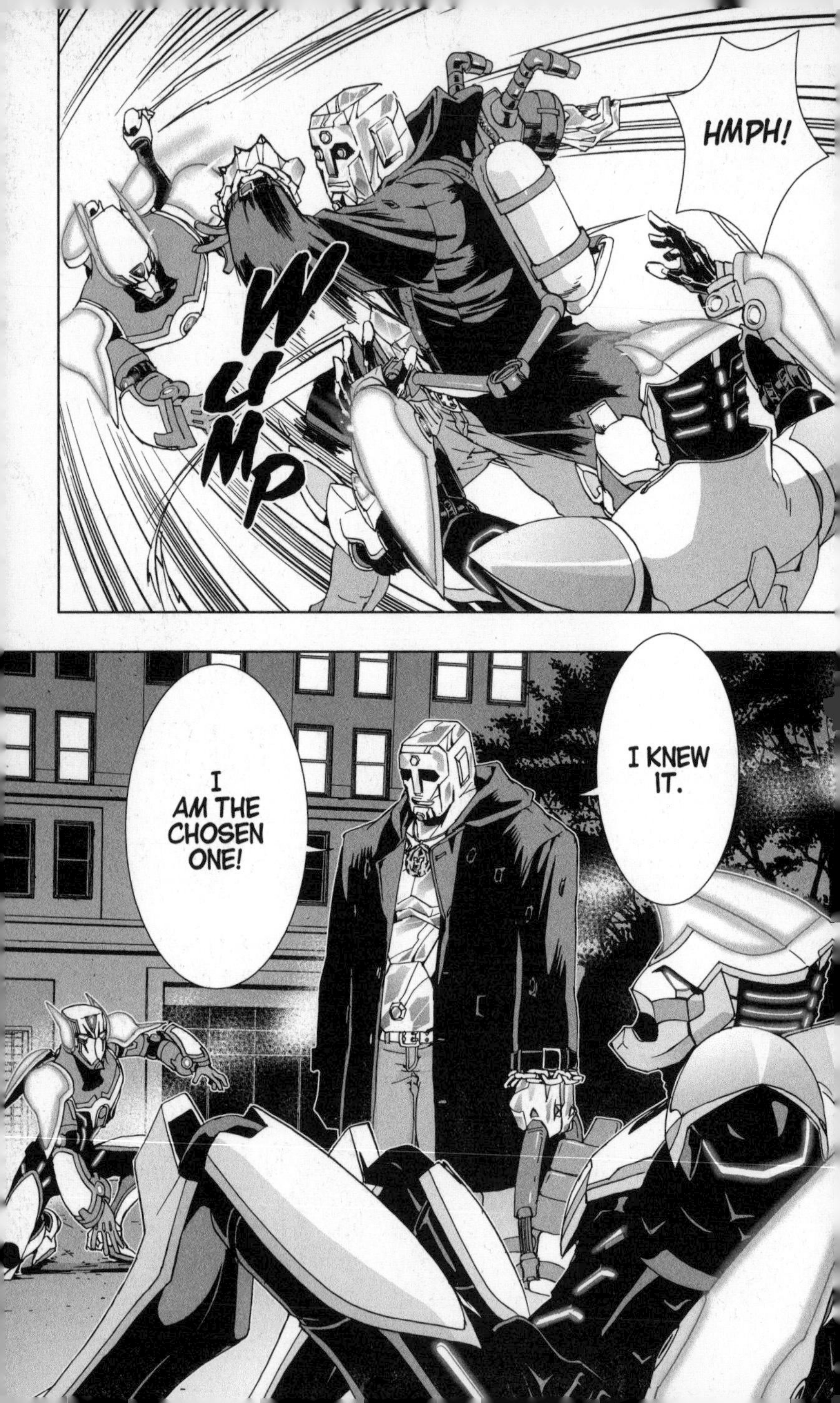
HMPH!
WUMP
I KNEW IT.
I AM THE CHOSEN ONE!

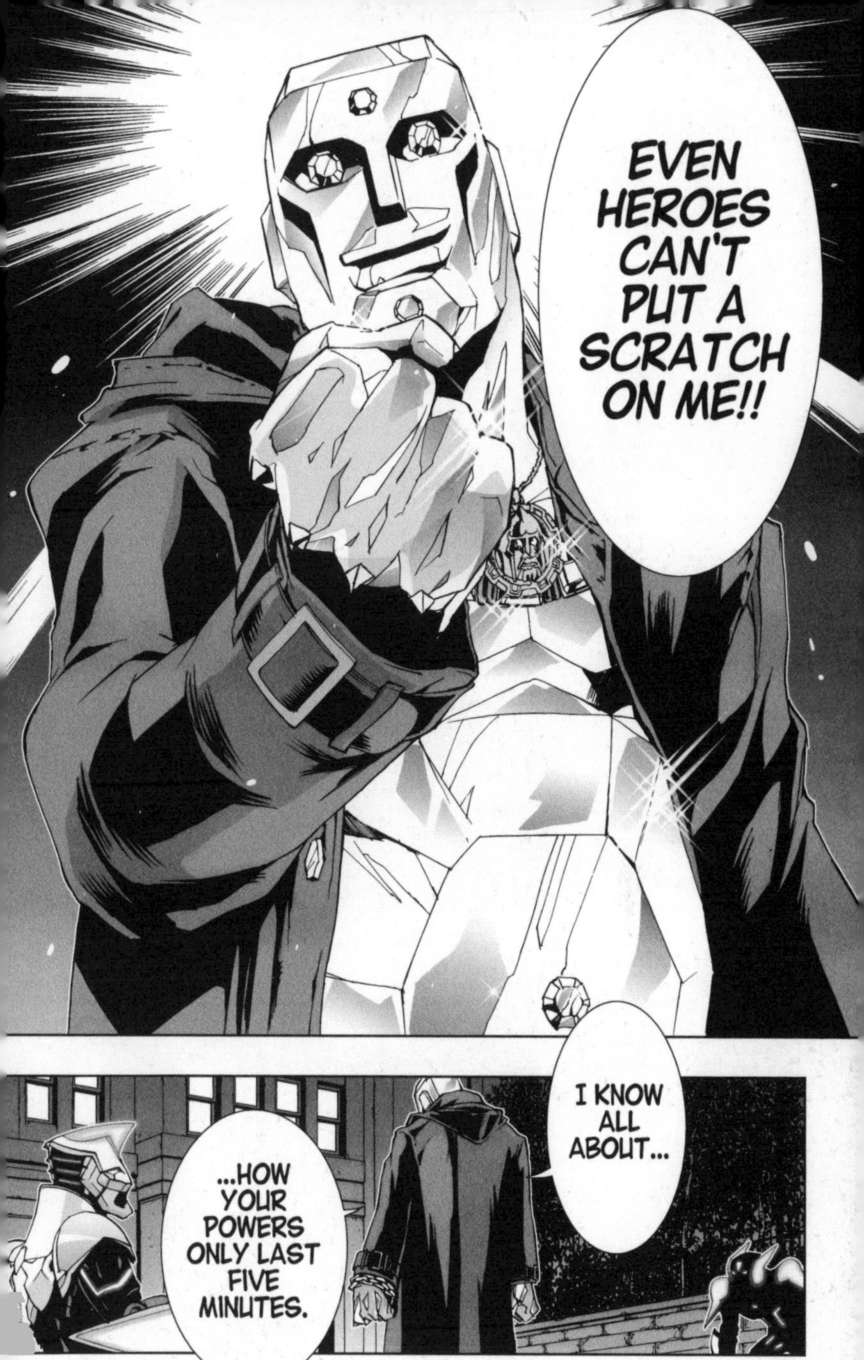
EVEN HEROES CAN'T PUT A SCRATCH ON ME!!
I KNOW ALL ABOUT...
...HOW YOUR POWERS ONLY LAST FIVE MINUTES.

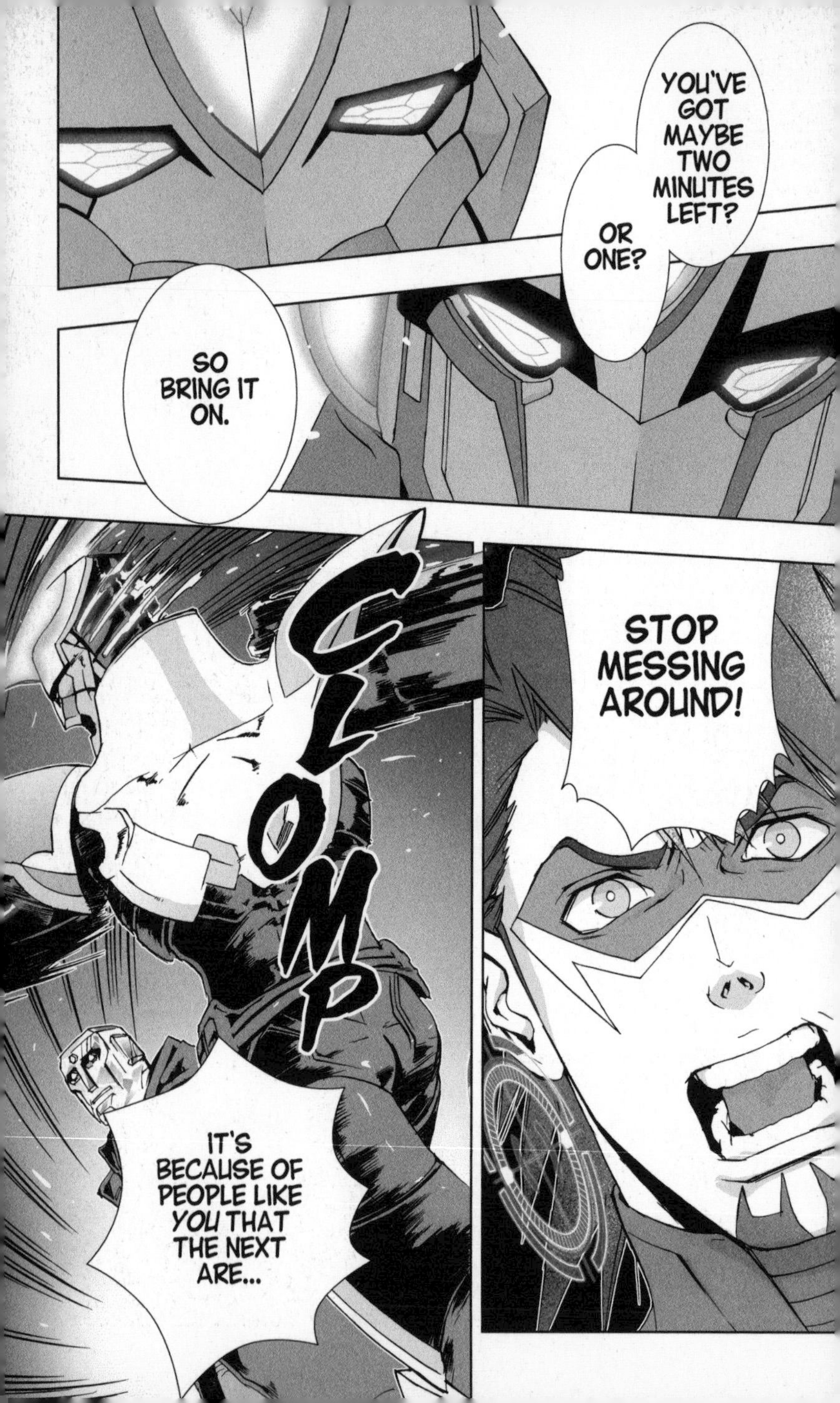
YOU'VE GOT MAYBE TWO MINUTES LEFT?
OR ONE?
SO BRING IT ON.
STOP MESSING AROUND!
CLOMP
IT'S BECAUSE OF PEOPLE LIKE YOU THAT THE NEXT ARE...

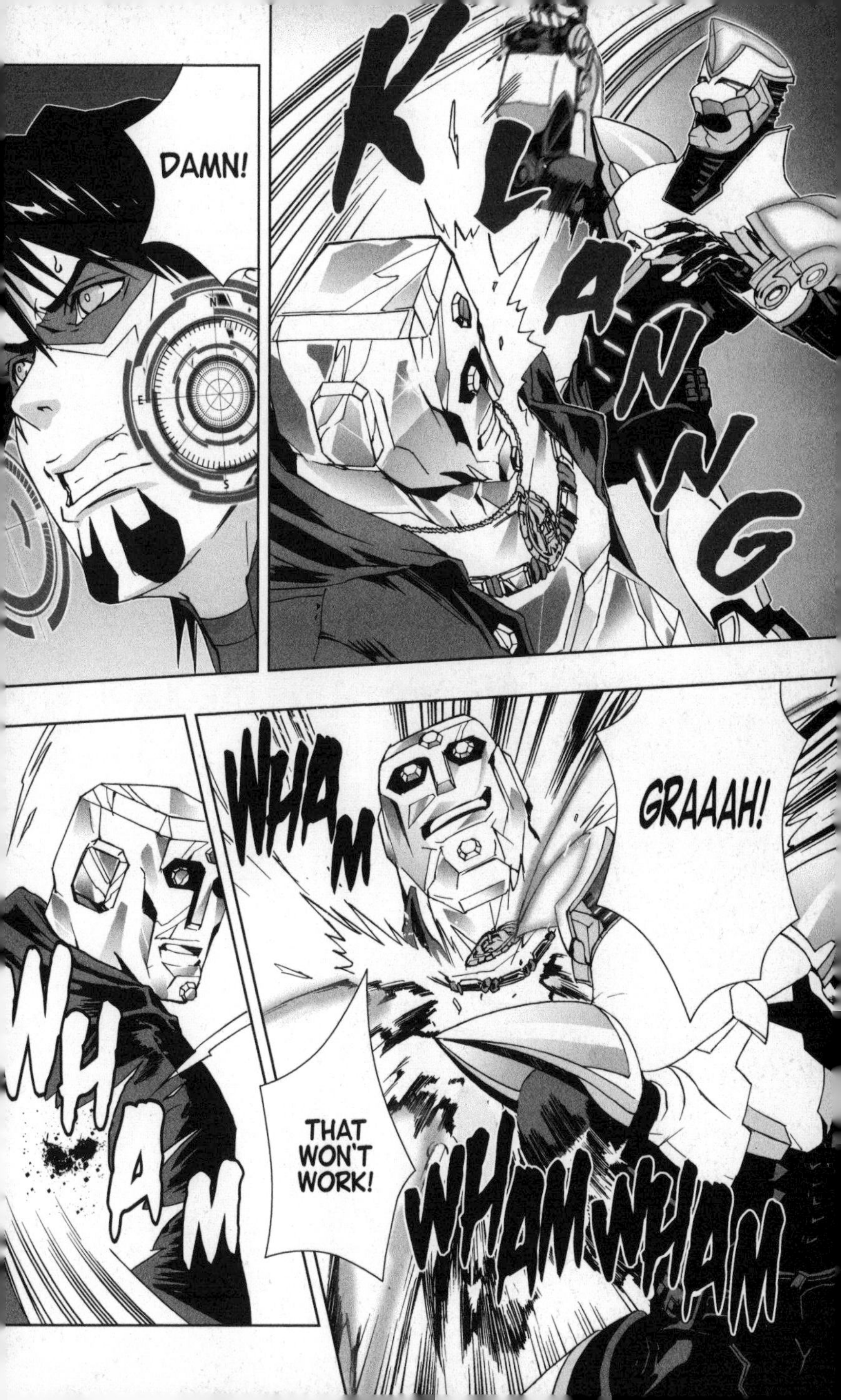
KLANNG
DAMN!
GRAAAH!
WHAM
THAT WON'T WORK!
WHAM WHAM
WHAM

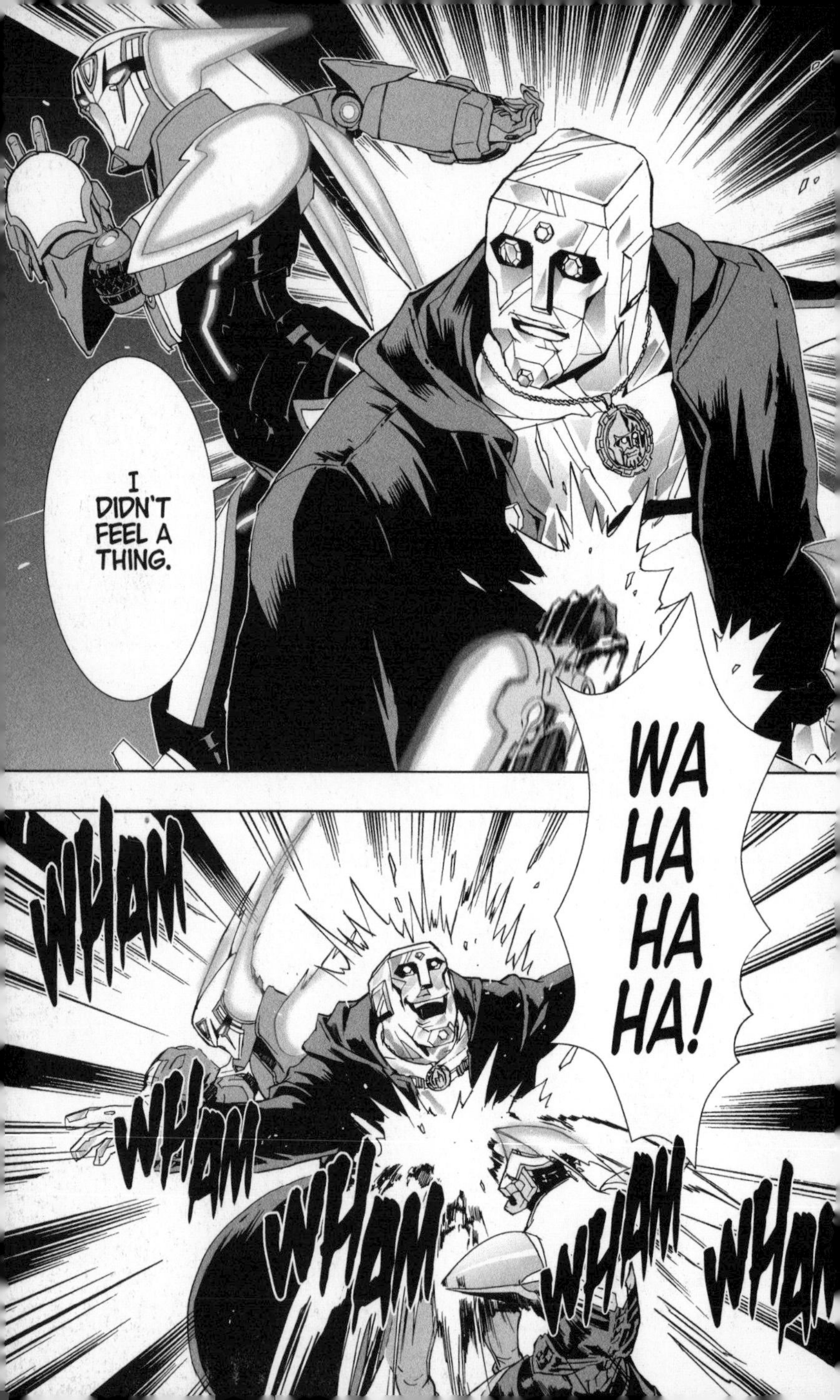
I DIDN'T FEEL A THING.
WA HA HA HA HA!
WHAM
WHAM
WHAM
WHAM
WHAM
WHAM

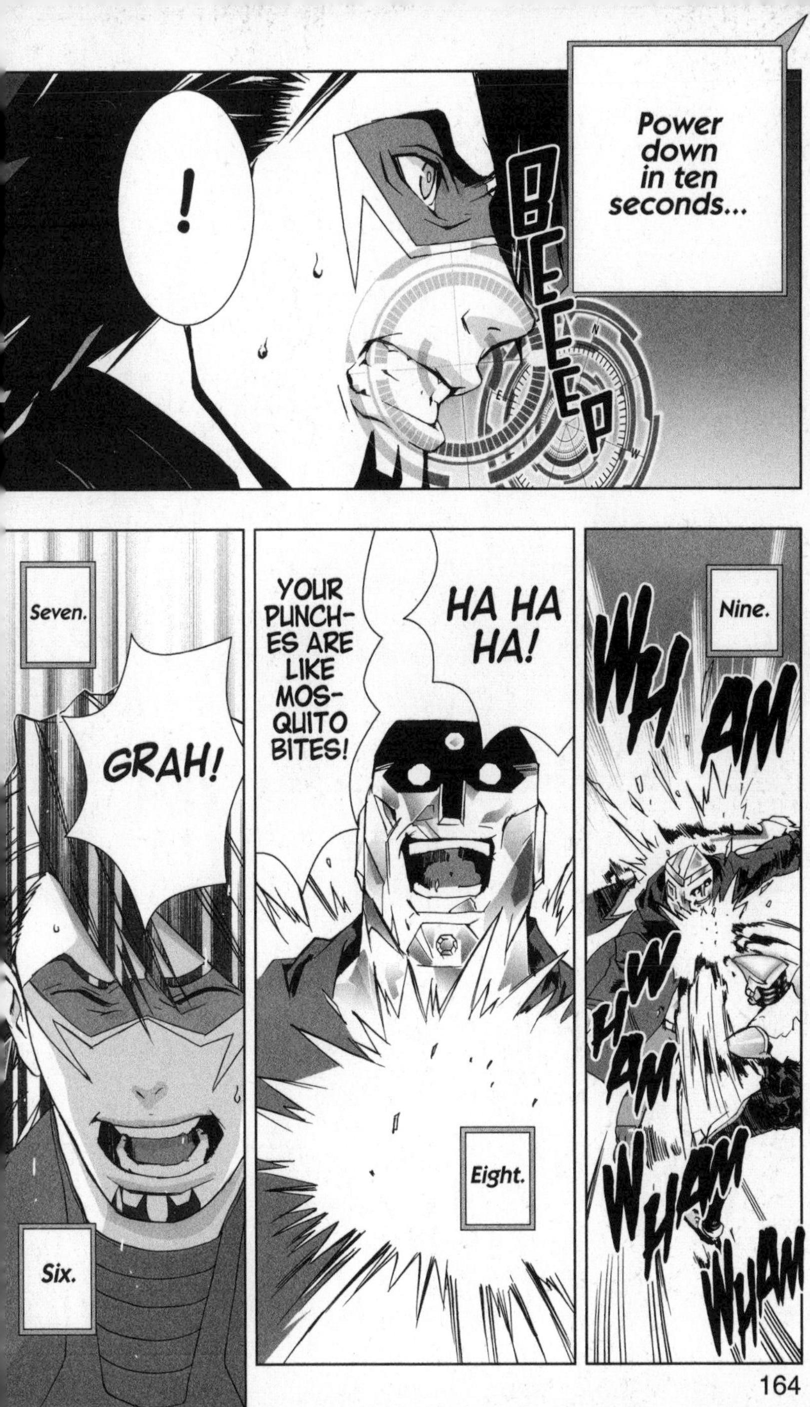
Power down in ten seconds...
BEEEEP
!
Nine.
WHAM
WHAM
WHAM
WHAM
HA HA HA!
YOUR PUNCHES ARE LIKE MOSQUITO BITES!
Eight.
Seven.
GRAH!
Six.

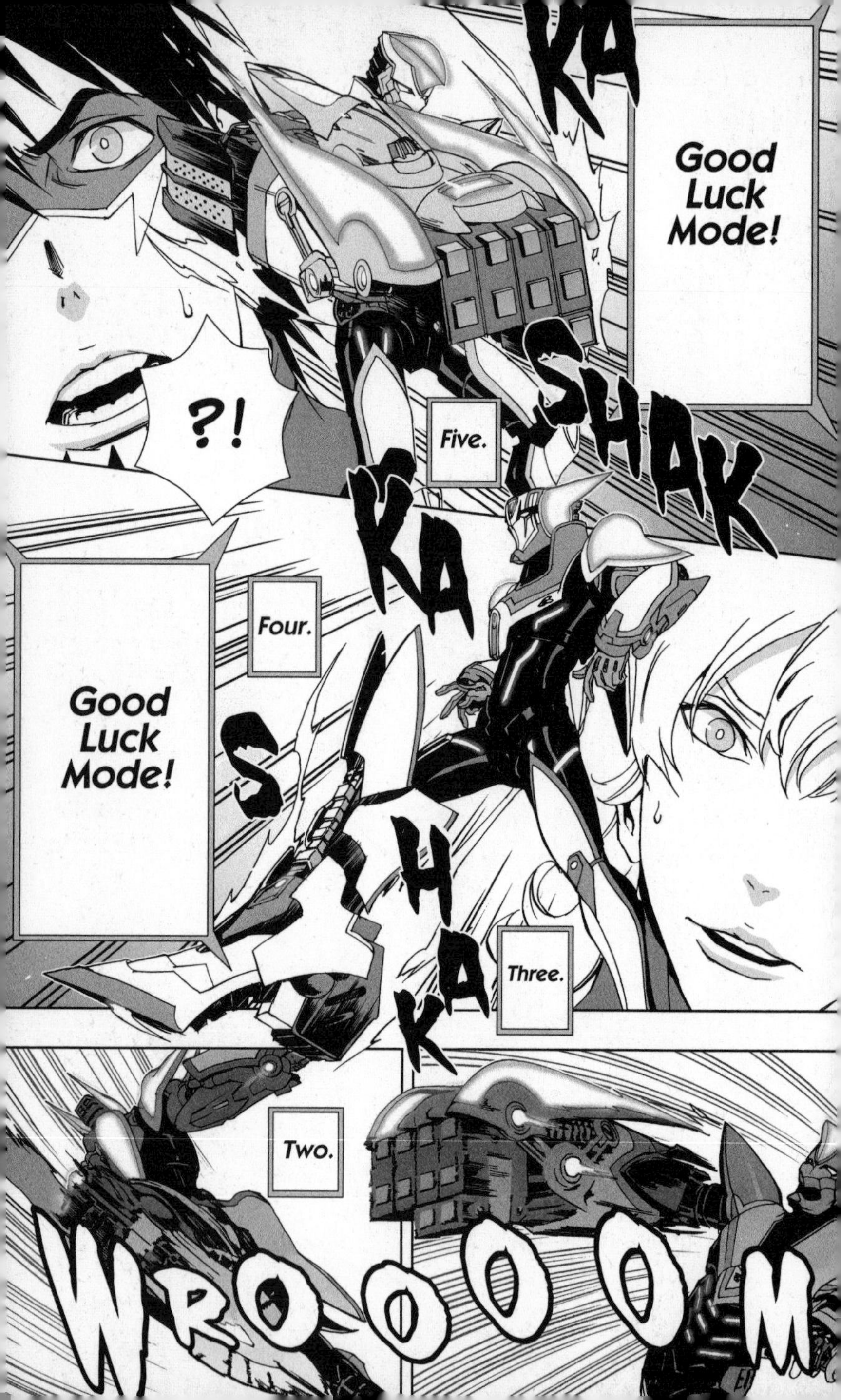
KA
Good Luck Mode!
SHAK
Five.
?!
Three.
KA
Four.
Good Luck Mode!
SHAK
Two.
WROOOOM

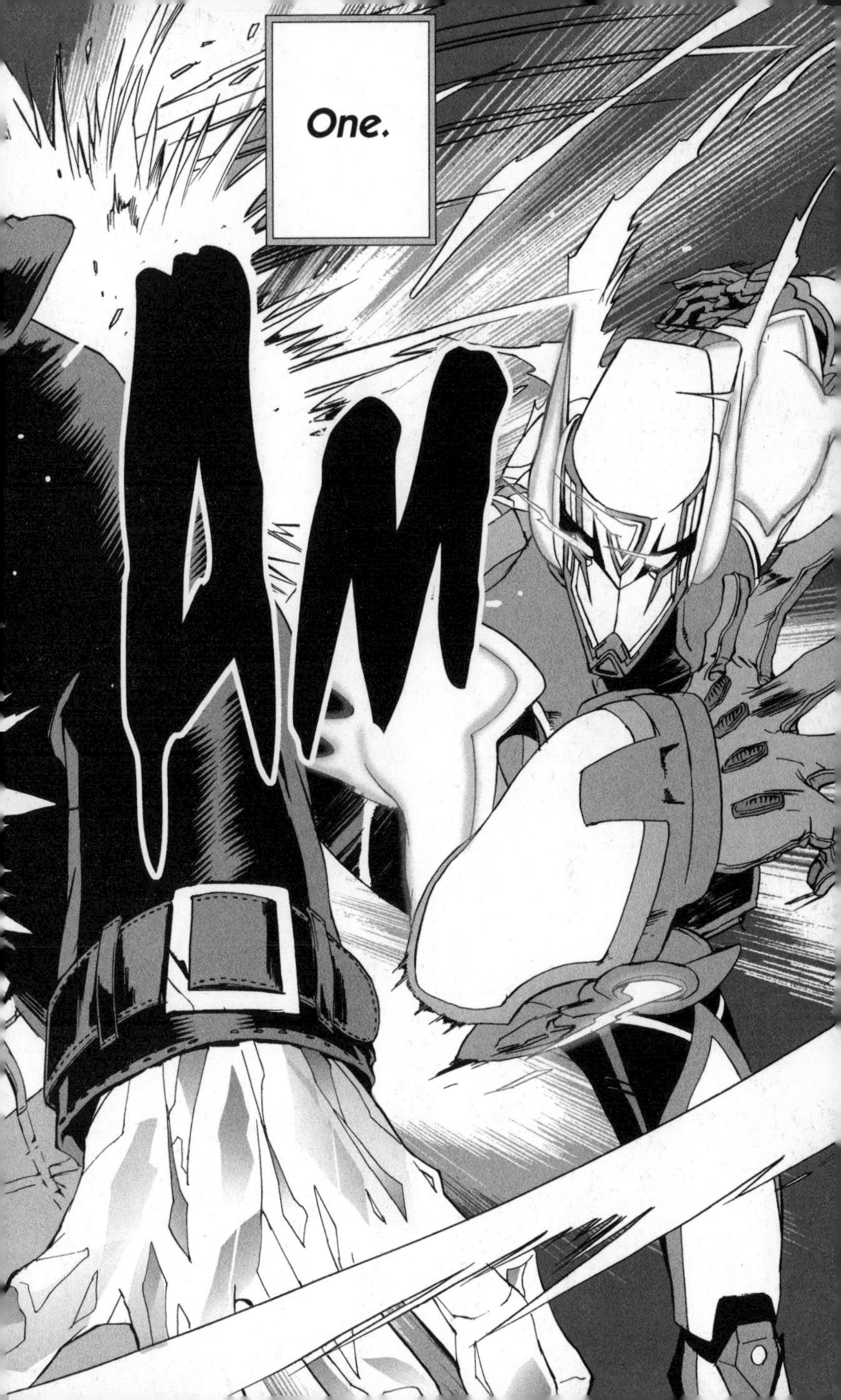
One.

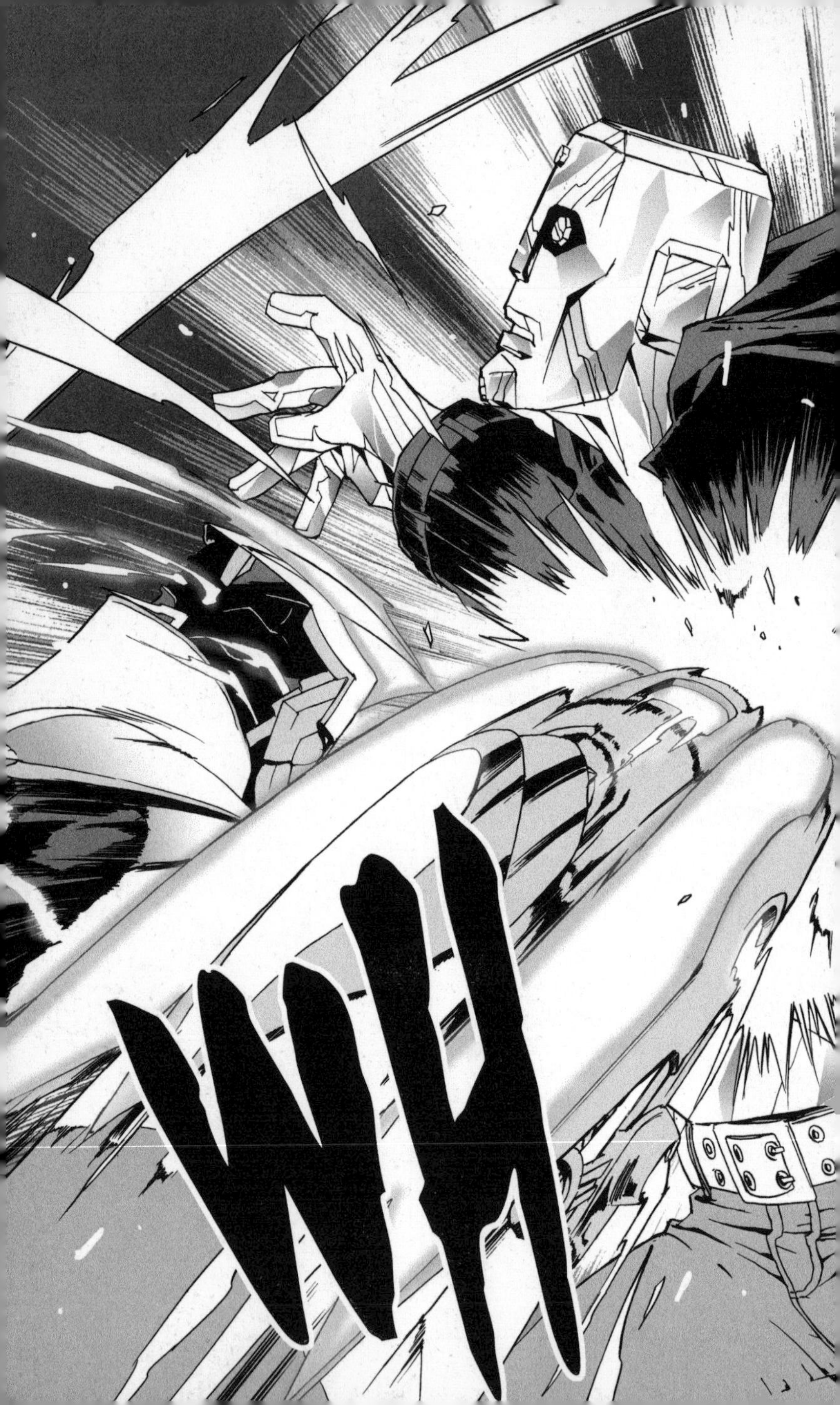
WH

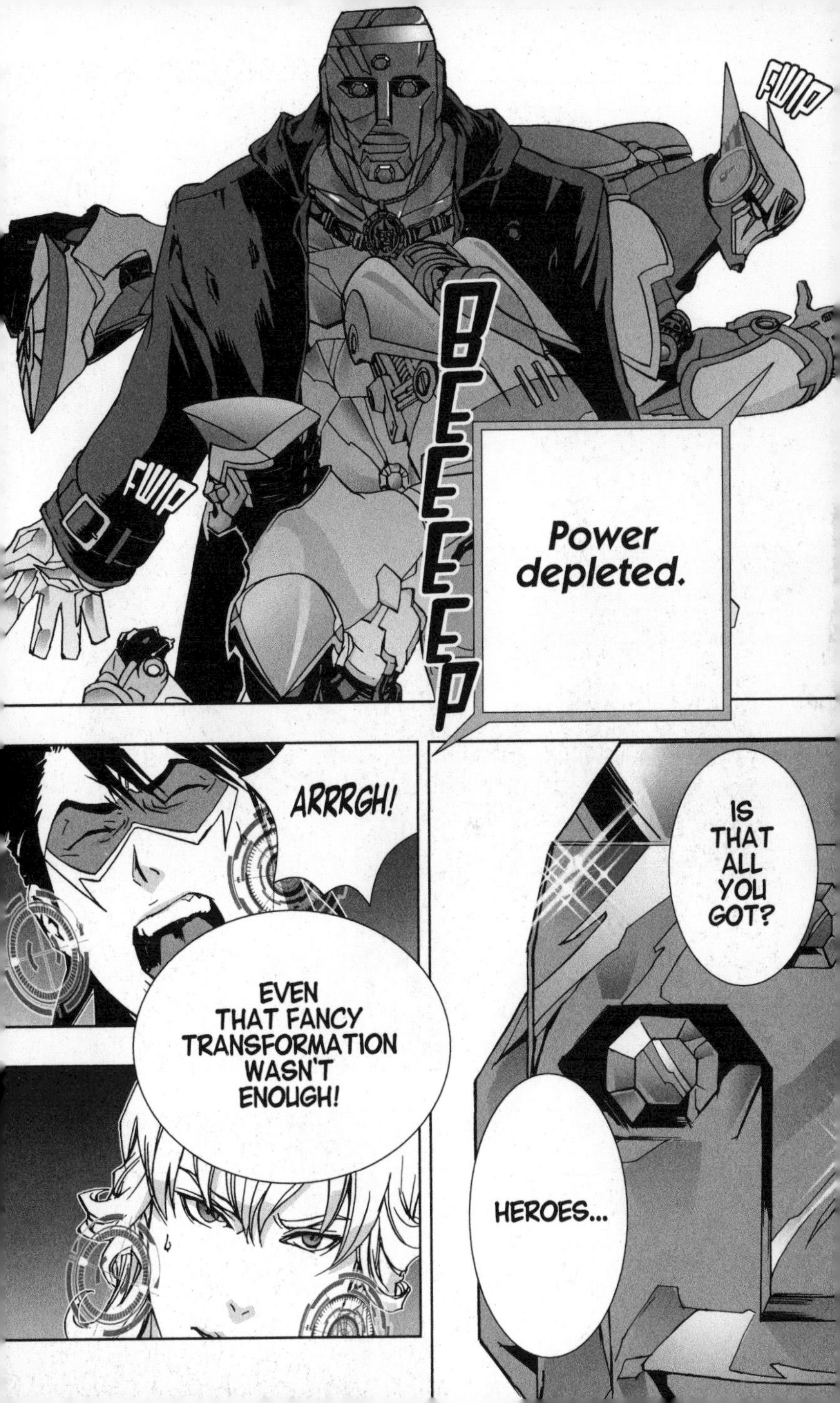
FWIP
BEEEEEP
Power depleted.
FWIP
IS THAT ALL YOU GOT?
HEROES...
ARRRGH!
EVEN THAT FANCY TRANSFORMATION WASN'T ENOUGH!

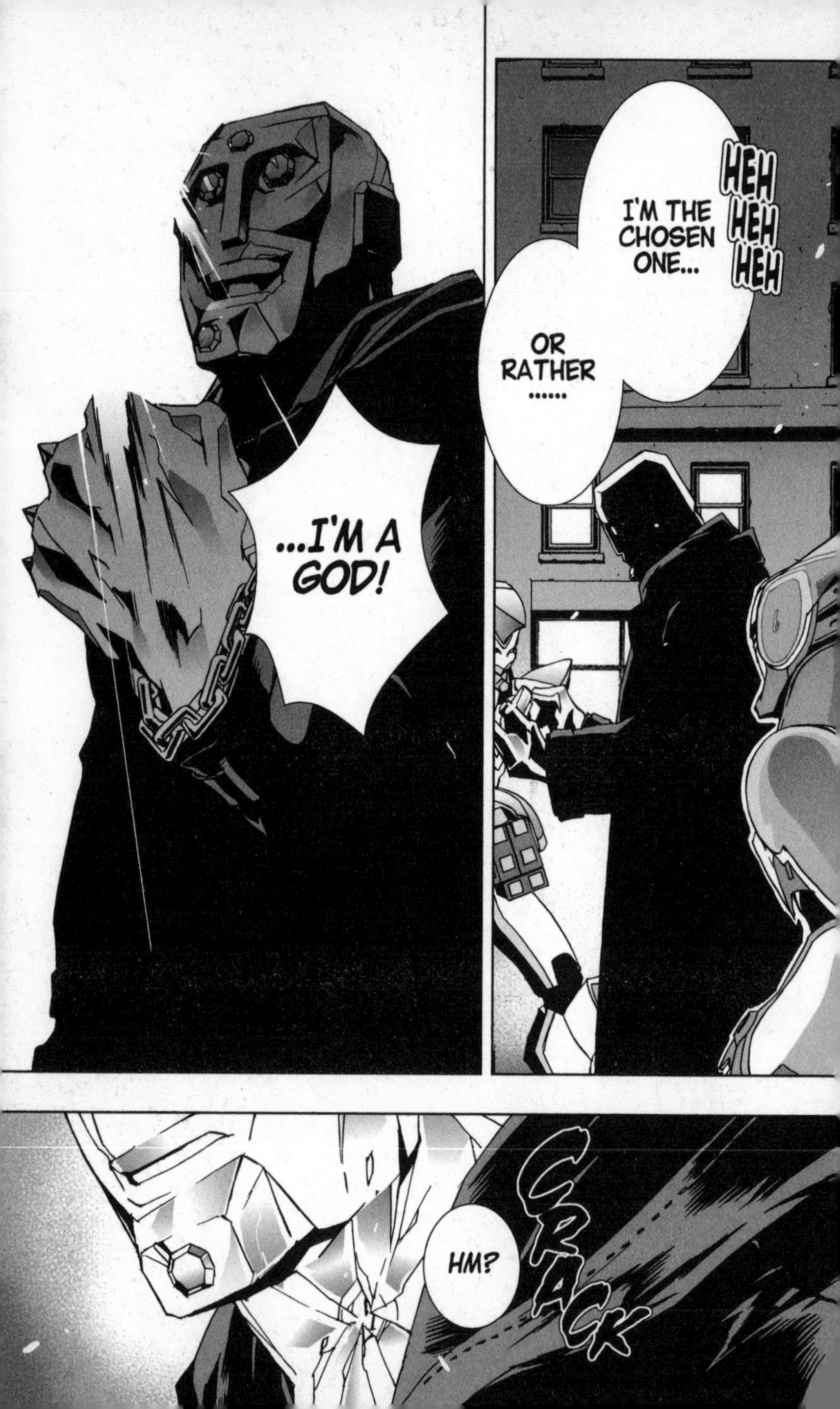
HEH HEH HEH
I'M THE CHOSEN ONE...
OR RATHER ......
...I'M A GOD!
CRACK
HM?

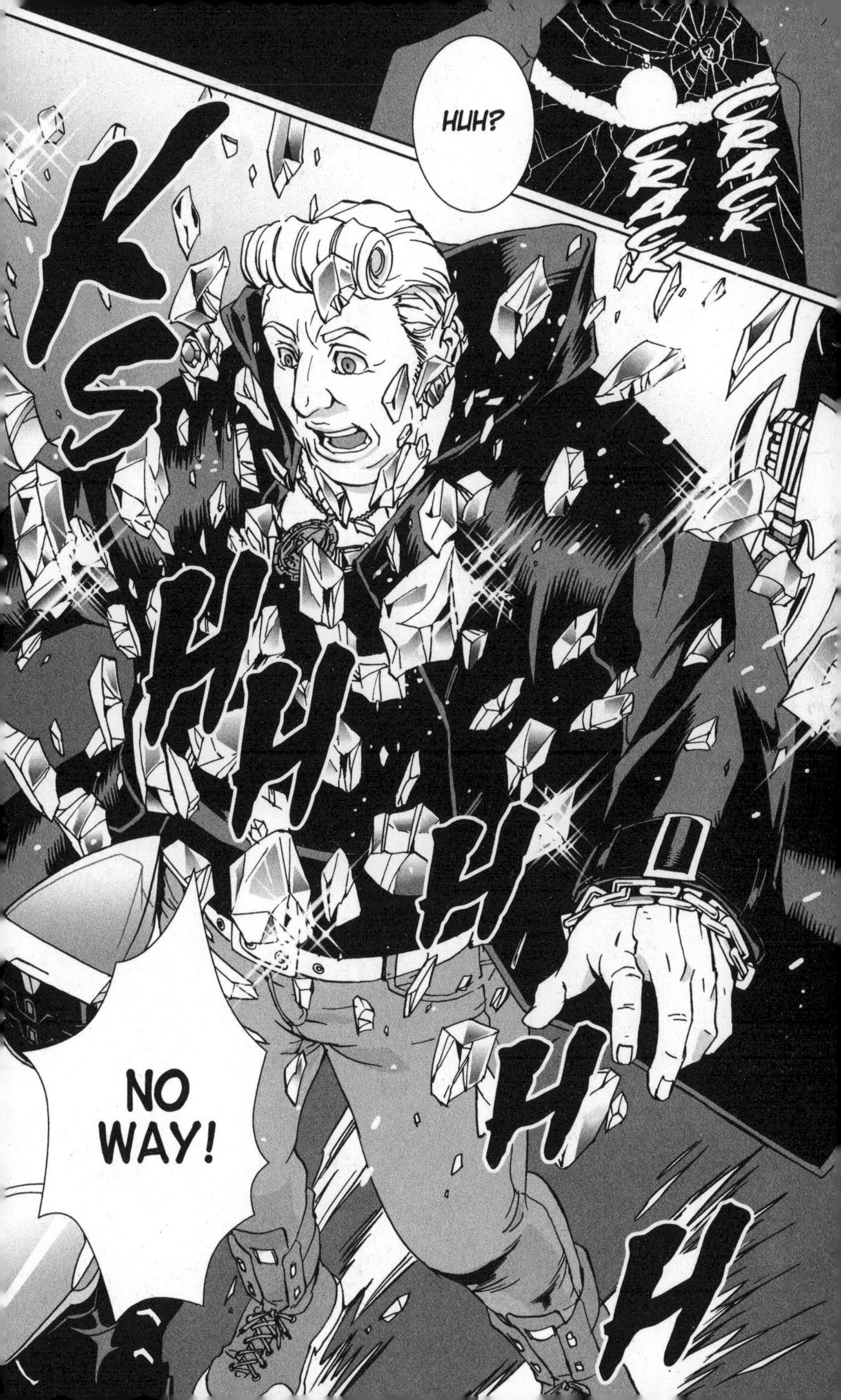

HUH?
CRACK CRACK
KSHHHHH
NO WAY!

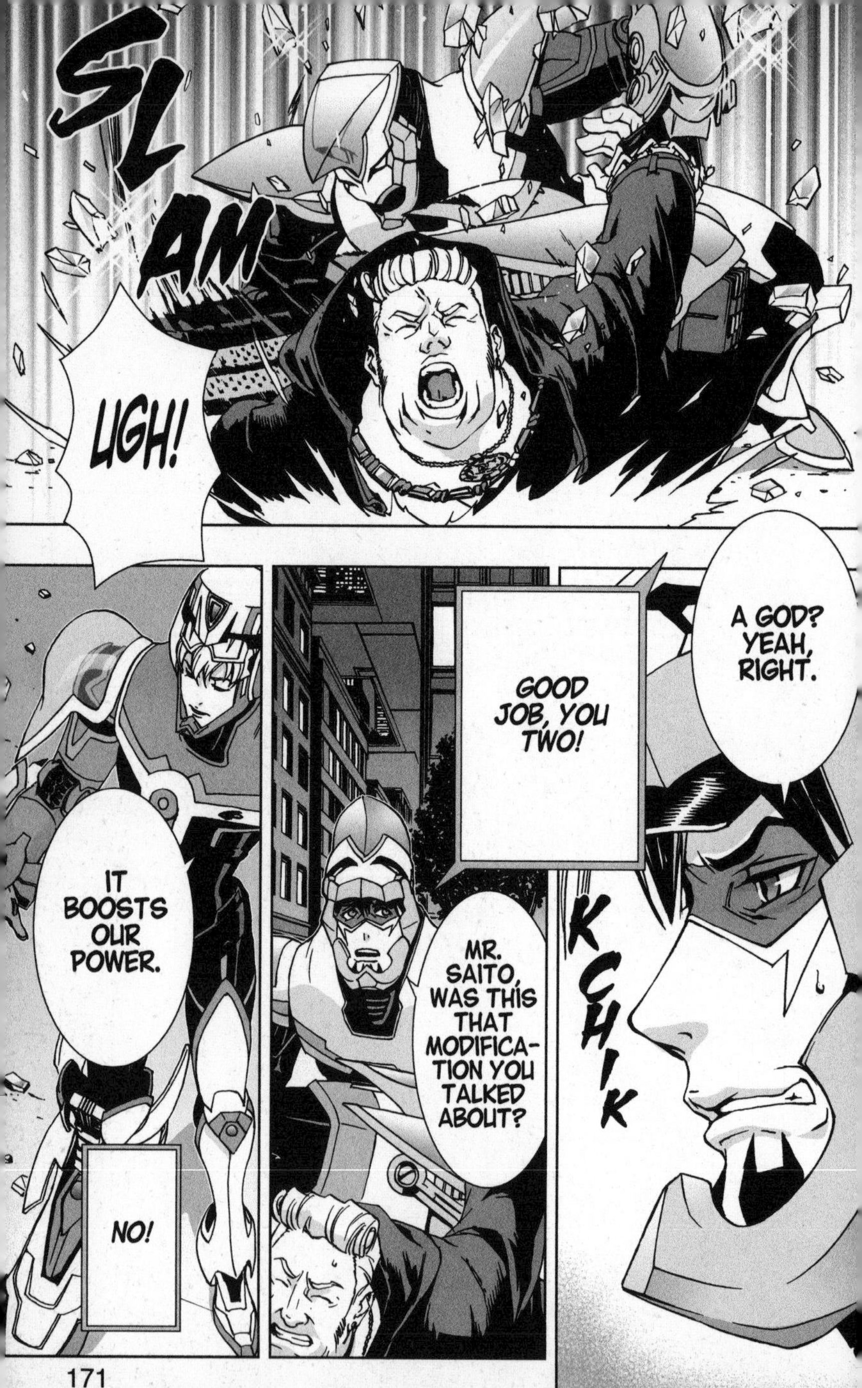
SLAM
UGH!
A GOD? YEAH, RIGHT.
KCHIK
GOOD JOB, YOU TWO!
MR. SAITO, WAS THIS THAT MODIFICATION YOU TALKED ABOUT?
IT BOOSTS OUR POWER.
NO!

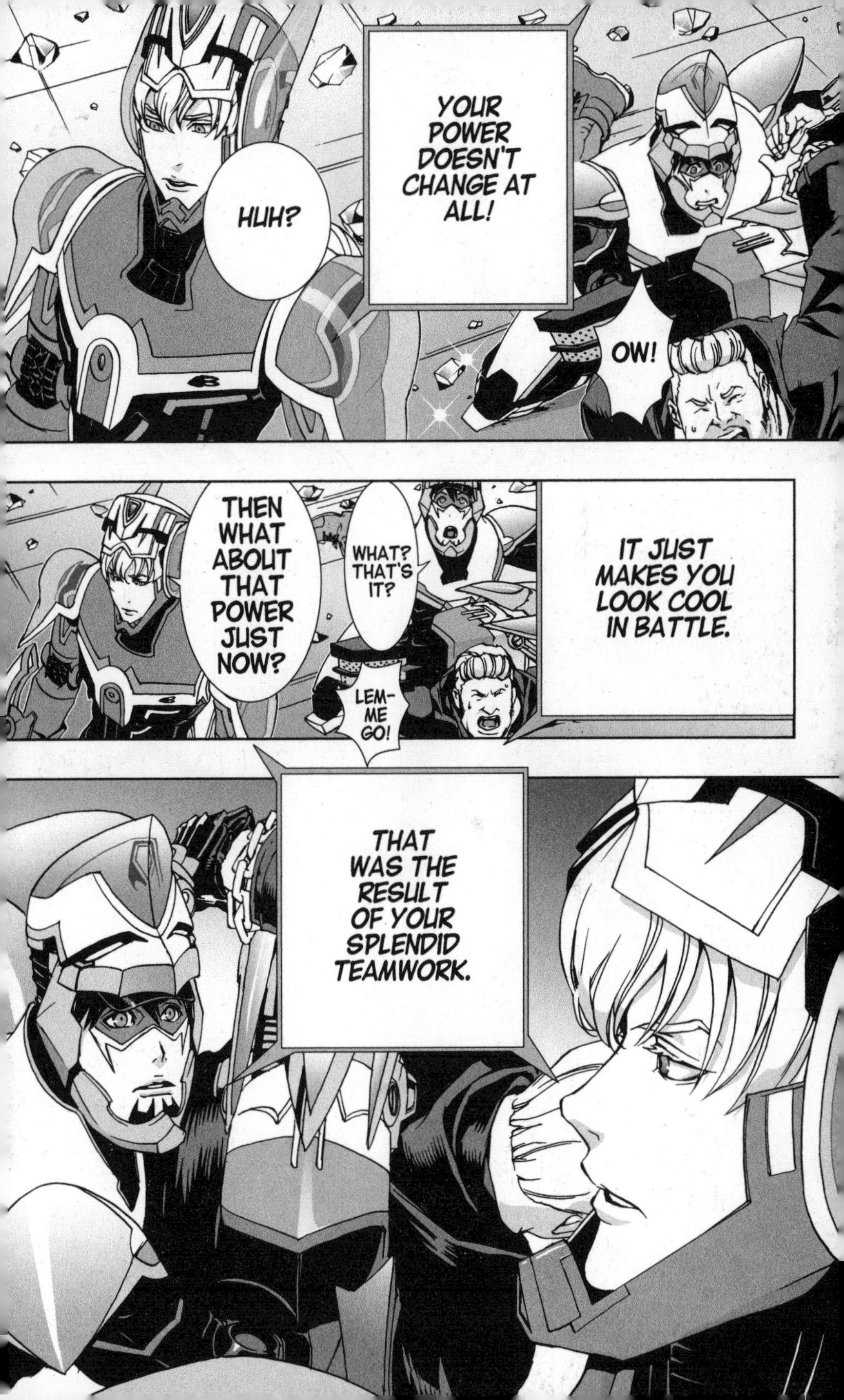

YOUR POWER DOESN'T CHANGE AT ALL!
HUH?
OW!
IT JUST MAKES YOU LOOK COOL IN BATTLE.
WHAT? THAT'S IT?
THEN WHAT ABOUT THAT POWER JUST NOW?
LEM-ME GO!
THAT WAS THE RESULT OF YOUR SPLENDID TEAMWORK.

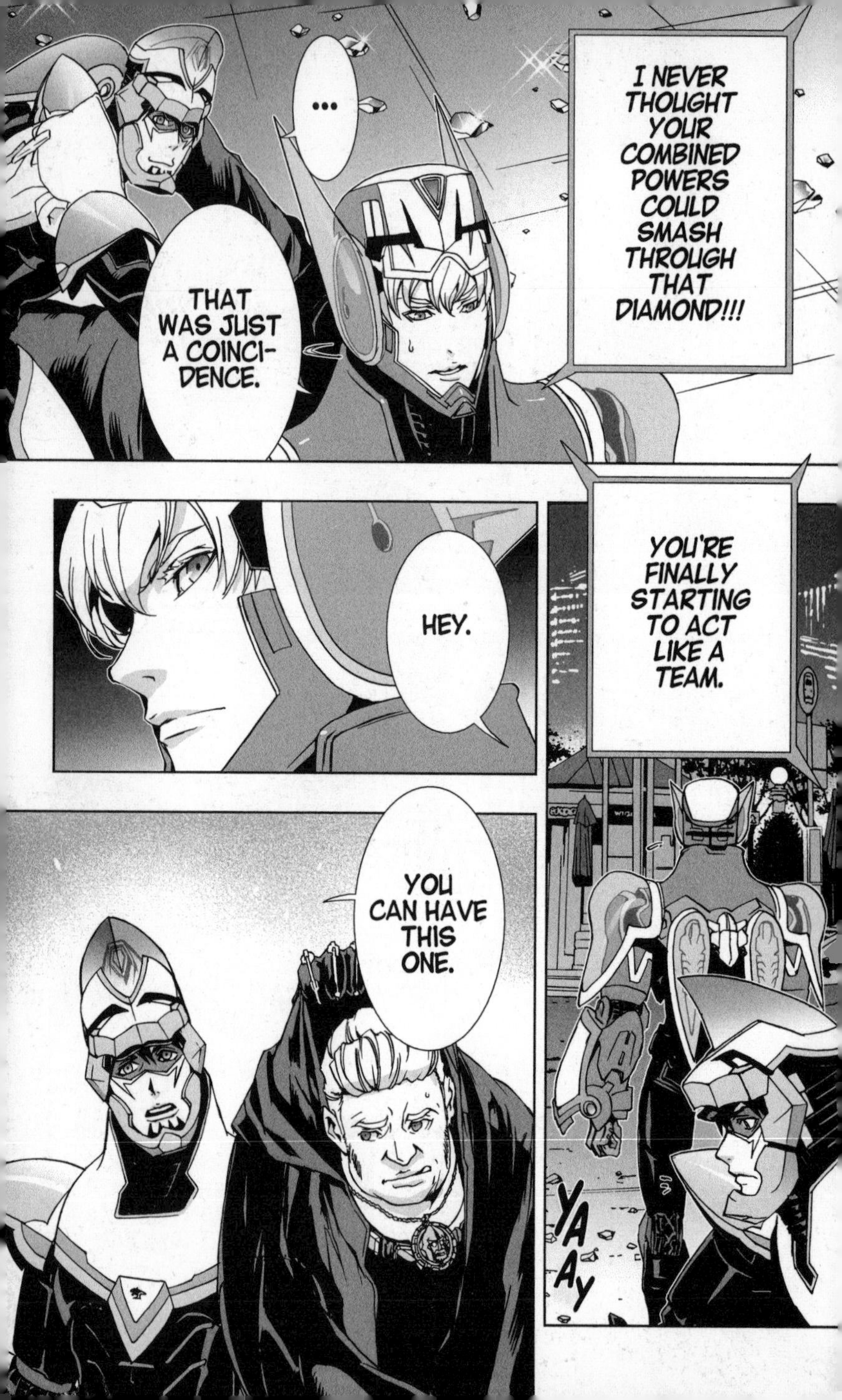
I NEVER THOUGHT YOUR COMBINED POWERS COULD SMASH THROUGH THAT DIAMOND!!!
...
THAT WAS JUST A COINCI-DENCE.
YOU'RE FINALLY STARTING TO ACT LIKE A TEAM.
YAAAy
HEY.
YOU CAN HAVE THIS ONE.

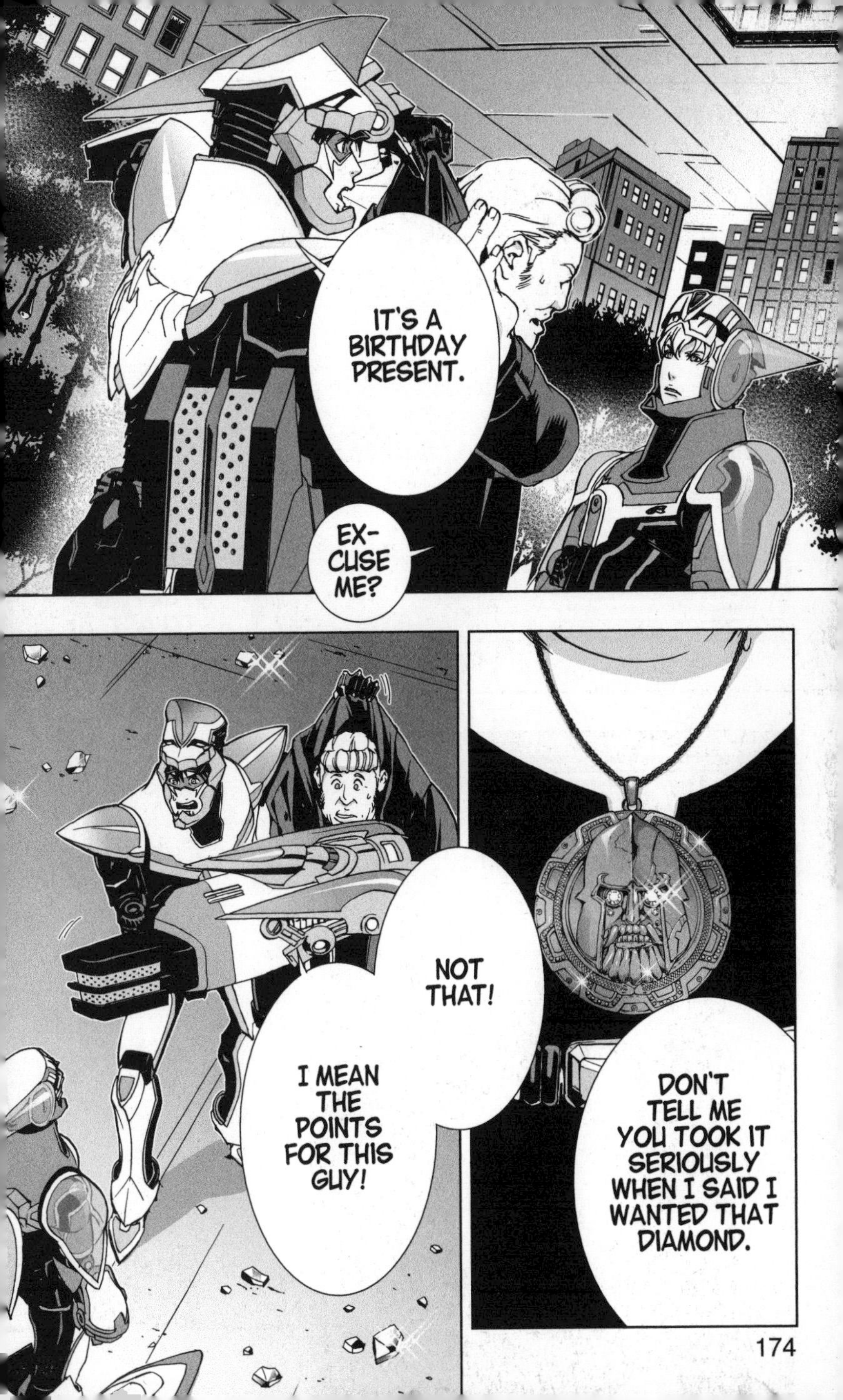

IT'S A BIRTHDAY PRESENT.
EX-CUSE ME?
DON'T TELL ME YOU TOOK IT SERIOUSLY WHEN I SAID I WANTED THAT DIAMOND.
NOT THAT!
I MEAN THE POINTS FOR THIS GUY!

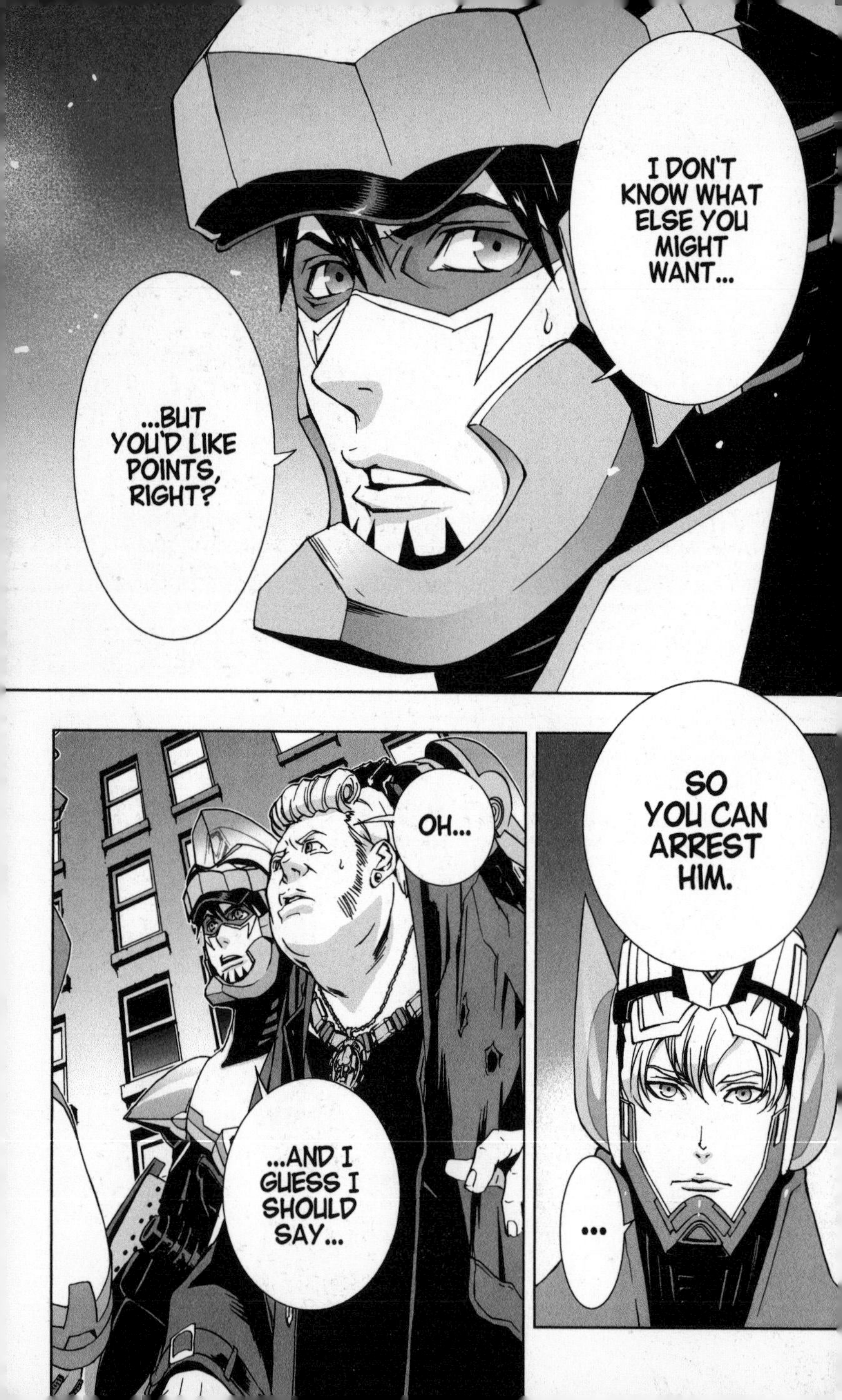
I DON'T KNOW WHAT ELSE YOU MIGHT WANT...
...BUT YOU'D LIKE POINTS, RIGHT?
SO YOU CAN ARREST HIM.
...
OH...
...AND I GUESS I SHOULD SAY...

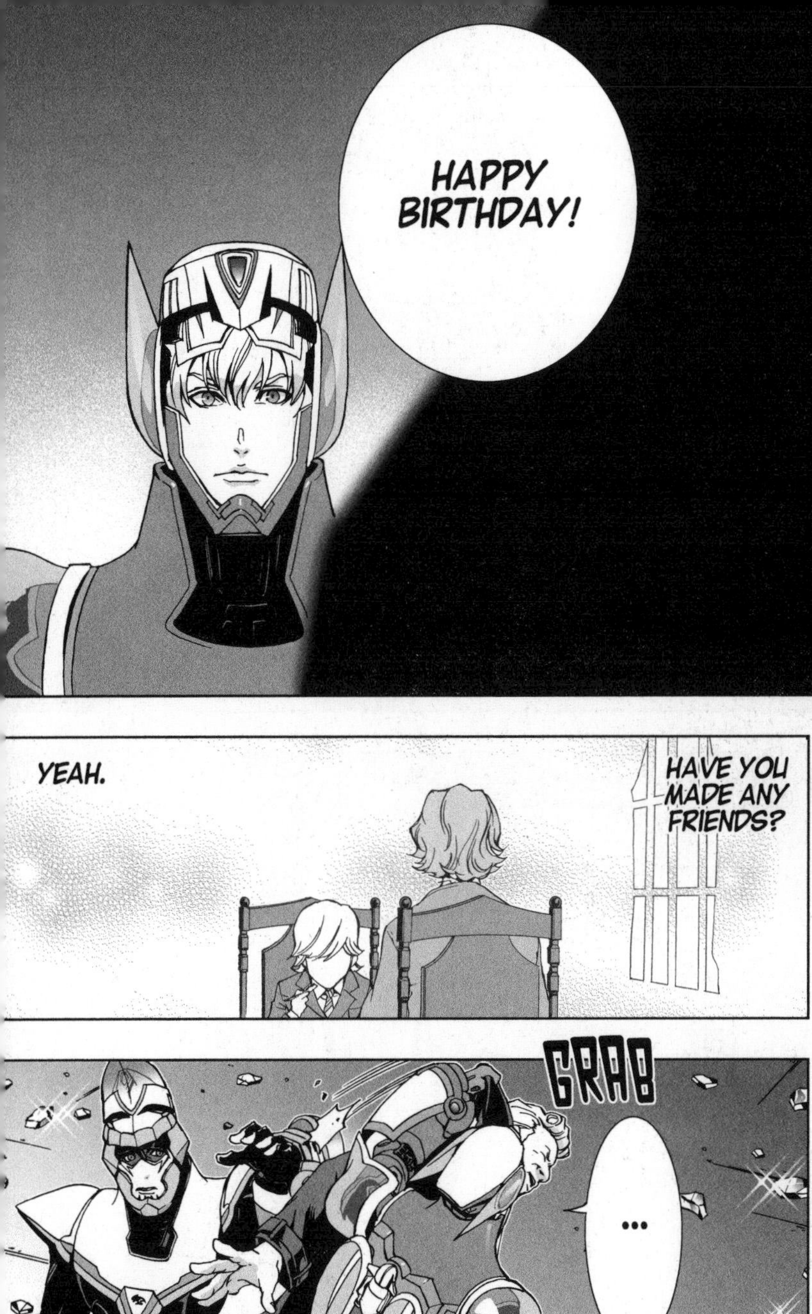
HAPPY BIRTHDAY!
HAVE YOU MADE ANY FRIENDS?
YEAH.
GRAB
...

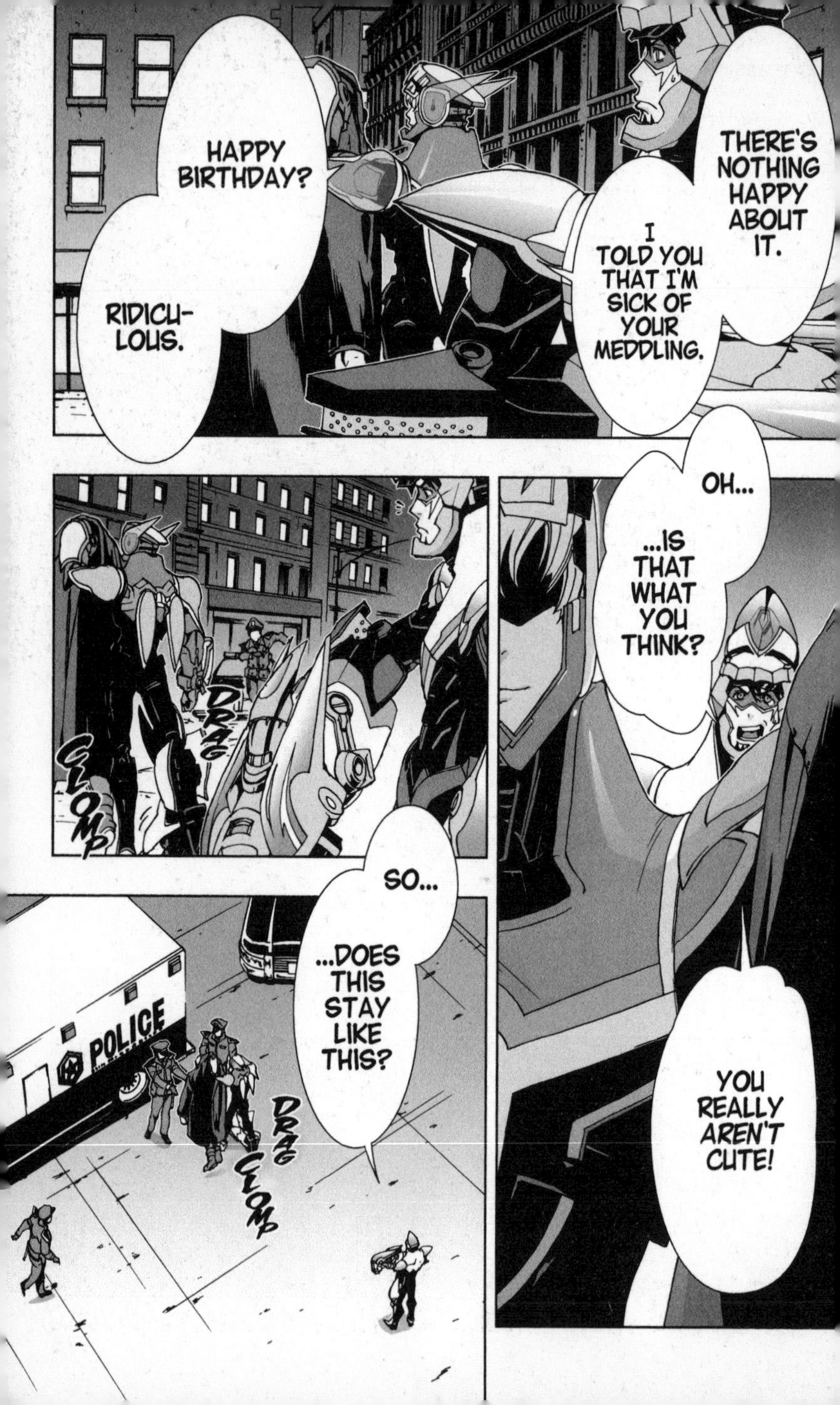
THERE'S NOTHING HAPPY ABOUT IT.
I TOLD YOU THAT I'M SICK OF YOUR MEDDLING.
HAPPY BIRTHDAY?
RIDICU-LOUS.
OH...
...IS THAT WHAT YOU THINK?
YOU REALLY AREN'T CUTE!
DRAG
CLOMP
SO...
...DOES THIS STAY LIKE THIS?
POLICE
DRAG
CLOMP

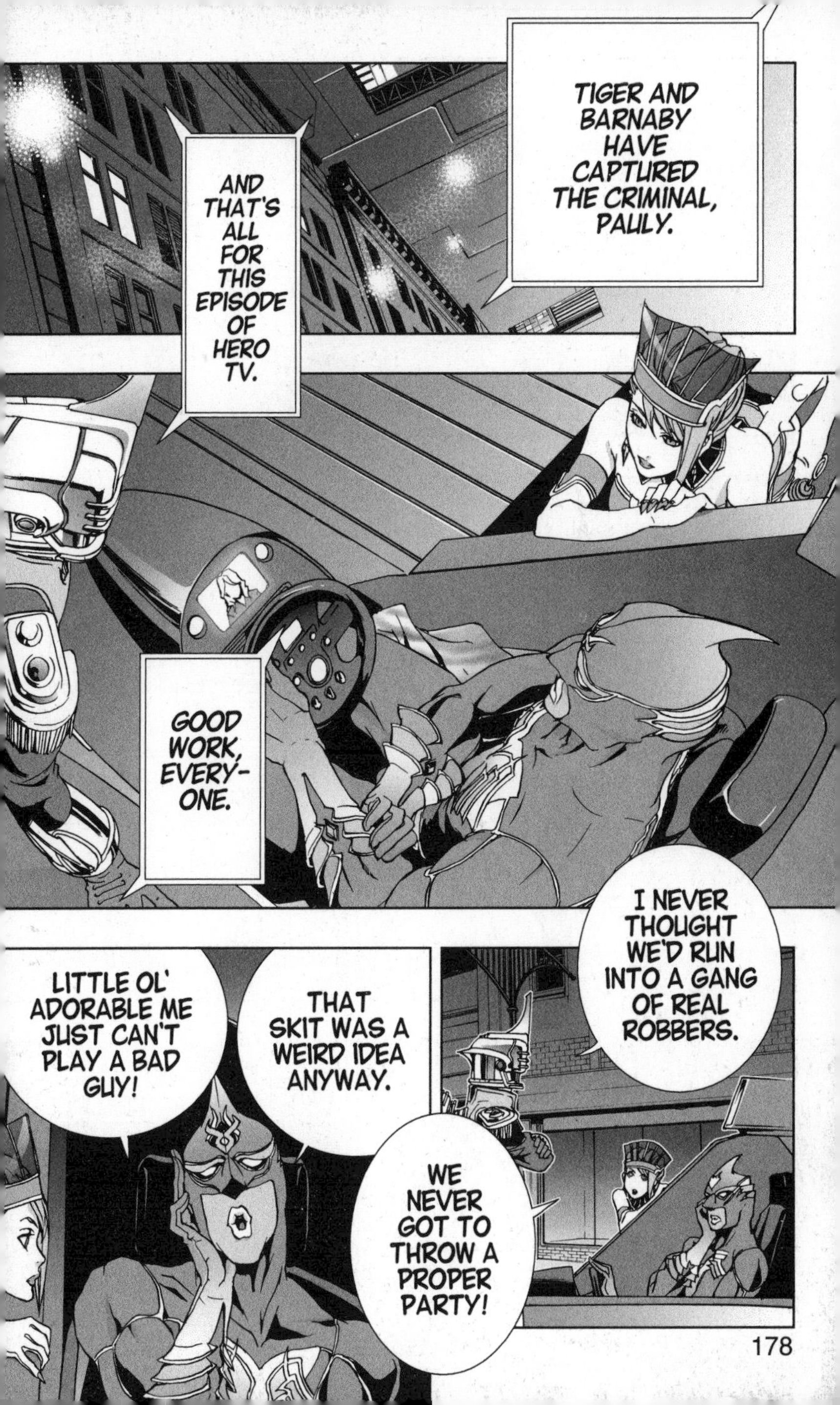
TIGER AND BARNABY HAVE CAPTURED THE CRIMINAL, PAULY.
AND THAT'S ALL FOR THIS EPISODE OF HERO TV.
GOOD WORK, EVERY-ONE.
I NEVER THOUGHT WE'D RUN INTO A GANG OF REAL ROBBERS.
WE NEVER GOT TO THROW A PROPER PARTY!
THAT SKIT WAS A WEIRD IDEA ANYWAY.
LITTLE OL' ADORABLE ME JUST CAN'T PLAY A BAD GUY!

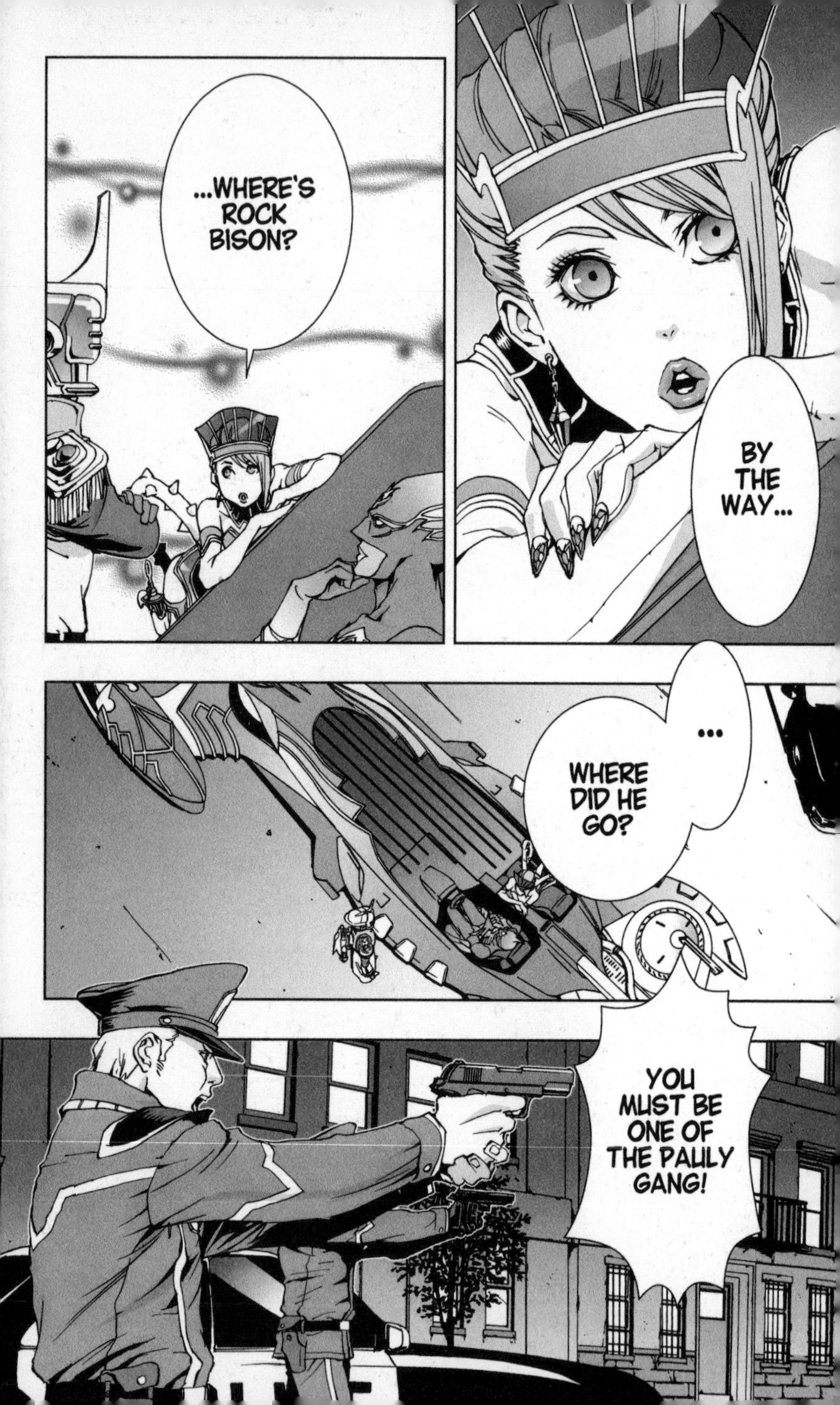

BY THE WAY...
...WHERE'S ROCK BISON?
... WHERE DID HE GO?
YOU MUST BE ONE OF THE PAULY GANG!

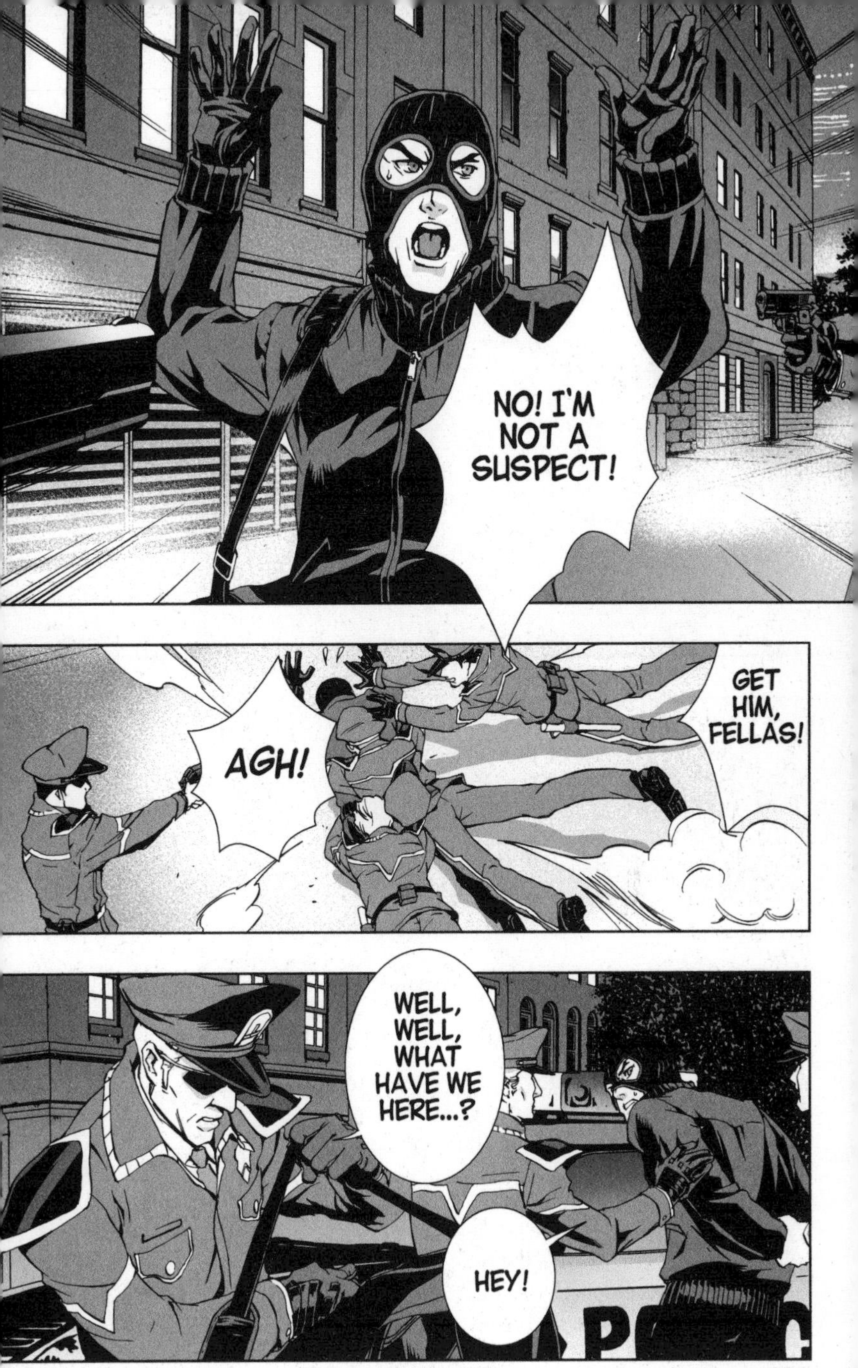
NO! I'M NOT A SUSPECT!
GET HIM, FELLAS!
AGH!
WELL, WELL, WHAT HAVE WE HERE...?
HEY!

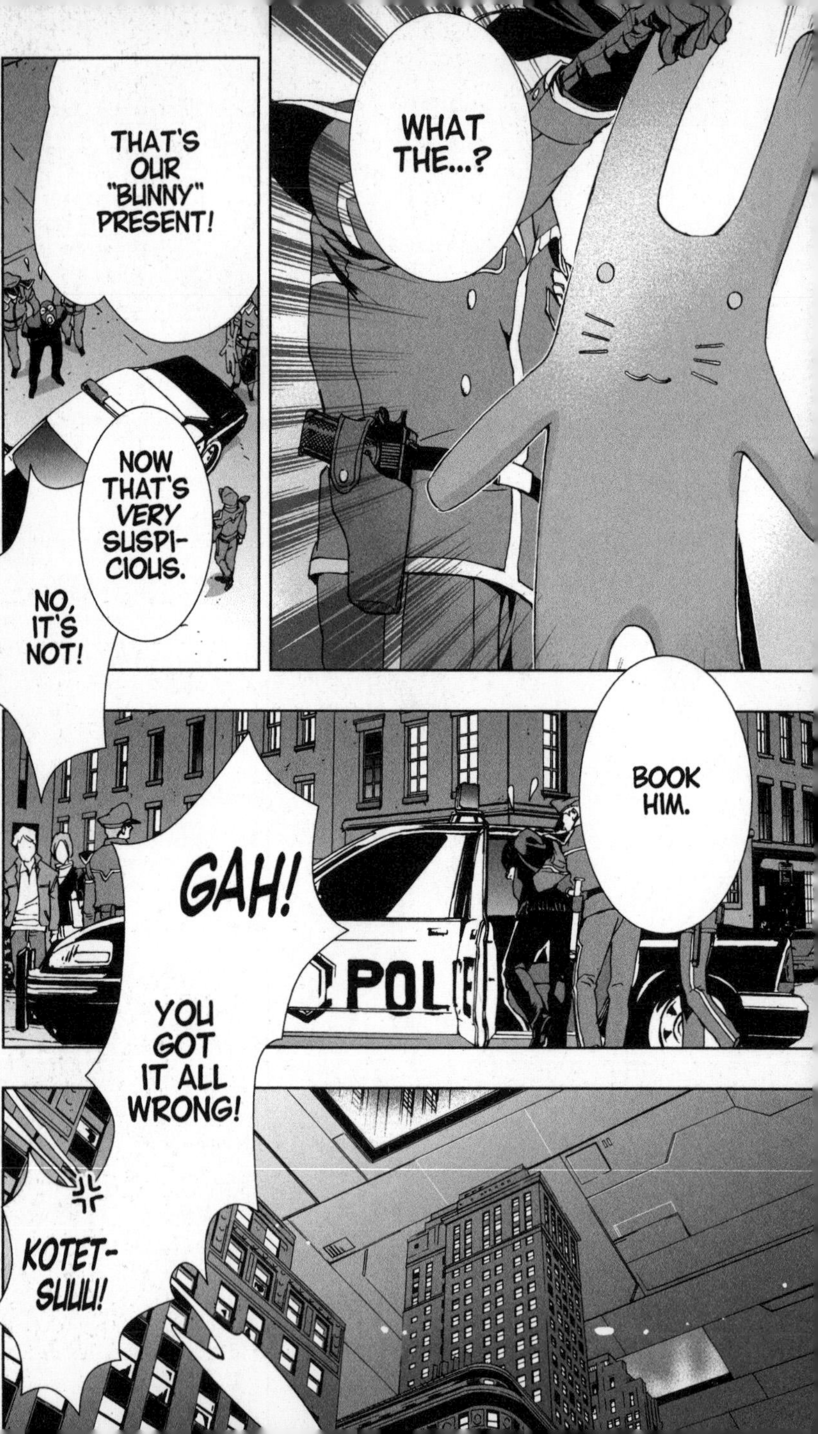
WHAT THE...?
THAT'S OUR "BUNNY" PRESENT!
NOW THAT'S VERY SUSPICIOUS.
NO, IT'S NOT!
BOOK HIM.
GAH!
YOU GOT IT ALL WRONG!
POL
KOTET-SUUU!

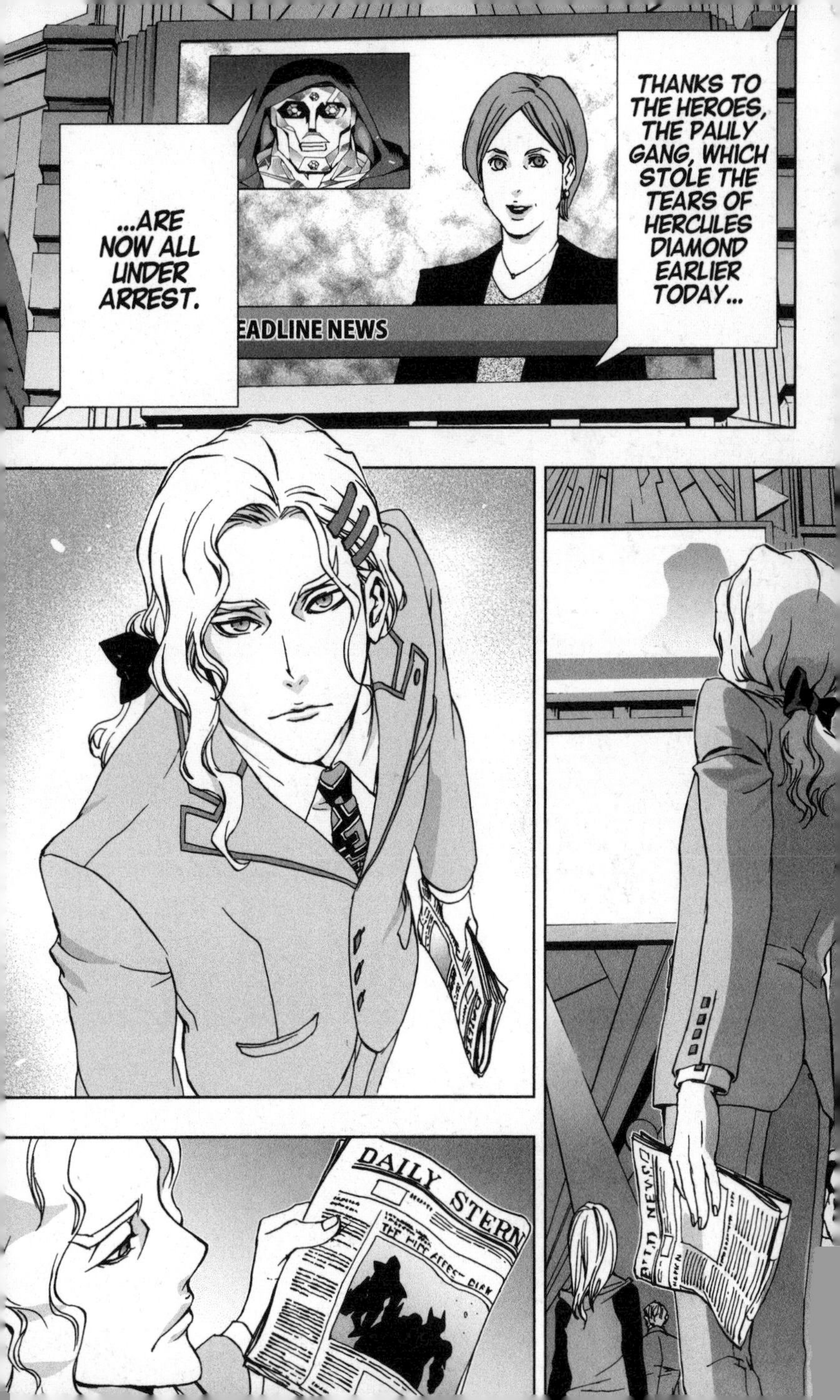
THANKS TO THE HEROES, THE PAULY GANG, WHICH STOLE THE TEARS OF HERCULES DIAMOND EARLIER TODAY...
...ARE NOW ALL UNDER ARREST.
EADLINE NEWS
DAILY STERN

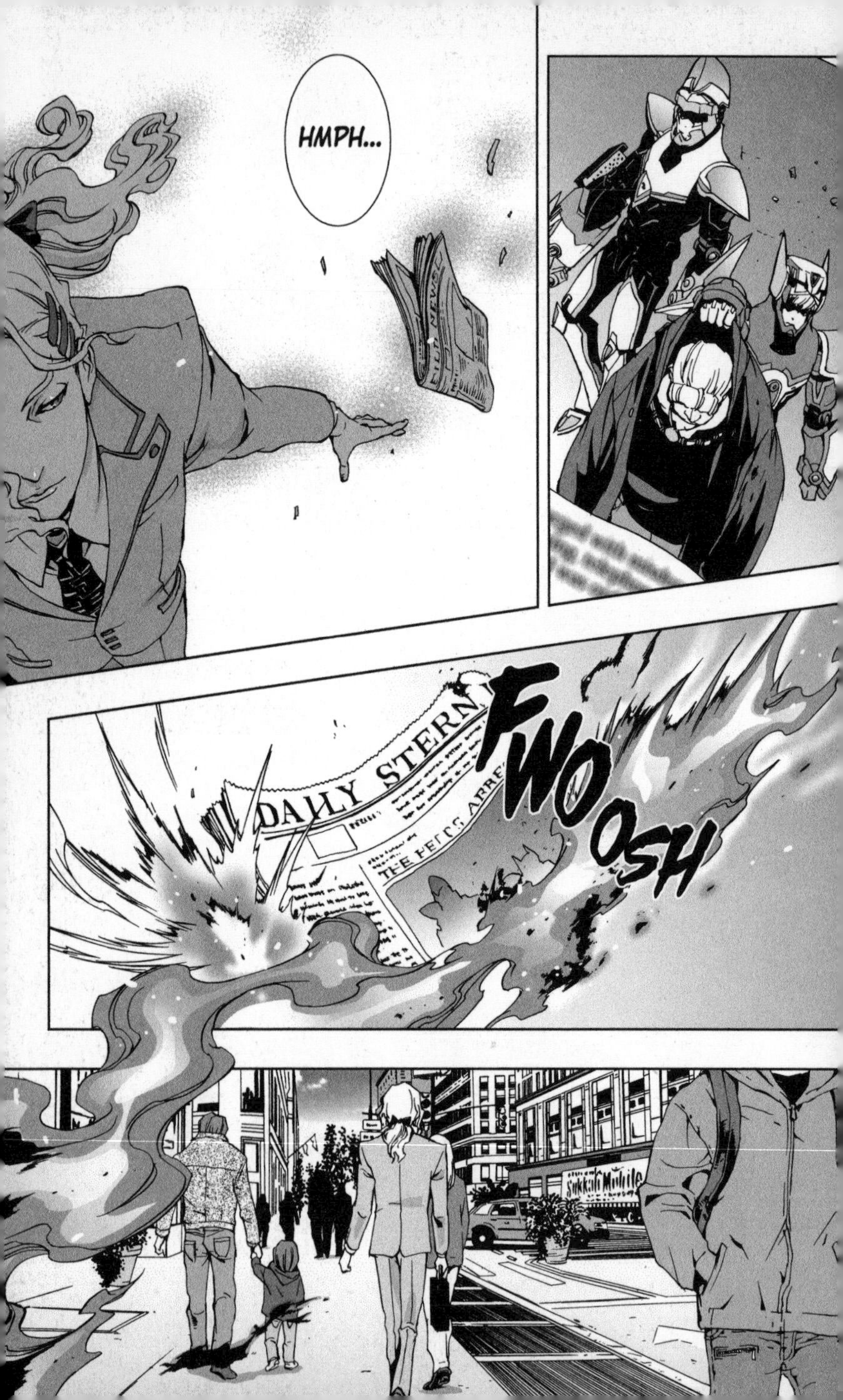
HMPH...
DAILY STERN
FWOOSH

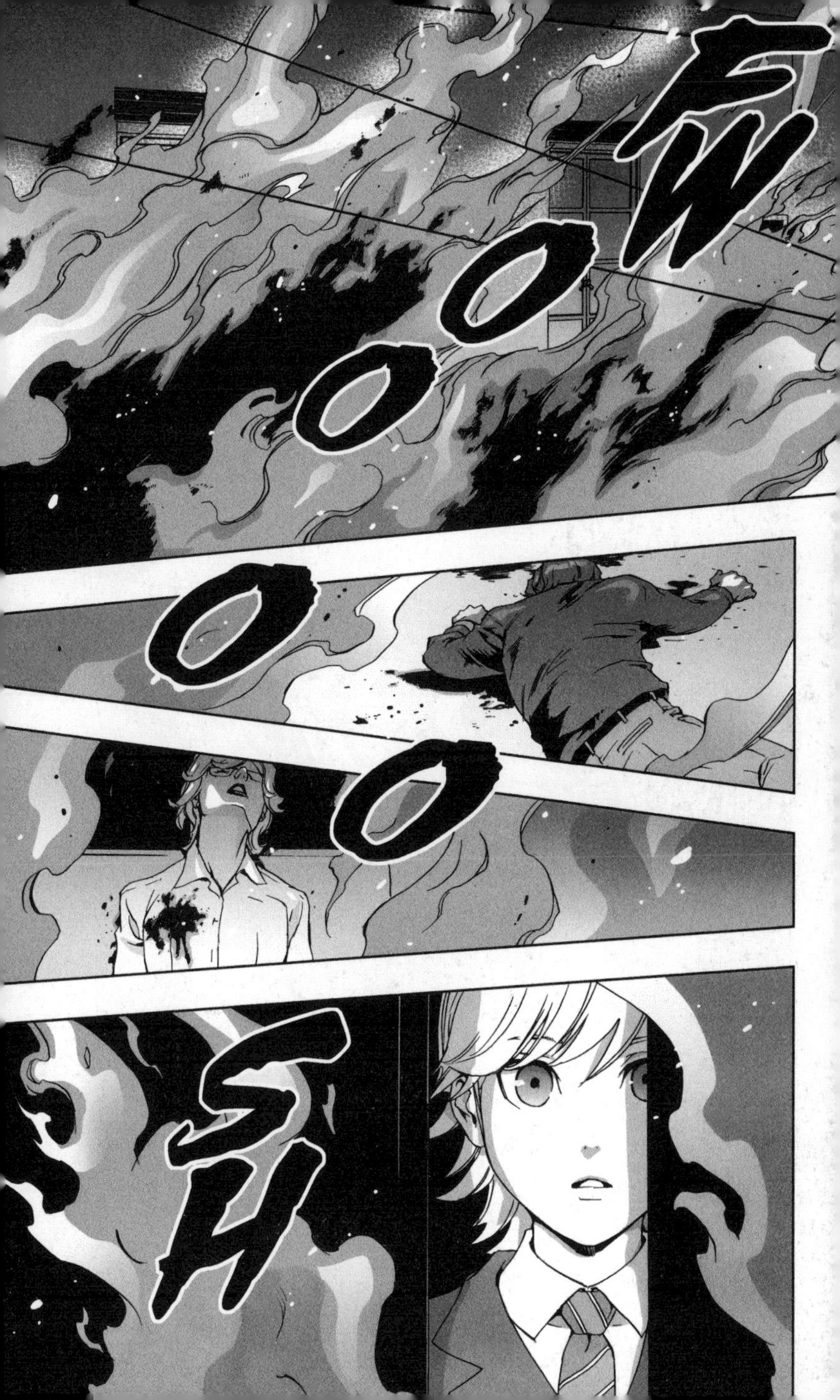
FWOOOO
SH

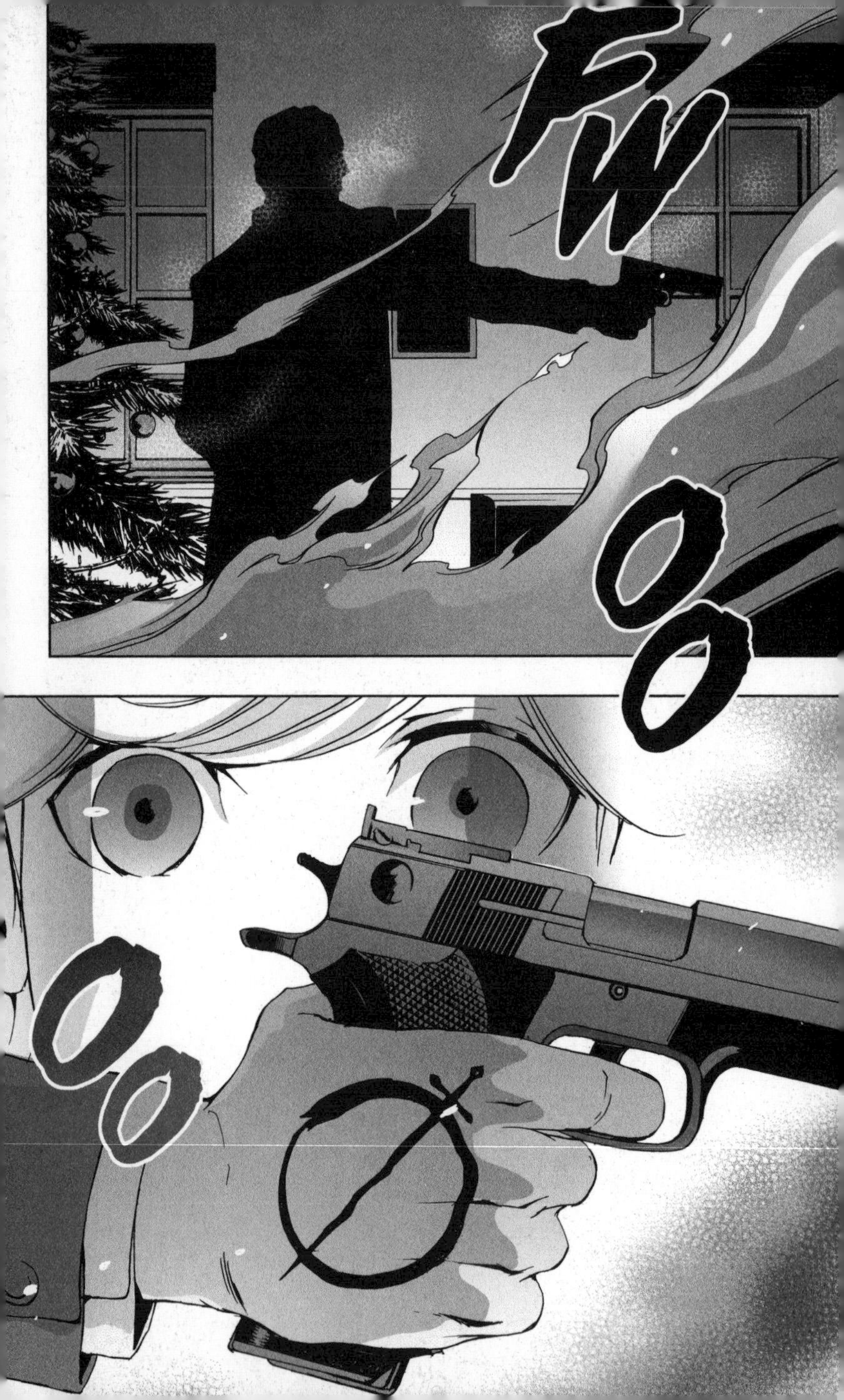
FWOO
OO

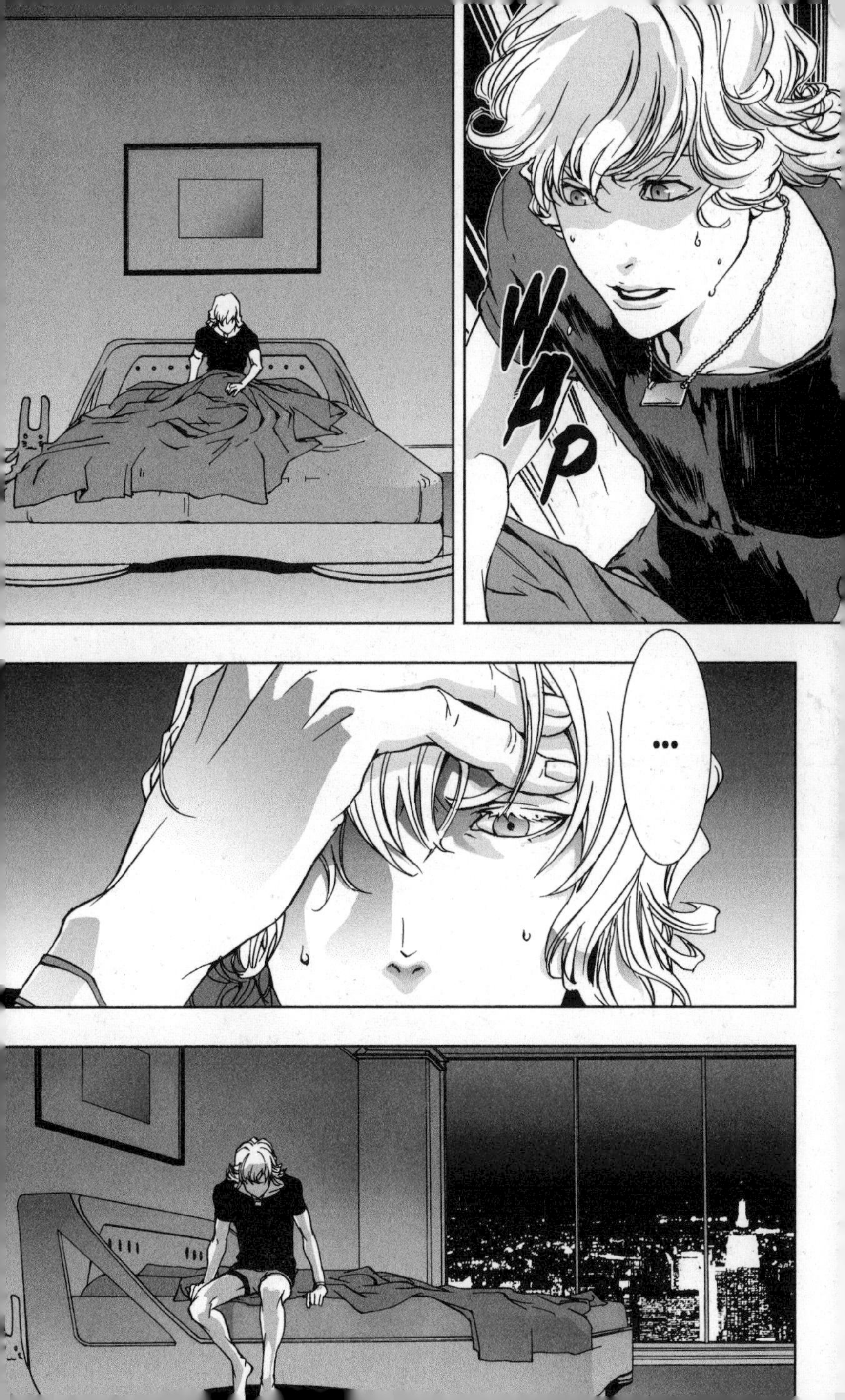
WAP
...

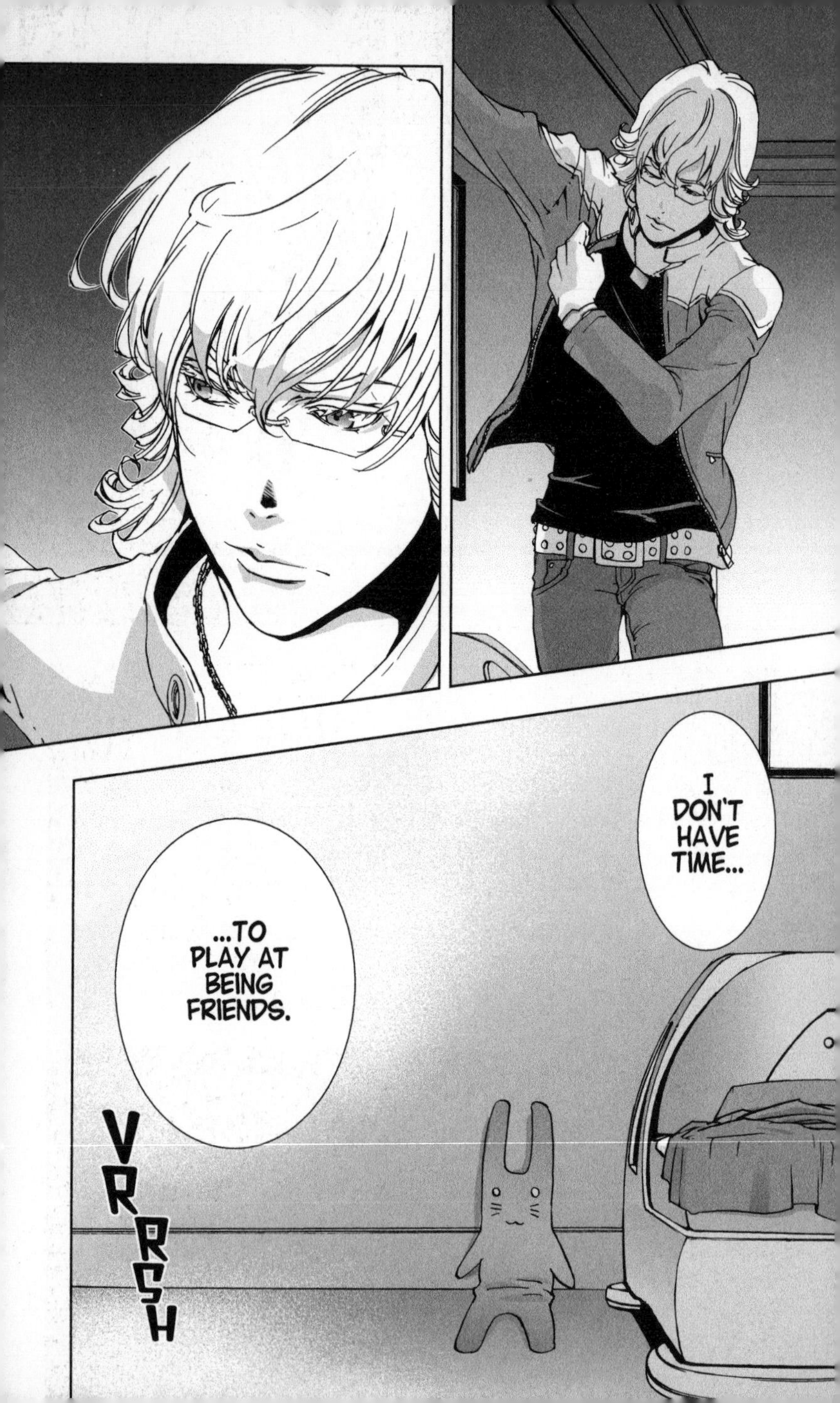
I DON'T HAVE TIME...
...TO PLAY AT BEING FRIENDS.
VRSH

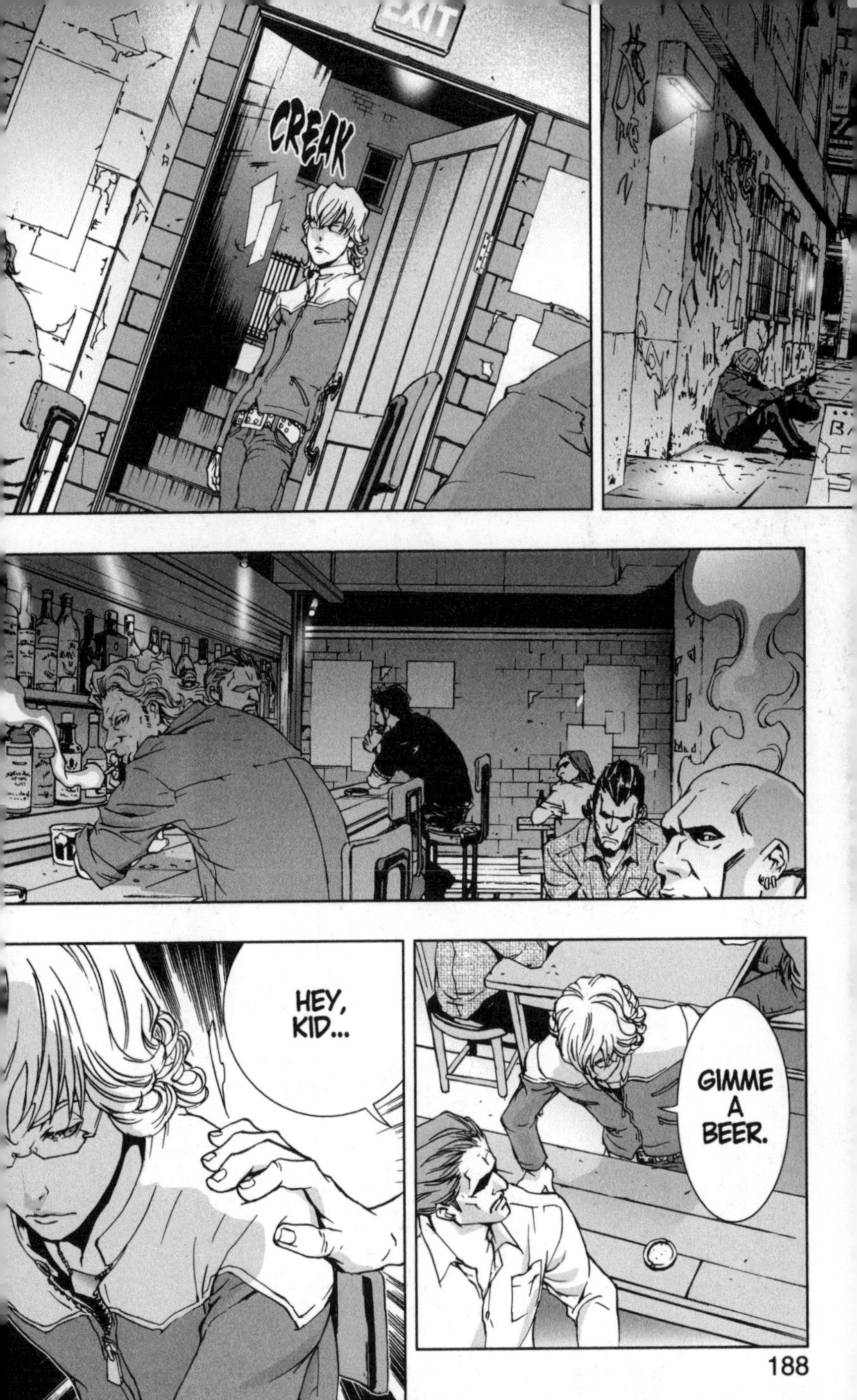
CREAK
GIMME A BEER.
HEY, KID...

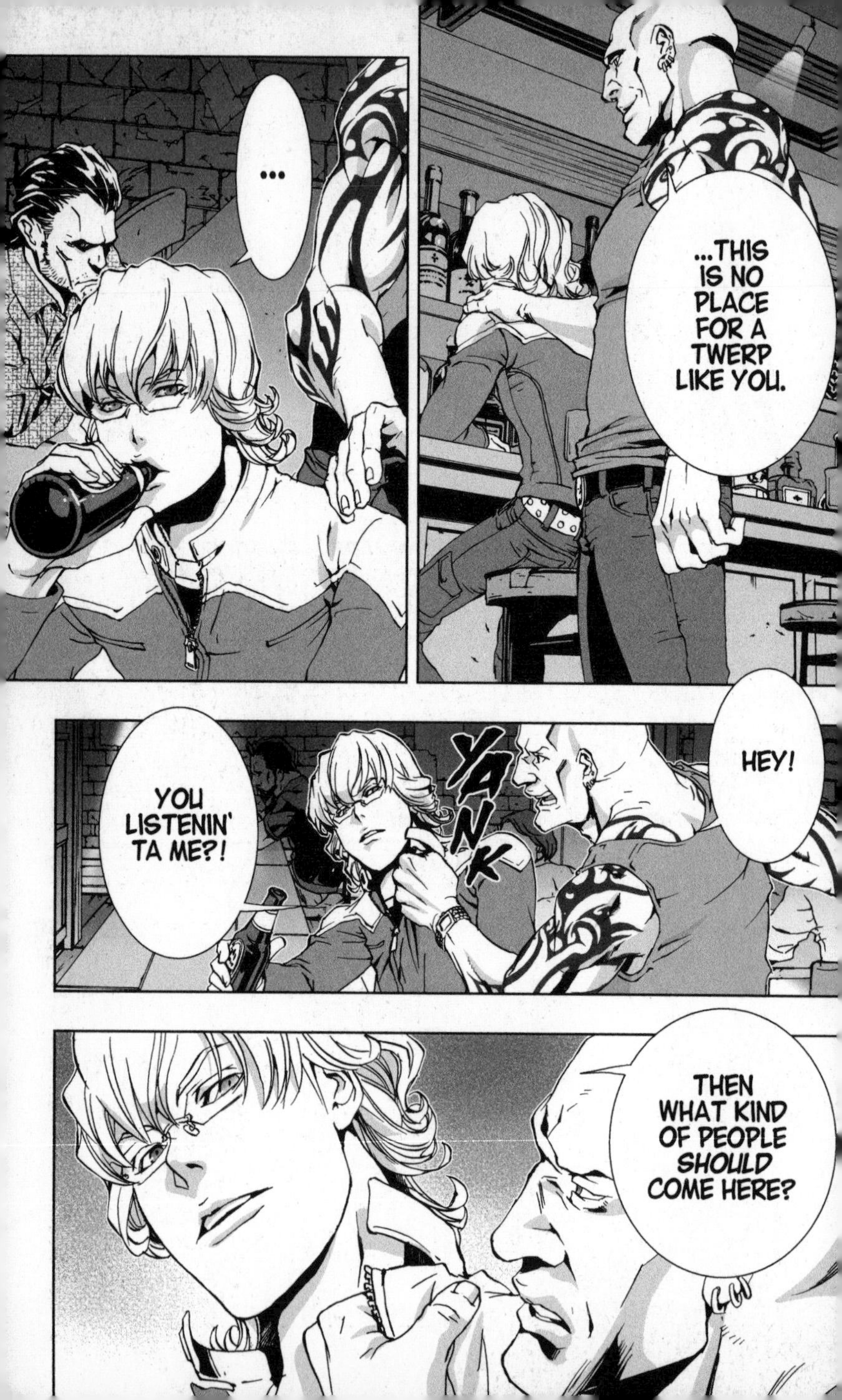
...THIS IS NO PLACE FOR A TWERP LIKE YOU.
...
HEY!
YANK
YOU LISTENIN' TA ME?!
THEN WHAT KIND OF PEOPLE SHOULD COME HERE?

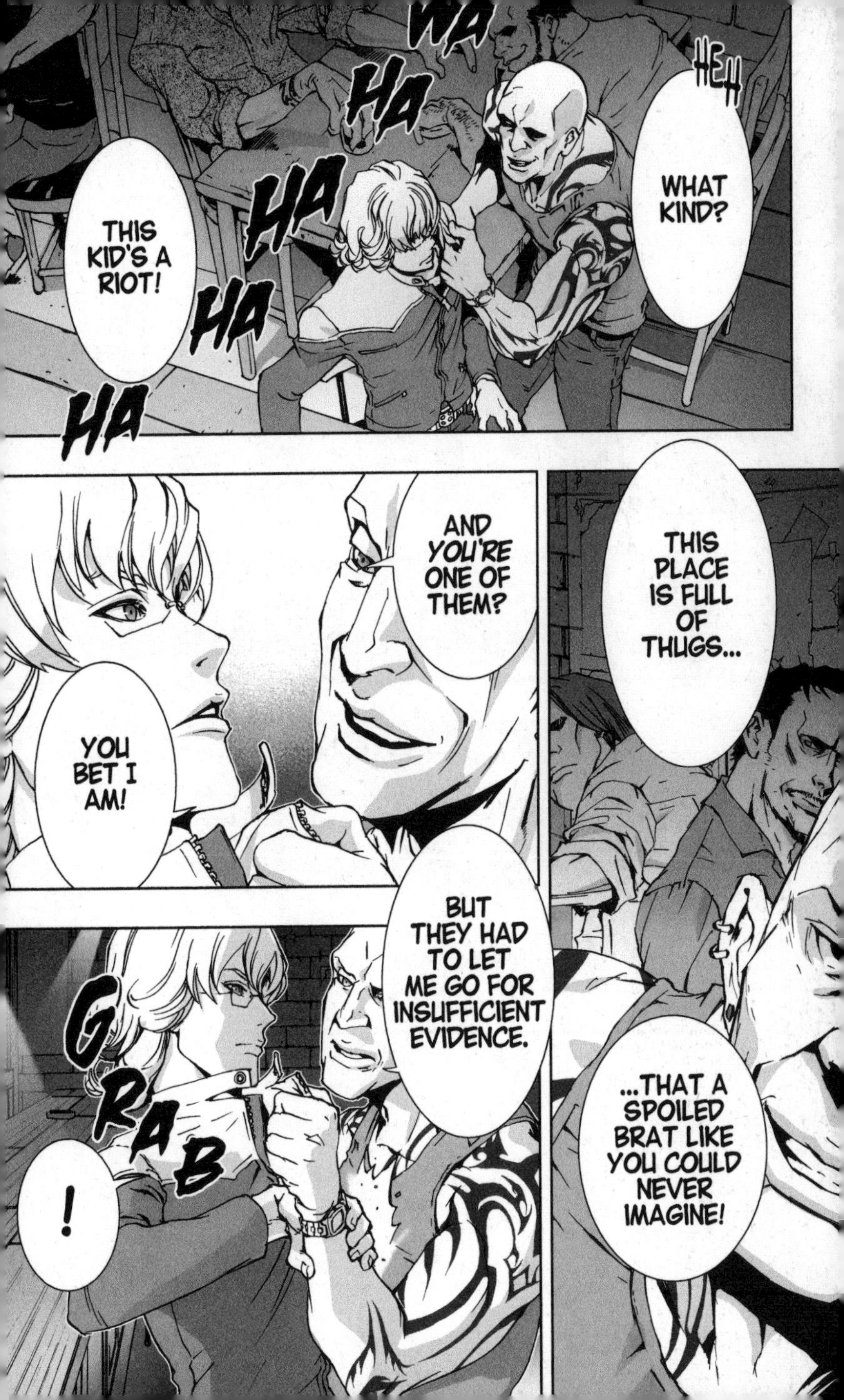
HEH
WHAT KIND?
WA HA HA HA HA HA
THIS KID'S A RIOT!
THIS PLACE IS FULL OF THUGS...
...THAT A SPOILED BRAT LIKE YOU COULD NEVER IMAGINE!
AND YOU'RE ONE OF THEM?
YOU BET I AM!
BUT THEY HAD TO LET ME GO FOR INSUFFICIENT EVIDENCE.
GRAB
!

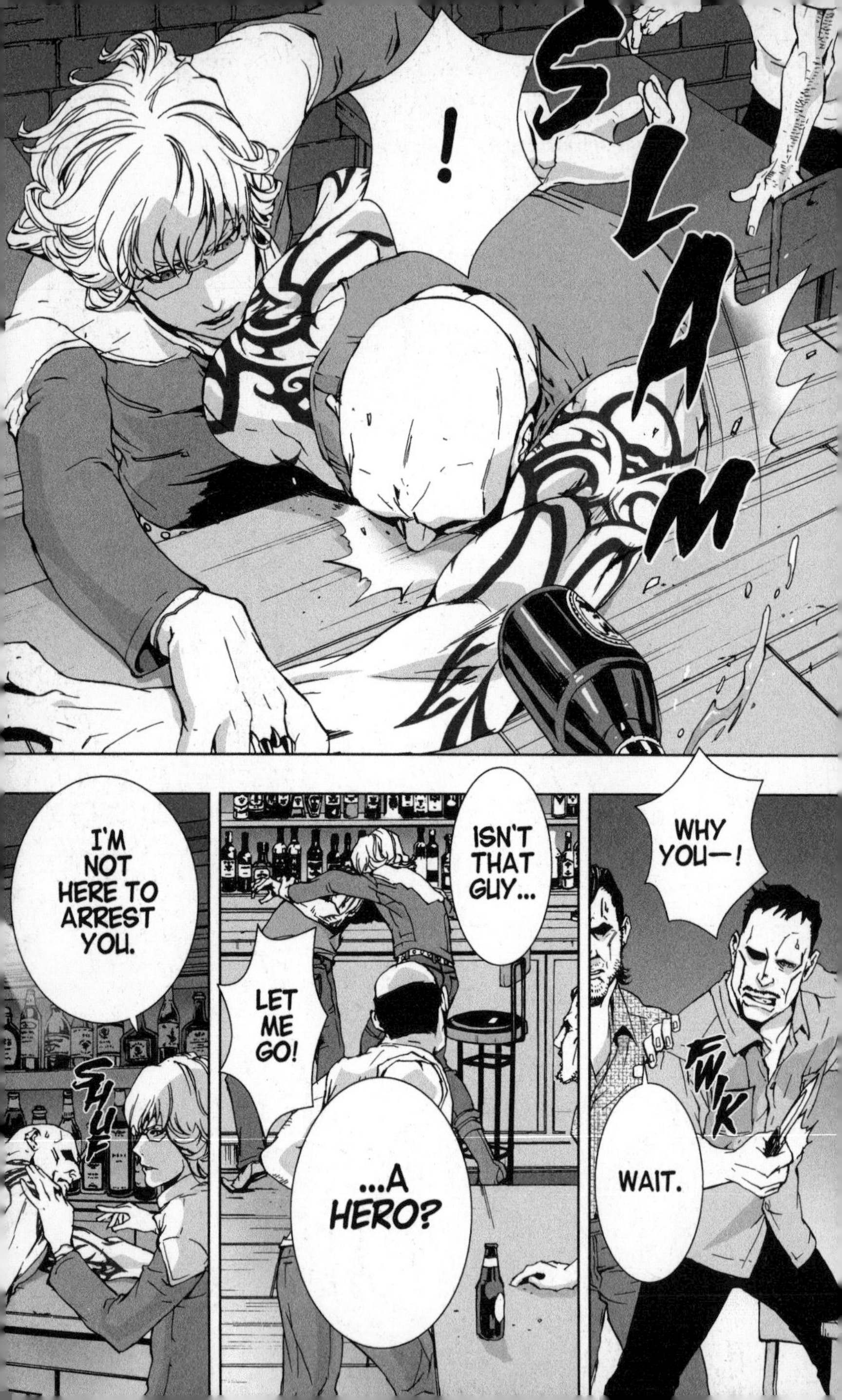
SLAM
!
WHY YOU—!
FWIK
WAIT.
ISN'T THAT GUY...
LET ME GO!
...A HERO?
I'M NOT HERE TO ARREST YOU.
SHUF

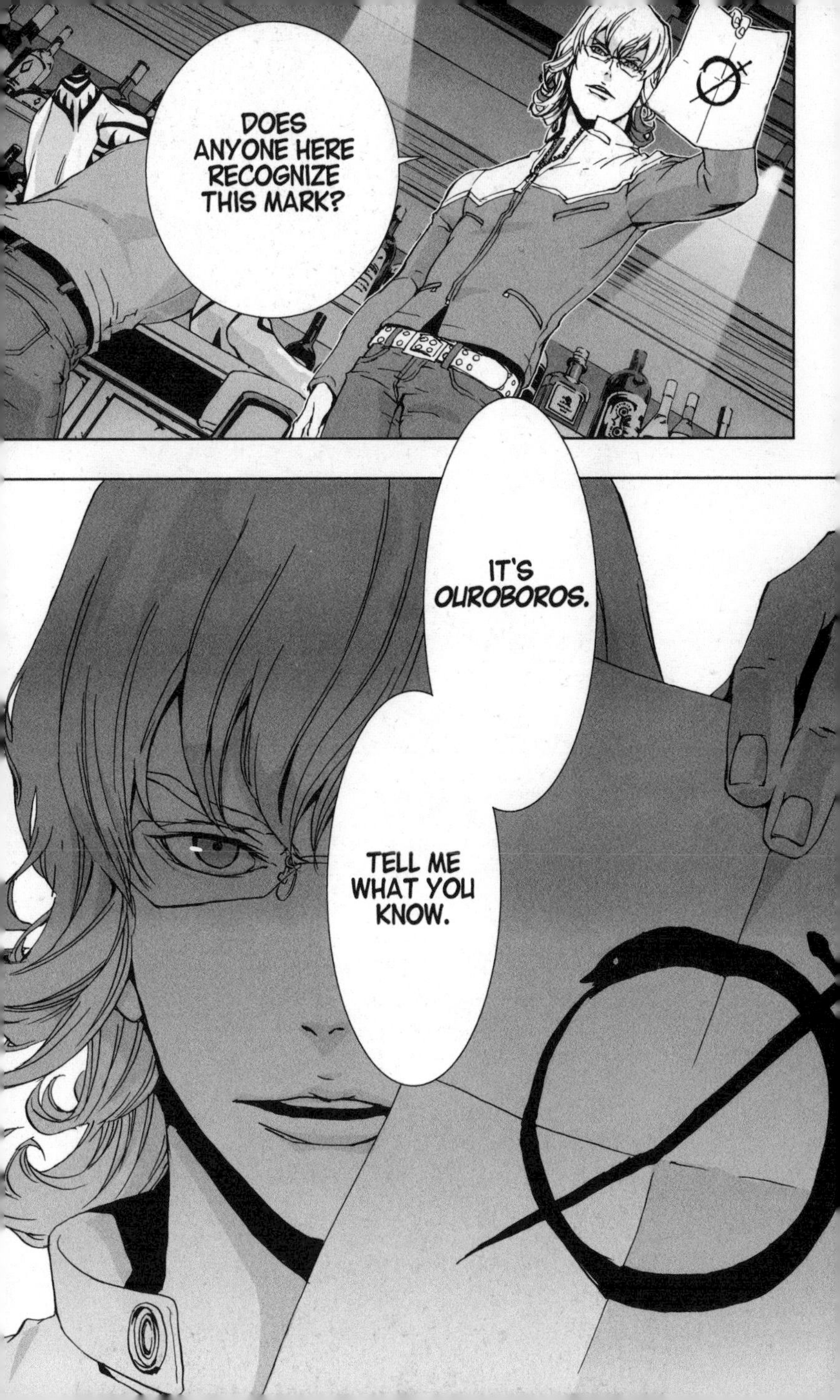
DOES ANYONE HERE RECOGNIZE THIS MARK?
IT'S OUROBOROS.
TELL ME WHAT YOU KNOW.

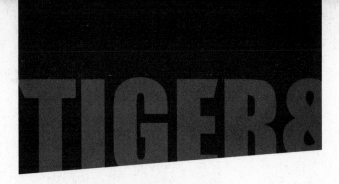

MIZUKI SAKAKIBARA

Mizuki Sakakibara's American comics debut was Marvel's *Exile* in 2002. Currently, *TIGER & BUNNY* is serialized in *Newtype Ace* magazine by Kadokawa Shoten.

MASAFUMI NISHIDA

Story director. TIGER & BUNNY was his first work as a TV animation scriptwriter. He is well known for the movie *Gachi☆Boy* and the Japanese TV dramas *Maoh*, *Kaibutsu-kun*, and *Youkai Ningen Bem*.

MASAKAZU KATSURA

Original character designer. Masakazu Katsura is well known for the manga series *WING MAN*, *Denei Shojo* (*Video Girl Ai*), *I"s*, and *ZETMAN*. Katsura's works have been translated into several languages, including Chinese and French, as well as English.

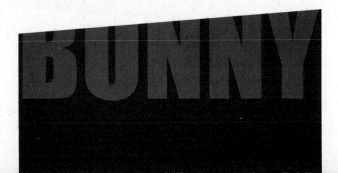

COMING **NEXT VOLUME**

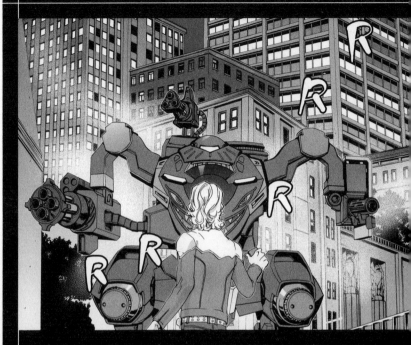

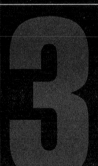

When he was a child, Barnaby lost his parents to a shadowy organization called Ouroboros. The search for his parents' killers may lead both Barnaby and Kotetsu into a dangerous conspiracy that has wider implications for everyone in Stern Bild City. Then the Heroes jump into action against rampaging mecha, renegade NEXTs and the secretive hand behind it all!

TIGER&BUNNY 2

VIZ Media Edition

Art **MIZUKI SAKAKIBARA**
Planning / Story **SUNRISE**
Original Script **MASAFUMI NISHIDA**
Original Character and Hero Design **MASAKAZU KATSURA**

TIGER & BUNNY Volume 2
© Mizuki SAKAKIBARA 2012
© SUNRISE/T&B PARTNERS, MBS
First published in Japan in 2012 by KADOKAWA SHOTEN Co., Ltd., Tokyo.
English translation rights arranged with KADOKAWA SHOTEN Co., Ltd., Tokyo.

Translation & English Adaptation **LABAAMEN & JOHN WERRY, HC LANGUAGE SOLUTIONS**
Touch-up Art & Lettering **STEPHEN DUTRO**
Design **FAWN LAU**
Editor **MIKE MONTESA**

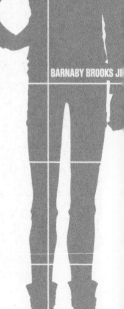

BARNABY BROOKS JR

Printed in the U.S.A.

Published by VIZ Media, LLC
P.O. Box 77010
San Francisco, CA 94107

10 9 8 7 6 5 4 3 2 1
First printing, July 2013

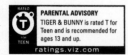

www.viz.com

YOU'RE READING THE
WRONG WAY!

Tiger & Bunny reads from right to left, starting in the upper-right corner. Japanese is read from right to left, meaning that action, sound effects, and word-balloon order are completely reversed from English order.

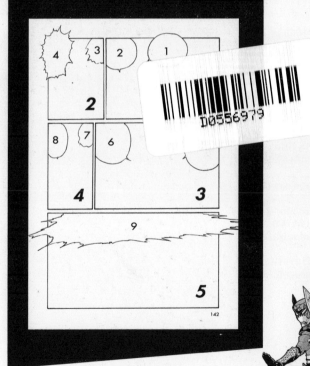

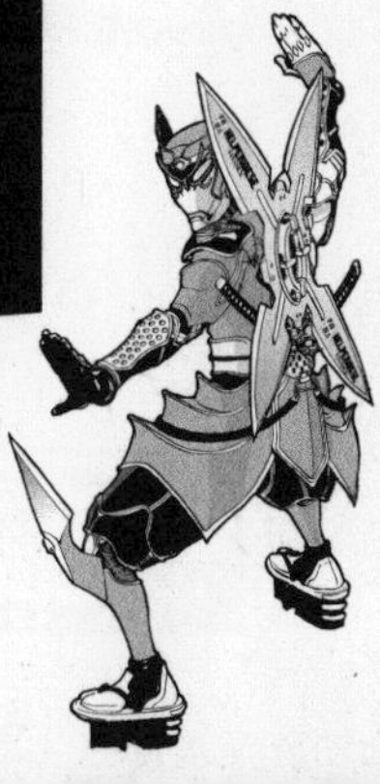